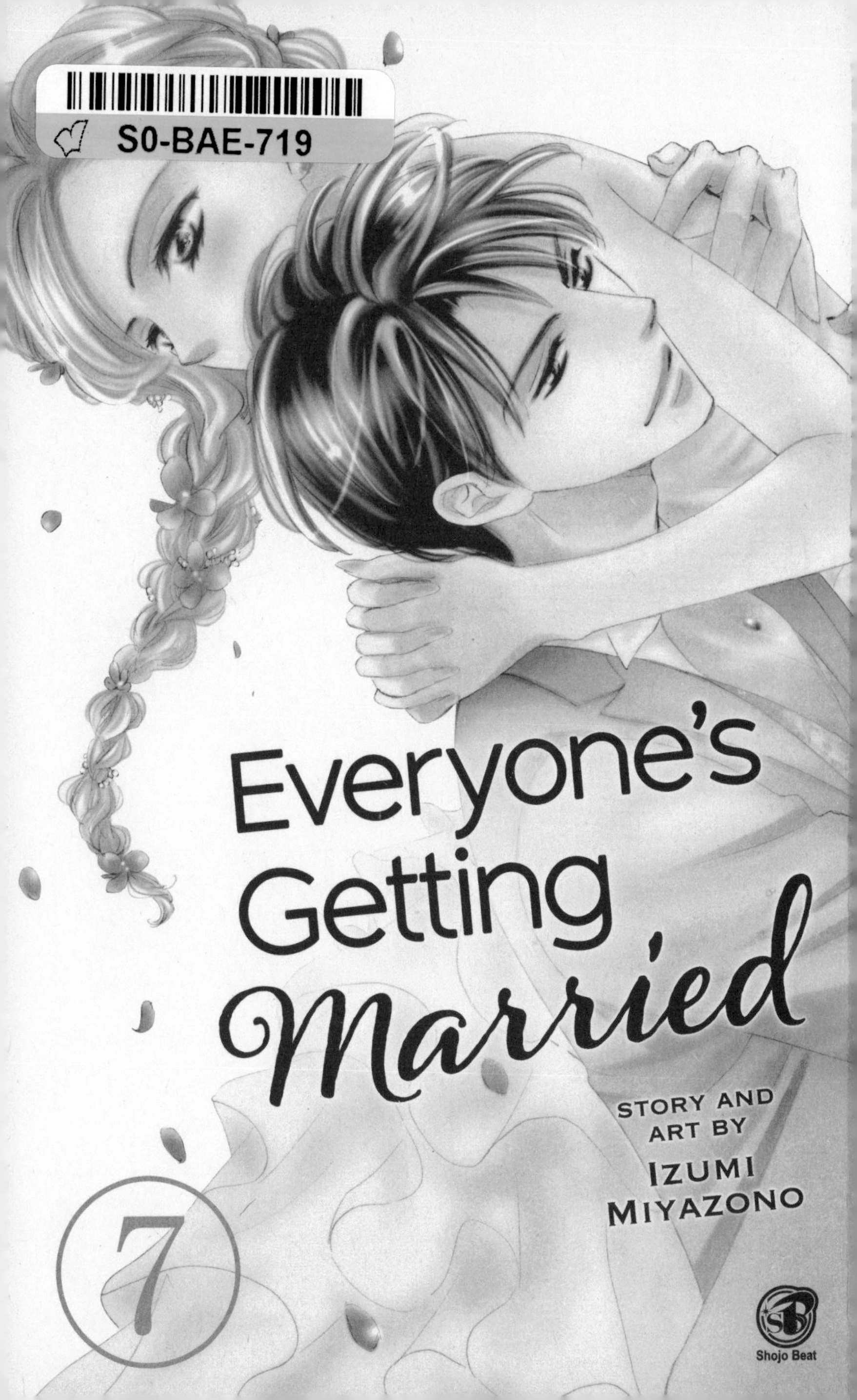
Everyone's Getting Married
STORY AND ART BY
IZUMI MIYAZONO
7
Shojo Beat

CHARACTERS

THE MAN WHO DOESN'T WANT TO GET MARRIED

Ryu Nanami
The handsome, up-and-coming newscaster at PTV. He's returned from the New York office.

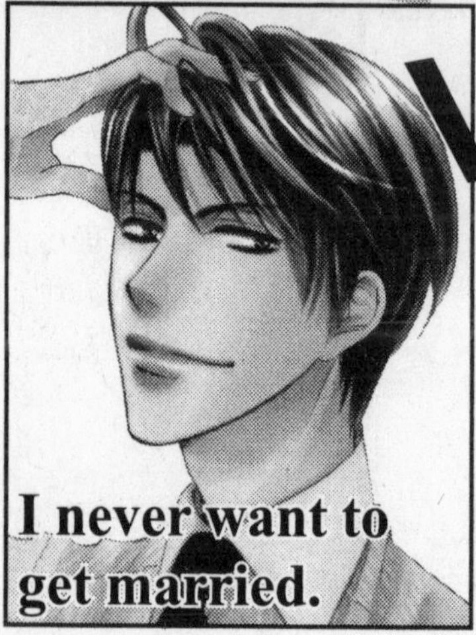
I never want to get married.

VS

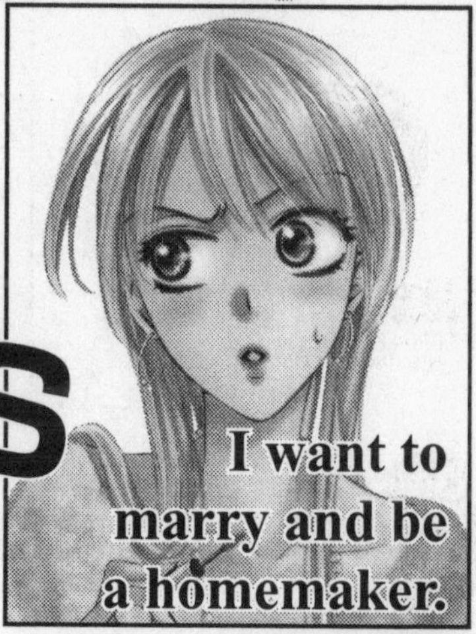
I want to marry and be a homemaker.

Asuka Takanashi
She takes pride in her career at a major bank, but feels strongly about getting married.

THE WOMAN WHO WANTS TO GET MARRIED

SIBLINGS

COLLEAGUES

THE LITTLE BROTHER WHO WANTS HIS SISTER TO BE HAPPY

Kaneda Takanashi
Asuka's younger brother. He cares a lot about her and is worried about her love life. He is blunt and tactless, but he also has a gentle side.

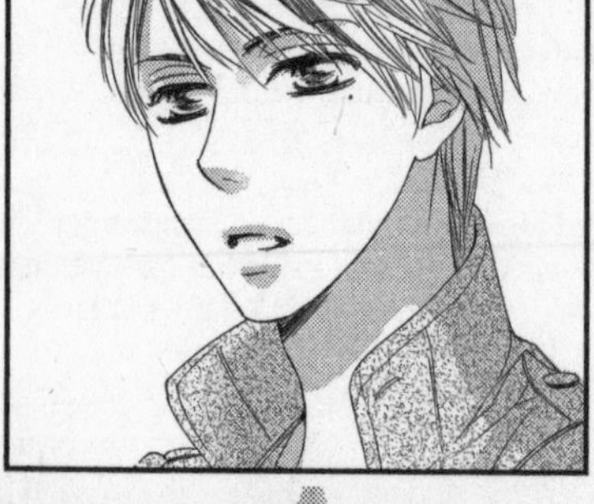

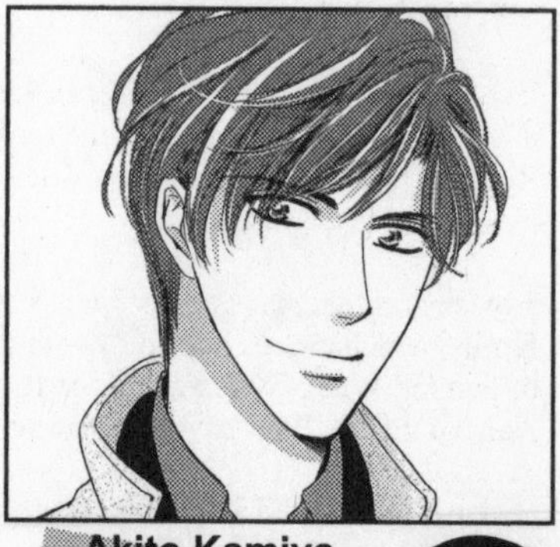

Akito Kamiya
The top salesman of a major bank. He's envisioned the woman he wants to be his wife, and he has set his sights on Asuka.

THE MAN WHO WANTS A BENEFICIAL MARRIAGE

HE WANTS TO
Hiroki Ono
A senior colleague of Asuka and Rio. He's friends with Nanami.
IN A RELATIONSHIP♥
(with no plans to marry in the future)
SHE DOESN'T WANT TO
Rio
Asuka's best friend. She's in a relationship with Hiroki.
HE DIDN'T WANT TO
Himuro
A producer at PTV.
COWORKERS
HE DID
Mikami
A news anchor at PTV.

STORY THUS FAR

Inspired by her mother, who was a full-time homemaker, Asuka aspires to get married and create a happy home too. She falls in love with the popular TV host Ryu, but he is against marriage. The two set aside their differing values and fall in love to the degree that they feel they would never be happy apart...

However, Asuka has been keeping her relationship with Ryu a secret from her family, which causes her little brother, Kanade, to be distrustful of her choice of partner. When Ryu meets Kanade and reveals their relationship, he promises Kanade that he'll make Asuka happy.

Ryu and Asuka find a new home to share and move in together. The apartment building just so happens to be the same one where Kamiya—who has his eye on Asuka—lives. Though this revelation is shocking, the couple still enjoys their new living situation. But what will happen when Ryu receives news that he's to be transferred overseas?!

Contents

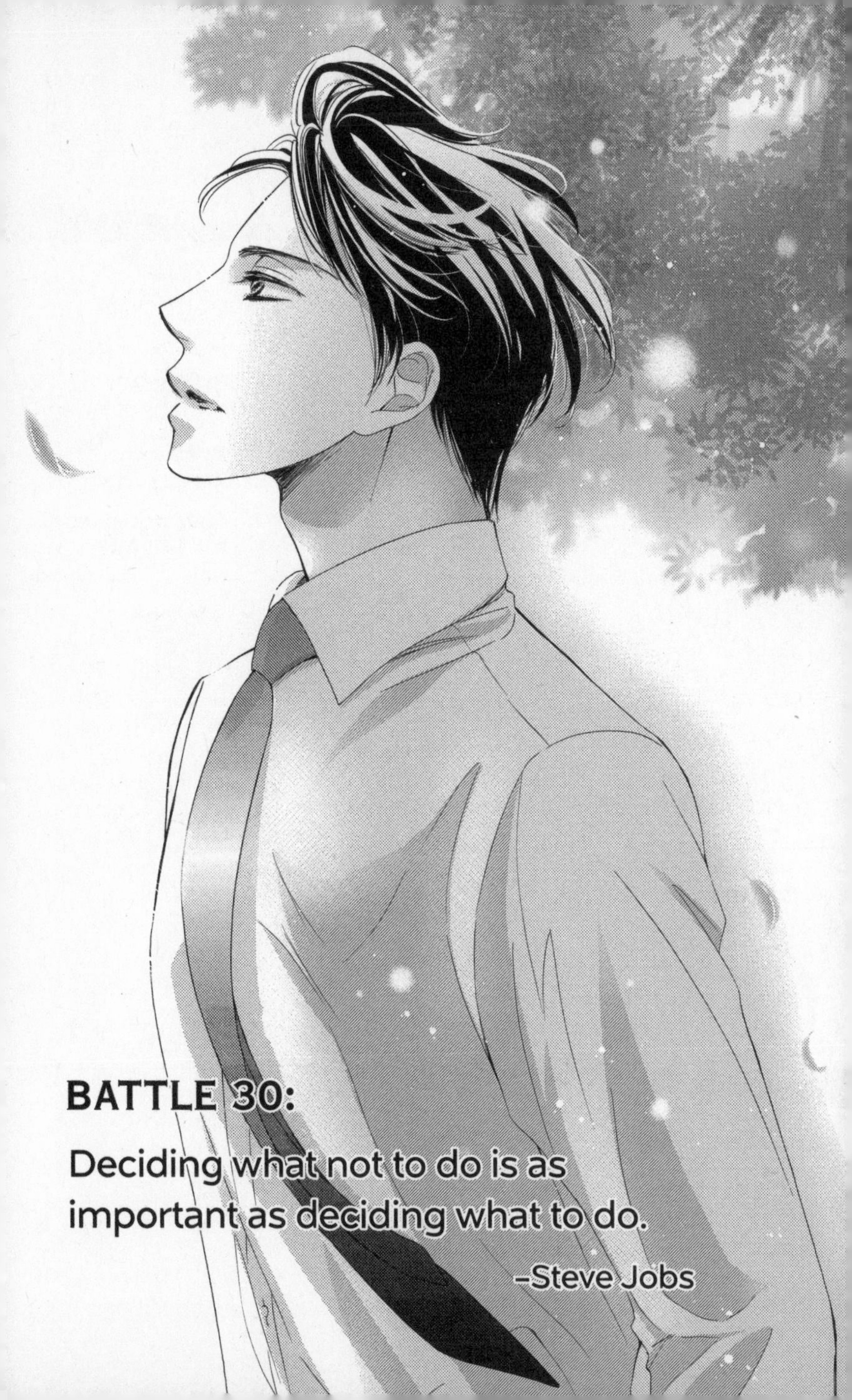

BATTLE 30:

Deciding what not to do is as important as deciding what to do.

–Steve Jobs

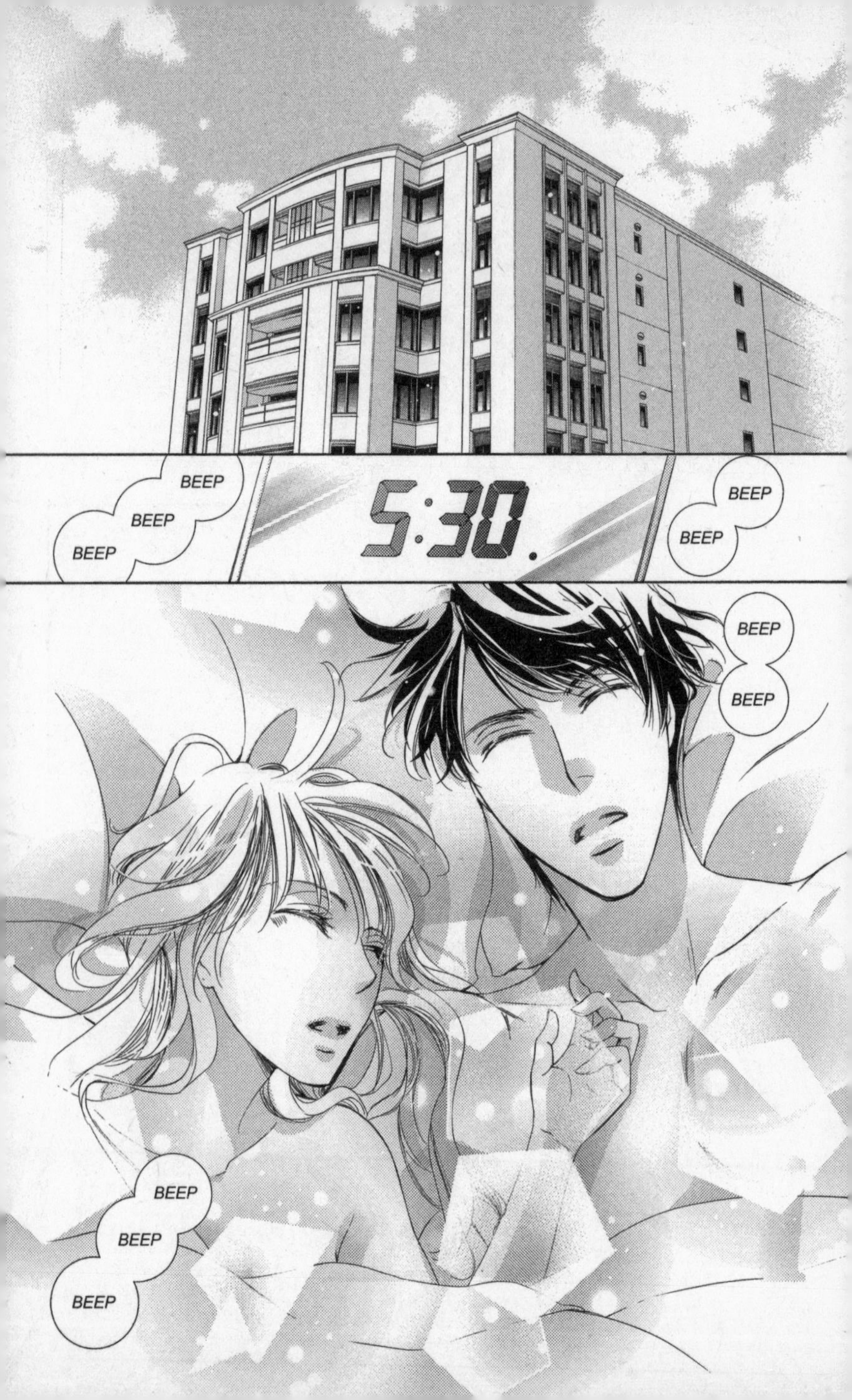
BEEP
BEEP
5:30
BEEP
BEEP
BEEP
BEEP
BEEP
BEEP
BEEP
BEEP

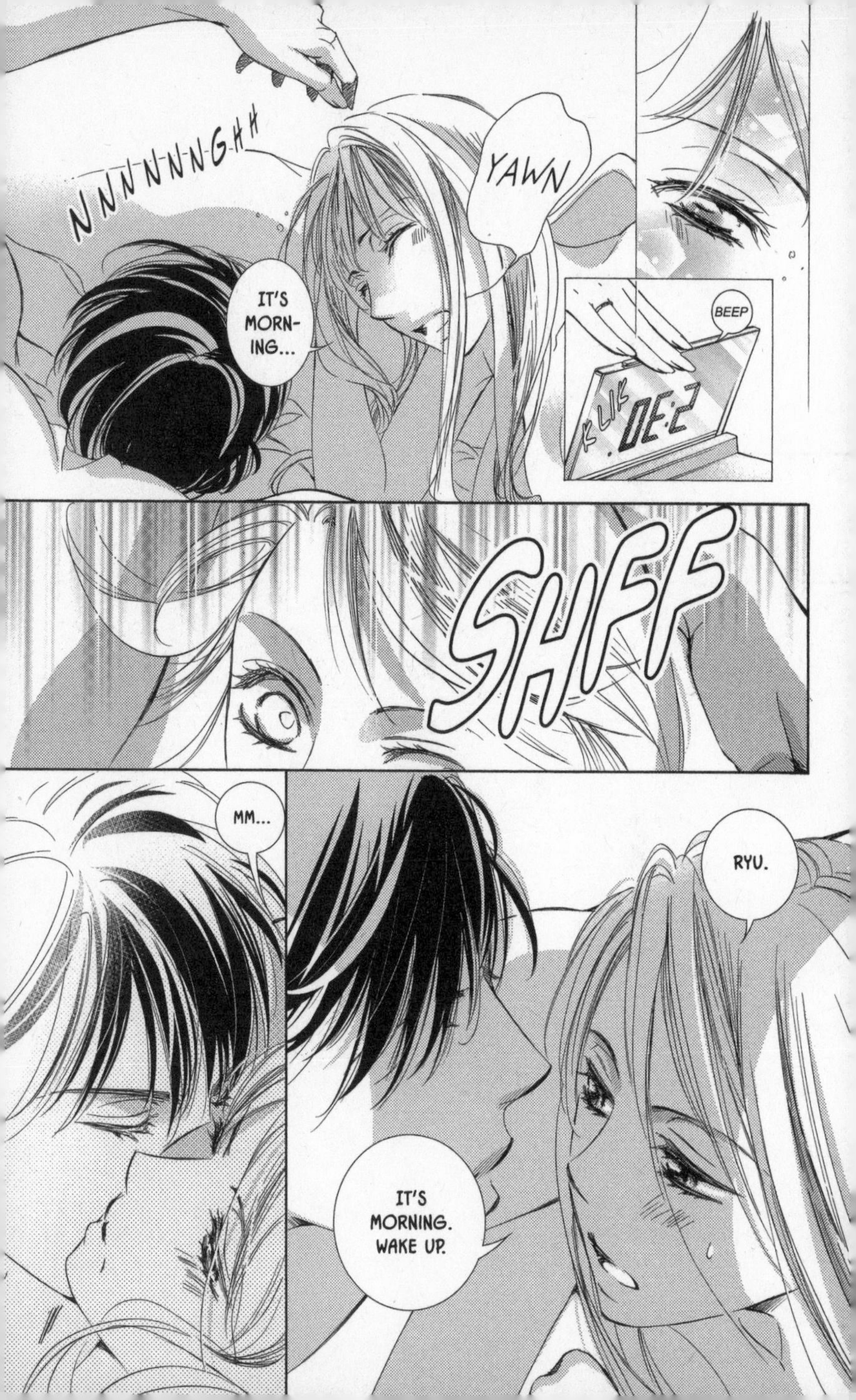
BEEP
YAWN
NNNNNNGHH
IT'S MORNING...
SHFF
RYU.
IT'S MORNING. WAKE UP.
MM...

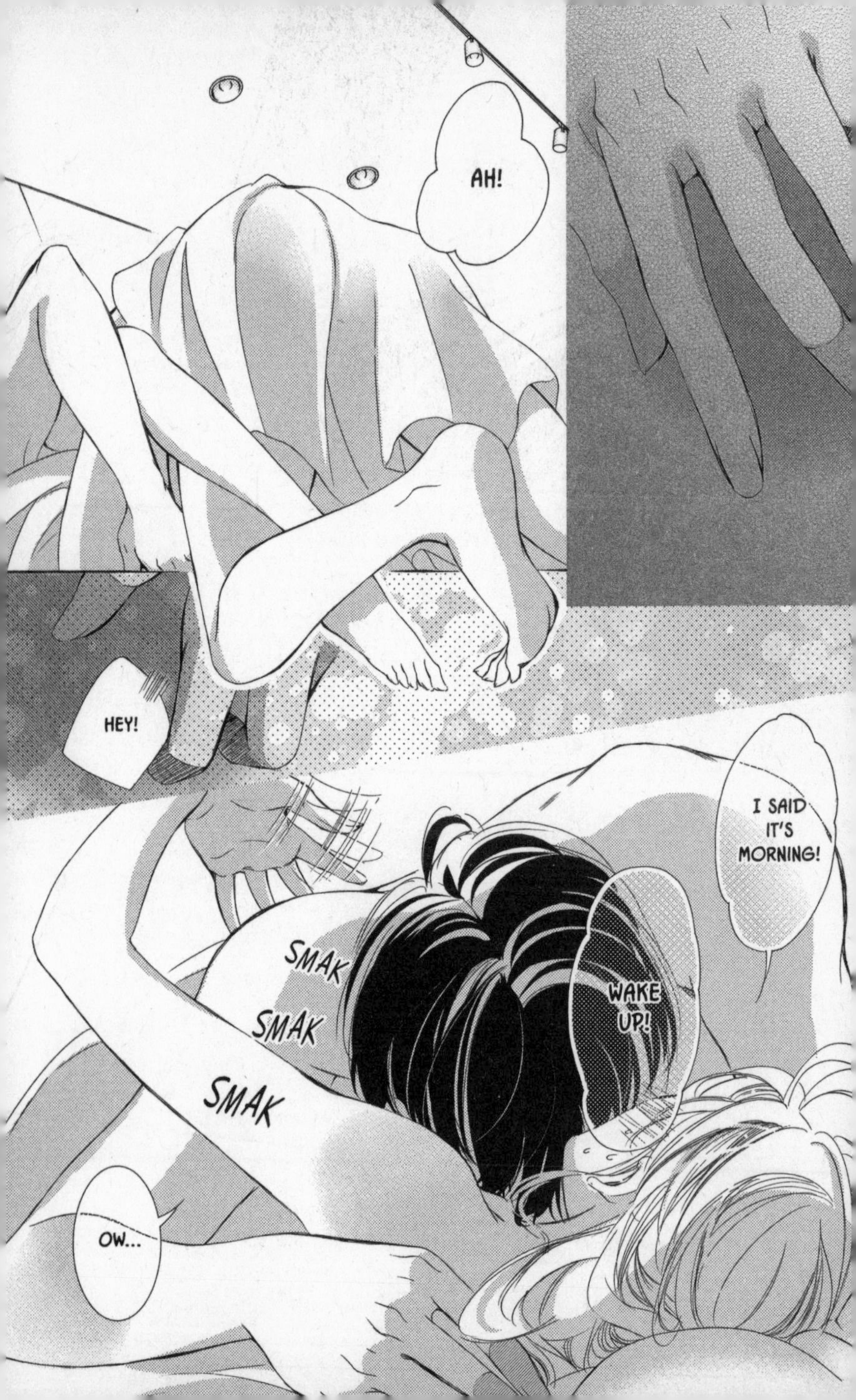
AH!
HEY!
I SAID IT'S MORNING!
WAKE UP!
SMAK
SMAK
SMAK
OW...

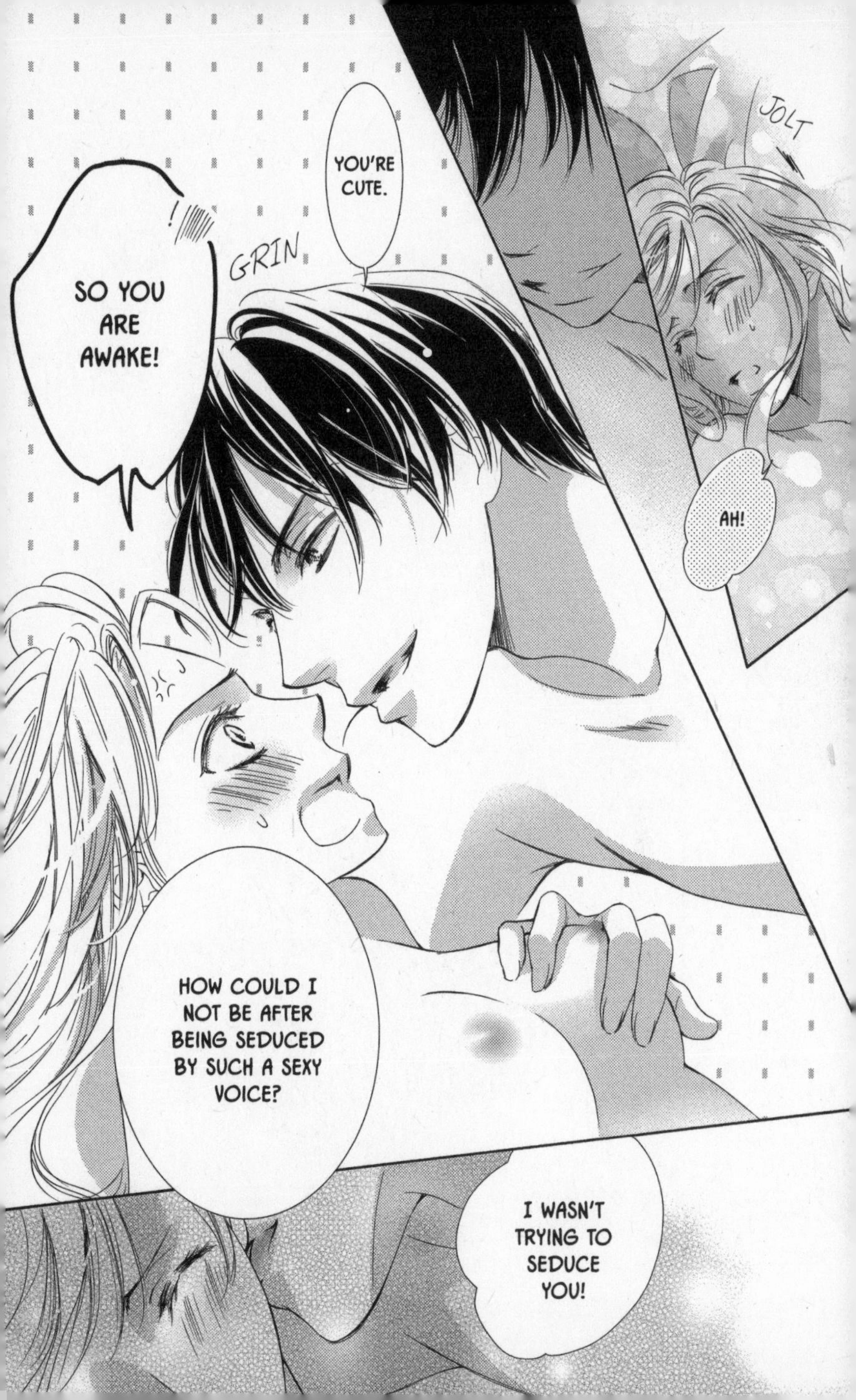
JOLT
AH!
YOU'RE CUTE.
GRIN
!
SO YOU ARE AWAKE!
HOW COULD I NOT BE AFTER BEING SEDUCED BY SUCH A SEXY VOICE?
I WASN'T TRYING TO SEDUCE YOU!

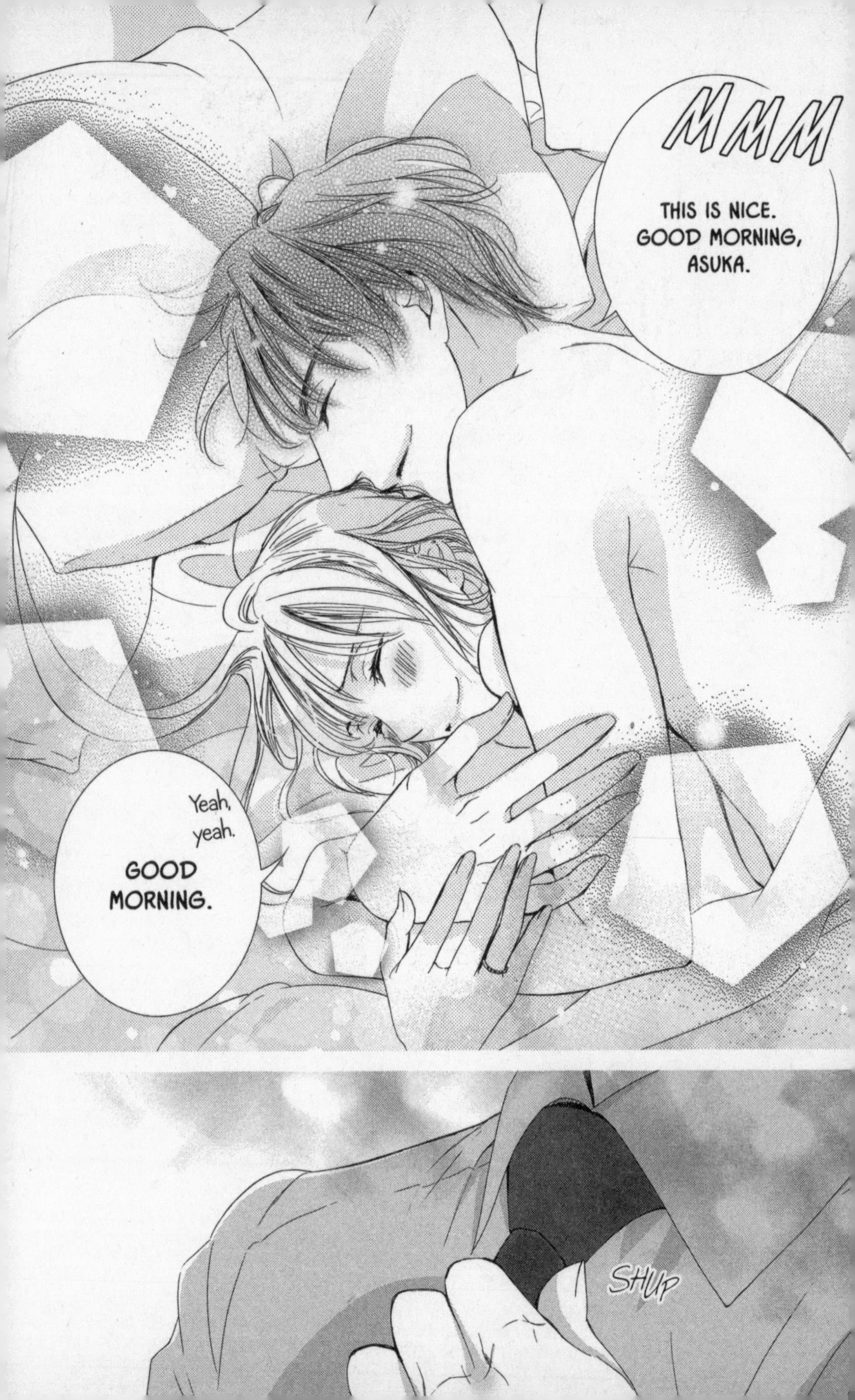
MMM
THIS IS NICE. GOOD MORNING, ASUKA.
Yeah, yeah. GOOD MORNING.
SHUP

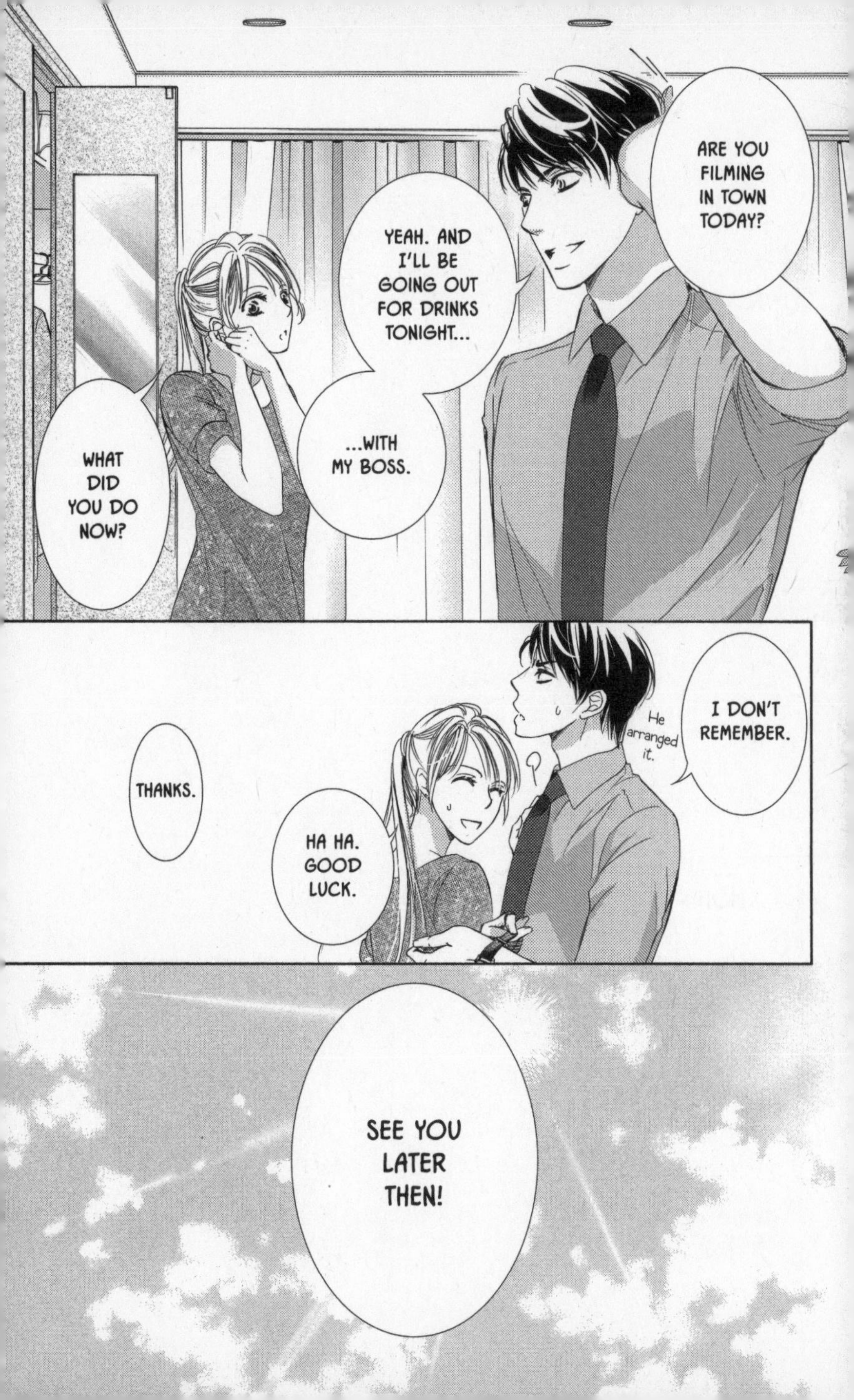
ARE YOU FILMING IN TOWN TODAY?
YEAH. AND I'LL BE GOING OUT FOR DRINKS TONIGHT...
...WITH MY BOSS.
WHAT DID YOU DO NOW?
I DON'T REMEMBER.
He arranged it.
HA HA. GOOD LUCK.
THANKS.
SEE YOU LATER THEN!

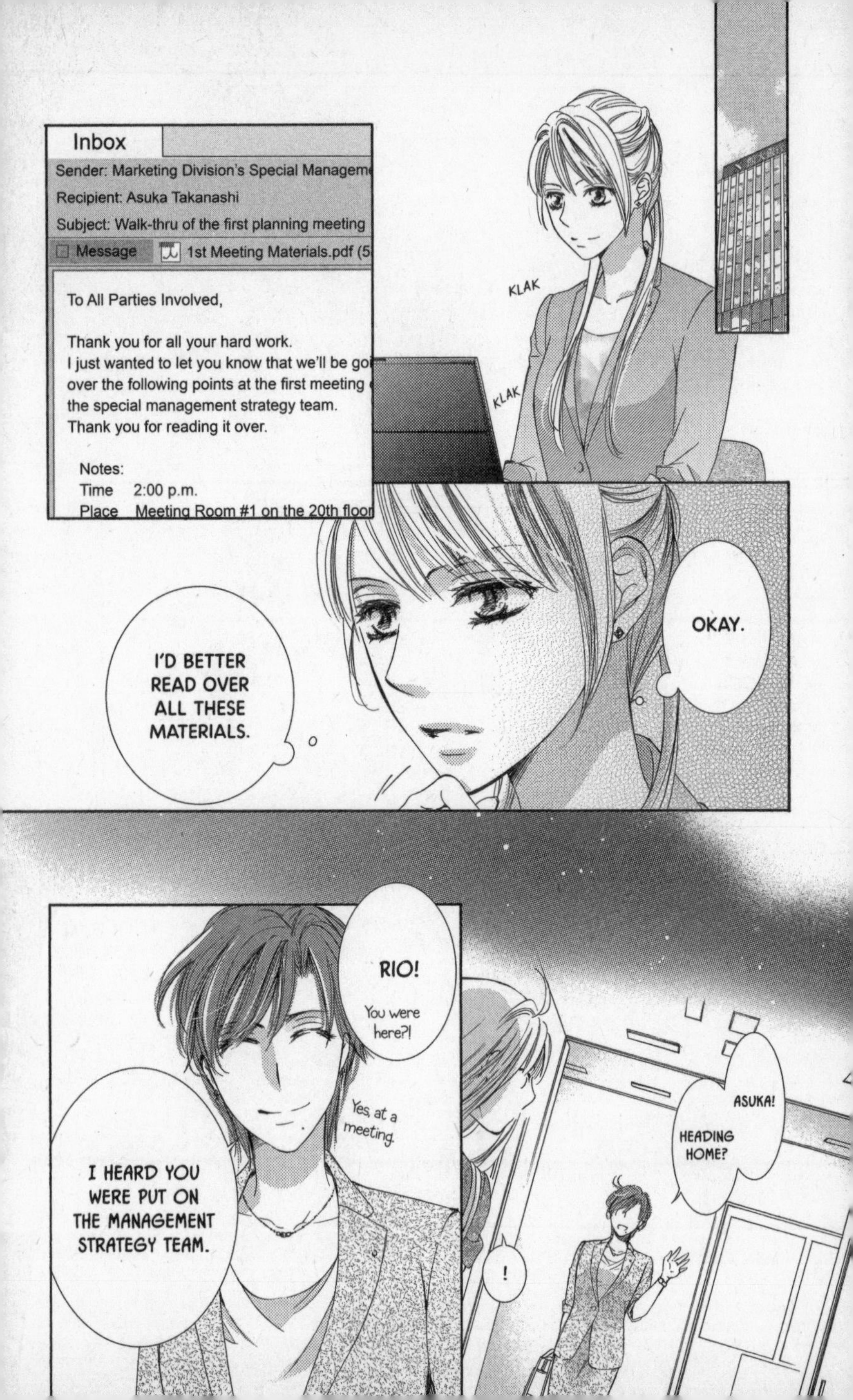
KLAK
KLAK
Inbox
Sender: Marketing Division's Special Manageme
Recipient: Asuka Takanashi
Subject: Walk-thru of the first planning meeting
Message
1st Meeting Materials.pdf (5
To All Parties Involved,
Thank you for all your hard work.
I just wanted to let you know that we'll be goi
over the following points at the first meeting
the special management strategy team.
Thank you for reading it over.
Notes:
Time 2:00 p.m.
Place Meeting Room #1 on the 20th floor
OKAY.
I'D BETTER READ OVER ALL THESE MATERIALS.
ASUKA!
HEADING HOME?
!
RIO!
You were here?!
Yes, at a meeting.
I HEARD YOU WERE PUT ON THE MANAGEMENT STRATEGY TEAM.

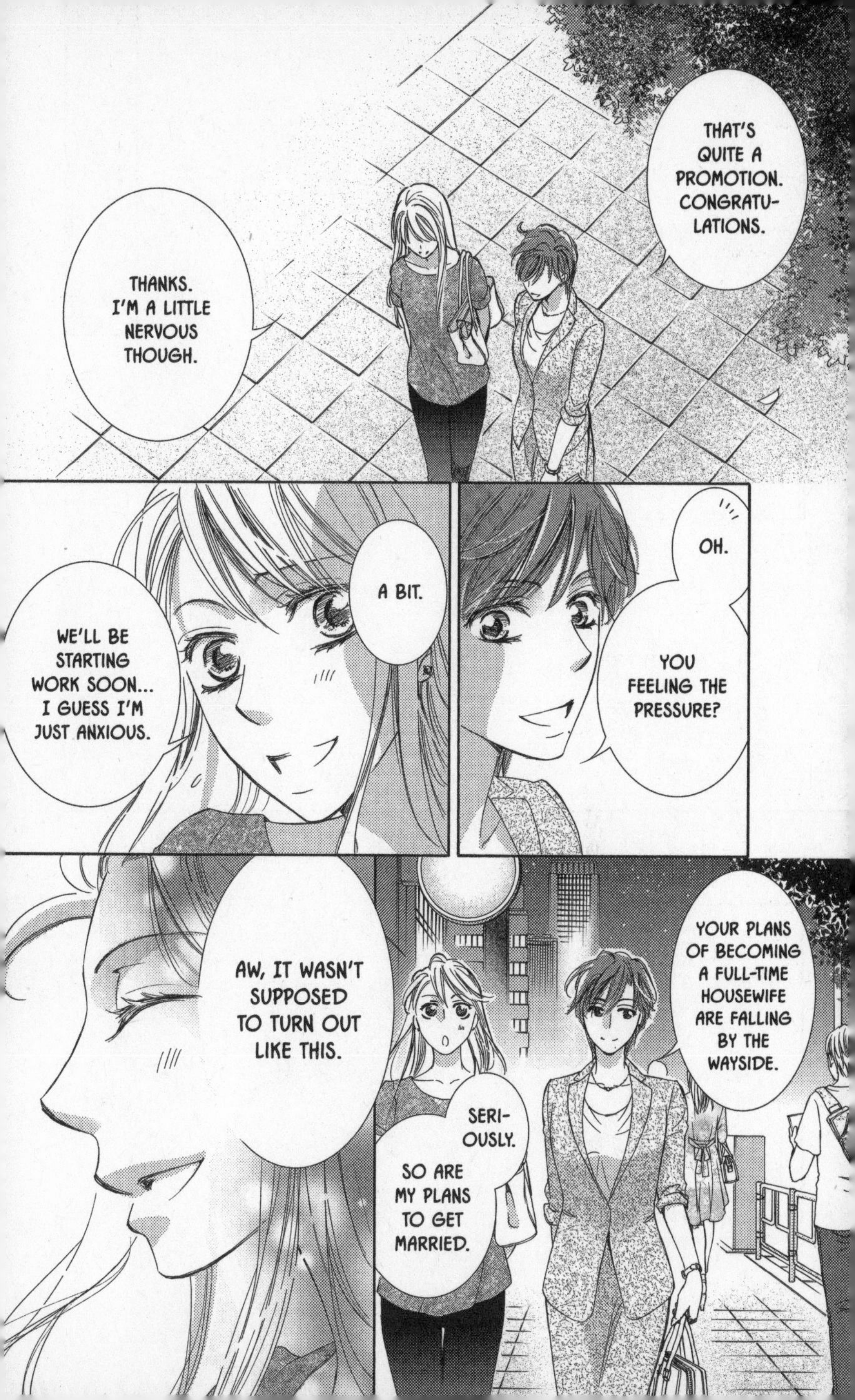
THAT'S QUITE A PROMOTION. CONGRATULATIONS.
THANKS. I'M A LITTLE NERVOUS THOUGH.
OH.
YOU FEELING THE PRESSURE?
A BIT.
WE'LL BE STARTING WORK SOON... I GUESS I'M JUST ANXIOUS.
YOUR PLANS OF BECOMING A FULL-TIME HOUSEWIFE ARE FALLING BY THE WAYSIDE.
SERIOUSLY.
SO ARE MY PLANS TO GET MARRIED.
AW, IT WASN'T SUPPOSED TO TURN OUT LIKE THIS.

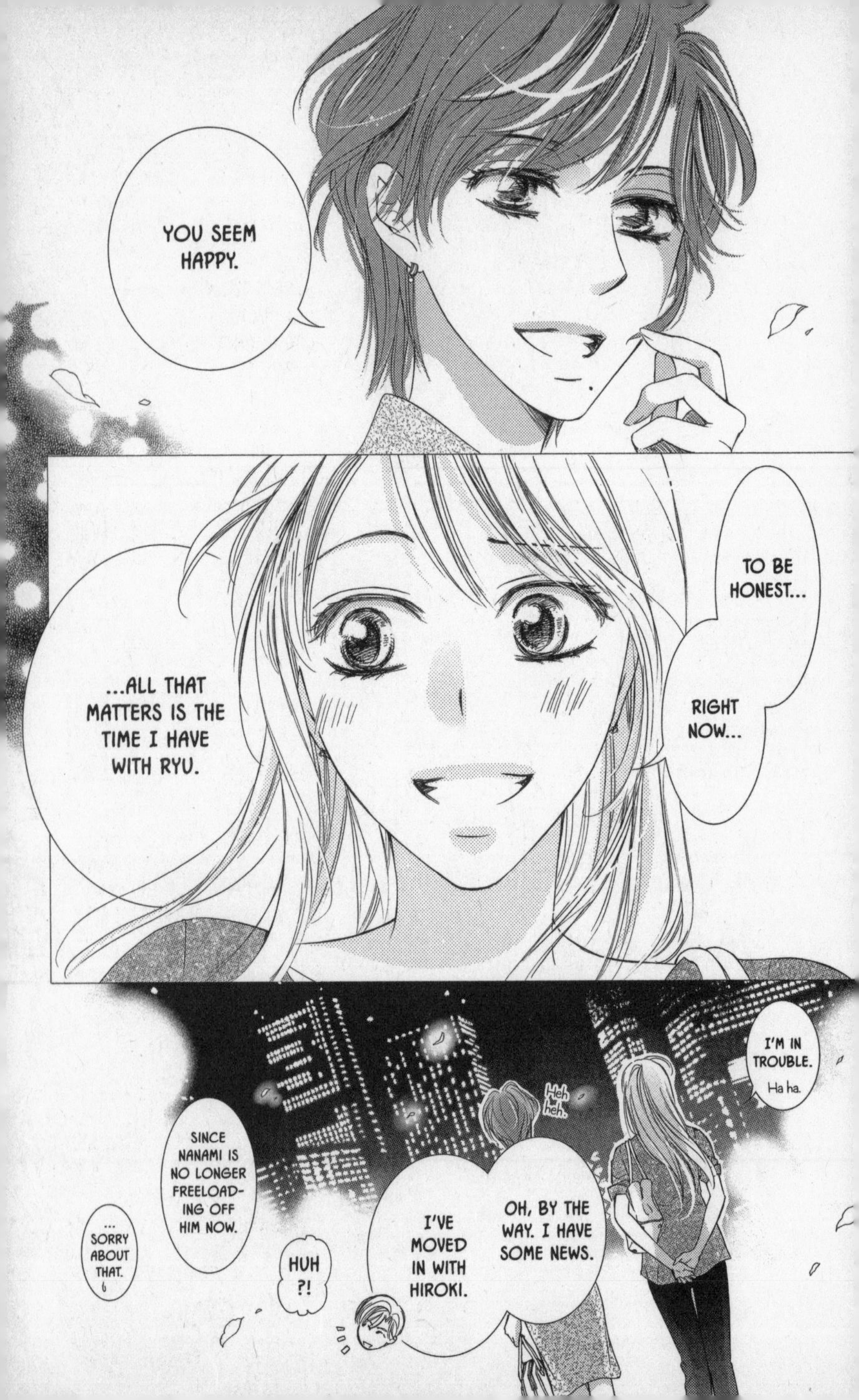
YOU SEEM HAPPY.
TO BE HONEST... RIGHT NOW...
...ALL THAT MATTERS IS THE TIME I HAVE WITH RYU.
I'M IN TROUBLE.
Ha ha.
Heh heh.
OH, BY THE WAY. I HAVE SOME NEWS.
I'VE MOVED IN WITH HIROKI.
HUH?!
SINCE NANAMI IS NO LONGER FREELOADING OFF HIM NOW.
...SORRY ABOUT THAT.

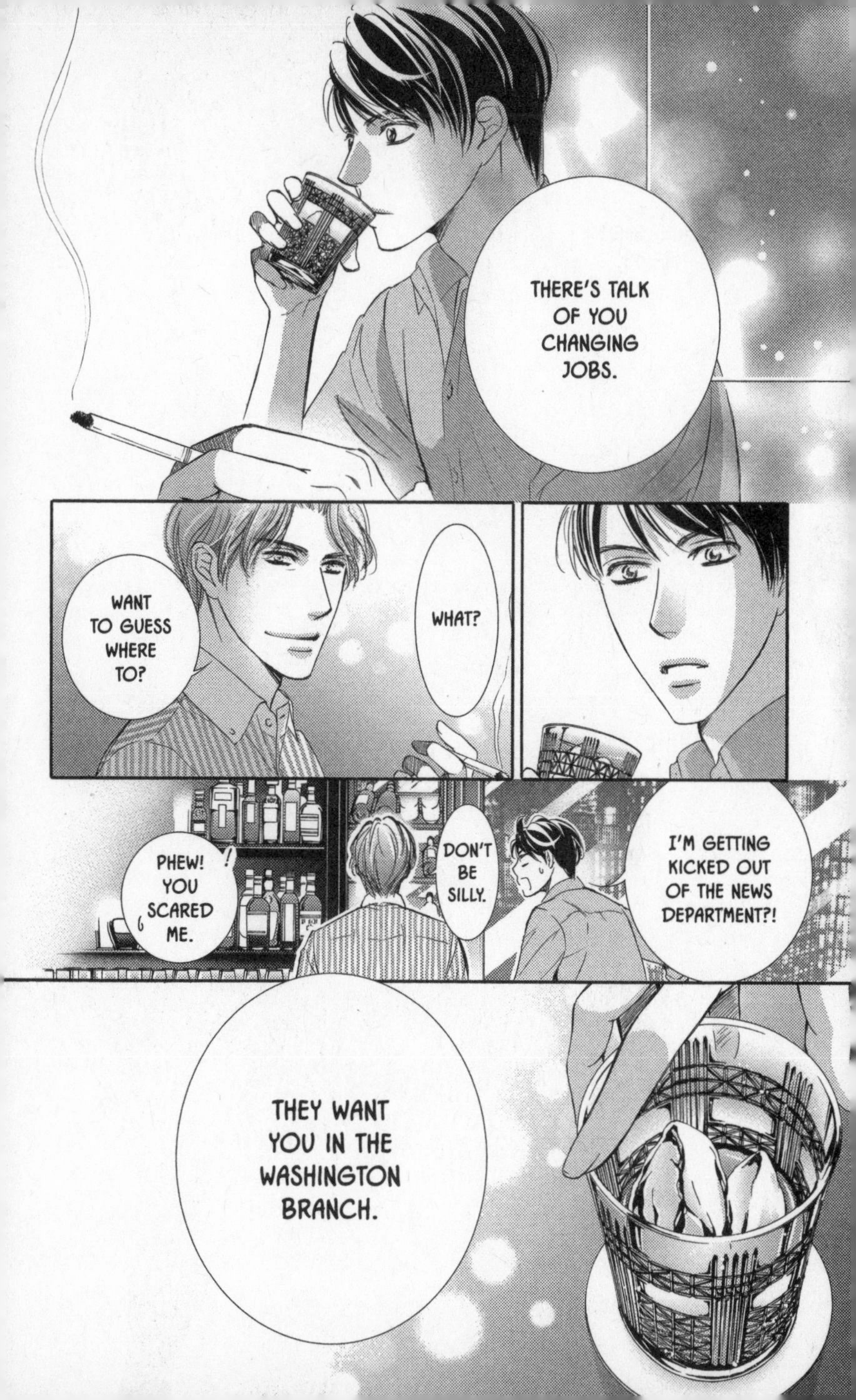
THERE'S TALK OF YOU CHANGING JOBS.
WHAT?
WANT TO GUESS WHERE TO?
I'M GETTING KICKED OUT OF THE NEWS DEPARTMENT?!
DON'T BE SILLY.
PHEW! YOU SCARED ME.
THEY WANT YOU IN THE WASHINGTON BRANCH.

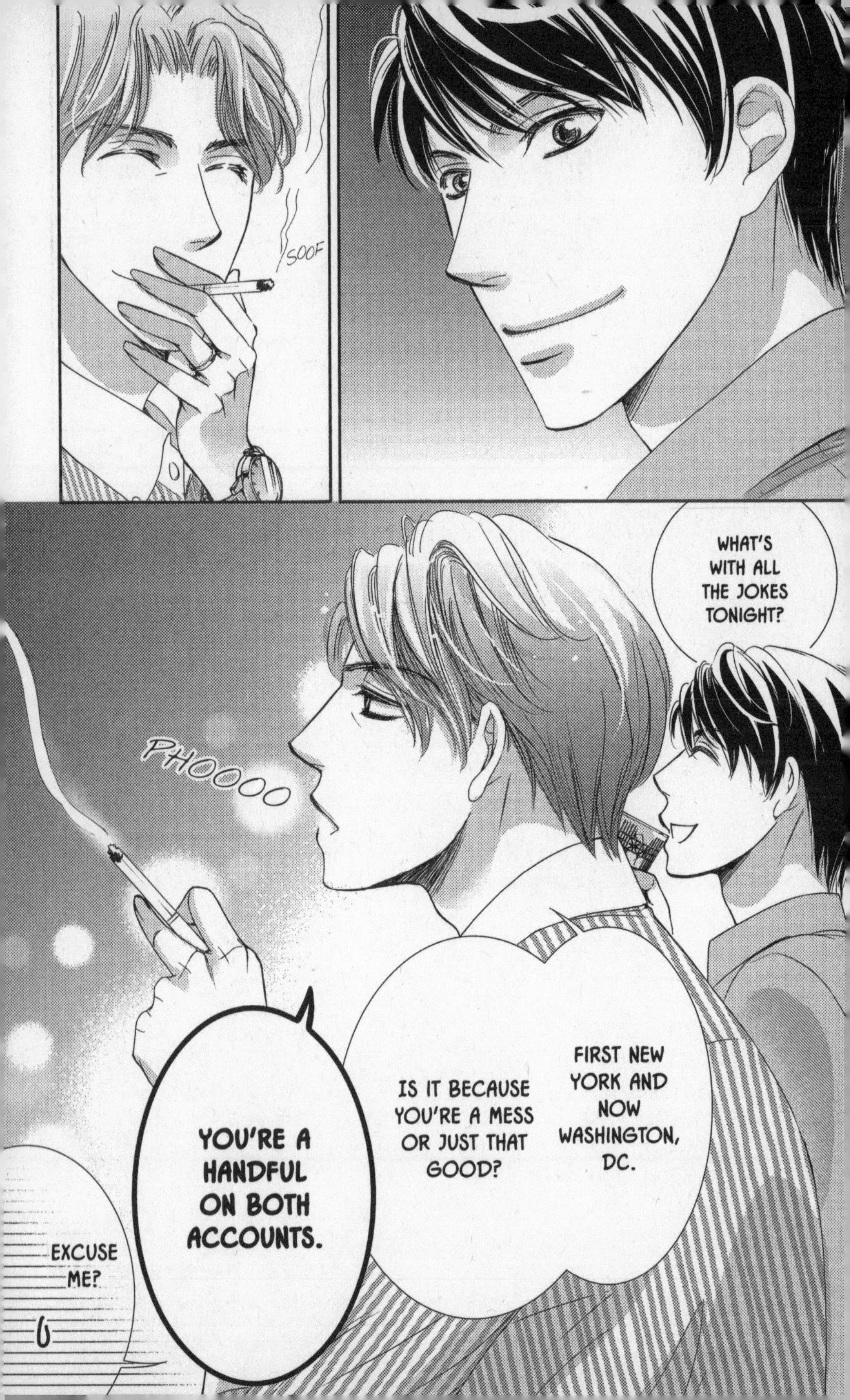
SOOF
WHAT'S WITH ALL THE JOKES TONIGHT?
PHOOOOO
FIRST NEW YORK AND NOW WASHINGTON, DC.
IS IT BECAUSE YOU'RE A MESS OR JUST THAT GOOD?
YOU'RE A HANDFUL ON BOTH ACCOUNTS.
EXCUSE ME?

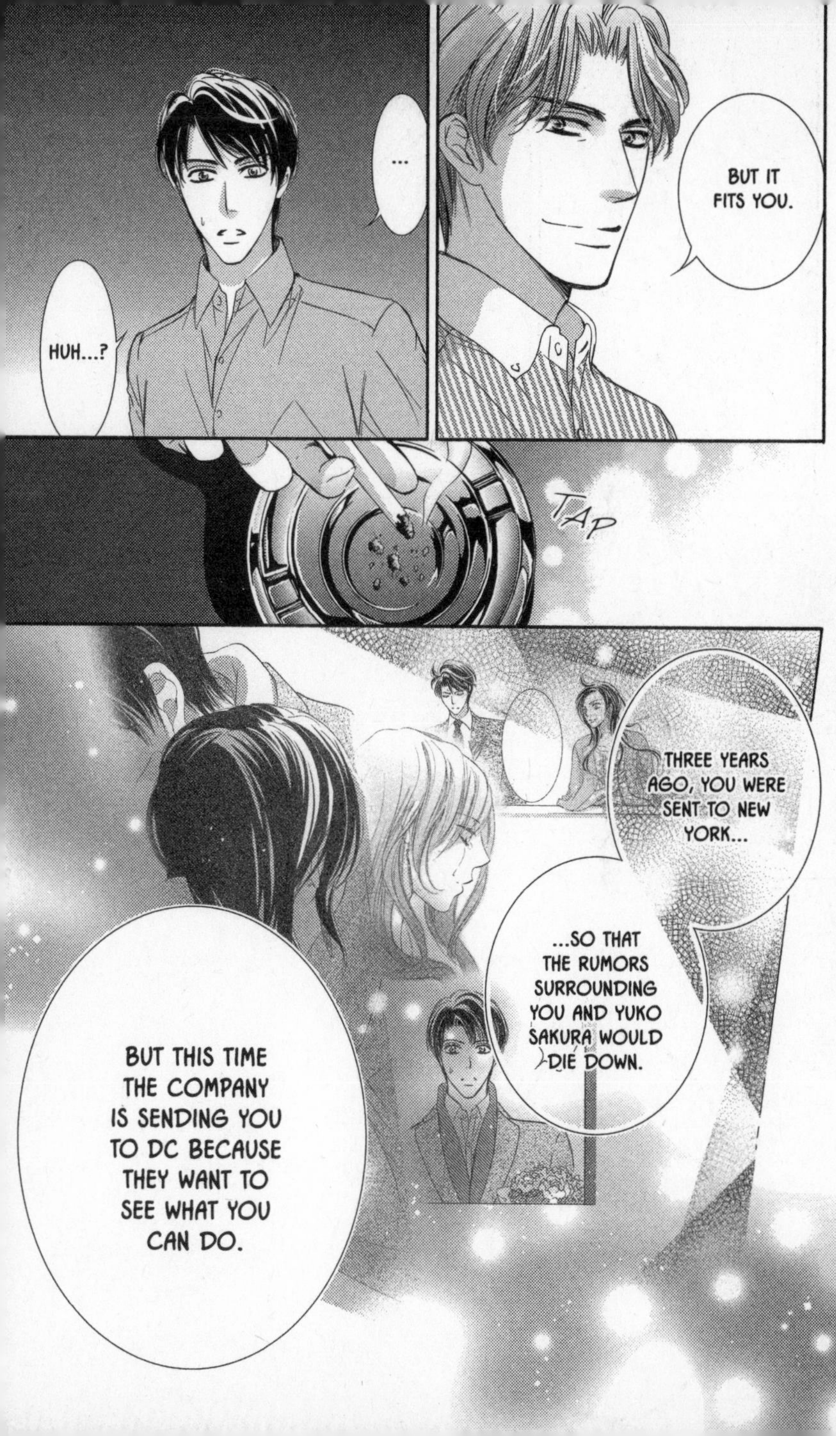
BUT IT FITS YOU.
...
HUH...?
TAP
THREE YEARS AGO, YOU WERE SENT TO NEW YORK...
...SO THAT THE RUMORS SURROUNDING YOU AND YUKO SAKURA WOULD DIE DOWN.
BUT THIS TIME THE COMPANY IS SENDING YOU TO DC BECAUSE THEY WANT TO SEE WHAT YOU CAN DO.

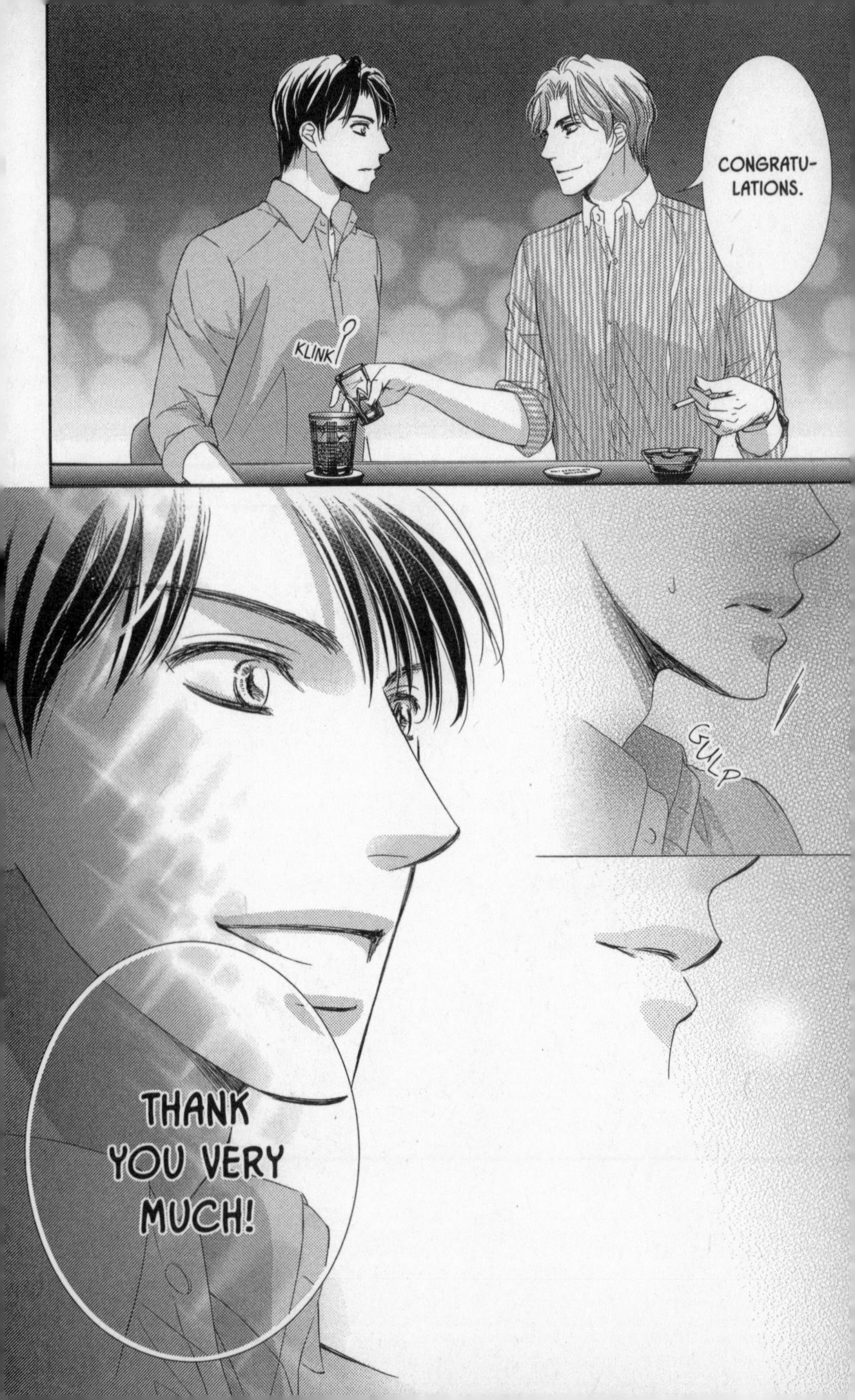
CONGRATULATIONS.
KLINK
GULP
THANK YOU VERY MUCH!

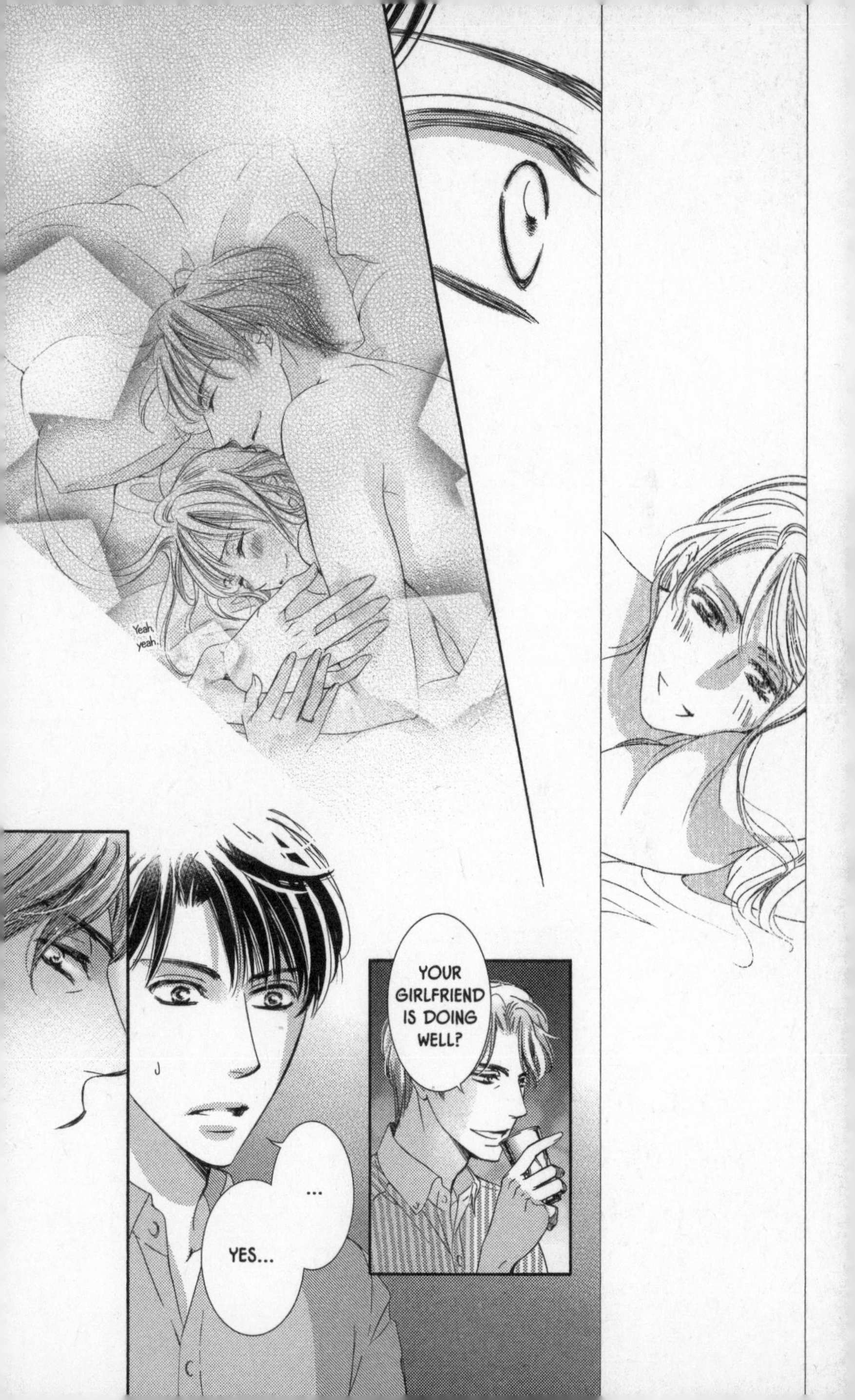
Yeah, yeah.
YOUR GIRLFRIEND IS DOING WELL?
...
YES...

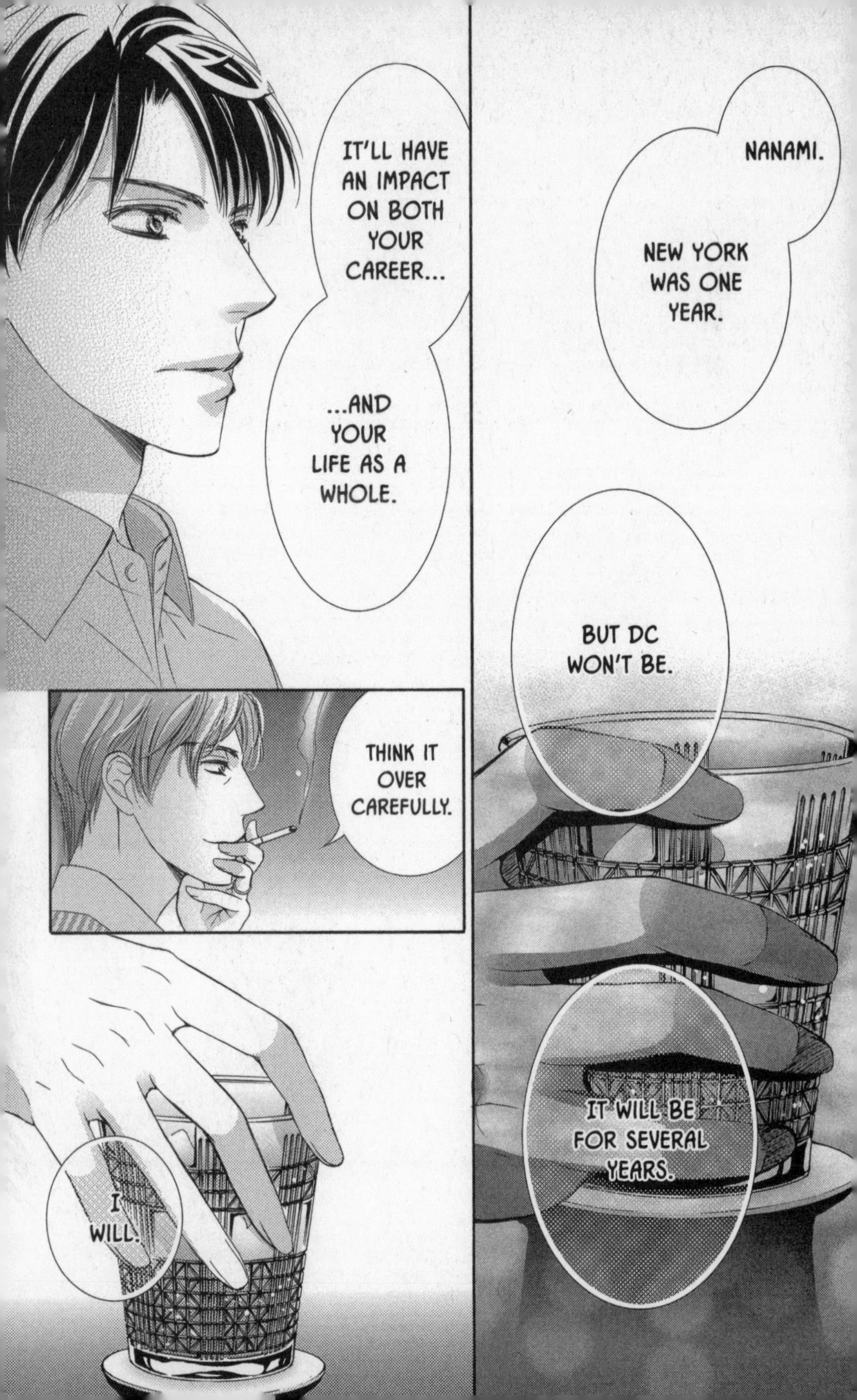
NANAMI.
NEW YORK WAS ONE YEAR.
BUT DC WON'T BE.
IT WILL BE FOR SEVERAL YEARS.
IT'LL HAVE AN IMPACT ON BOTH YOUR CAREER...
...AND YOUR LIFE AS A WHOLE.
THINK IT OVER CAREFULLY.
I WILL.

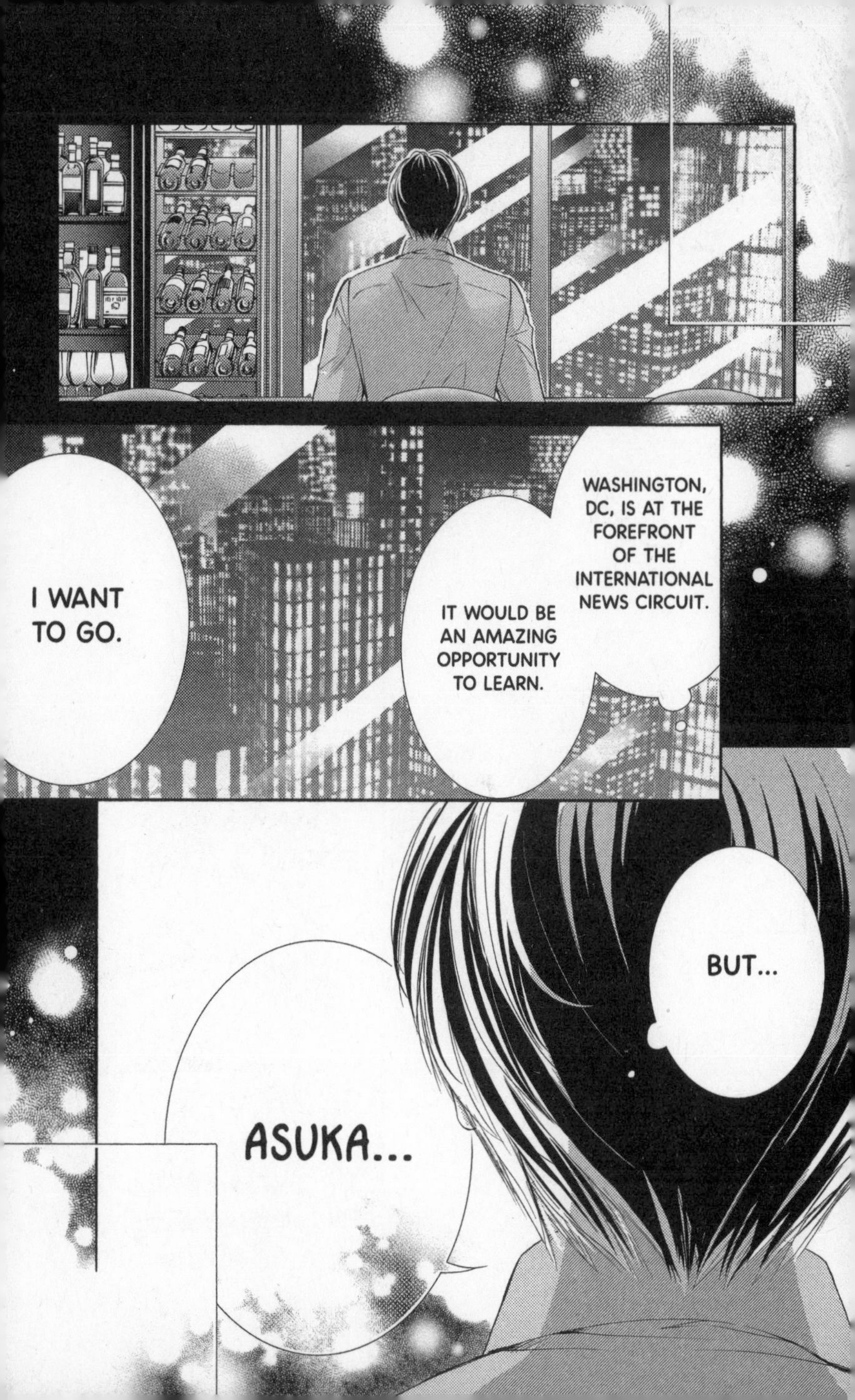
WASHINGTON, DC, IS AT THE FOREFRONT OF THE INTERNATIONAL NEWS CIRCUIT.
IT WOULD BE AN AMAZING OPPORTUNITY TO LEARN.
I WANT TO GO.
BUT...
ASUKA...

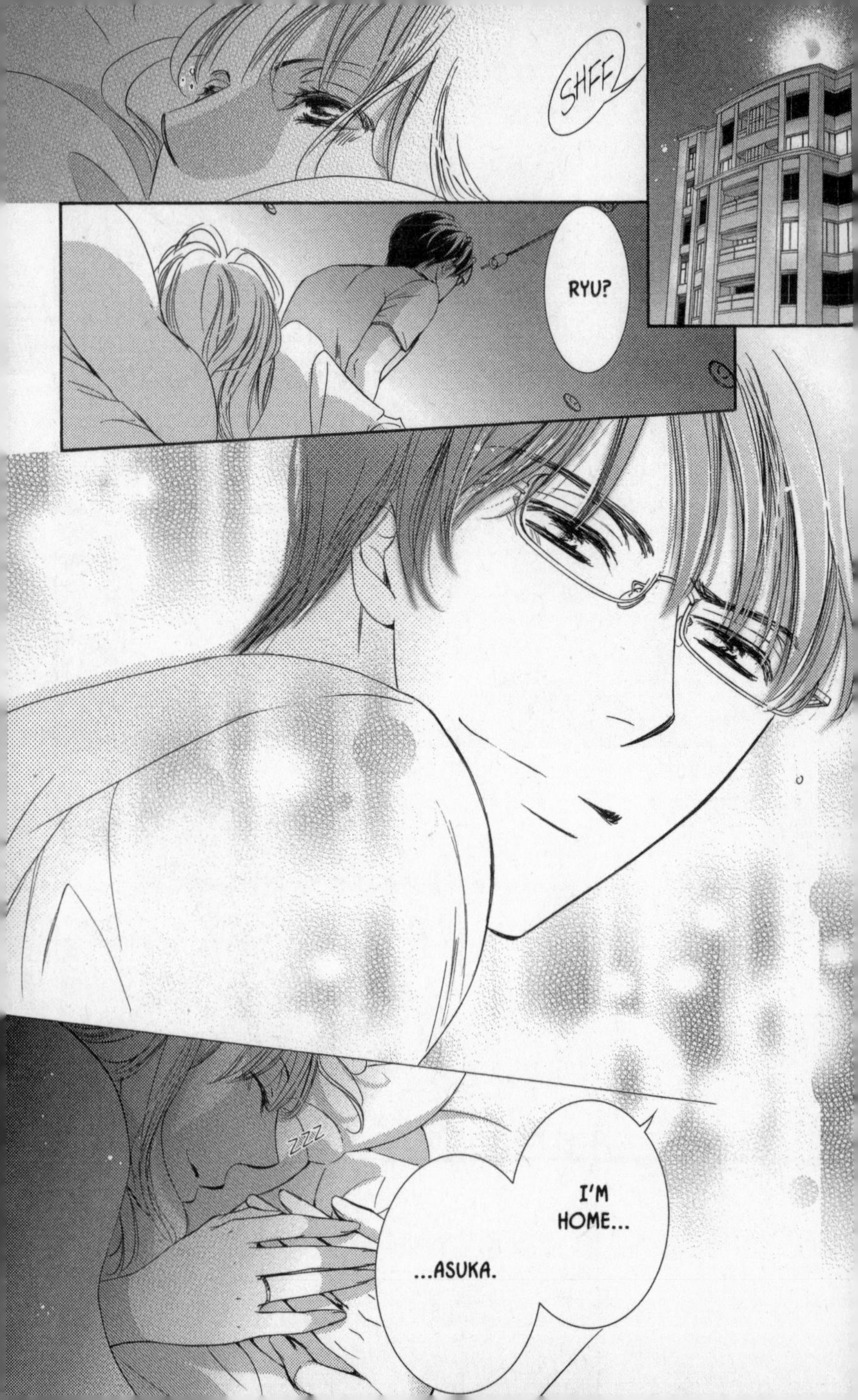
SHFF
RYU?
ZZZ
I'M HOME...
...ASUKA.

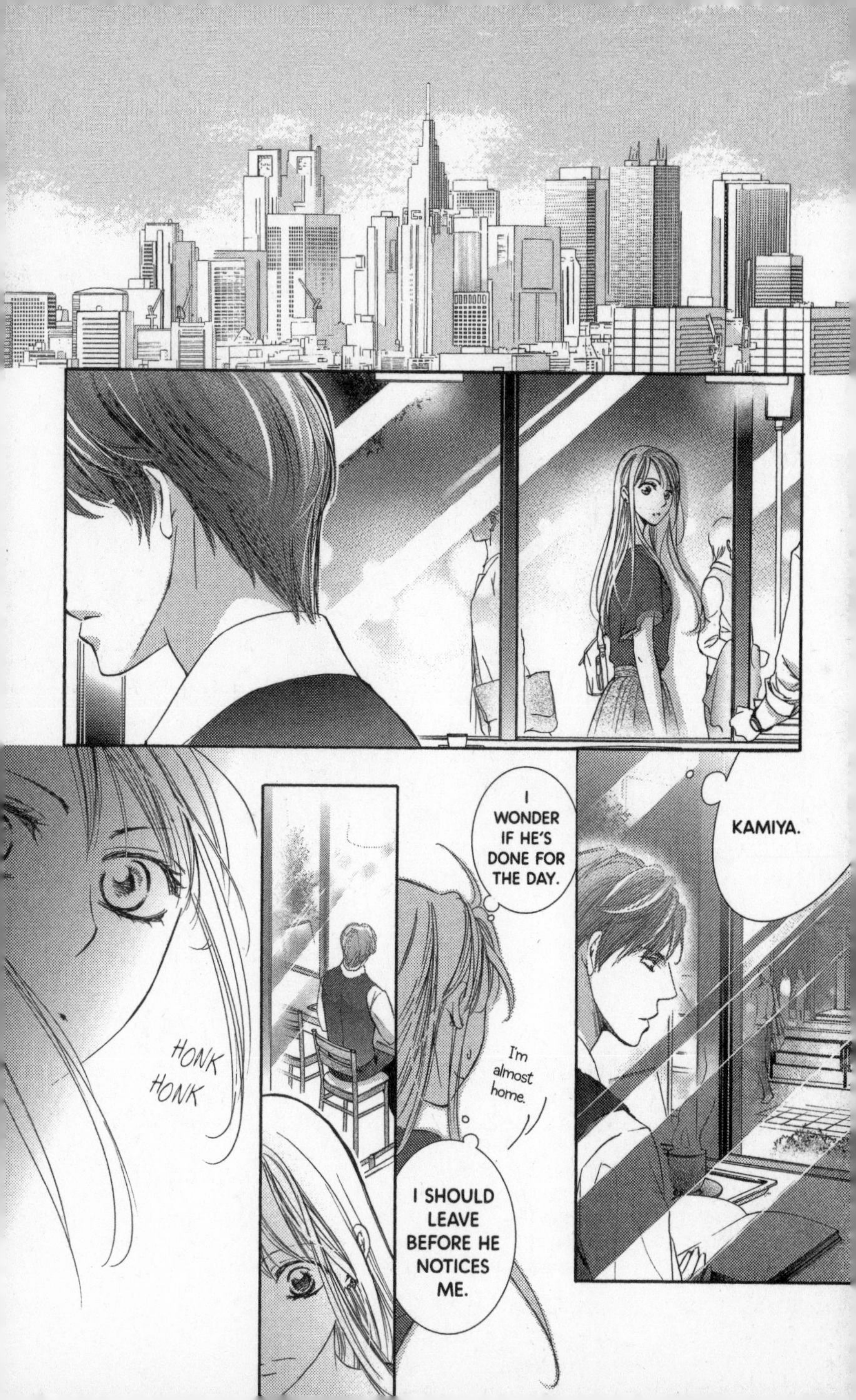
KAMIYA.
I WONDER IF HE'S DONE FOR THE DAY.
I'm almost home.
I SHOULD LEAVE BEFORE HE NOTICES ME.
HONK HONK

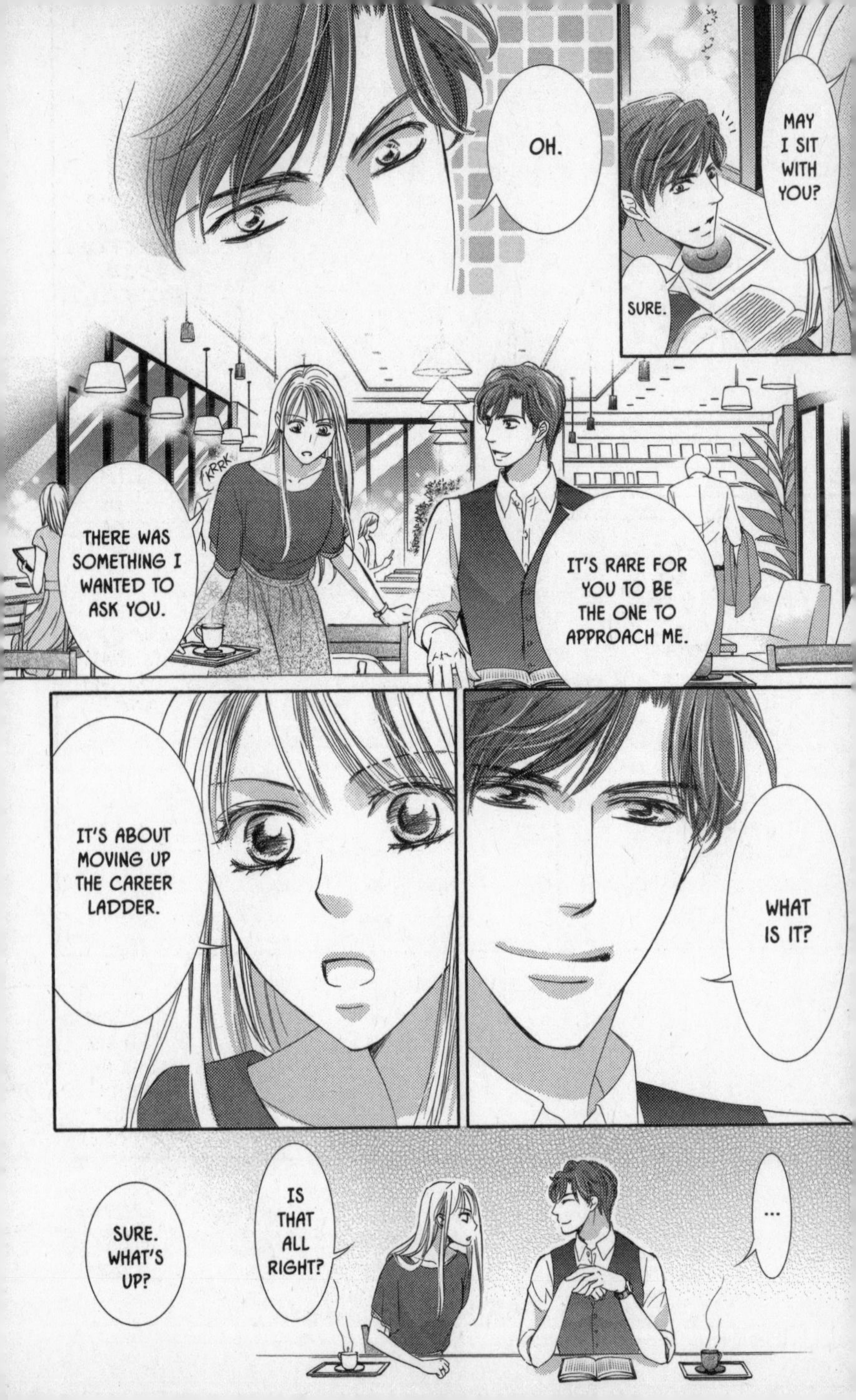
MAY I SIT WITH YOU?
SURE.
OH.
IT'S RARE FOR YOU TO BE THE ONE TO APPROACH ME.
KRRK
THERE WAS SOMETHING I WANTED TO ASK YOU.
WHAT IS IT?
IT'S ABOUT MOVING UP THE CAREER LADDER.
...
IS THAT ALL RIGHT?
SURE. WHAT'S UP?

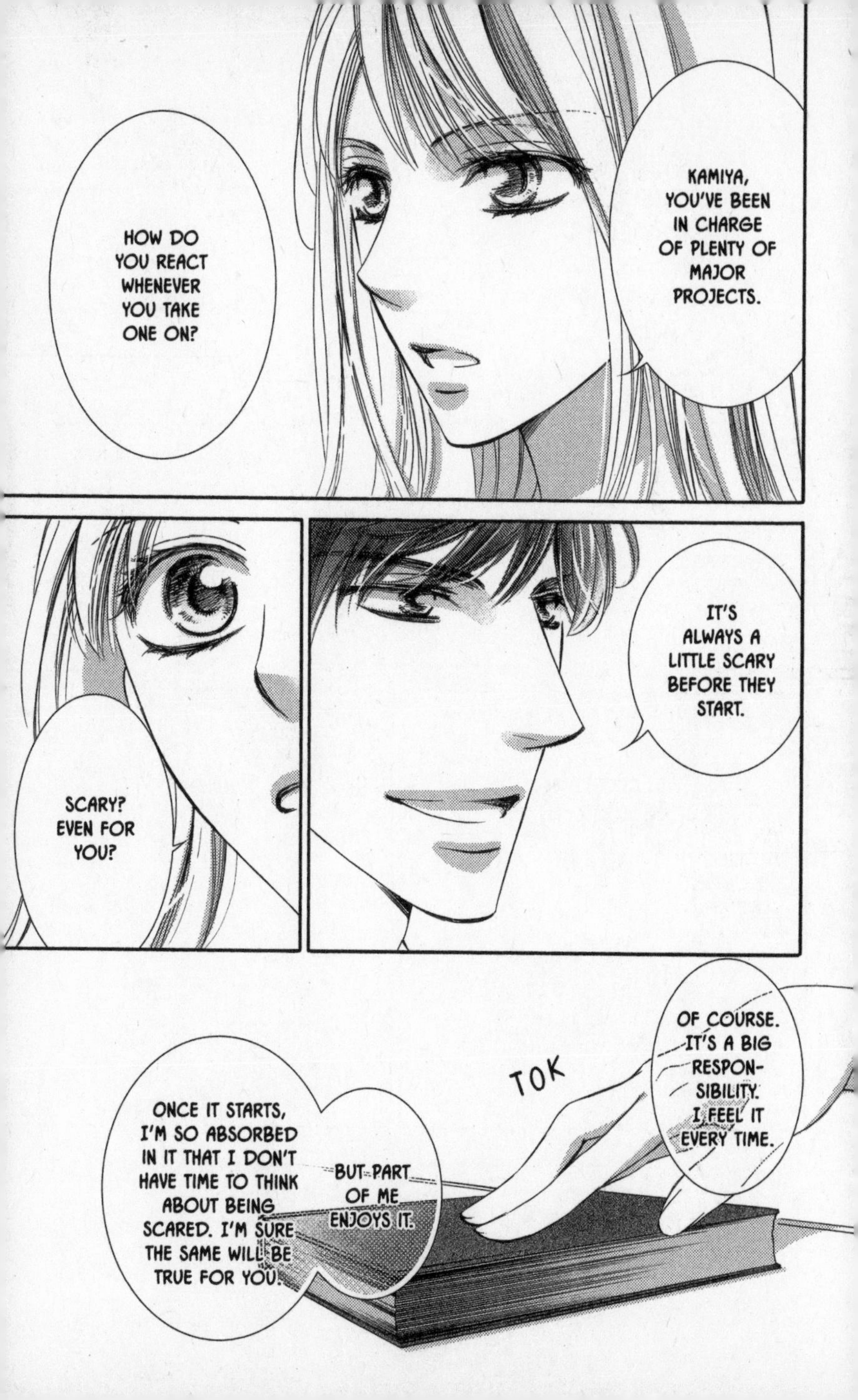
KAMIYA, YOU'VE BEEN IN CHARGE OF PLENTY OF MAJOR PROJECTS.
HOW DO YOU REACT WHENEVER YOU TAKE ONE ON?
IT'S ALWAYS A LITTLE SCARY BEFORE THEY START.
SCARY? EVEN FOR YOU?
OF COURSE. IT'S A BIG RESPON-SIBILITY. I FEEL IT EVERY TIME.
TOK
BUT PART OF ME ENJOYS IT.
ONCE IT STARTS, I'M SO ABSORBED IN IT THAT I DON'T HAVE TIME TO THINK ABOUT BEING SCARED. I'M SURE THE SAME WILL BE TRUE FOR YOU.

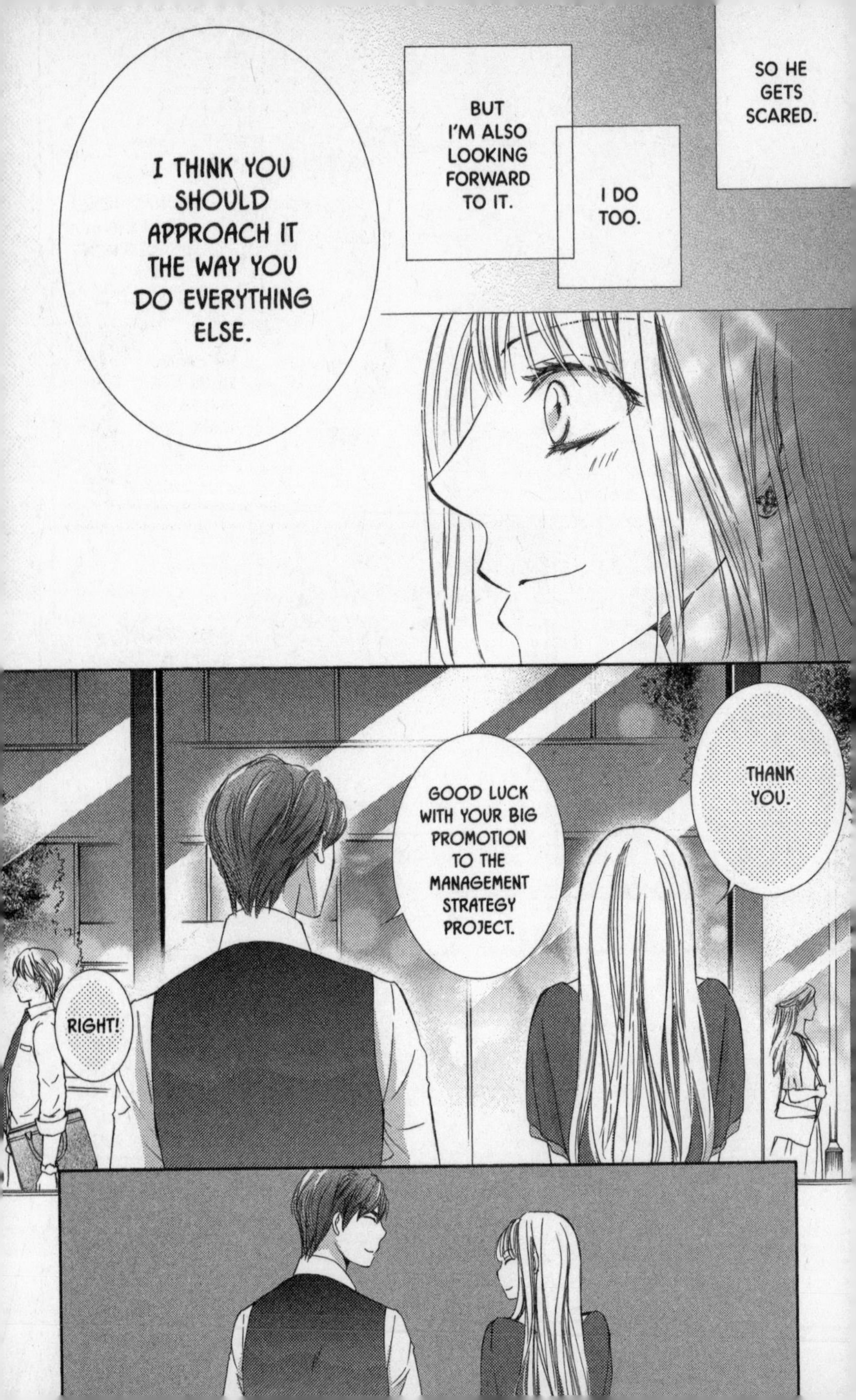
SO HE GETS SCARED.
I DO TOO.
BUT I'M ALSO LOOKING FORWARD TO IT.
I THINK YOU SHOULD APPROACH IT THE WAY YOU DO EVERYTHING ELSE.
THANK YOU.
GOOD LUCK WITH YOUR BIG PROMOTION TO THE MANAGEMENT STRATEGY PROJECT.
RIGHT!

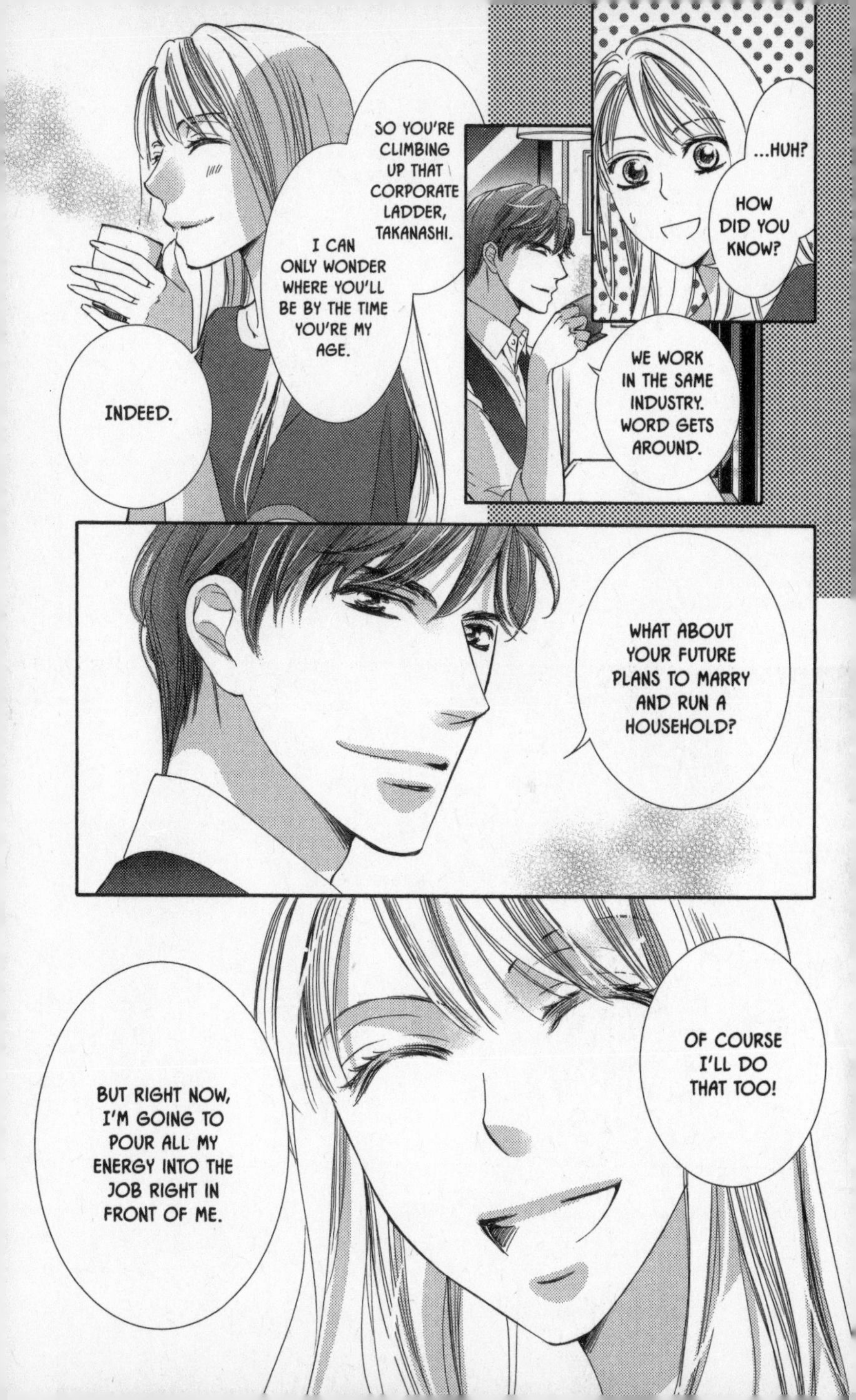
...HUH?
HOW DID YOU KNOW?
WE WORK IN THE SAME INDUSTRY. WORD GETS AROUND.
SO YOU'RE CLIMBING UP THAT CORPORATE LADDER, TAKANASHI.
I CAN ONLY WONDER WHERE YOU'LL BE BY THE TIME YOU'RE MY AGE.
INDEED.
WHAT ABOUT YOUR FUTURE PLANS TO MARRY AND RUN A HOUSEHOLD?
OF COURSE I'LL DO THAT TOO!
BUT RIGHT NOW, I'M GOING TO POUR ALL MY ENERGY INTO THE JOB RIGHT IN FRONT OF ME.

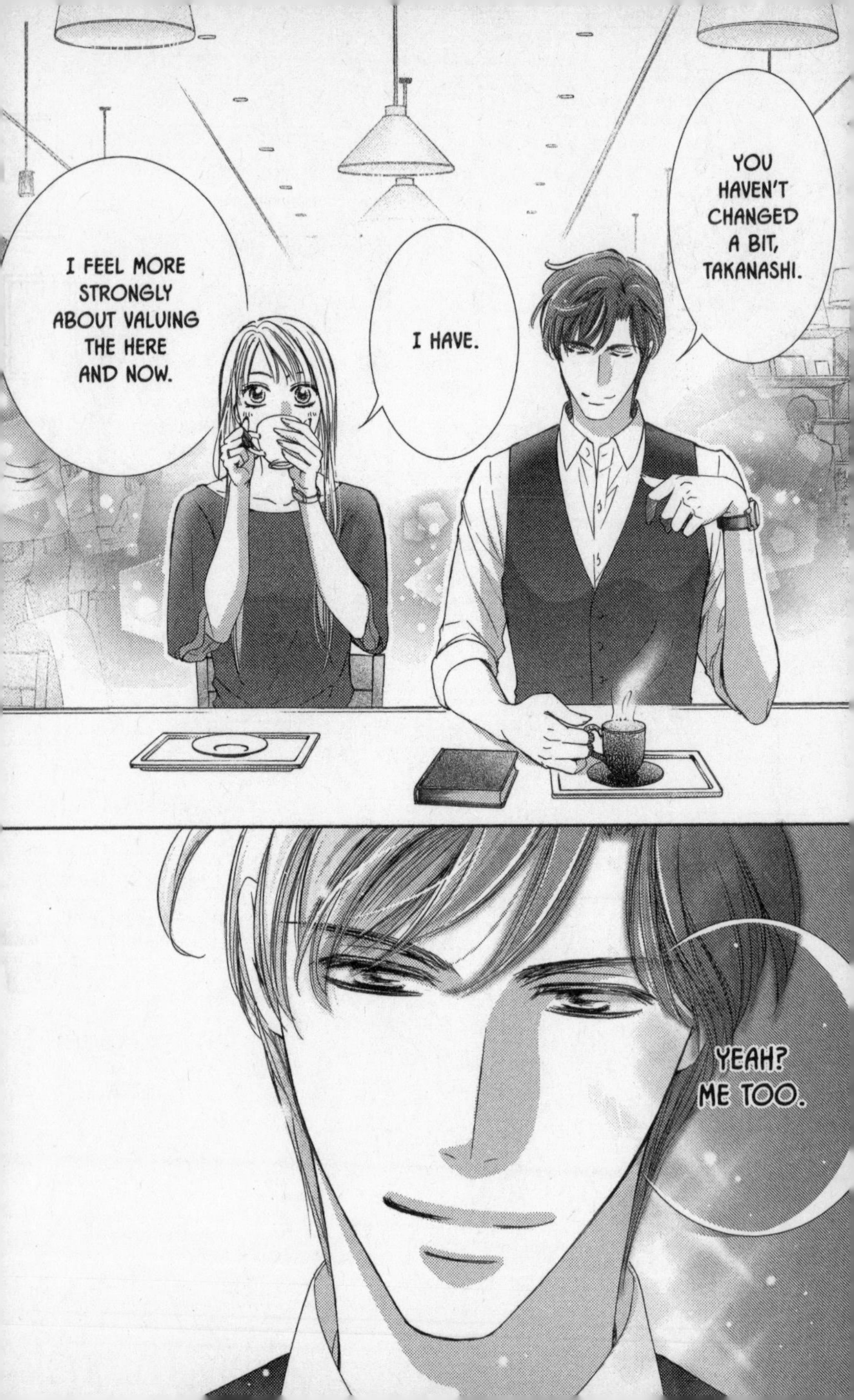
YOU HAVEN'T CHANGED A BIT, TAKANASHI.
I HAVE.
I FEEL MORE STRONGLY ABOUT VALUING THE HERE AND NOW.
YEAH? ME TOO.

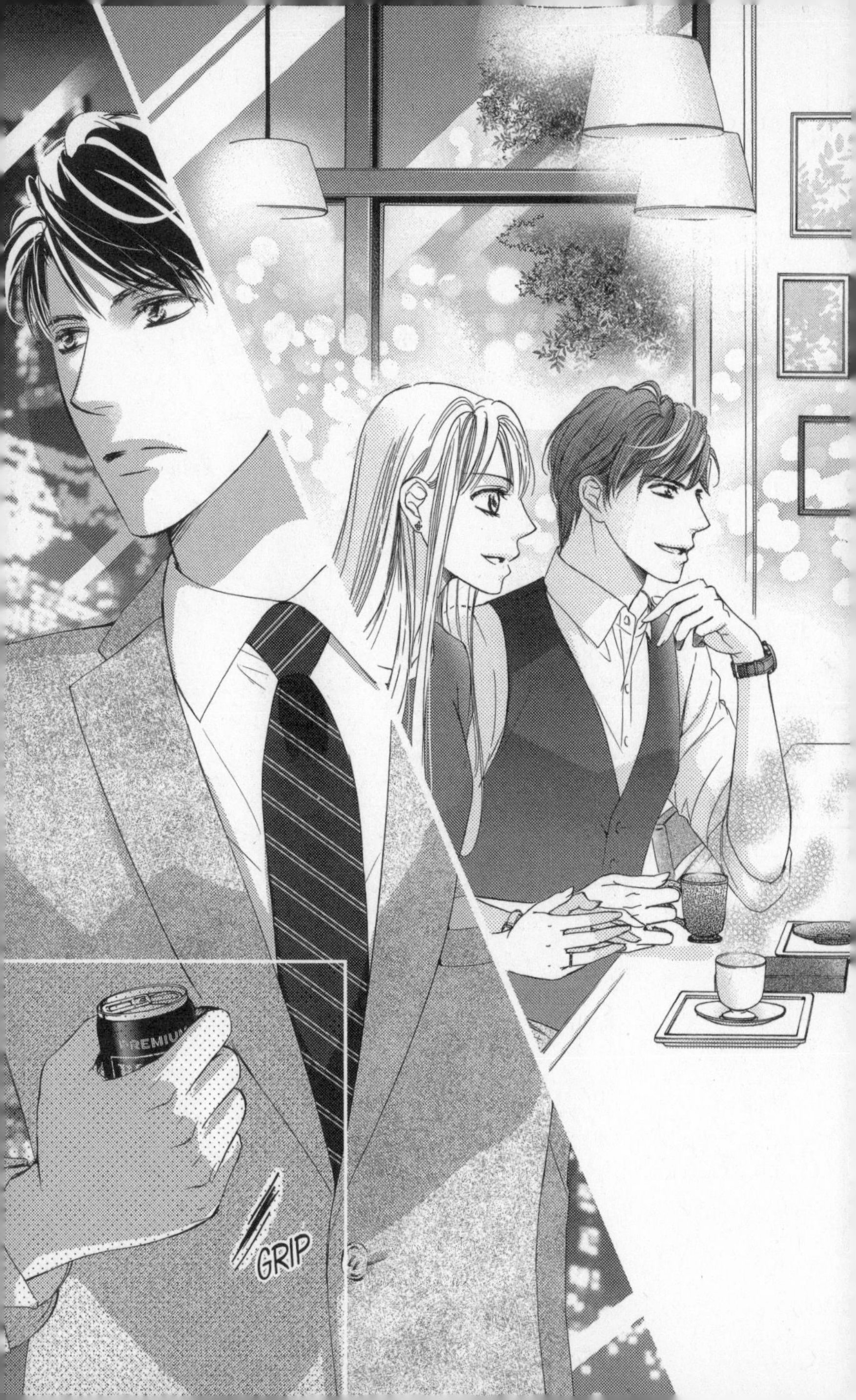
GRIP

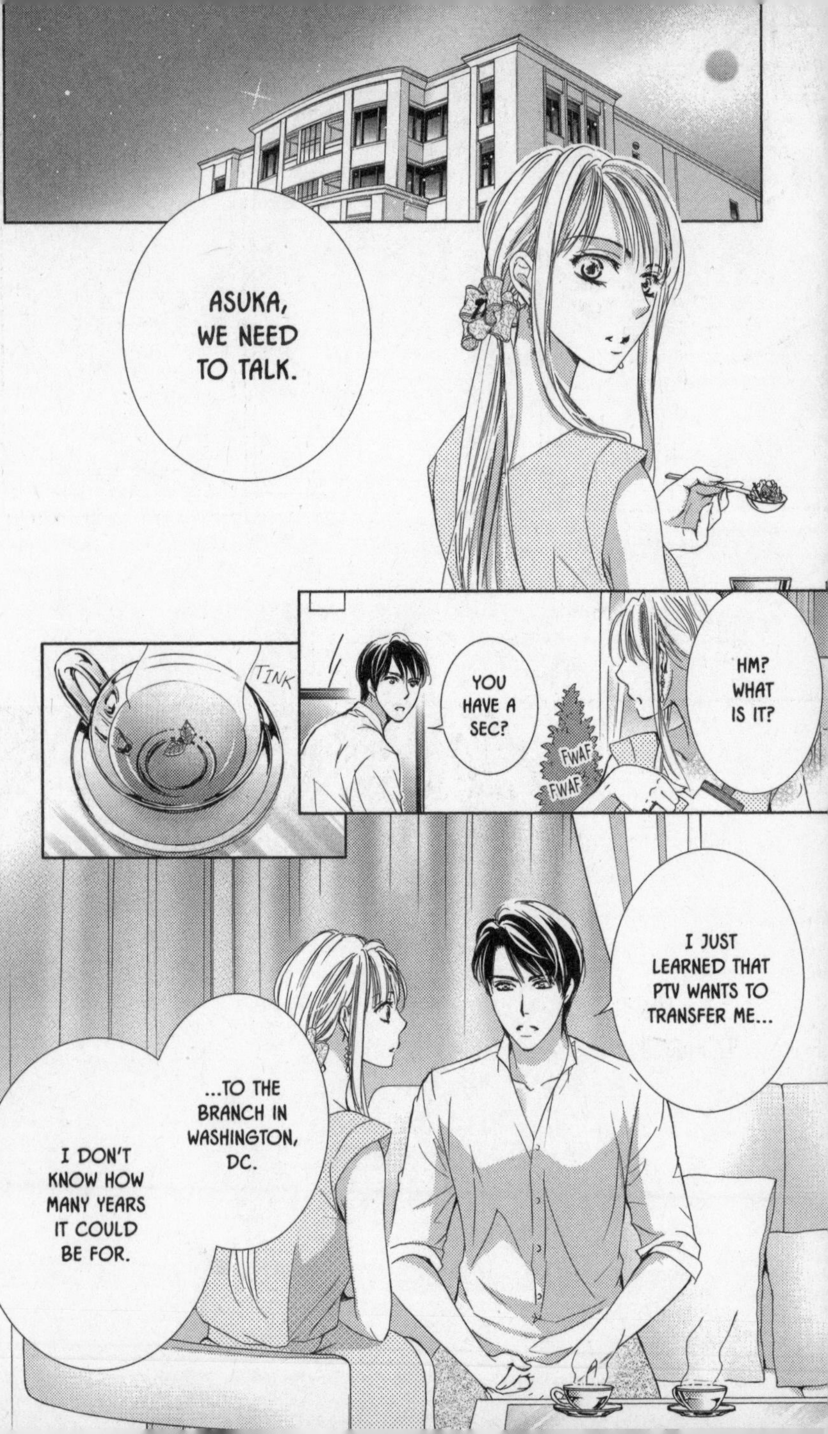
ASUKA, WE NEED TO TALK.
YOU HAVE A SEC?
FWAF
FWAF
HM? WHAT IS IT?
TINK
I JUST LEARNED THAT PTV WANTS TO TRANSFER ME...
...TO THE BRANCH IN WASHINGTON, DC.
I DON'T KNOW HOW MANY YEARS IT COULD BE FOR.

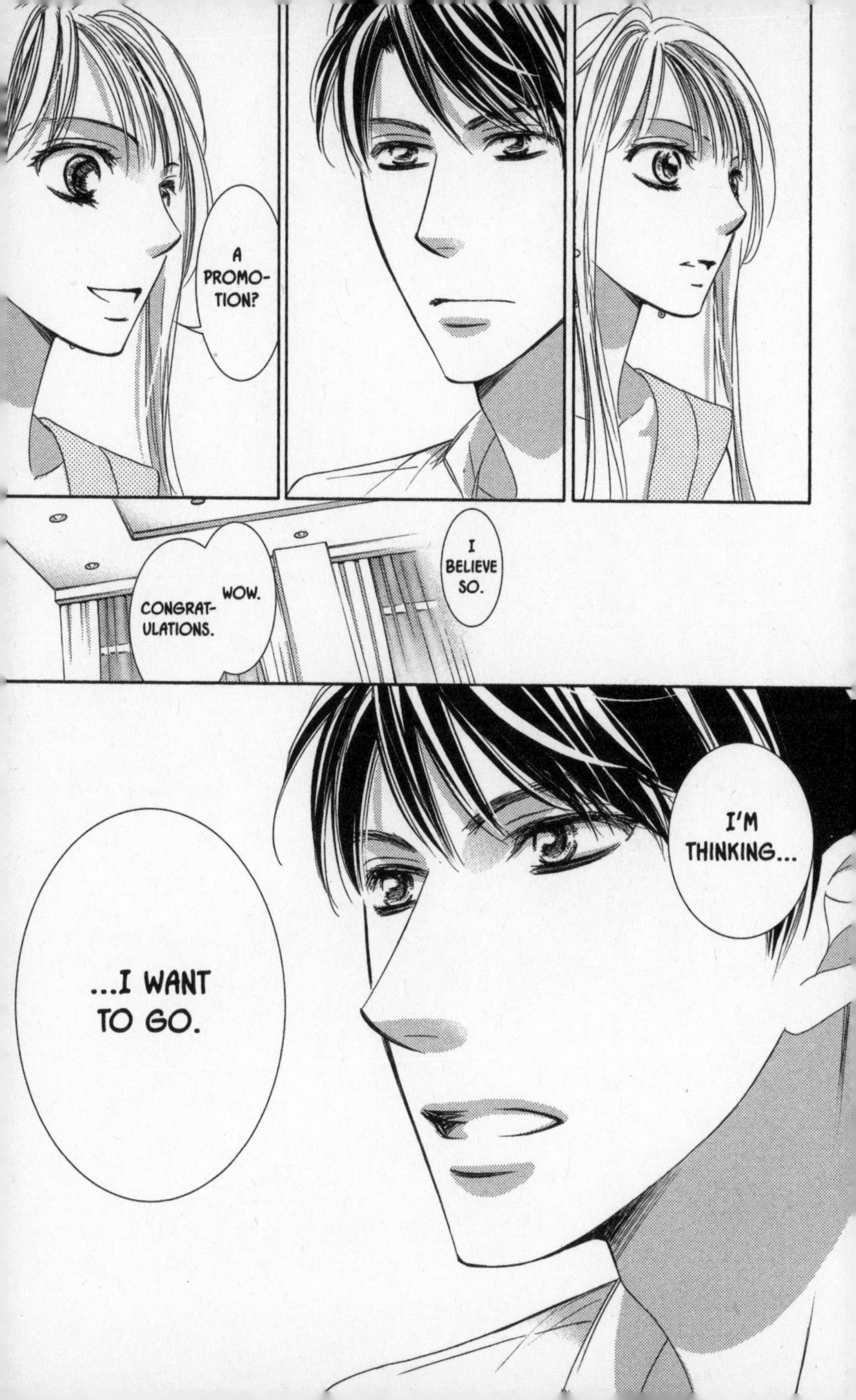

A PROMOTION?
I BELIEVE SO.
WOW. CONGRATULATIONS.
I'M THINKING...
...I WANT TO GO.

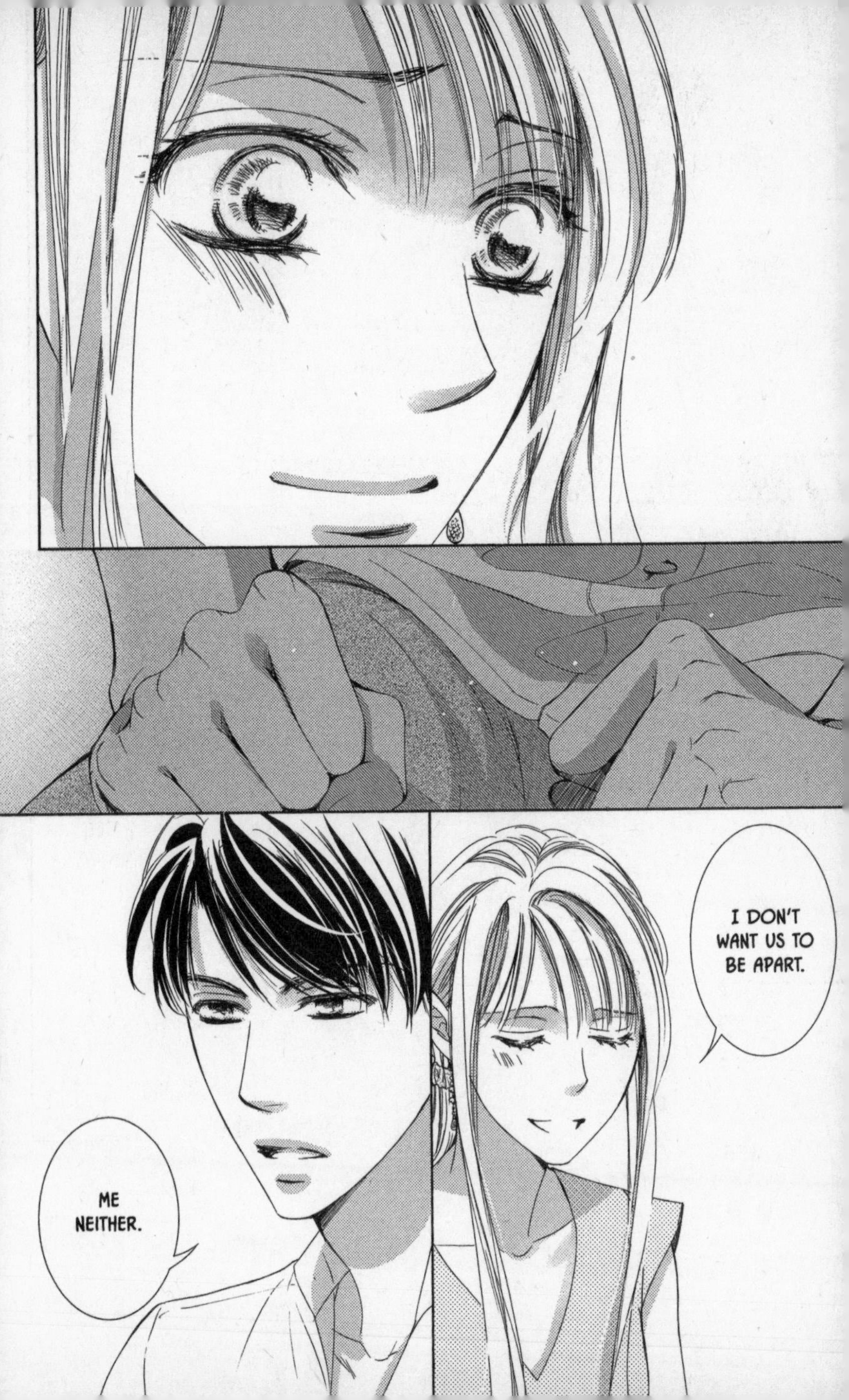
I DON'T WANT US TO BE APART.
ME NEITHER.

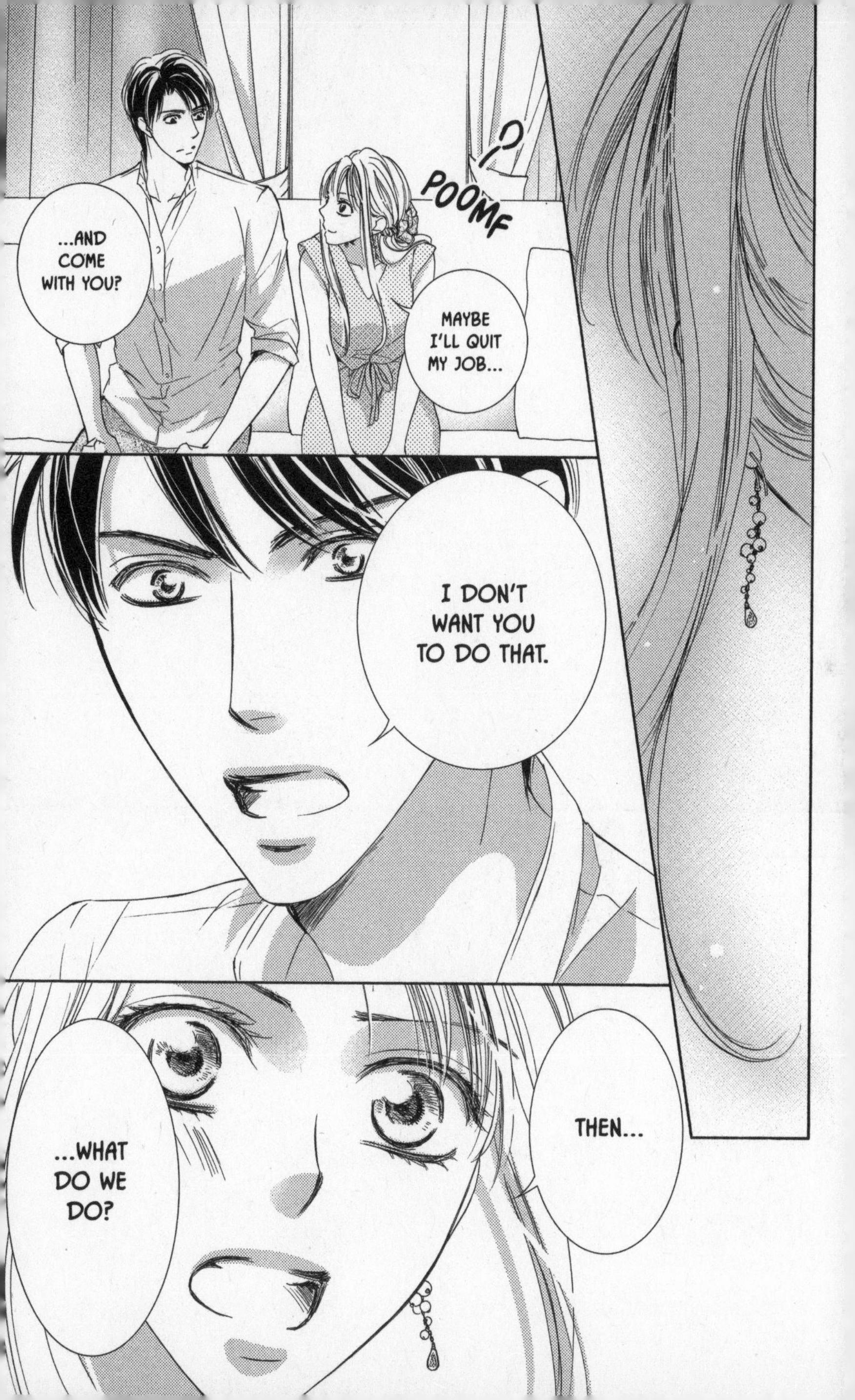
?
POOMF
MAYBE I'LL QUIT MY JOB...
...AND COME WITH YOU?
I DON'T WANT YOU TO DO THAT.
THEN...
...WHAT DO WE DO?

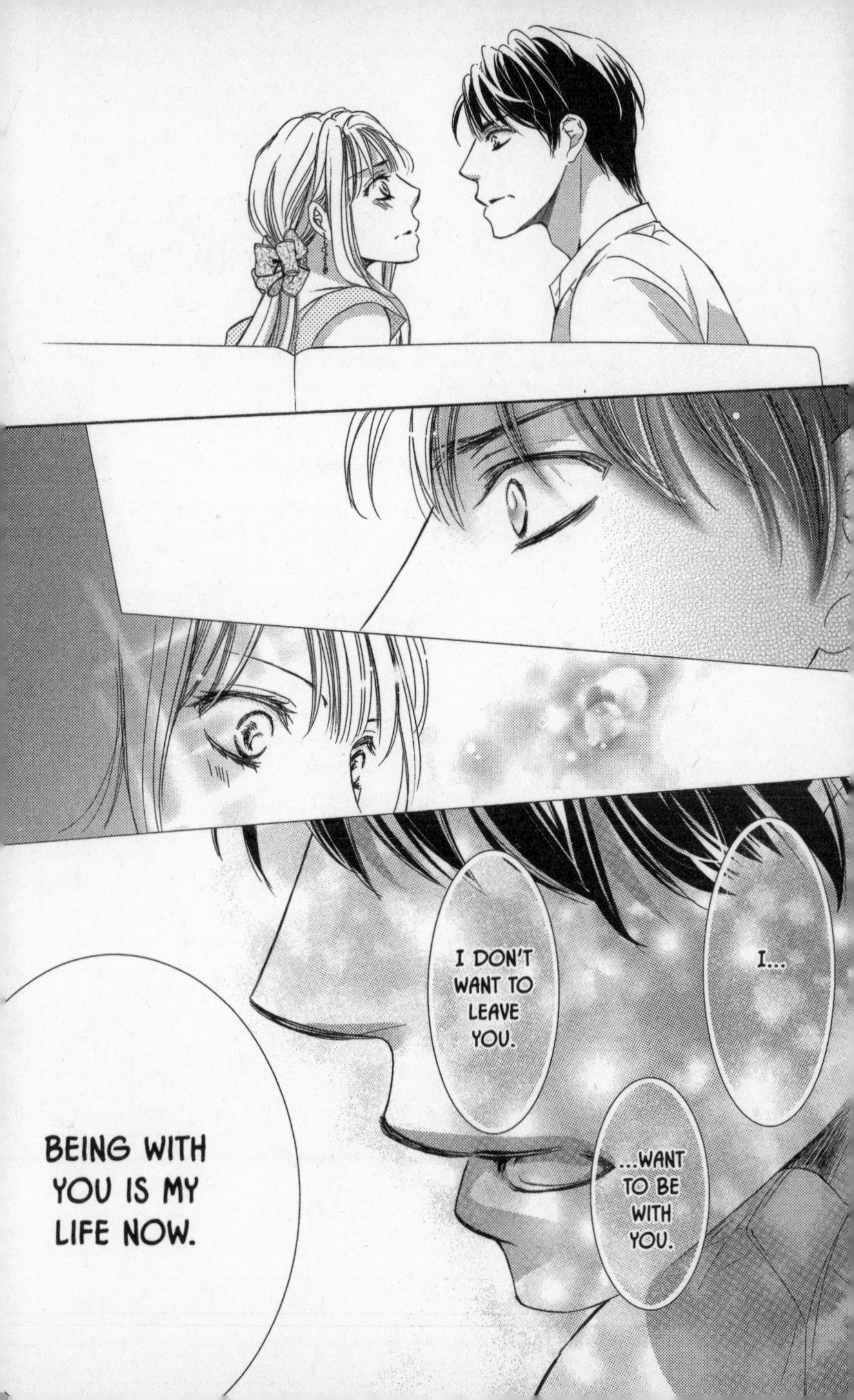
I...
...WANT TO BE WITH YOU.
I DON'T WANT TO LEAVE YOU.
BEING WITH YOU IS MY LIFE NOW.

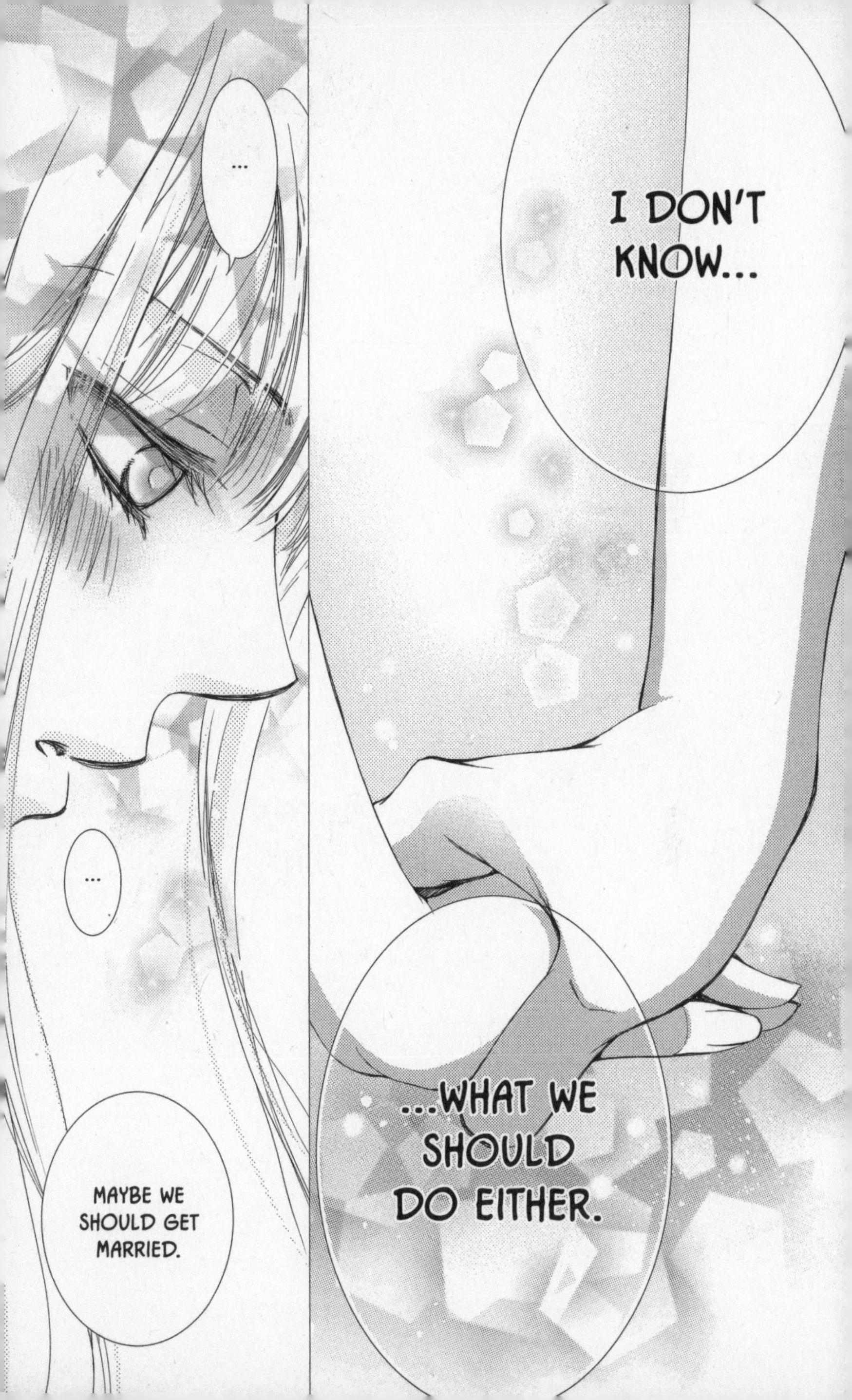
I DON'T KNOW...
...WHAT WE SHOULD DO EITHER.
...
...
MAYBE WE SHOULD GET MARRIED.

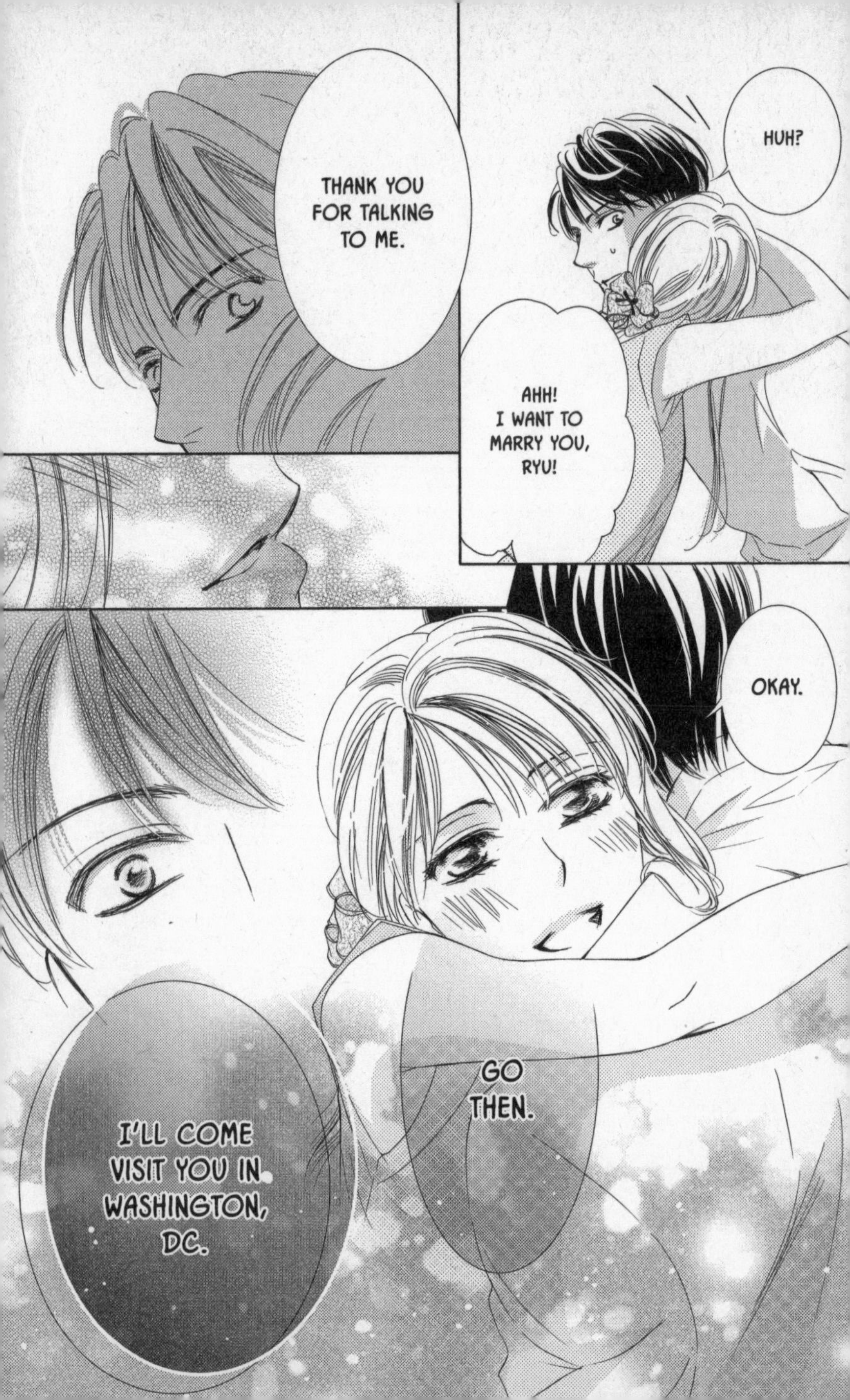
HUH?
AHH! I WANT TO MARRY YOU, RYU!
THANK YOU FOR TALKING TO ME.
OKAY.
GO THEN.
I'LL COME VISIT YOU IN WASHINGTON, DC.

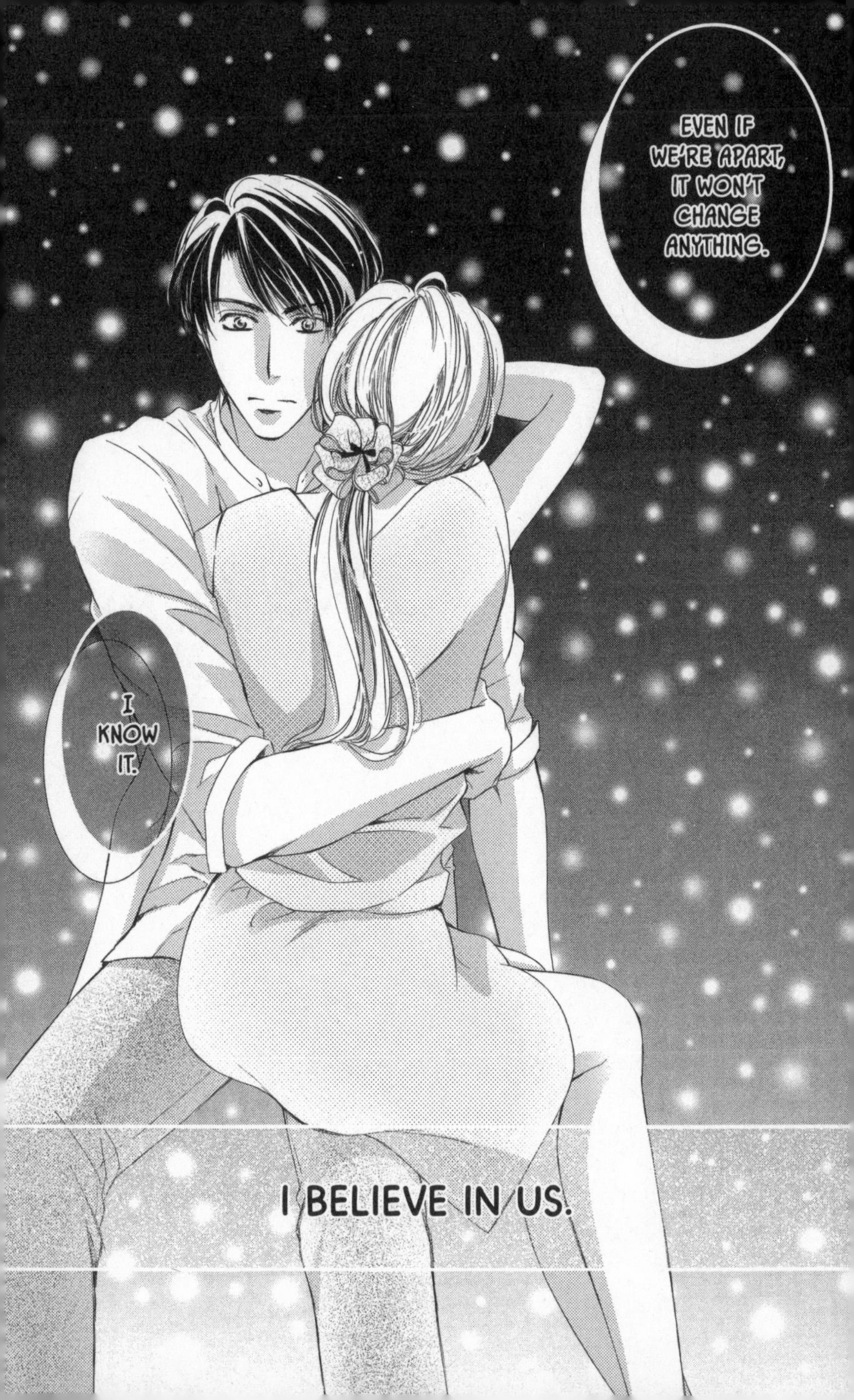
EVEN IF WE'RE APART, IT WON'T CHANGE ANYTHING.
I KNOW IT.
I BELIEVE IN US.

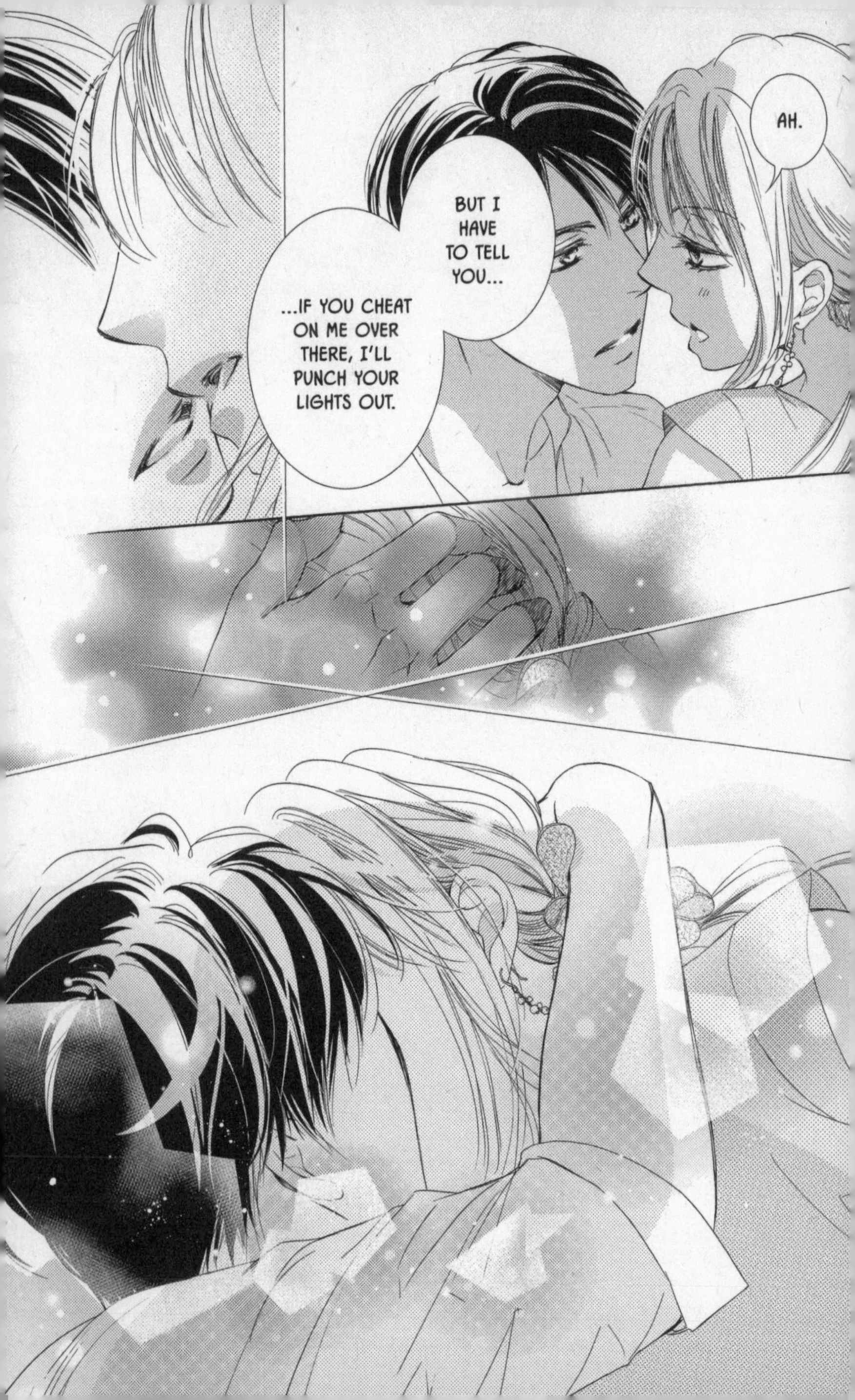
AH.
BUT I HAVE TO TELL YOU...
...IF YOU CHEAT ON ME OVER THERE, I'LL PUNCH YOUR LIGHTS OUT.

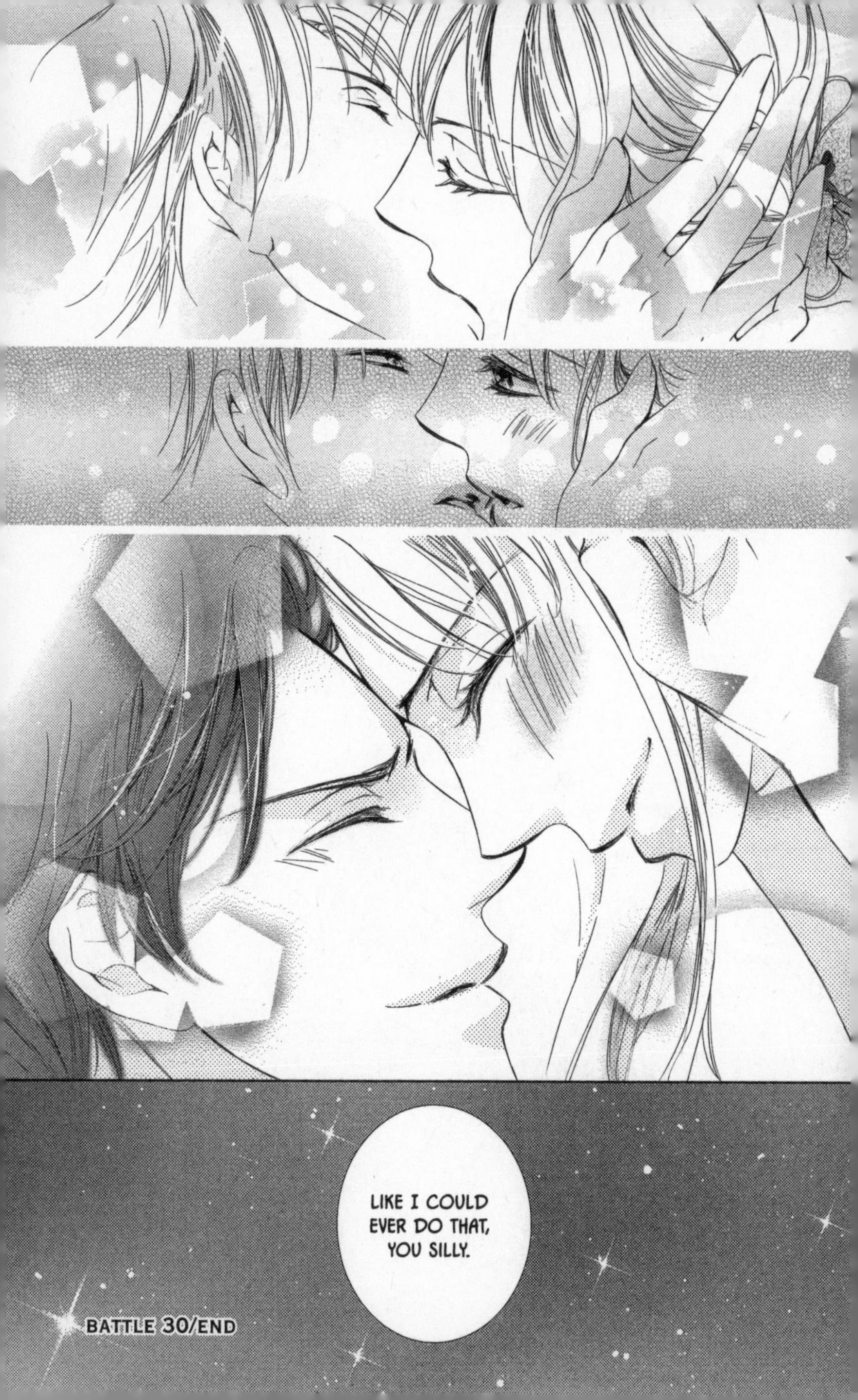
LIKE I COULD EVER DO THAT, YOU SILLY.
BATTLE 30/END

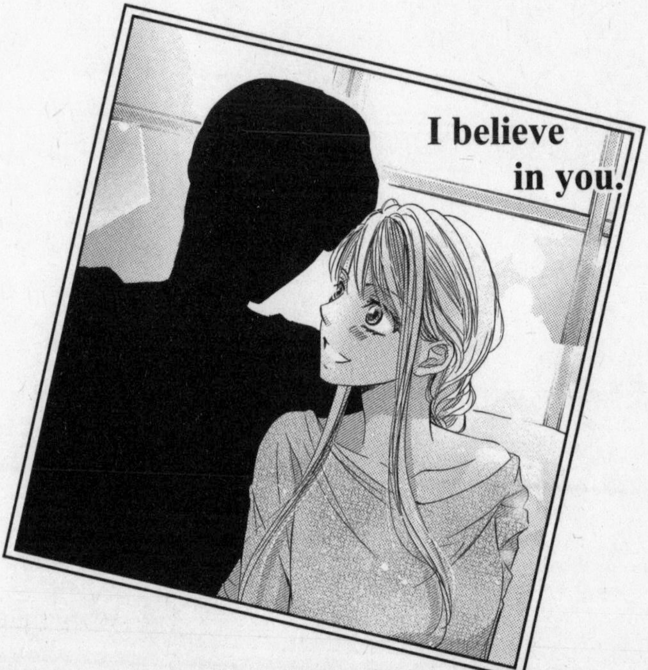
I believe in you.

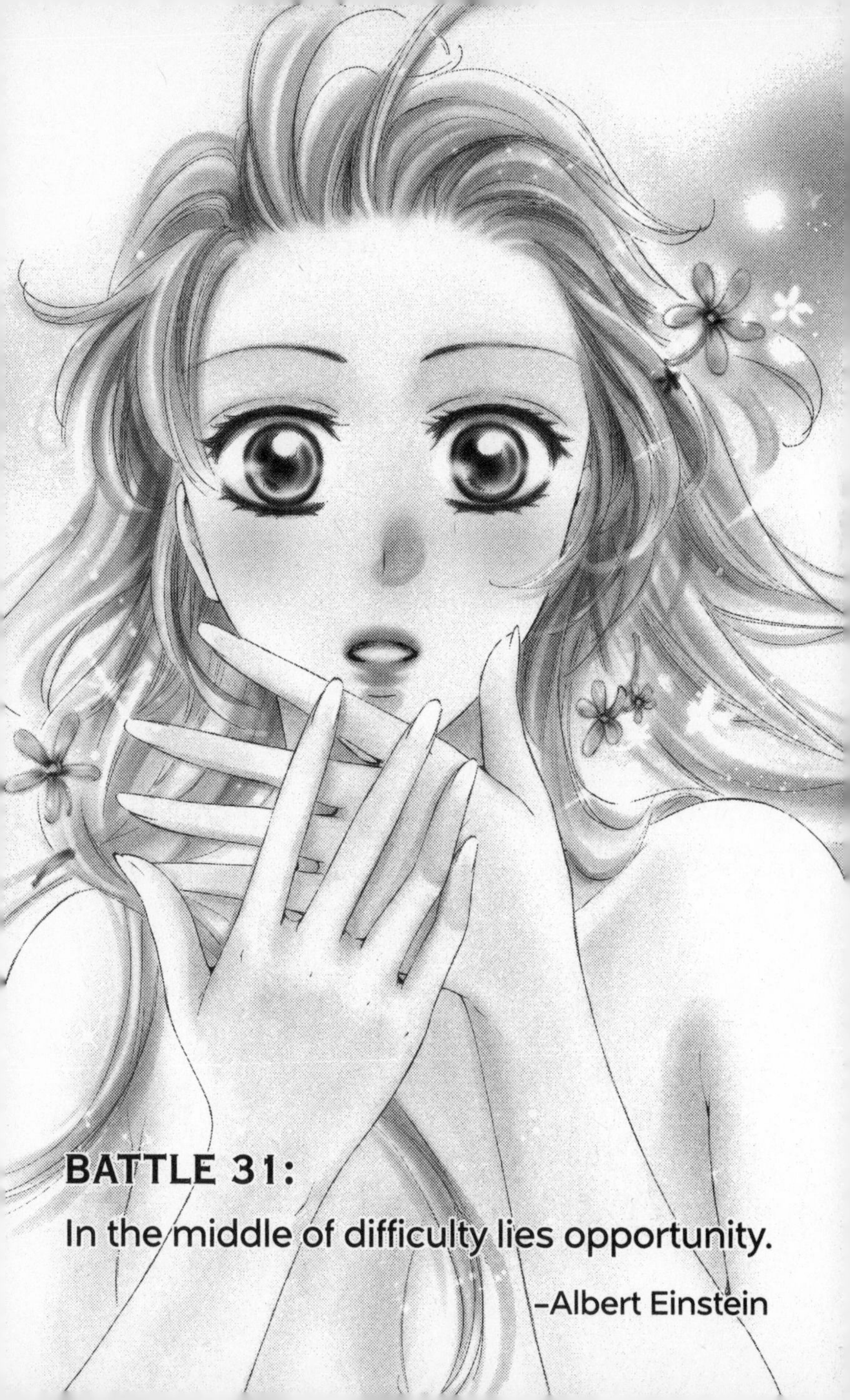

BATTLE 31:

In the middle of difficulty lies opportunity.

–Albert Einstein

Everyone's
Getting
Married

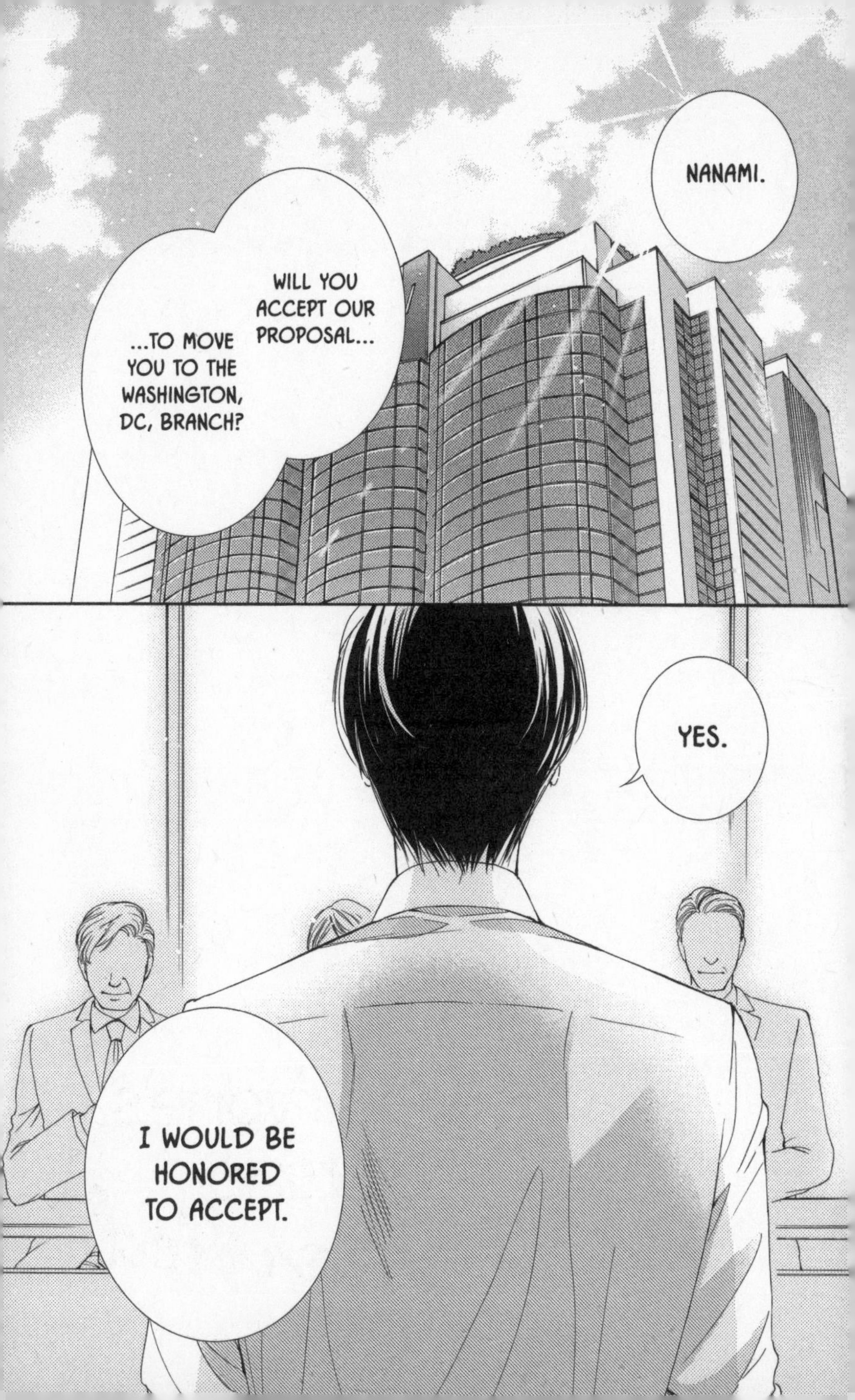
NANAMI.
WILL YOU ACCEPT OUR PROPOSAL...
...TO MOVE YOU TO THE WASHINGTON, DC, BRANCH?
YES.
I WOULD BE HONORED TO ACCEPT.

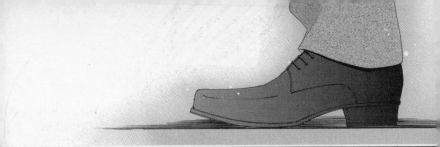

HEY.

YOU LOOK HAPPY.

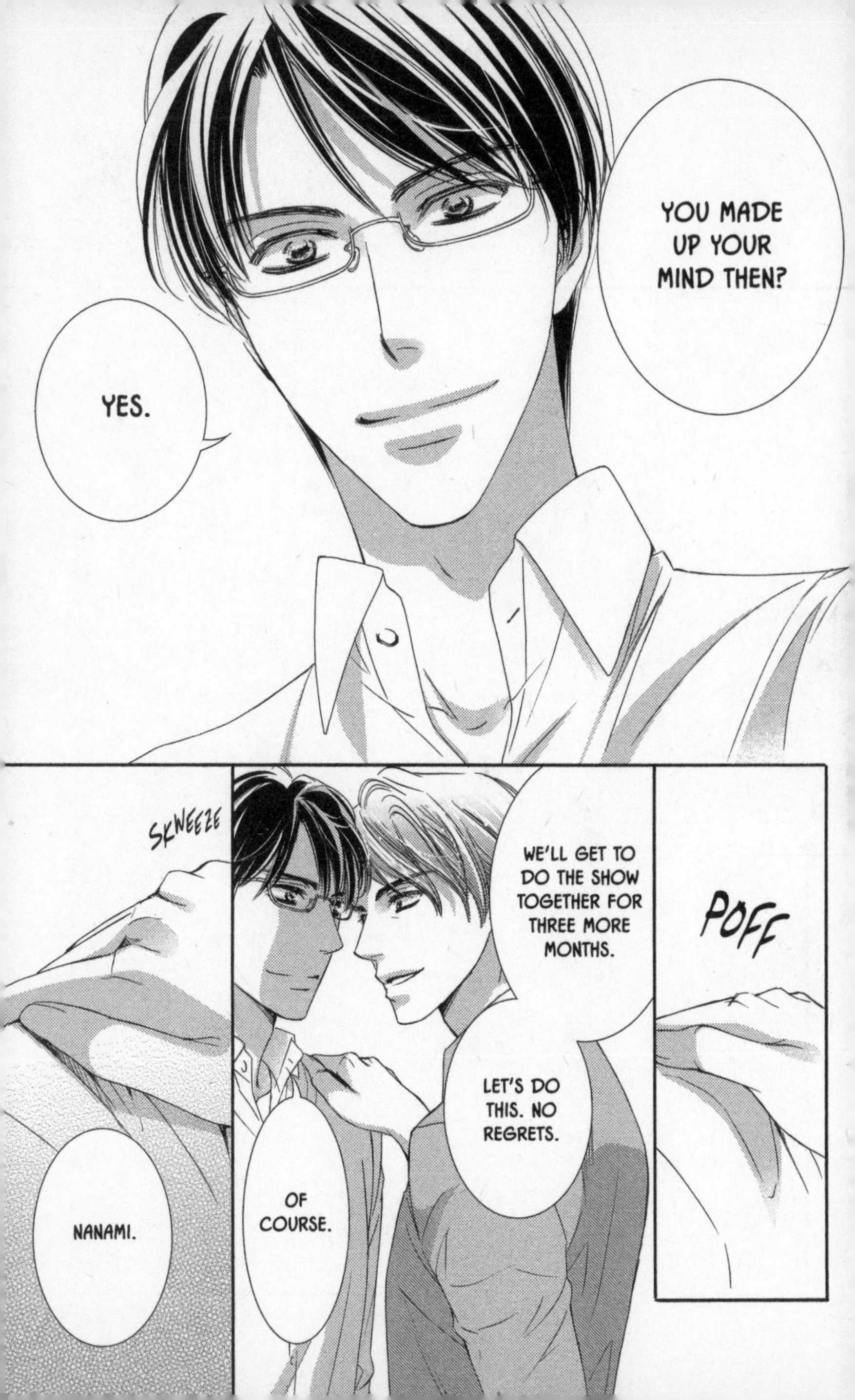
YOU MADE UP YOUR MIND THEN?
YES.
POFF
WE'LL GET TO DO THE SHOW TOGETHER FOR THREE MORE MONTHS.
LET'S DO THIS. NO REGRETS.
OF COURSE.
SKWEEZE
NANAMI.

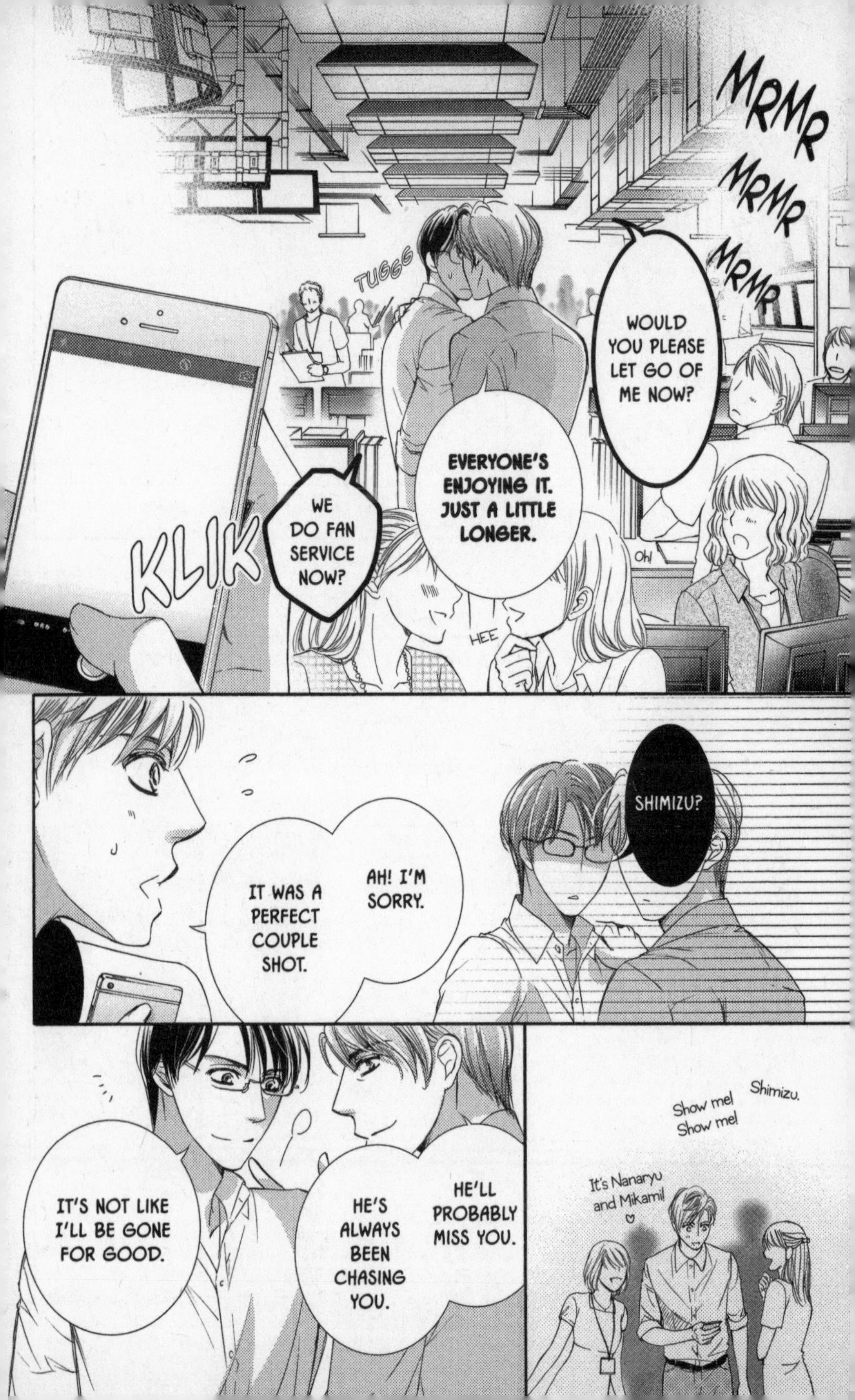
MRMR
MRMR
MRMR
WOULD YOU PLEASE LET GO OF ME NOW?
Oh!
EVERYONE'S ENJOYING IT. JUST A LITTLE LONGER.
TUGGG
HEE
WE DO FAN SERVICE NOW?
KLIK
SHIMIZU?
AH! I'M SORRY.
IT WAS A PERFECT COUPLE SHOT.
Shimizu.
Show me! Show me!
It's Nanaryu and Mikami!
HE'LL PROBABLY MISS YOU.
HE'S ALWAYS BEEN CHASING YOU.
IT'S NOT LIKE I'LL BE GONE FOR GOOD.

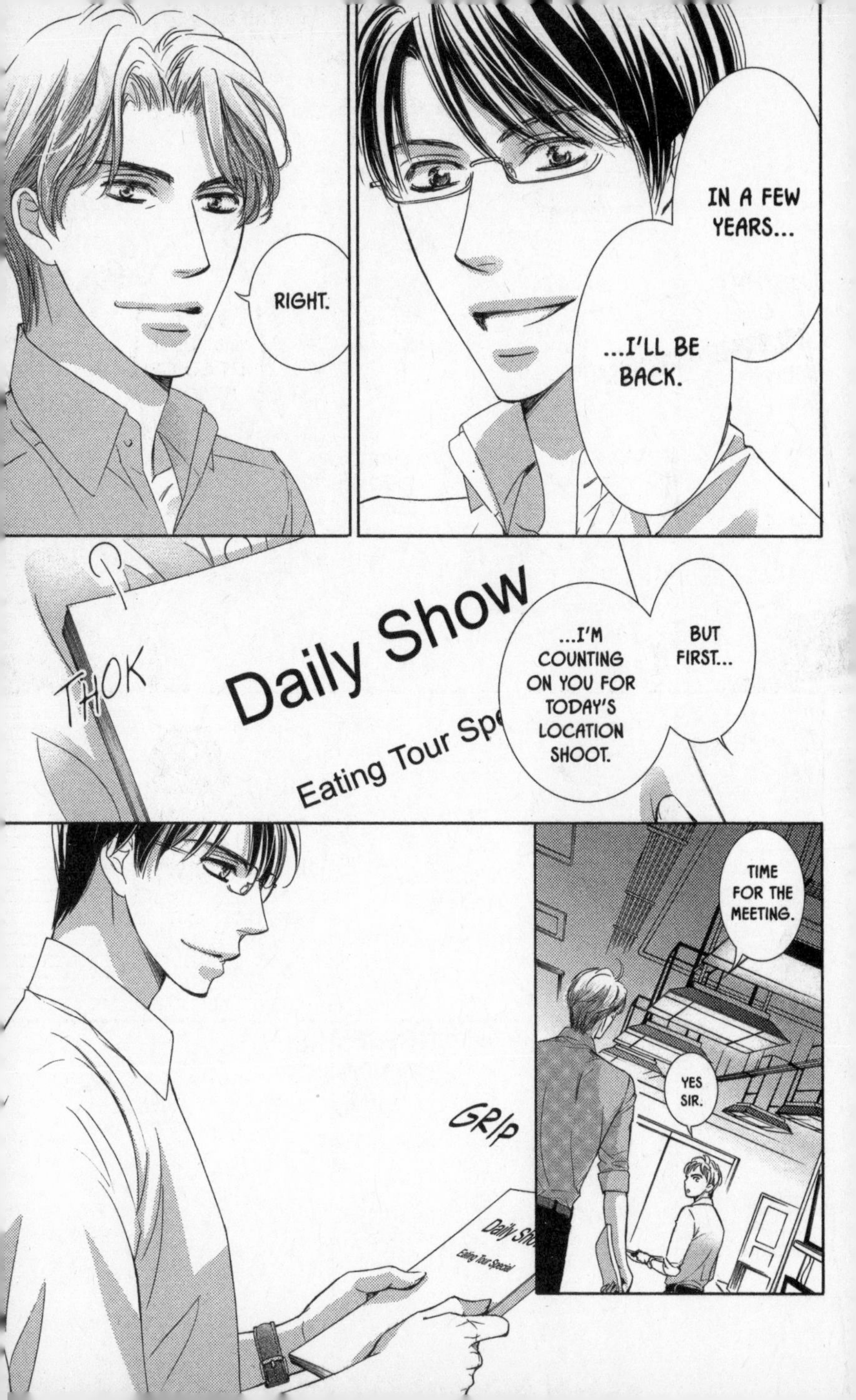
IN A FEW YEARS...
...I'LL BE BACK.
RIGHT.
BUT FIRST...
...I'M COUNTING ON YOU FOR TODAY'S LOCATION SHOOT.
Daily Show
Eating Tour Spe
THOK
TIME FOR THE MEETING.
YES SIR.
GRIP
Daily Sho
Eating Tour Special

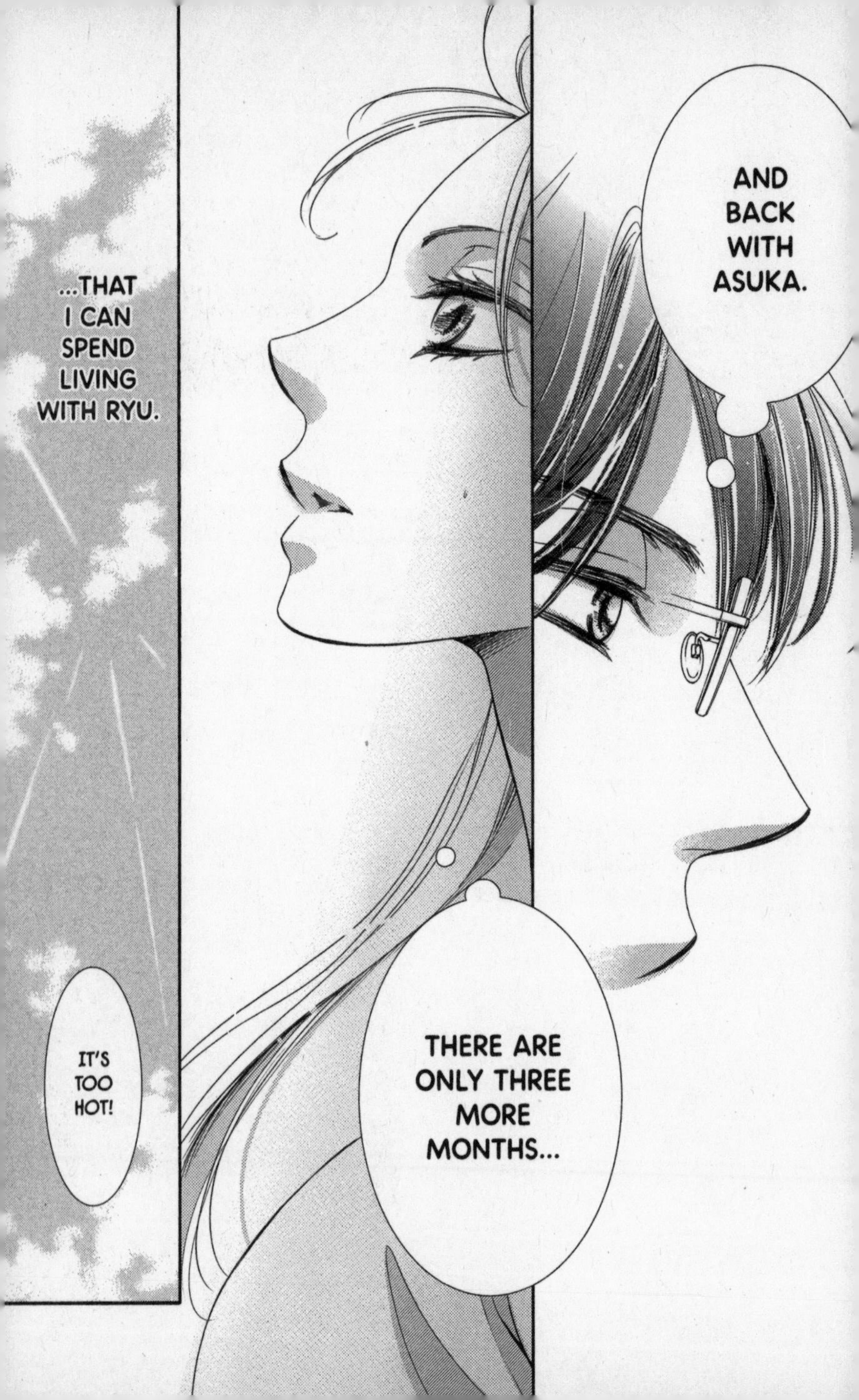
AND BACK WITH ASUKA.
THERE ARE ONLY THREE MORE MONTHS...
...THAT I CAN SPEND LIVING WITH RYU.
IT'S TOO HOT!

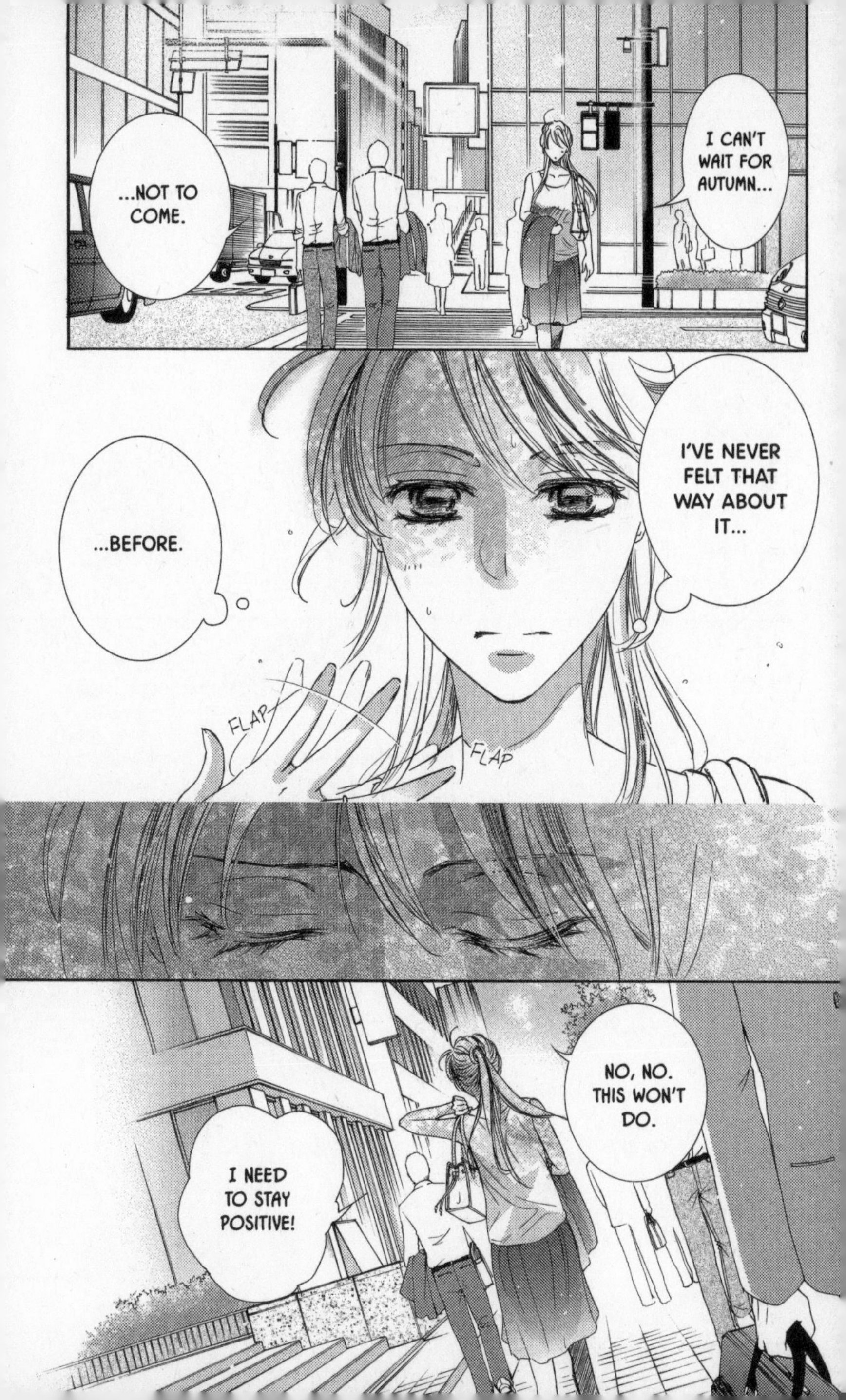
I CAN'T WAIT FOR AUTUMN...
...NOT TO COME.
I'VE NEVER FELT THAT WAY ABOUT IT...
...BEFORE.
FLAP
FLAP
NO, NO. THIS WON'T DO.
I NEED TO STAY POSITIVE!

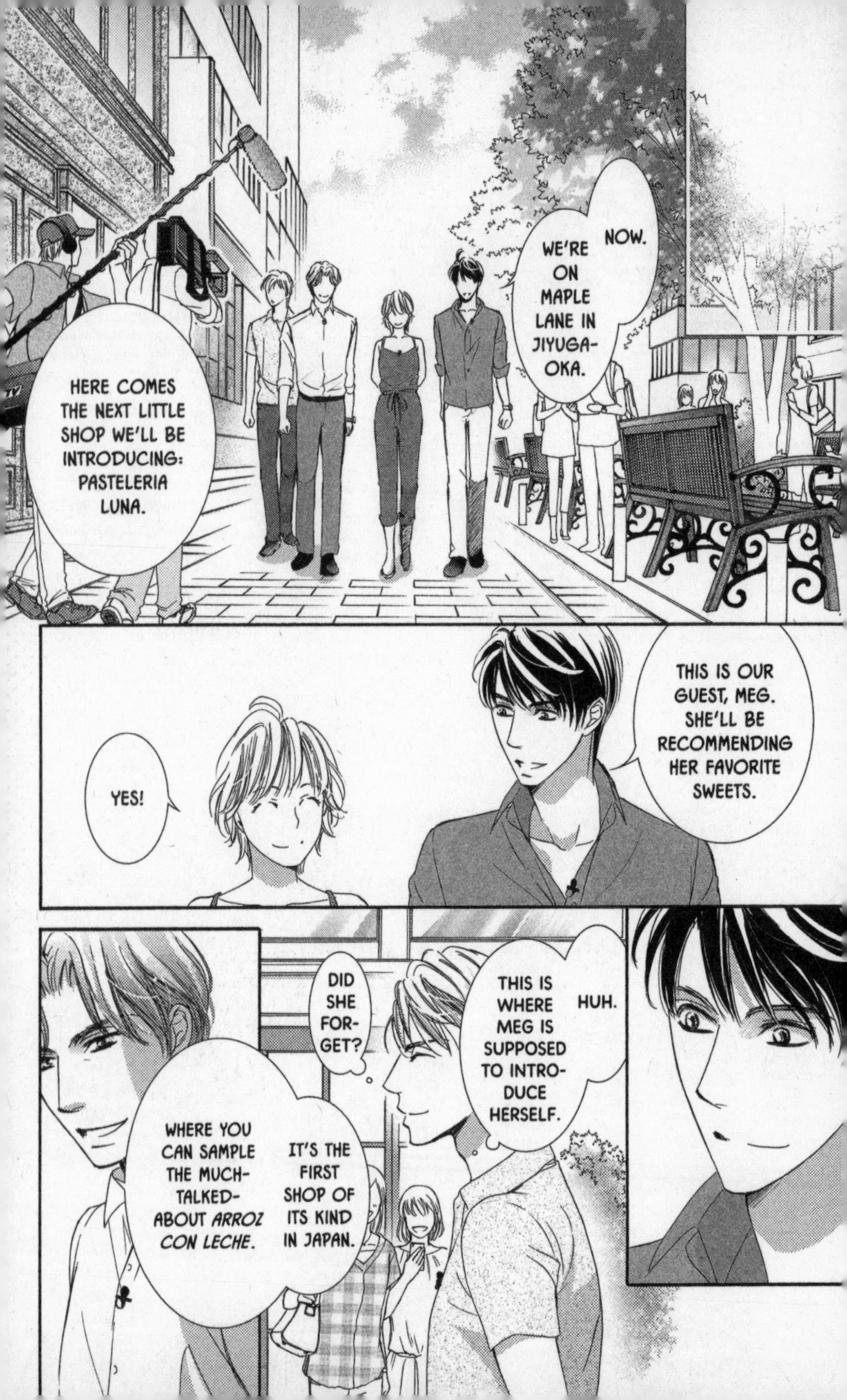
NOW.
WE'RE ON MAPLE LANE IN JIYUGA-OKA.
HERE COMES THE NEXT LITTLE SHOP WE'LL BE INTRODUCING: PASTELERIA LUNA.
THIS IS OUR GUEST, MEG. SHE'LL BE RECOMMENDING HER FAVORITE SWEETS.
YES!
HUH.
THIS IS WHERE MEG IS SUPPOSED TO INTRODUCE HERSELF.
DID SHE FORGET?
IT'S THE FIRST SHOP OF ITS KIND IN JAPAN.
WHERE YOU CAN SAMPLE THE MUCH-TALKED-ABOUT *ARROZ CON LECHE*.

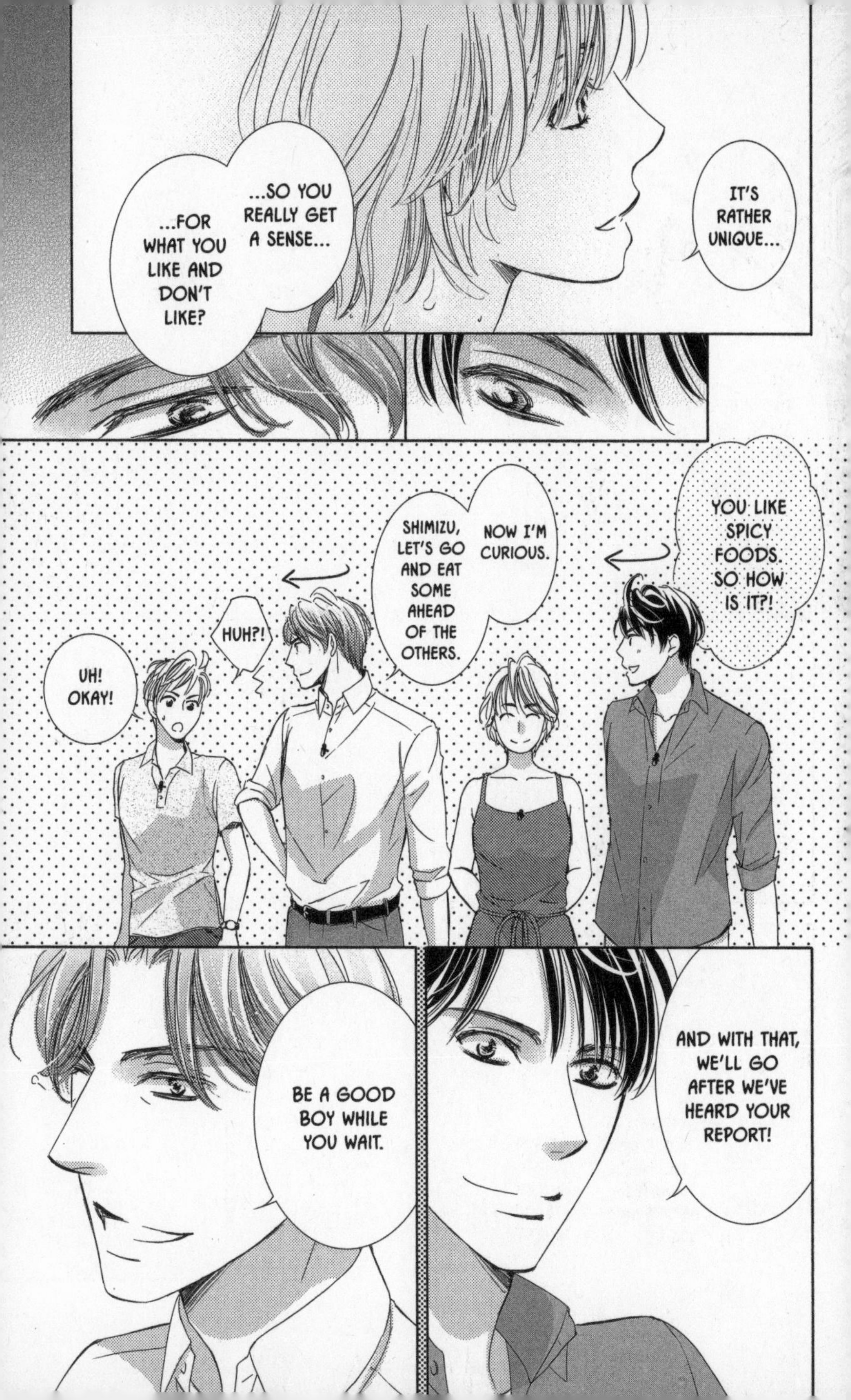
IT'S RATHER UNIQUE...
...SO YOU REALLY GET A SENSE...
...FOR WHAT YOU LIKE AND DON'T LIKE?
YOU LIKE SPICY FOODS. SO HOW IS IT?!
NOW I'M CURIOUS.
SHIMIZU, LET'S GO AND EAT SOME AHEAD OF THE OTHERS.
HUH?!
UH! OKAY!
AND WITH THAT, WE'LL GO AFTER WE'VE HEARD YOUR REPORT!
BE A GOOD BOY WHILE YOU WAIT.

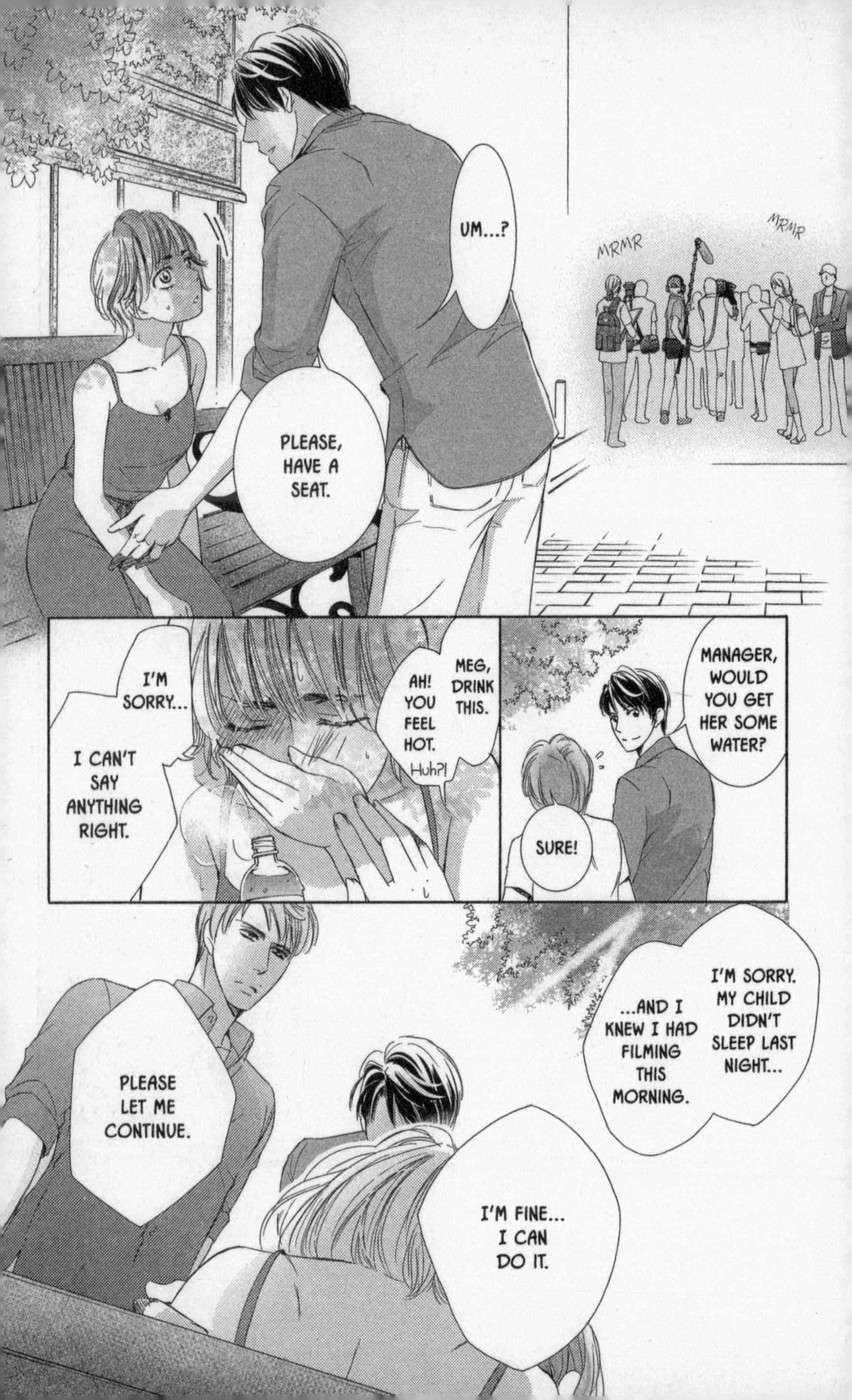
MRMR
MRMR
UM...?
PLEASE, HAVE A SEAT.
MANAGER, WOULD YOU GET HER SOME WATER?
SURE!
MEG, DRINK THIS.
AH! YOU FEEL HOT.
Huh?!
I'M SORRY...
I CAN'T SAY ANYTHING RIGHT.
I'M SORRY. MY CHILD DIDN'T SLEEP LAST NIGHT...
...AND I KNEW I HAD FILMING THIS MORNING.
PLEASE LET ME CONTINUE.
I'M FINE... I CAN DO IT.

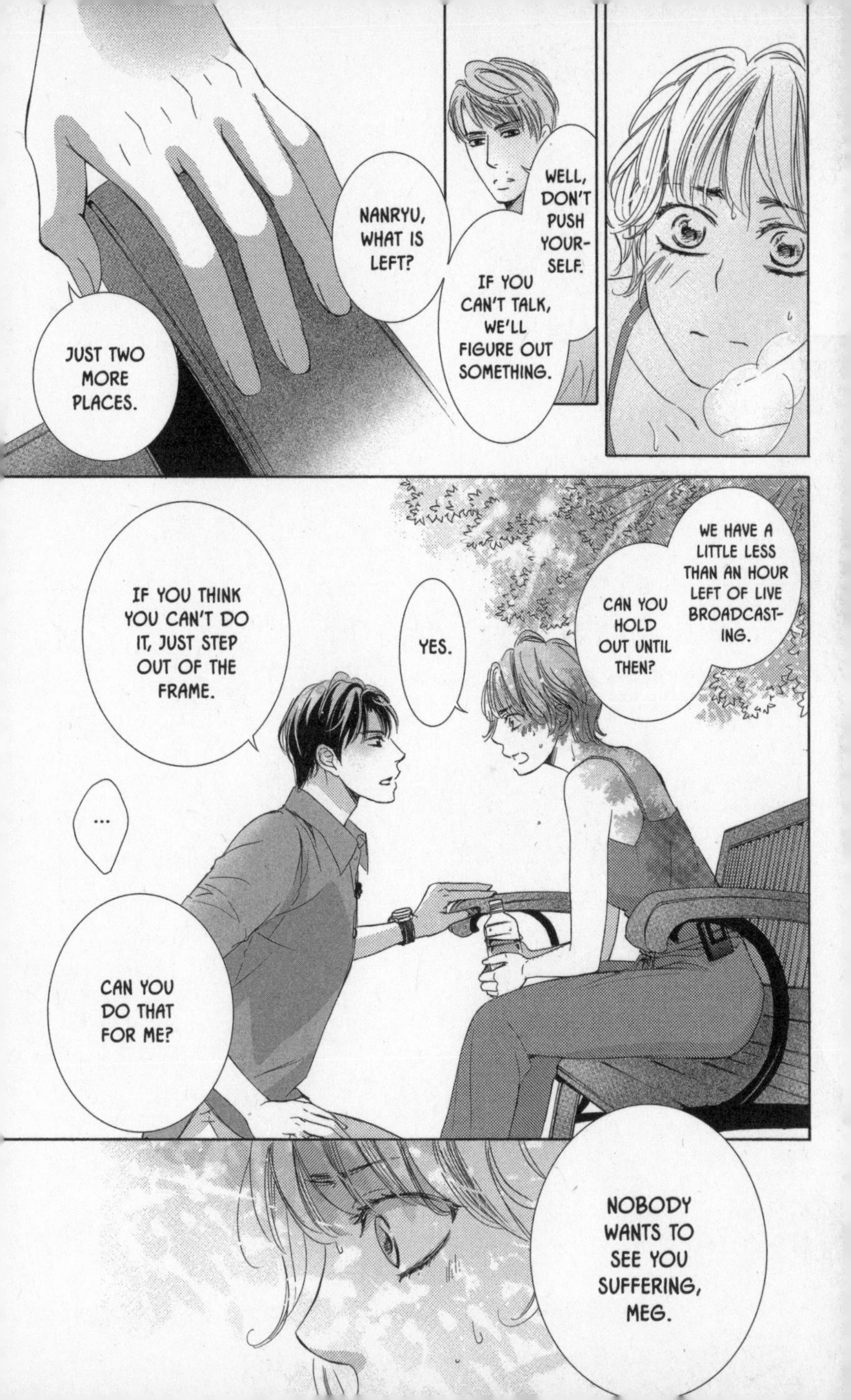
WELL, DON'T PUSH YOURSELF.
IF YOU CAN'T TALK, WE'LL FIGURE OUT SOMETHING.
NANRYU, WHAT IS LEFT?
JUST TWO MORE PLACES.
WE HAVE A LITTLE LESS THAN AN HOUR LEFT OF LIVE BROADCASTING.
CAN YOU HOLD OUT UNTIL THEN?
YES.
IF YOU THINK YOU CAN'T DO IT, JUST STEP OUT OF THE FRAME.
...
CAN YOU DO THAT FOR ME?
NOBODY WANTS TO SEE YOU SUFFERING, MEG.

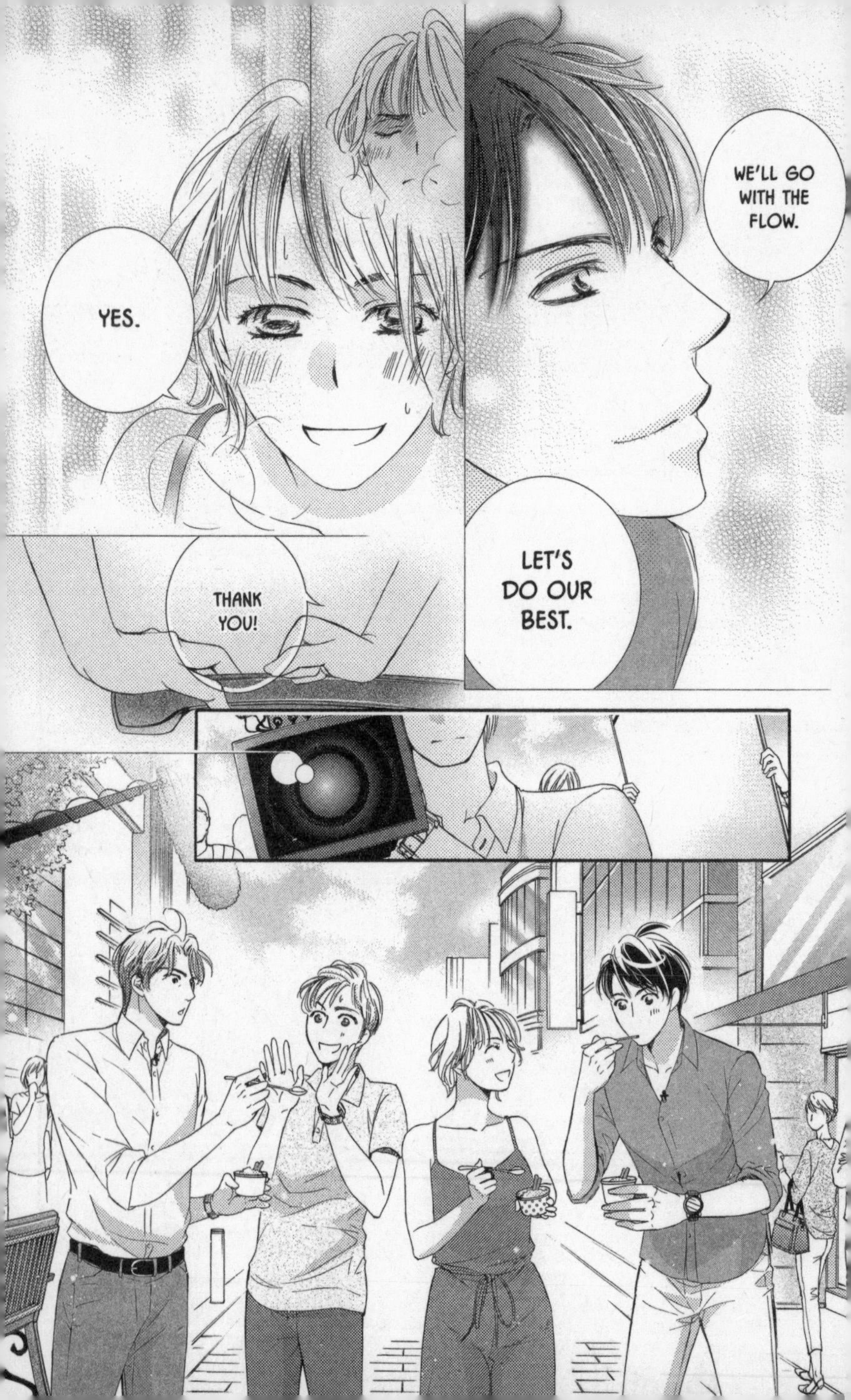
WE'LL GO WITH THE FLOW.
LET'S DO OUR BEST.
YES.
THANK YOU!

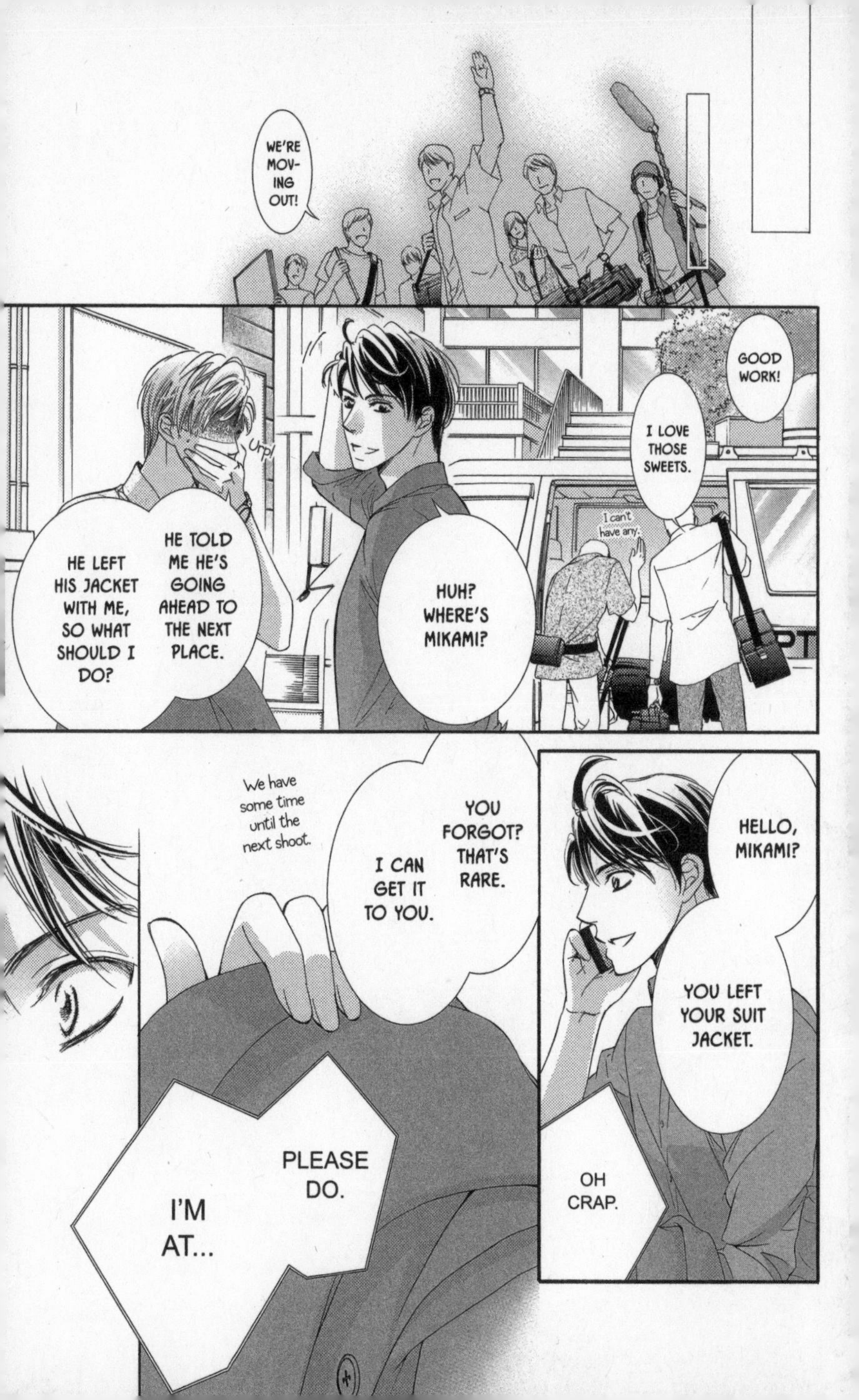

WE'RE MOV-ING OUT!
GOOD WORK!
I LOVE THOSE SWEETS.
I can't have any.
HUH? WHERE'S MIKAMI?
Urp!
HE TOLD ME HE'S GOING AHEAD TO THE NEXT PLACE.
HE LEFT HIS JACKET WITH ME, SO WHAT SHOULD I DO?
HELLO, MIKAMI?
YOU LEFT YOUR SUIT JACKET.
OH CRAP.
YOU FORGOT? THAT'S RARE.
I CAN GET IT TO YOU.
We have some time until the next shoot.
PLEASE DO.
I'M AT...

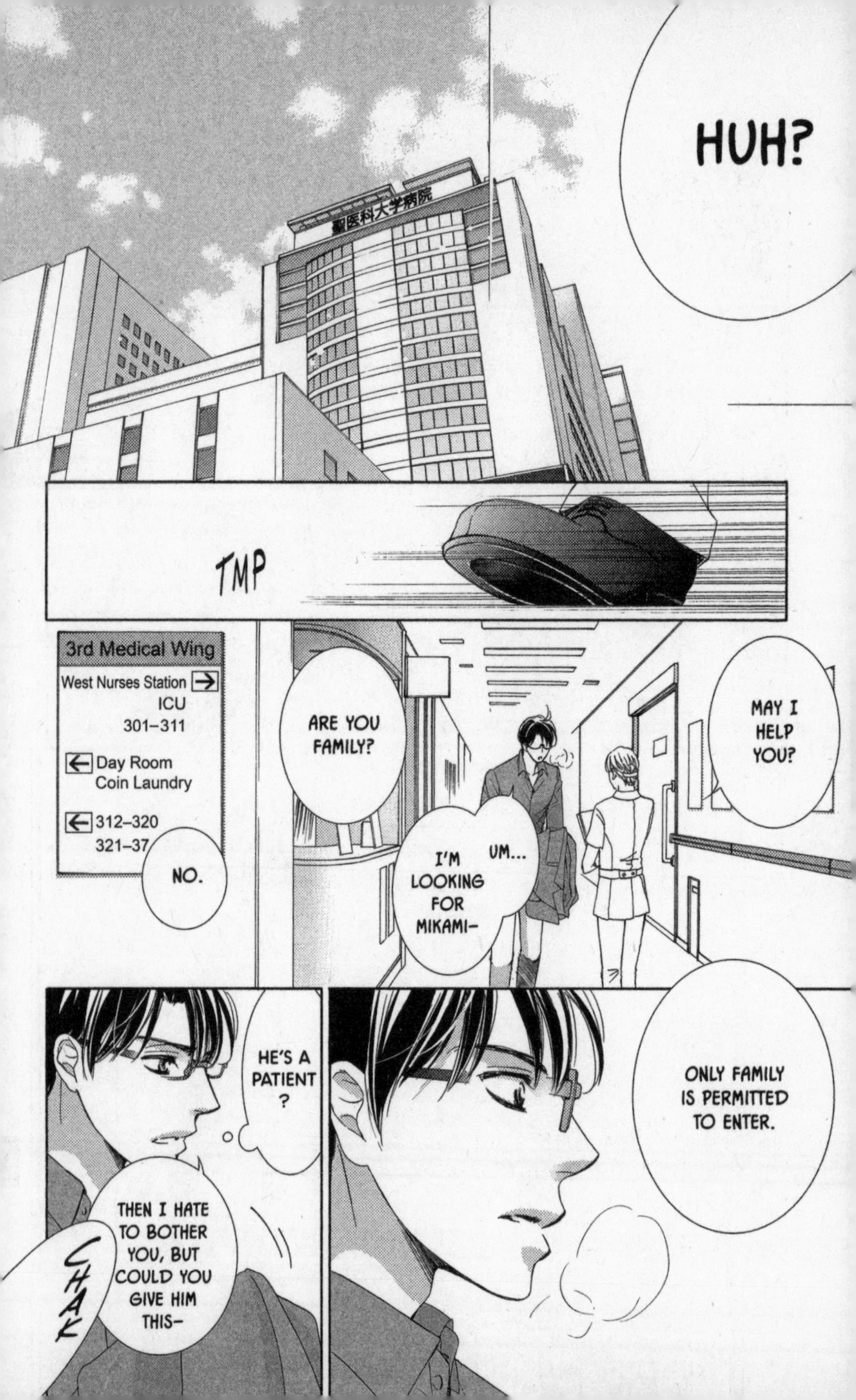
HUH?
聖医科大学病院
TMP
MAY I HELP YOU?
UM...
I'M LOOKING FOR MIKAMI-
ARE YOU FAMILY?
3rd Medical Wing
West Nurses Station ICU 301–311
Day Room Coin Laundry
312–320 321–37
NO.
ONLY FAMILY IS PERMITTED TO ENTER.
HE'S A PATIENT?
THEN I HATE TO BOTHER YOU, BUT COULD YOU GIVE HIM THIS-
CHAK

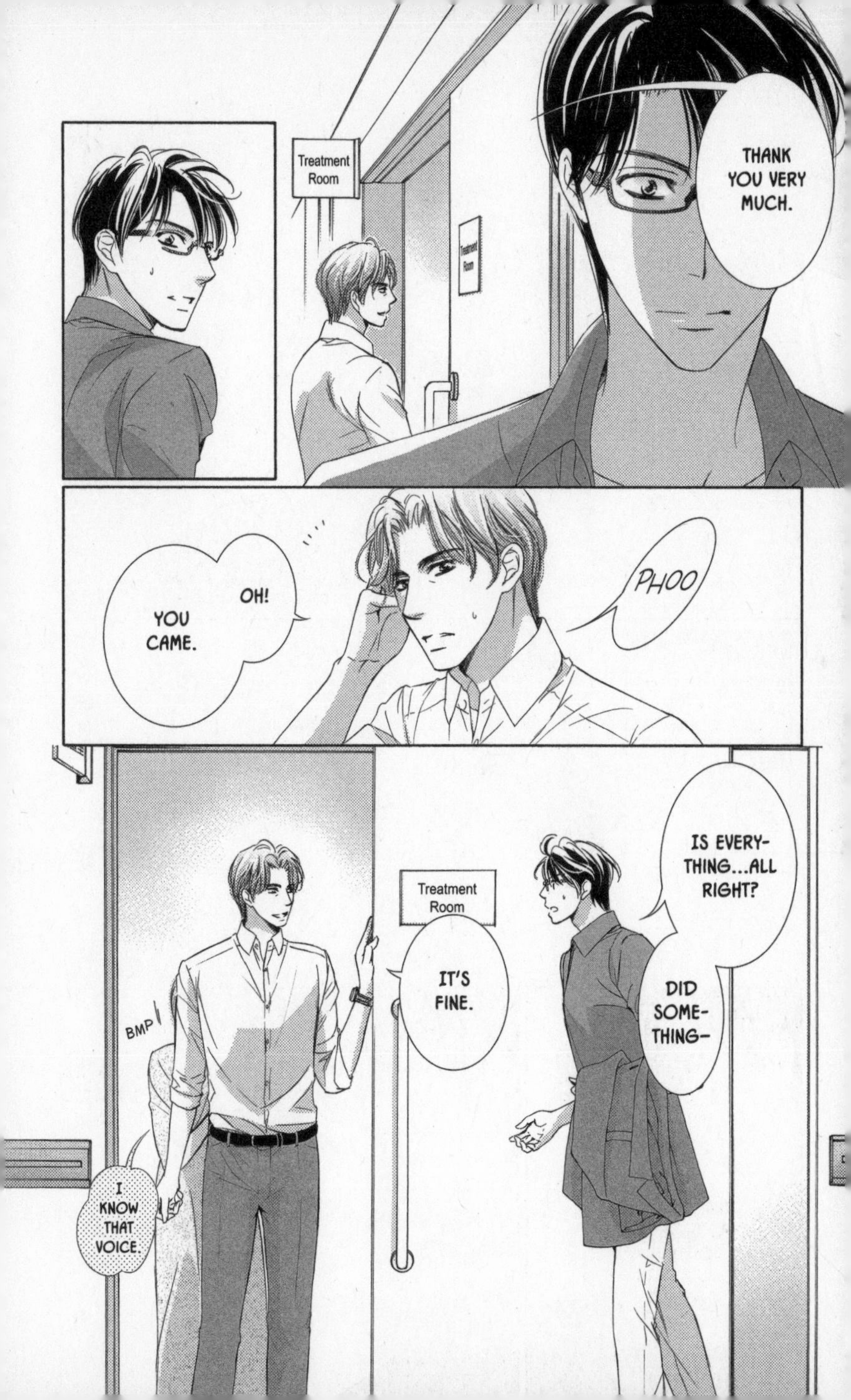
THANK YOU VERY MUCH.
Treatment Room
PHOO
OH! YOU CAME.
IS EVERY-THING...ALL RIGHT?
DID SOME-THING–
Treatment Room
IT'S FINE.
BMP
I KNOW THAT VOICE.

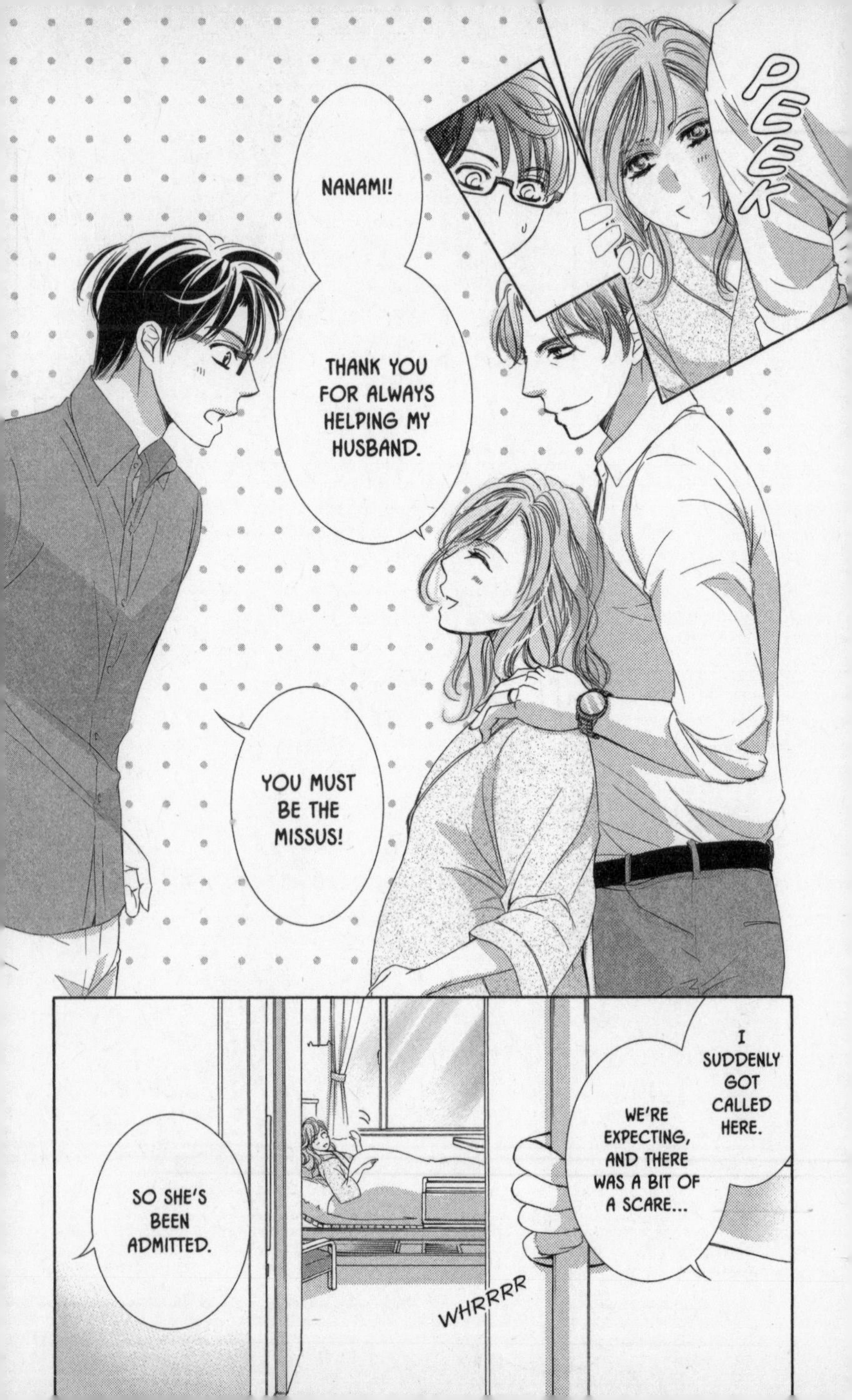
PEEK
NANAMI!
THANK YOU FOR ALWAYS HELPING MY HUSBAND.
YOU MUST BE THE MISSUS!
I SUDDENLY GOT CALLED HERE.
WE'RE EXPECTING, AND THERE WAS A BIT OF A SCARE...
WHRRRR
SO SHE'S BEEN ADMITTED.

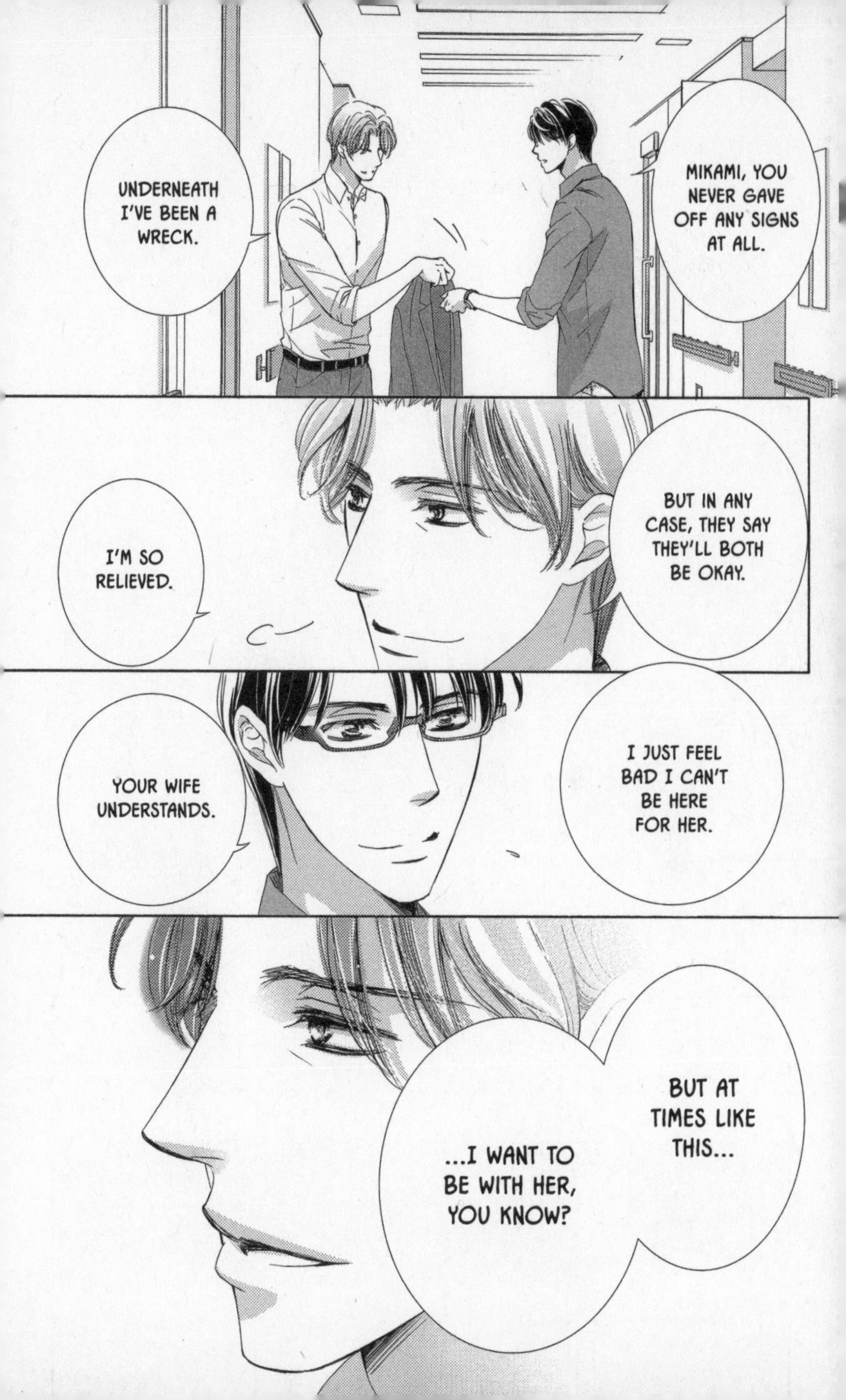
MIKAMI, YOU NEVER GAVE OFF ANY SIGNS AT ALL.
UNDERNEATH I'VE BEEN A WRECK.
BUT IN ANY CASE, THEY SAY THEY'LL BOTH BE OKAY.
I'M SO RELIEVED.
I JUST FEEL BAD I CAN'T BE HERE FOR HER.
YOUR WIFE UNDERSTANDS.
BUT AT TIMES LIKE THIS...
...I WANT TO BE WITH HER, YOU KNOW?

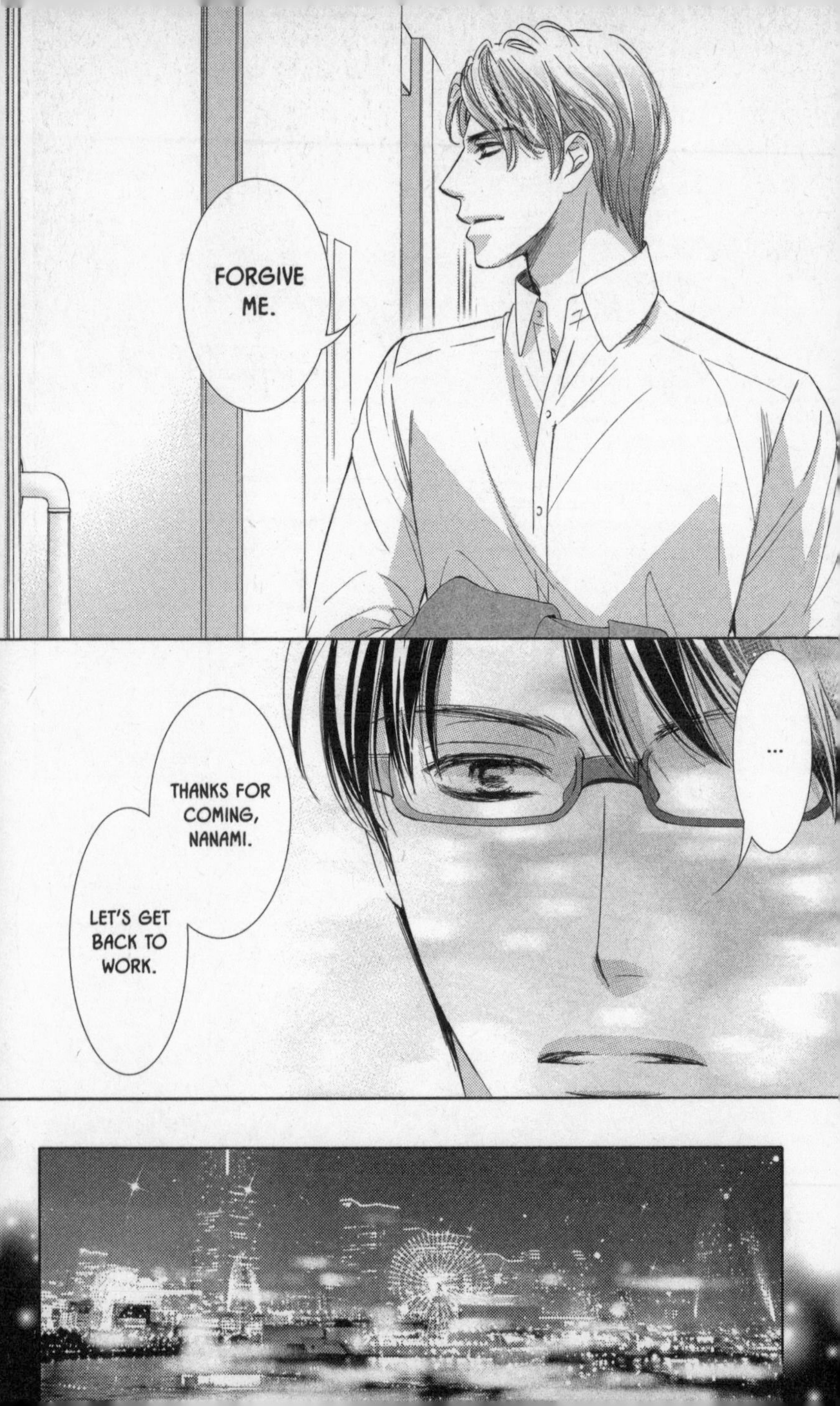
FORGIVE ME.
...
THANKS FOR COMING, NANAMI.
LET'S GET BACK TO WORK.

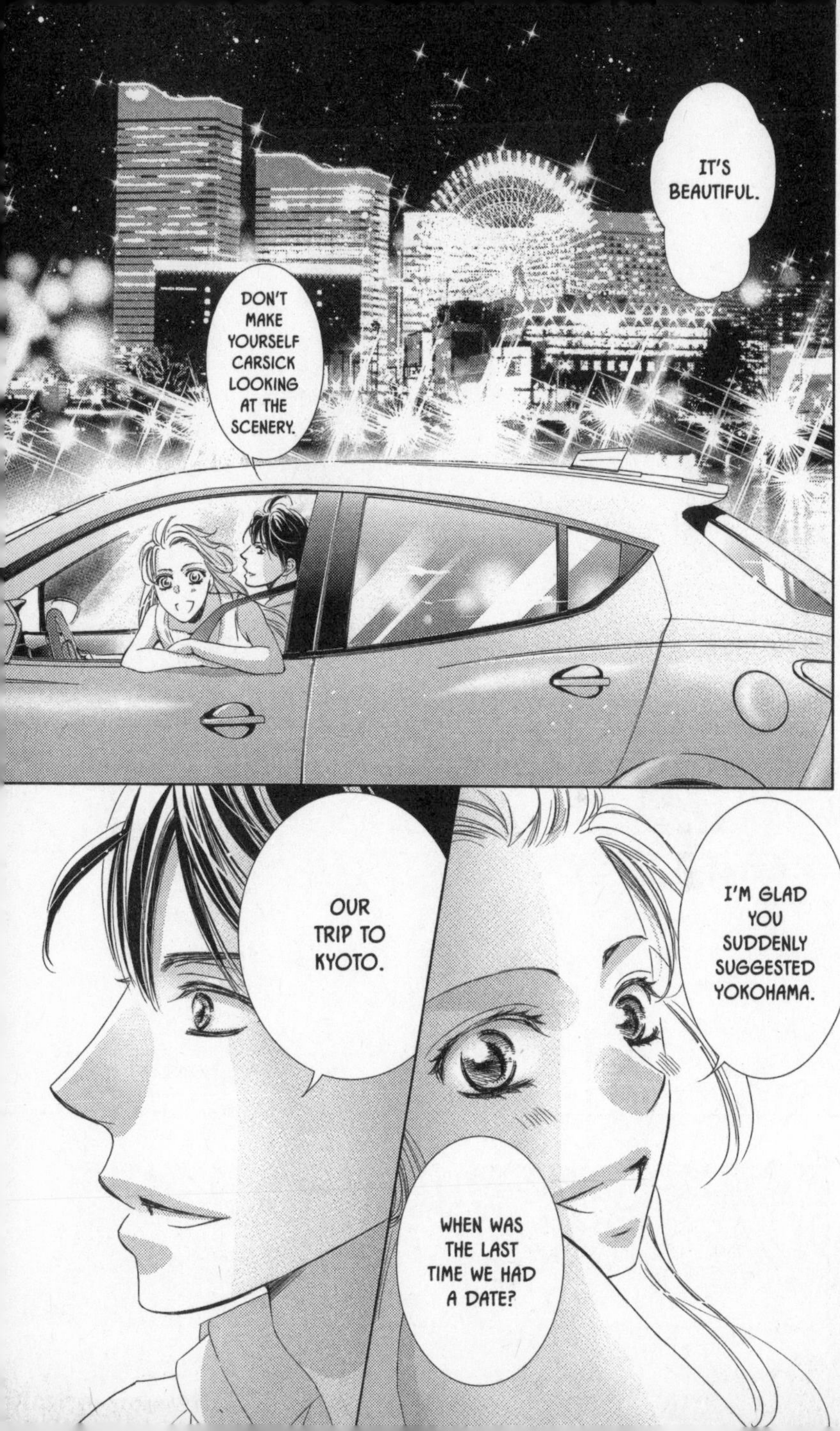
IT'S BEAUTIFUL.
DON'T MAKE YOURSELF CARSICK LOOKING AT THE SCENERY.
I'M GLAD YOU SUDDENLY SUGGESTED YOKOHAMA.
WHEN WAS THE LAST TIME WE HAD A DATE?
OUR TRIP TO KYOTO.

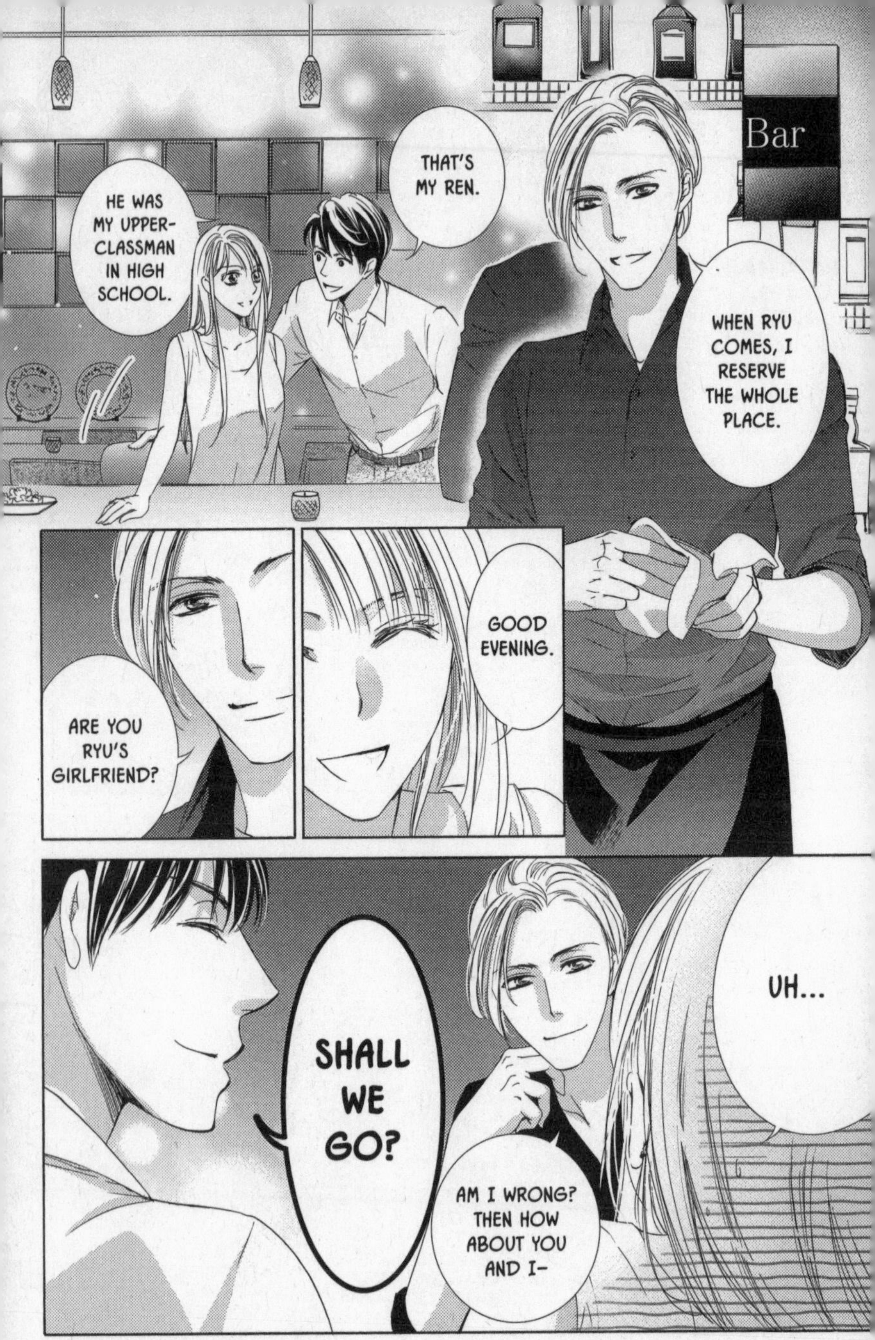
Bar
WHEN RYU COMES, I RESERVE THE WHOLE PLACE.
THAT'S MY REN.
HE WAS MY UPPER-CLASSMAN IN HIGH SCHOOL.
GOOD EVENING.
ARE YOU RYU'S GIRLFRIEND?
UH...
AM I WRONG? THEN HOW ABOUT YOU AND I-
SHALL WE GO?

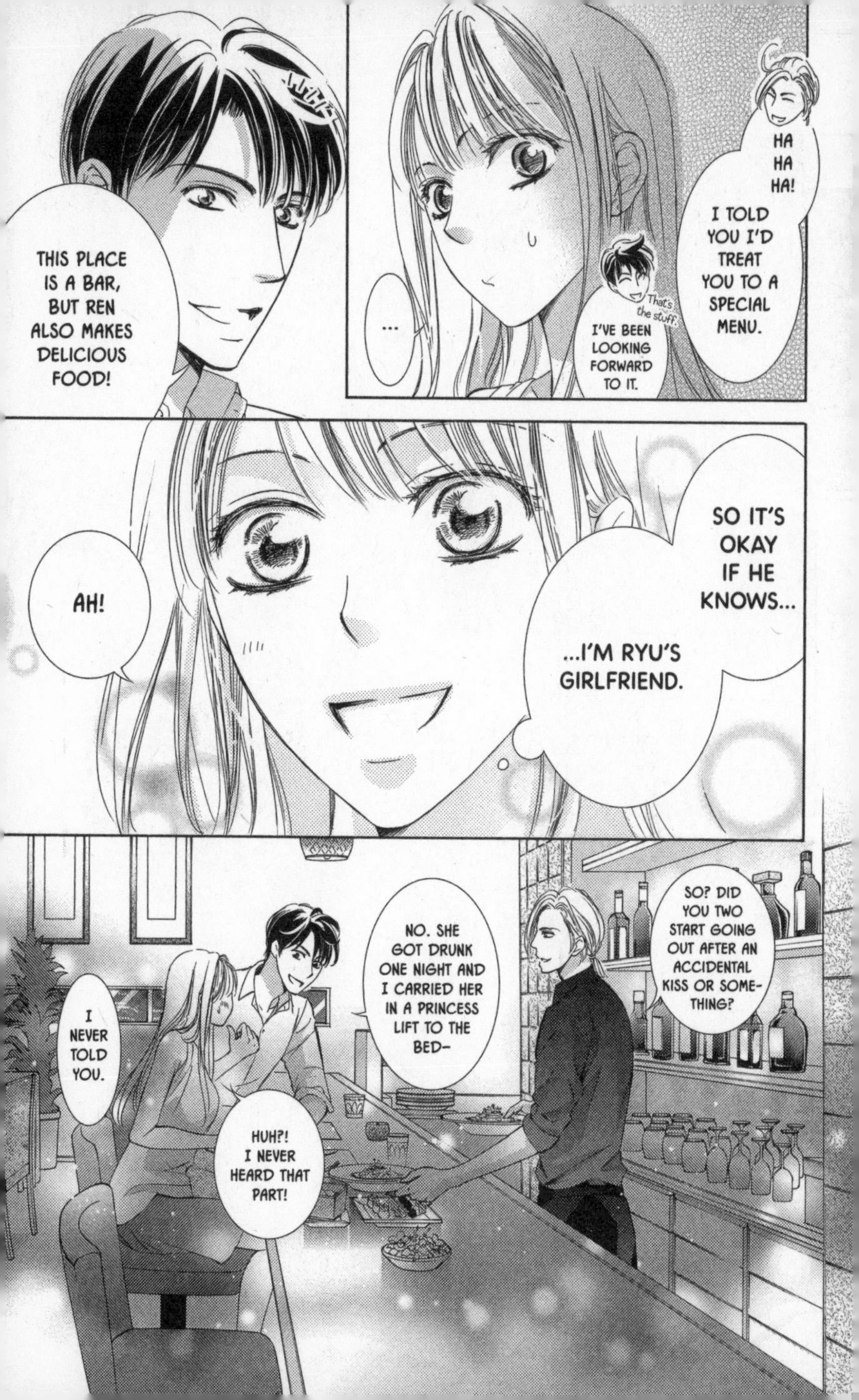
HA HA HA! I TOLD YOU I'D TREAT YOU TO A SPECIAL MENU.
That's the stuff.
I'VE BEEN LOOKING FORWARD TO IT.
...
THIS PLACE IS A BAR, BUT REN ALSO MAKES DELICIOUS FOOD!
SO IT'S OKAY IF HE KNOWS...
...I'M RYU'S GIRLFRIEND.
AH!
SO? DID YOU TWO START GOING OUT AFTER AN ACCIDENTAL KISS OR SOME-THING?
NO. SHE GOT DRUNK ONE NIGHT AND I CARRIED HER IN A PRINCESS LIFT TO THE BED–
HUH?! I NEVER HEARD THAT PART!
I NEVER TOLD YOU.

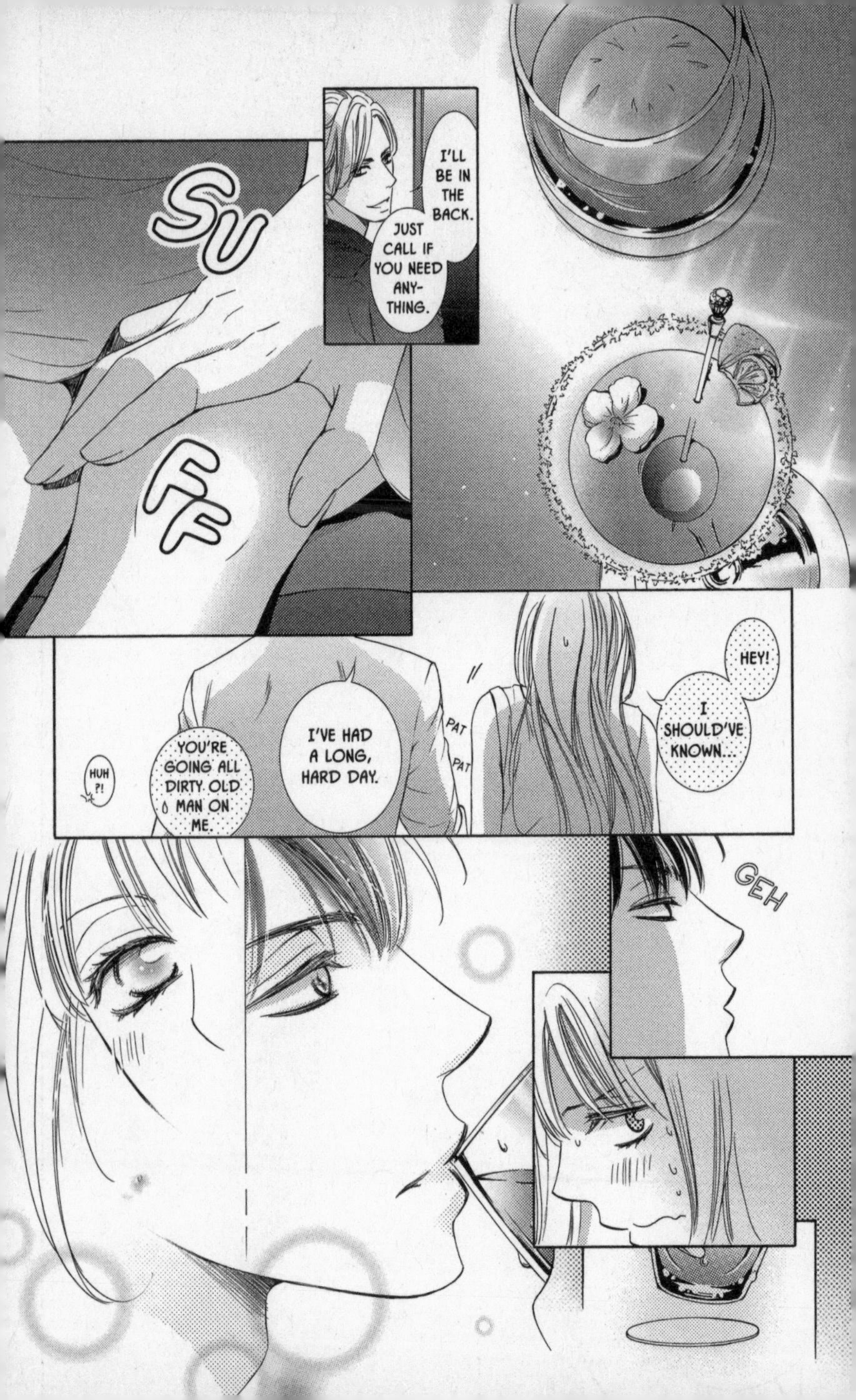
I'LL BE IN THE BACK.
JUST CALL IF YOU NEED ANY-THING.
SUFF
HEY!
I SHOULD'VE KNOWN...
PAT PAT
I'VE HAD A LONG, HARD DAY.
YOU'RE GOING ALL DIRTY OLD MAN ON ME.
HUH?!
GEH

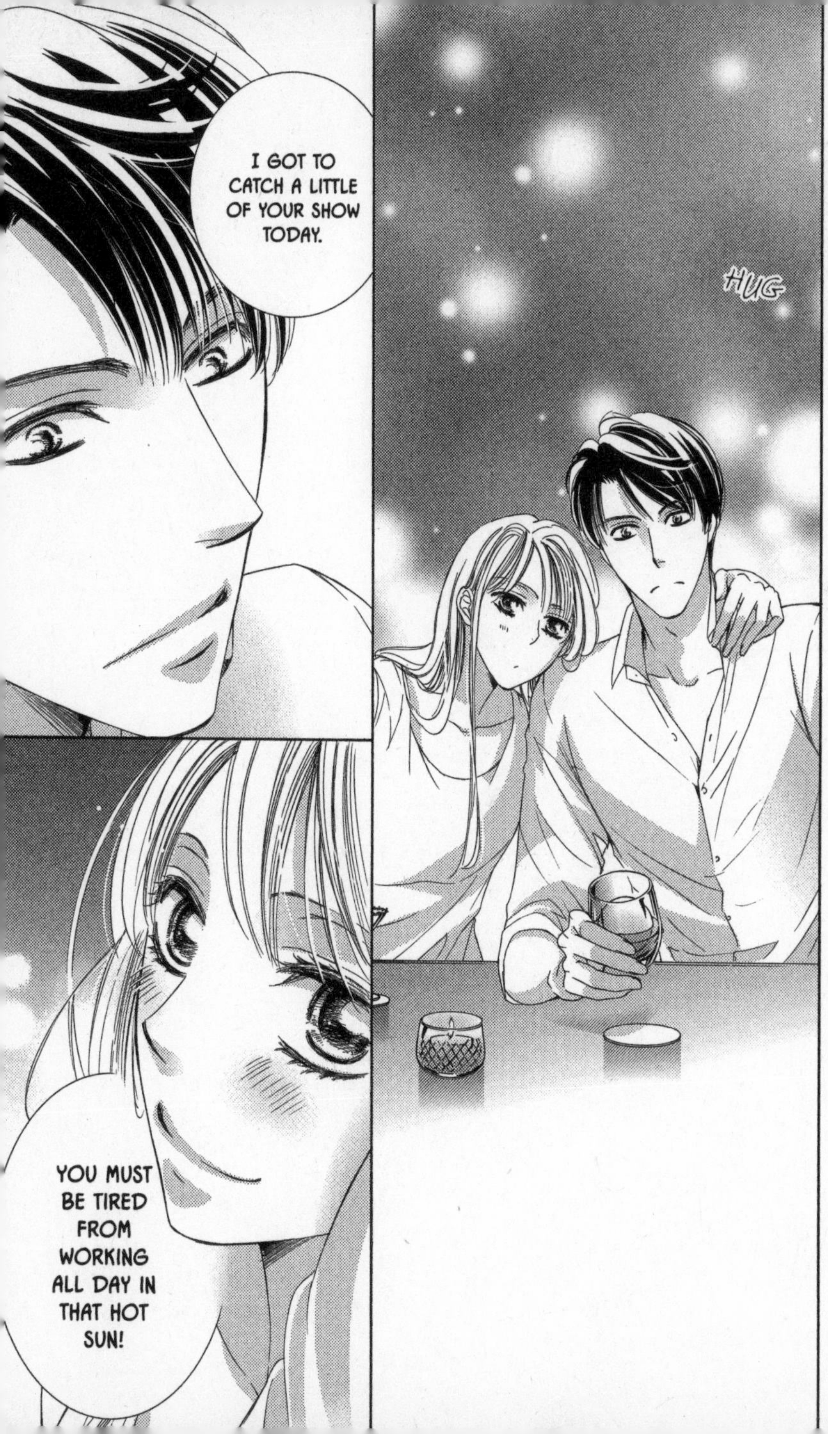
HUG
I GOT TO CATCH A LITTLE OF YOUR SHOW TODAY.
YOU MUST BE TIRED FROM WORKING ALL DAY IN THAT HOT SUN!

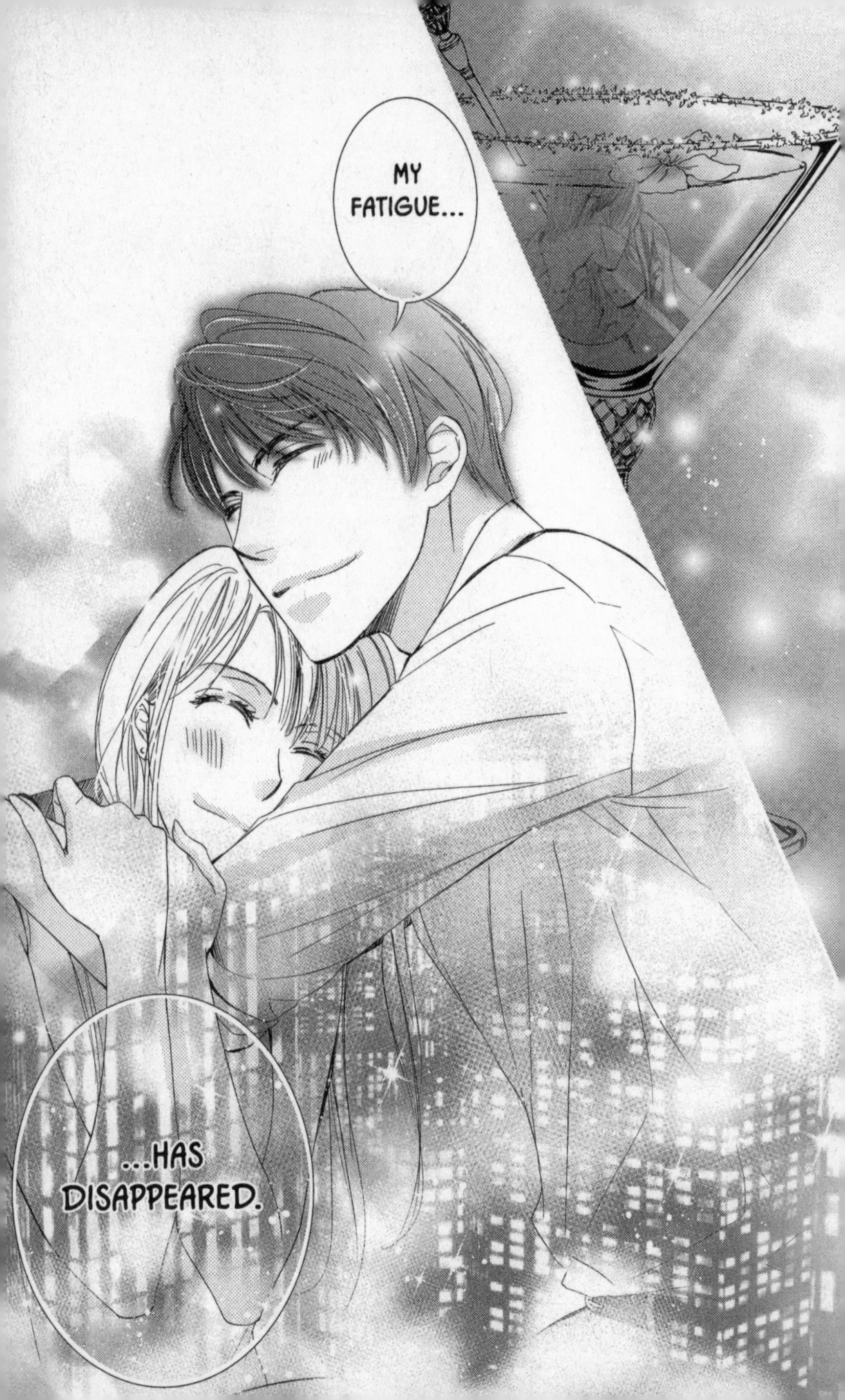
MY FATIGUE...
...HAS DISAPPEARED.

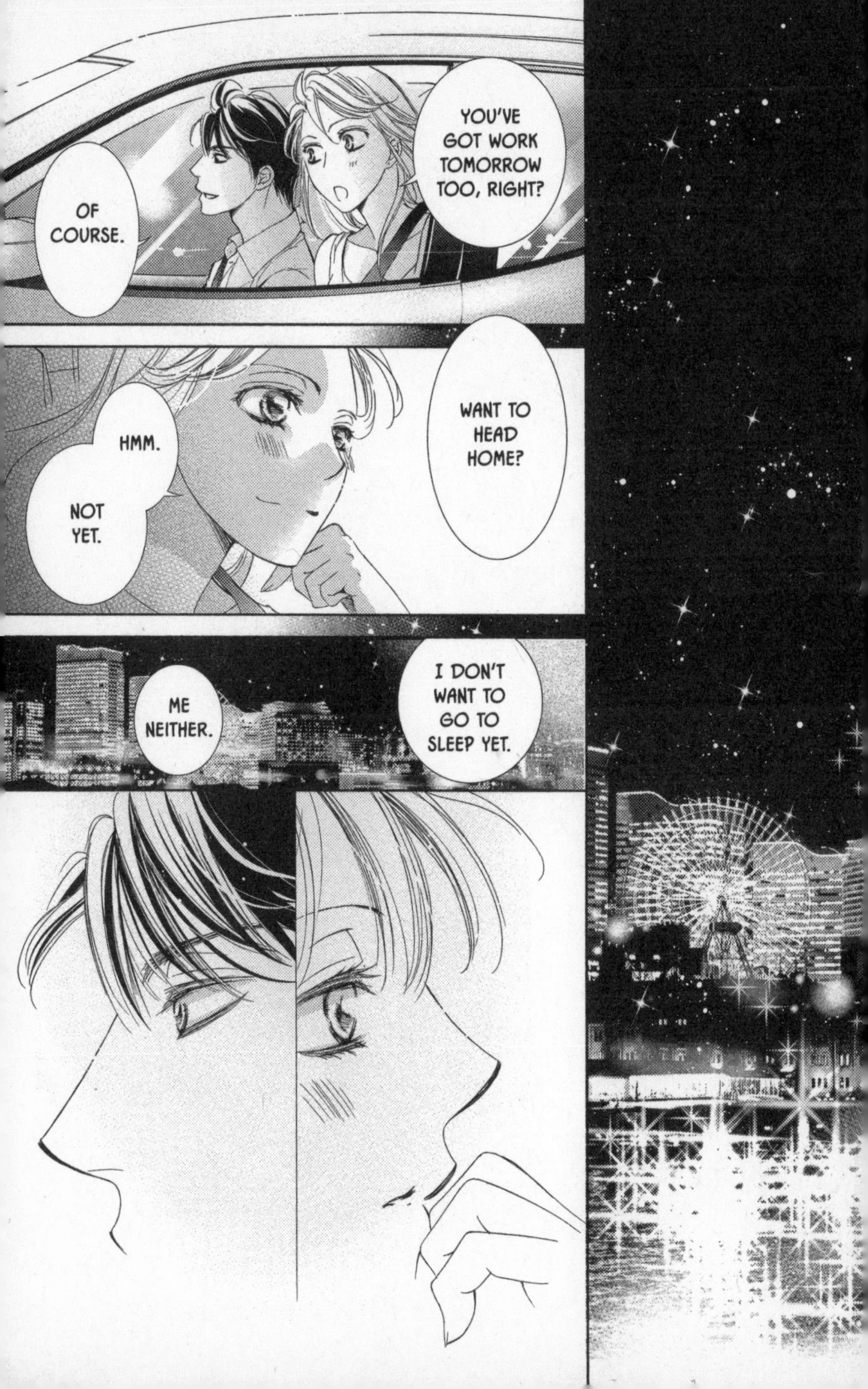
YOU'VE GOT WORK TOMORROW TOO, RIGHT?
OF COURSE.
WANT TO HEAD HOME?
HMM.
NOT YET.
I DON'T WANT TO GO TO SLEEP YET.
ME NEITHER.

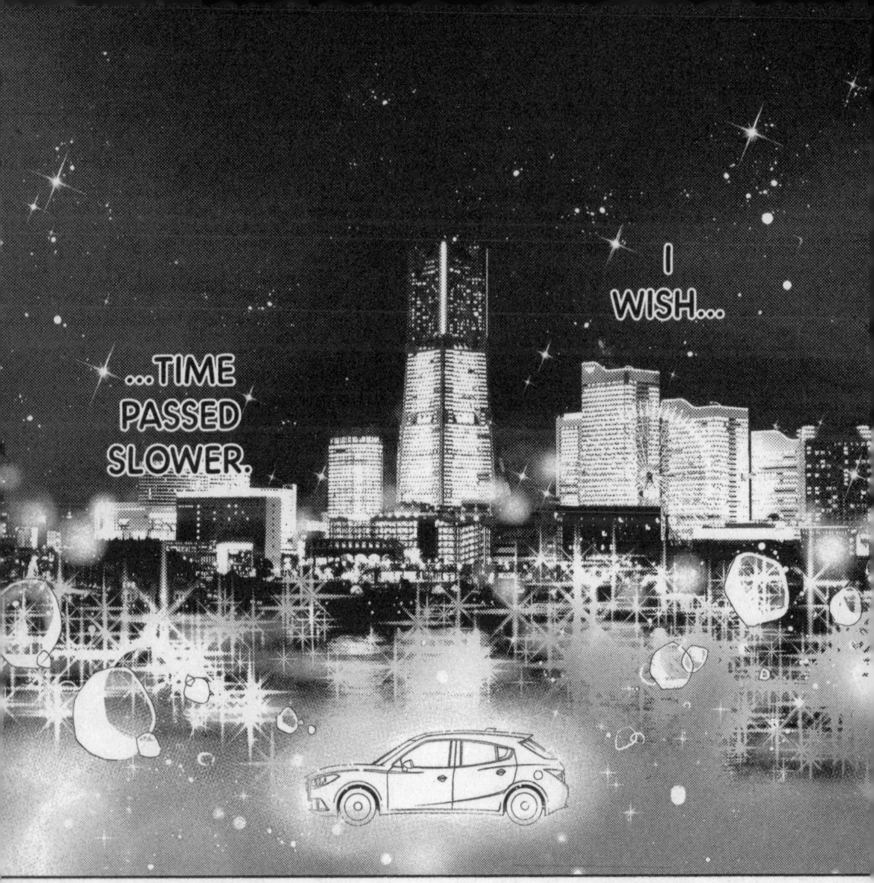
I WISH...
...TIME PASSED SLOWER.

I DON'T WANT US
TO BE APART.

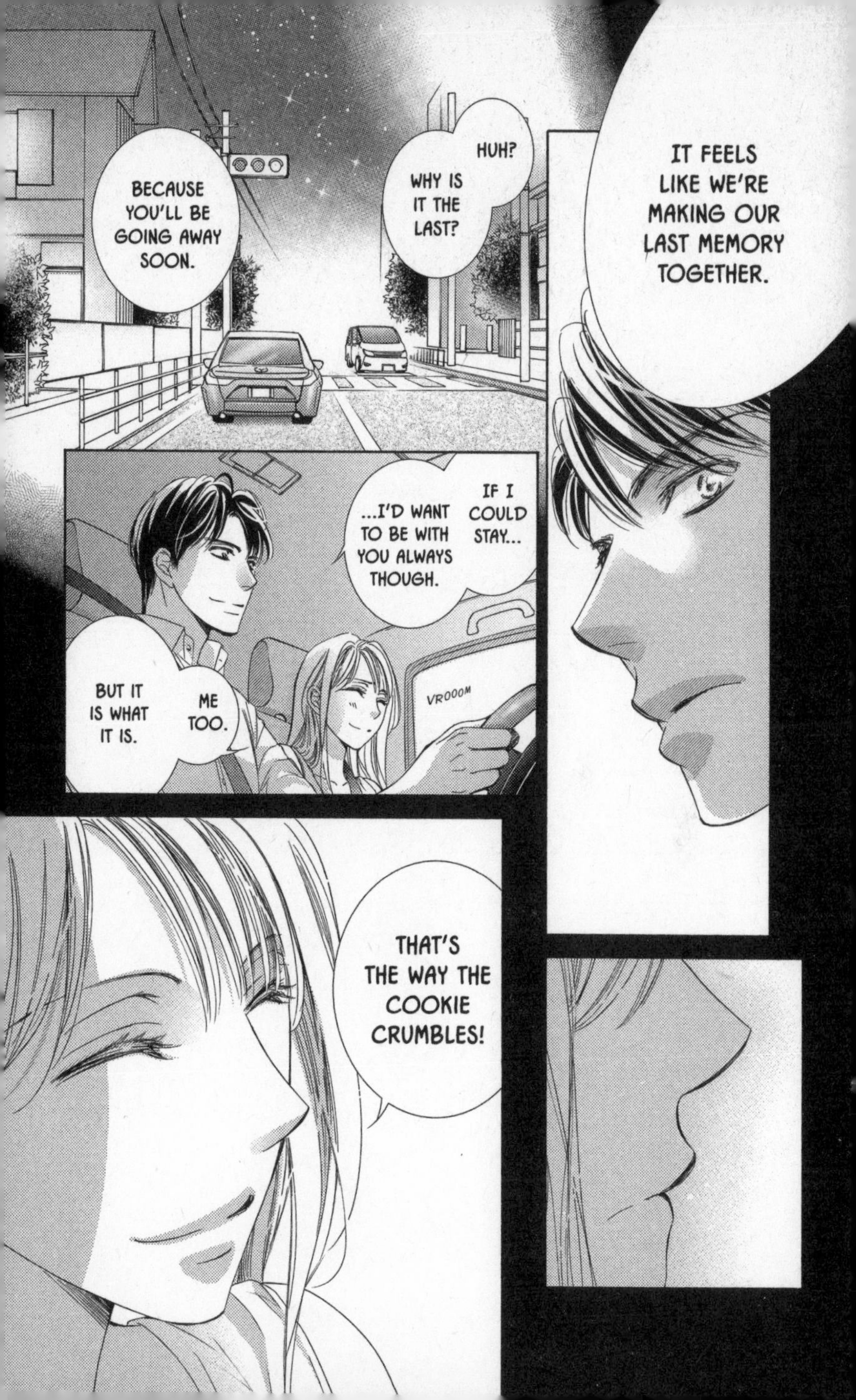
IT FEELS LIKE WE'RE MAKING OUR LAST MEMORY TOGETHER.
HUH?
WHY IS IT THE LAST?
BECAUSE YOU'LL BE GOING AWAY SOON.
IF I COULD STAY...
...I'D WANT TO BE WITH YOU ALWAYS THOUGH.
VROOOM
ME TOO.
BUT IT IS WHAT IT IS.
THAT'S THE WAY THE COOKIE CRUMBLES!

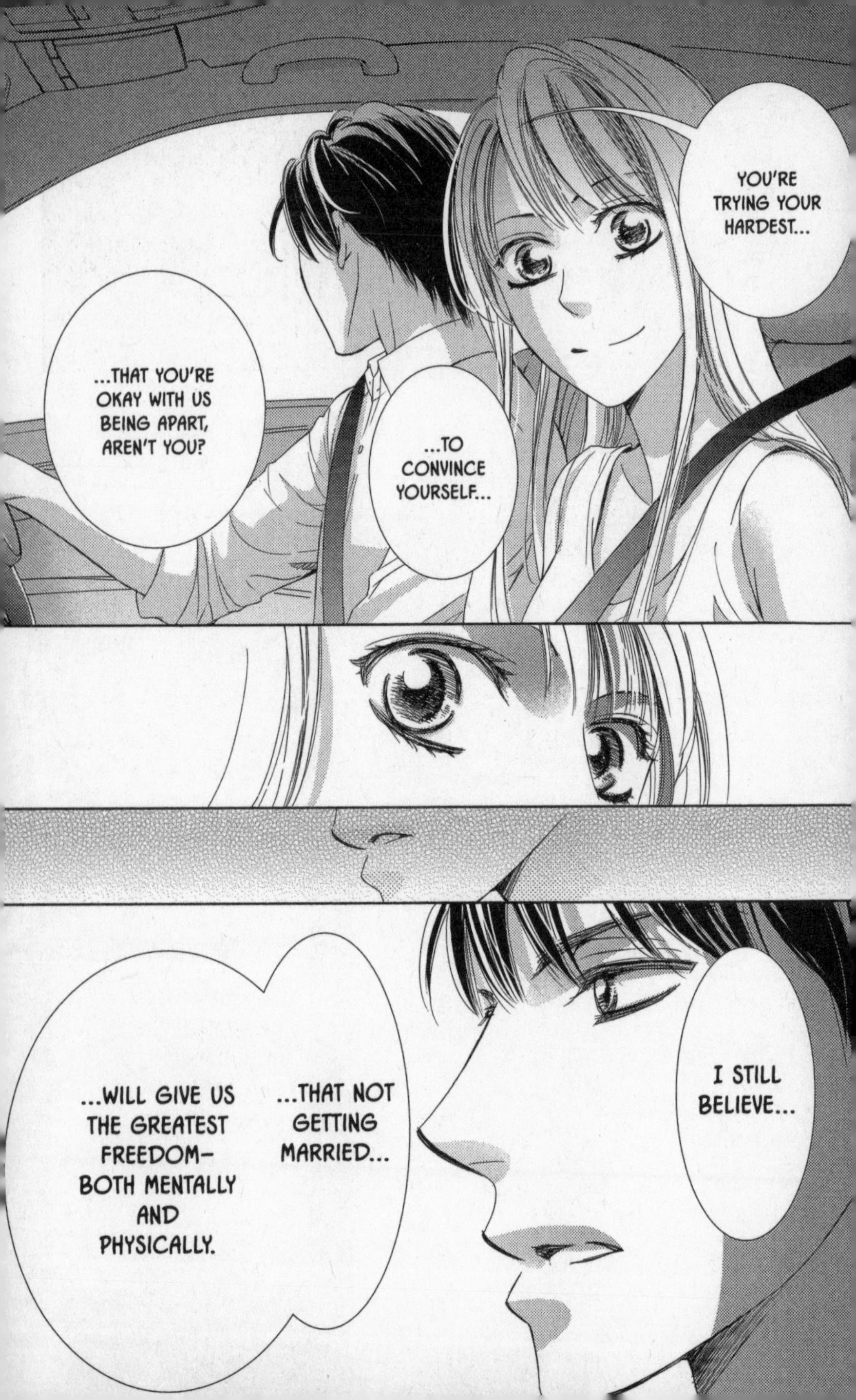
YOU'RE TRYING YOUR HARDEST...
...TO CONVINCE YOURSELF...
...THAT YOU'RE OKAY WITH US BEING APART, AREN'T YOU?
I STILL BELIEVE...
...THAT NOT GETTING MARRIED...
...WILL GIVE US THE GREATEST FREEDOM— BOTH MENTALLY AND PHYSICALLY.

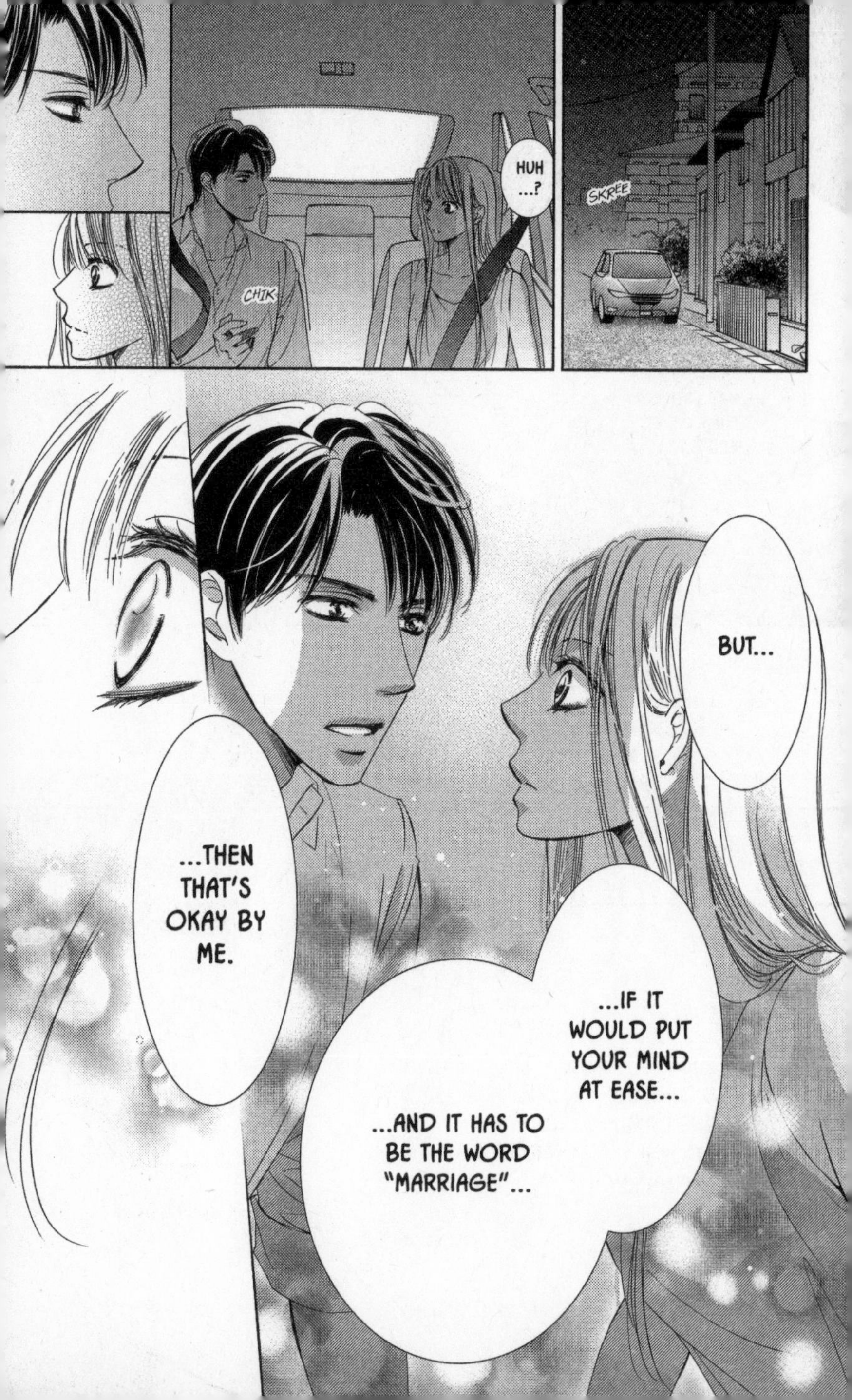
SKREE
HUH ...?
CHIK
BUT...
...IF IT WOULD PUT YOUR MIND AT EASE...
...AND IT HAS TO BE THE WORD "MARRIAGE"...
...THEN THAT'S OKAY BY ME.

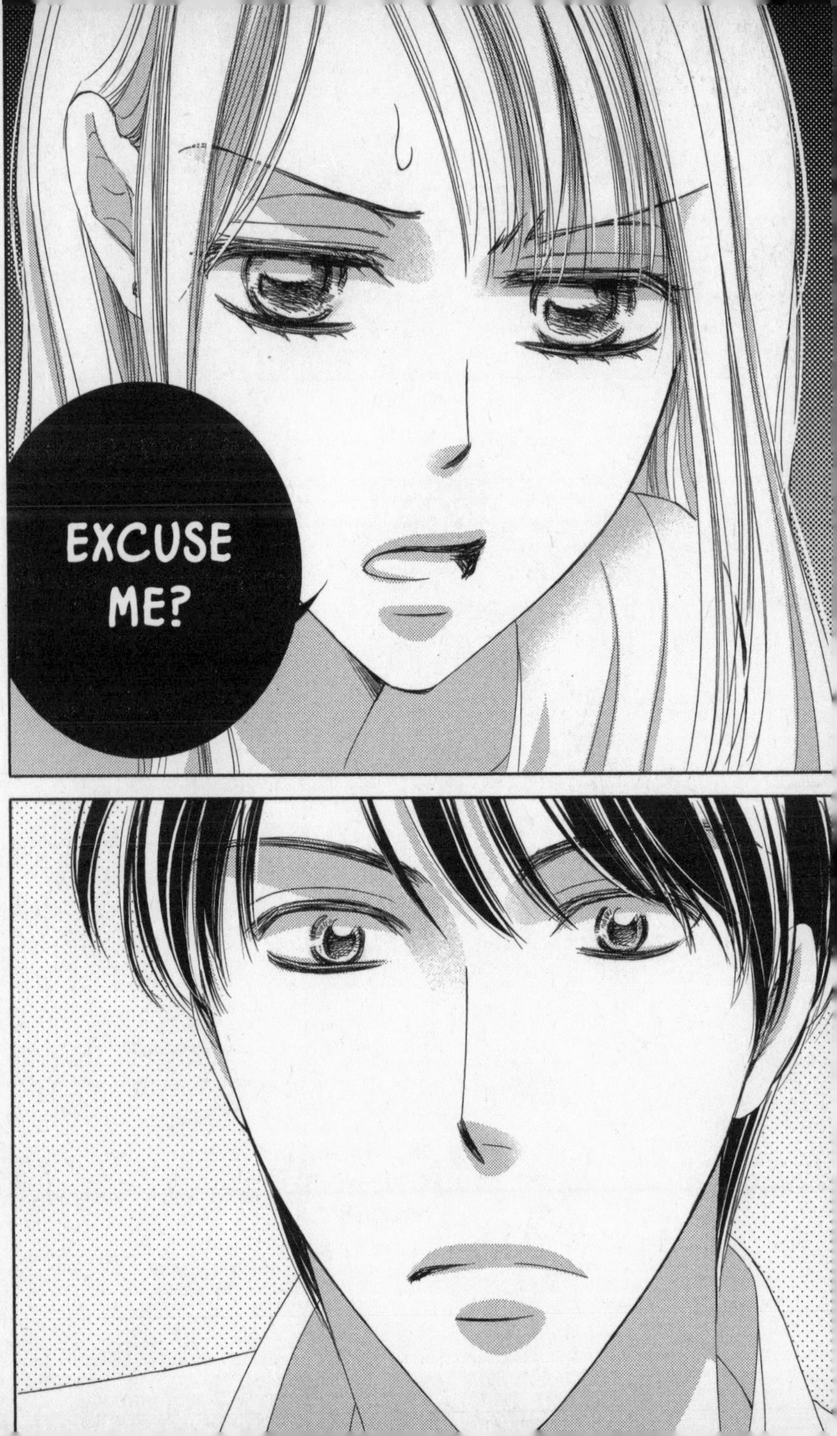
EXCUSE ME?

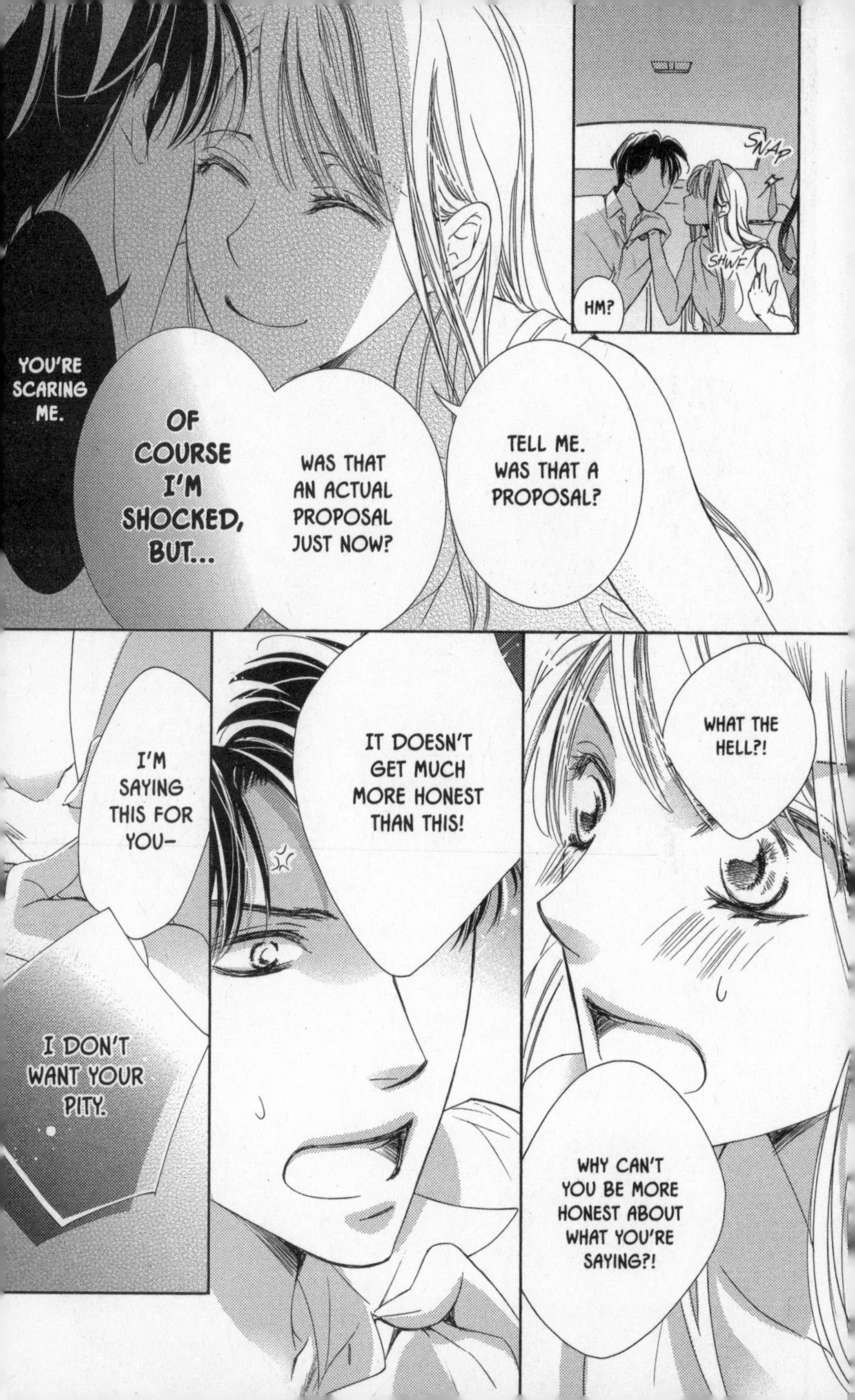
SNAP
SHWF
HM?
TELL ME. WAS THAT A PROPOSAL?
WAS THAT AN ACTUAL PROPOSAL JUST NOW?
OF COURSE I'M SHOCKED, BUT...
YOU'RE SCARING ME.
WHAT THE HELL?!
WHY CAN'T YOU BE MORE HONEST ABOUT WHAT YOU'RE SAYING?!
IT DOESN'T GET MUCH MORE HONEST THAN THIS!
I'M SAYING THIS FOR YOU–
I DON'T WANT YOUR PITY.

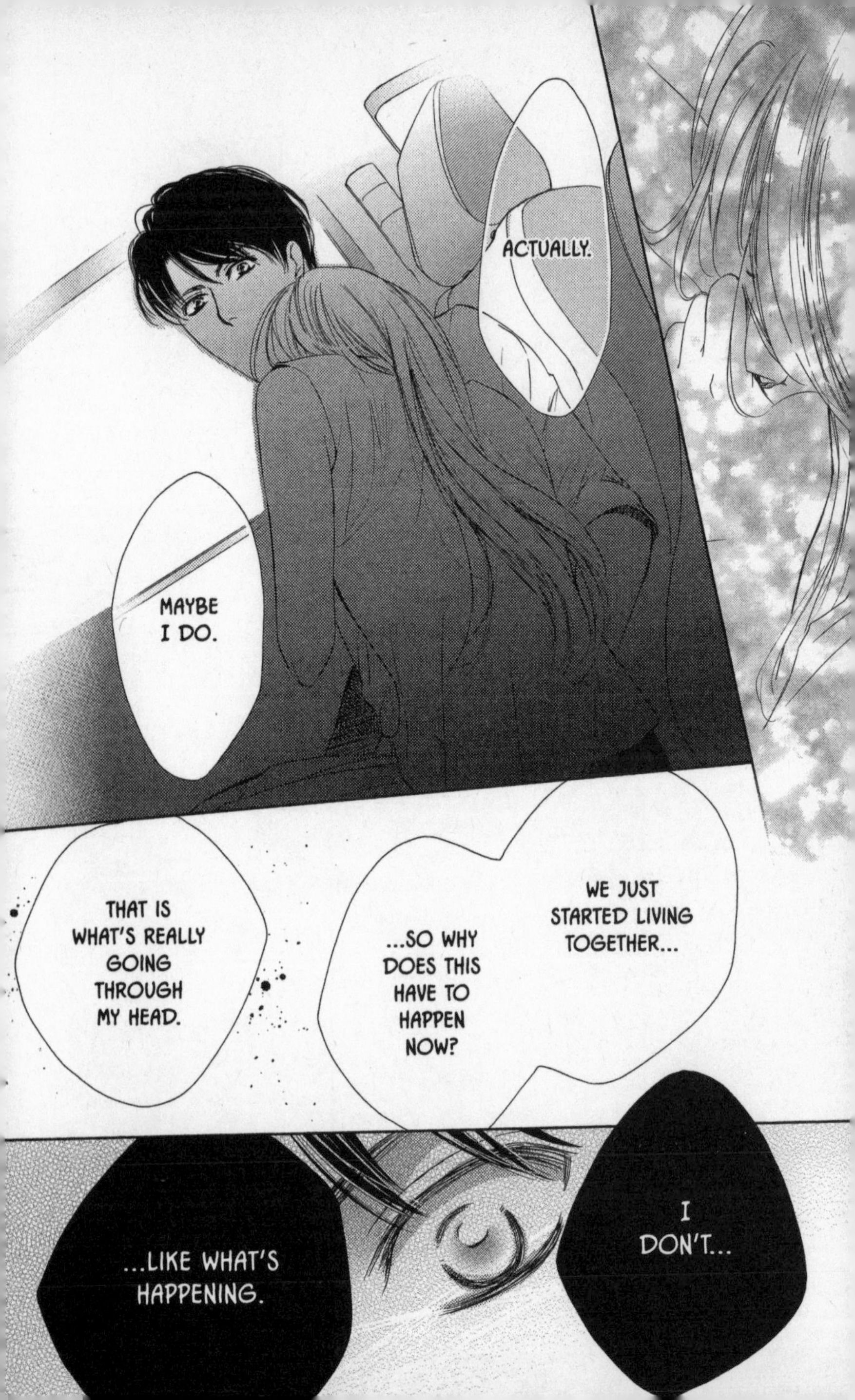
ACTUALLY.
MAYBE I DO.
WE JUST STARTED LIVING TOGETHER...
...SO WHY DOES THIS HAVE TO HAPPEN NOW?
THAT IS WHAT'S REALLY GOING THROUGH MY HEAD.
I DON'T...
...LIKE WHAT'S HAPPENING.

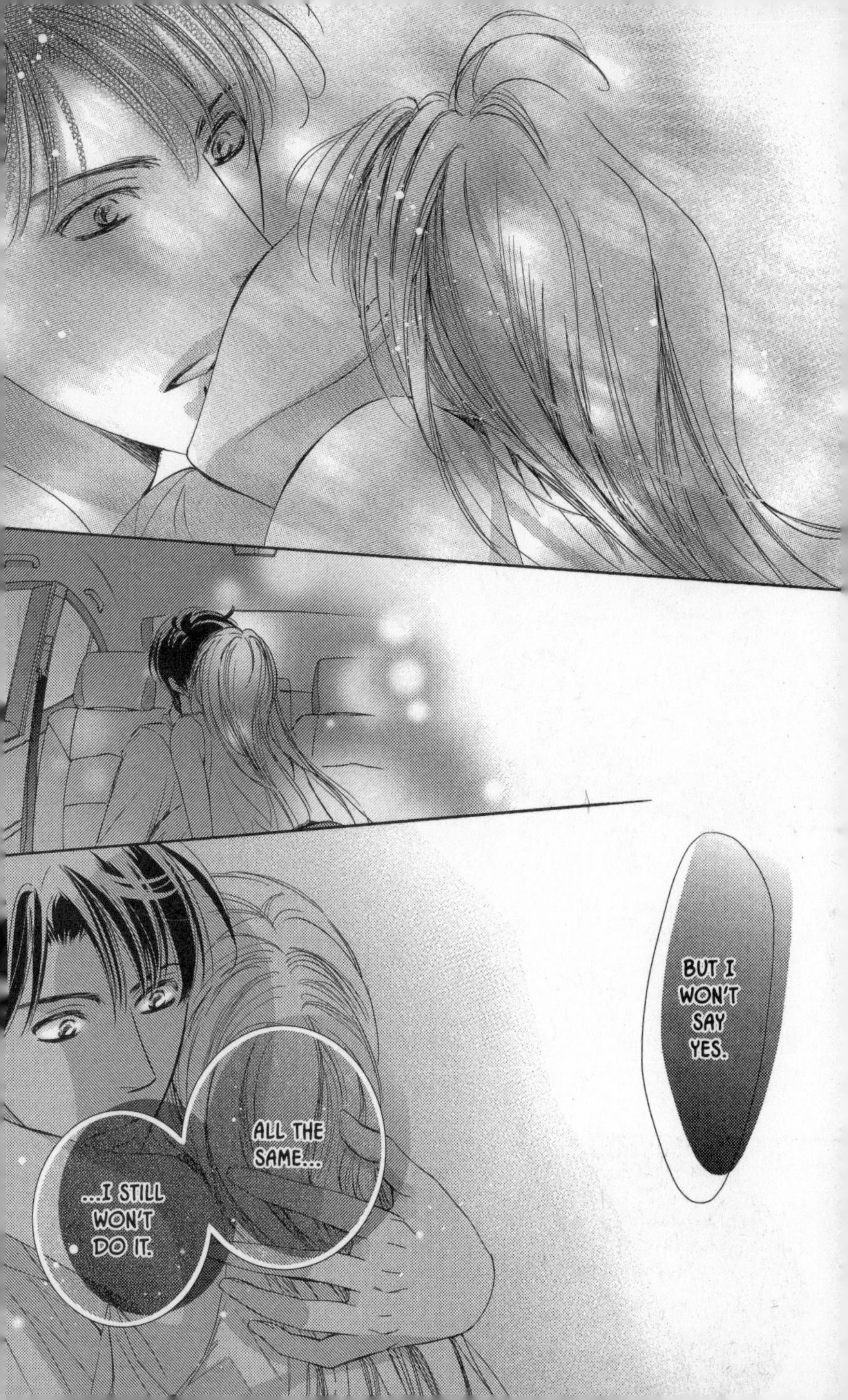
BUT I WON'T SAY YES.
ALL THE SAME...
...I STILL WON'T DO IT.

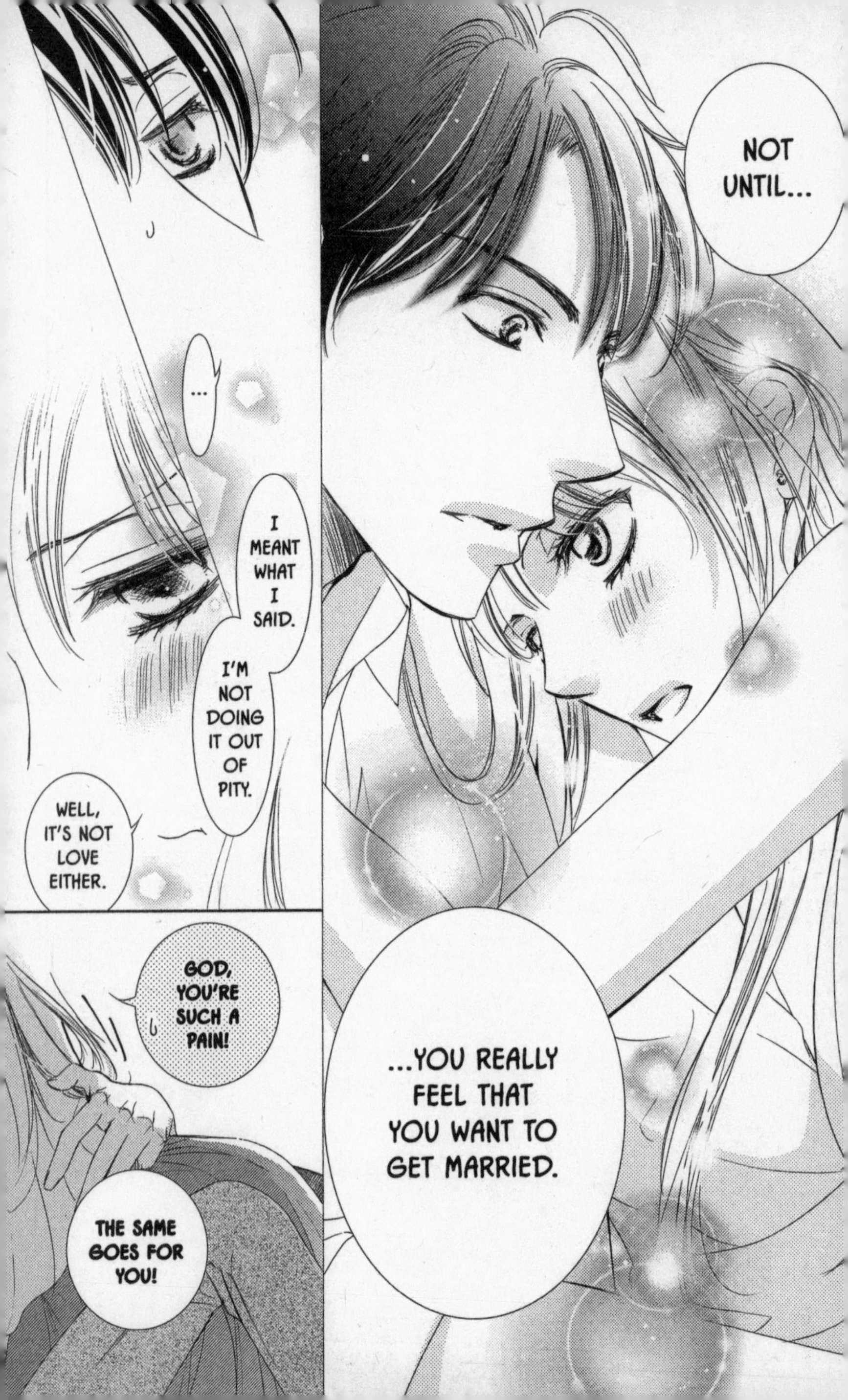
NOT UNTIL...
...YOU REALLY FEEL THAT YOU WANT TO GET MARRIED.
...
I MEANT WHAT I SAID.
I'M NOT DOING IT OUT OF PITY.
WELL, IT'S NOT LOVE EITHER.
GOD, YOU'RE SUCH A PAIN!
THE SAME GOES FOR YOU!

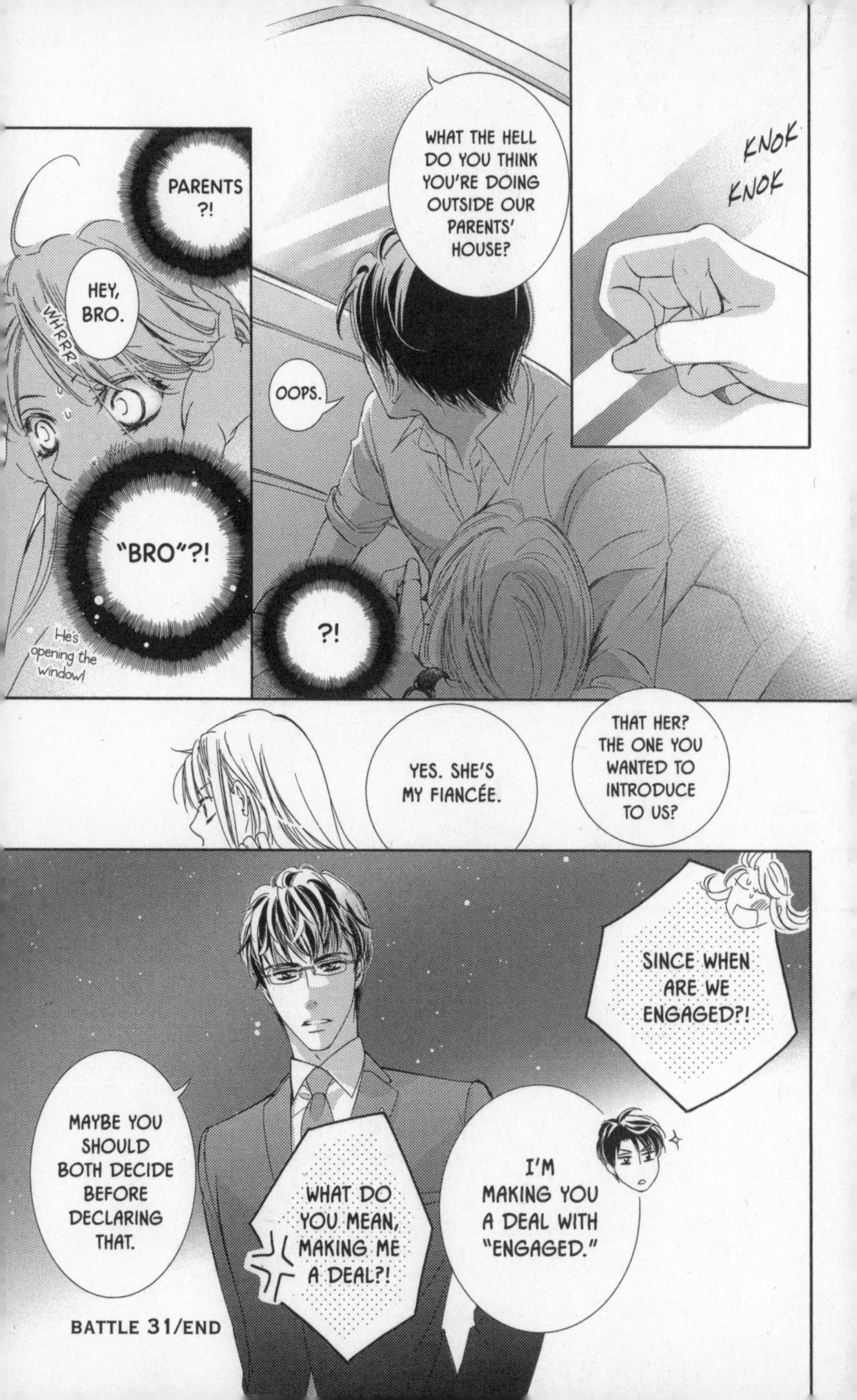
KNOK
KNOK
WHAT THE HELL DO YOU THINK YOU'RE DOING OUTSIDE OUR PARENTS' HOUSE?
OOPS.
?!
PARENTS ?!
HEY, BRO.
WHRRR
"BRO"?!
He's opening the window!
THAT HER? THE ONE YOU WANTED TO INTRODUCE TO US?
YES. SHE'S MY FIANCÉE.
SINCE WHEN ARE WE ENGAGED?!
I'M MAKING YOU A DEAL WITH "ENGAGED."
WHAT DO YOU MEAN, MAKING ME A DEAL?!
MAYBE YOU SHOULD BOTH DECIDE BEFORE DECLARING THAT.
BATTLE 31/END

I think of you
all the time.

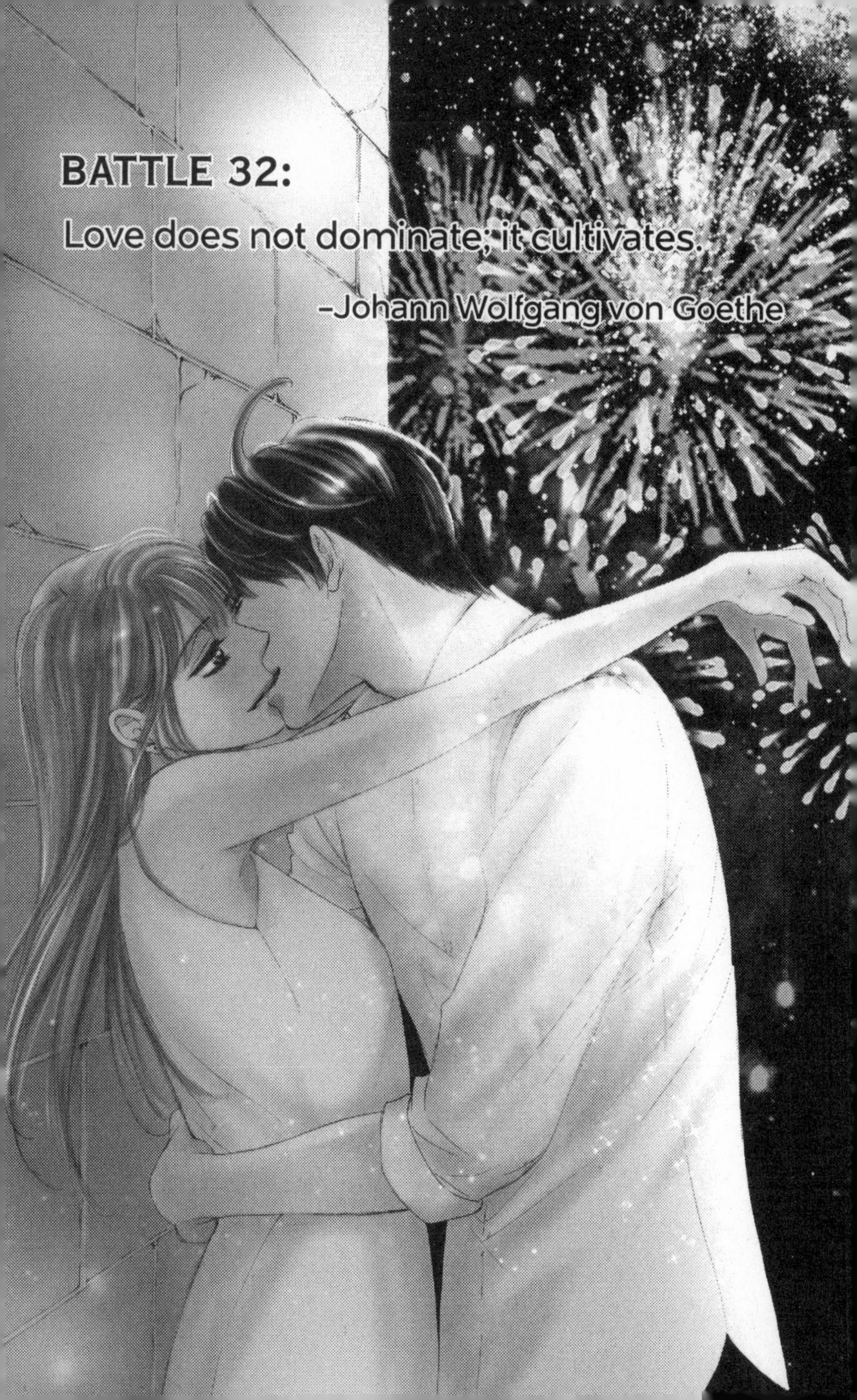
BATTLE 32:
Love does not dominate; it cultivates.
–Johann Wolfgang von Goethe

Everyone's
Getting
Married

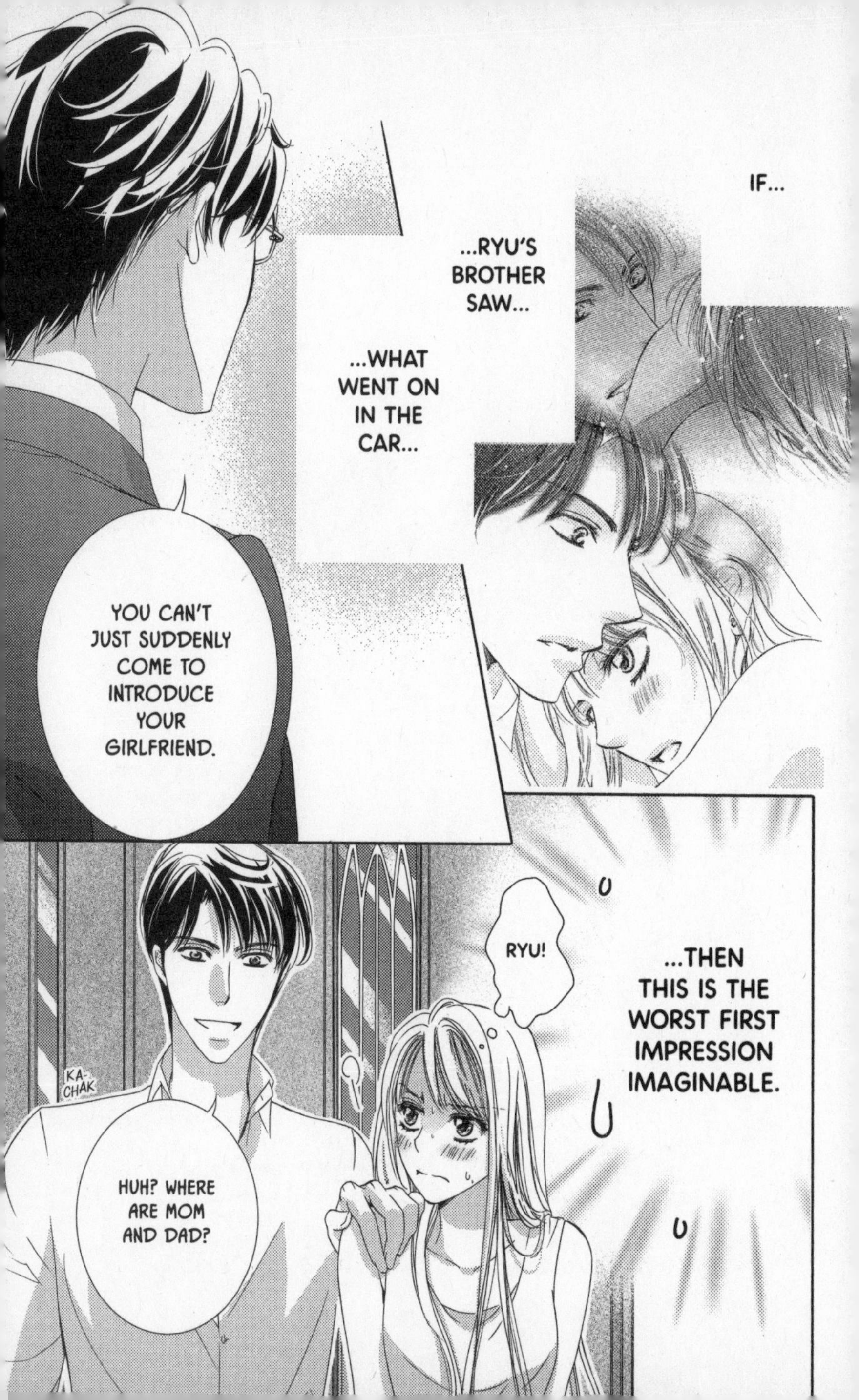
IF...
...RYU'S BROTHER SAW...
...WHAT WENT ON IN THE CAR...
YOU CAN'T JUST SUDDENLY COME TO INTRODUCE YOUR GIRLFRIEND.
...THEN THIS IS THE WORST FIRST IMPRESSION IMAGINABLE.
RYU!
KA-CHAK
HUH? WHERE ARE MOM AND DAD?

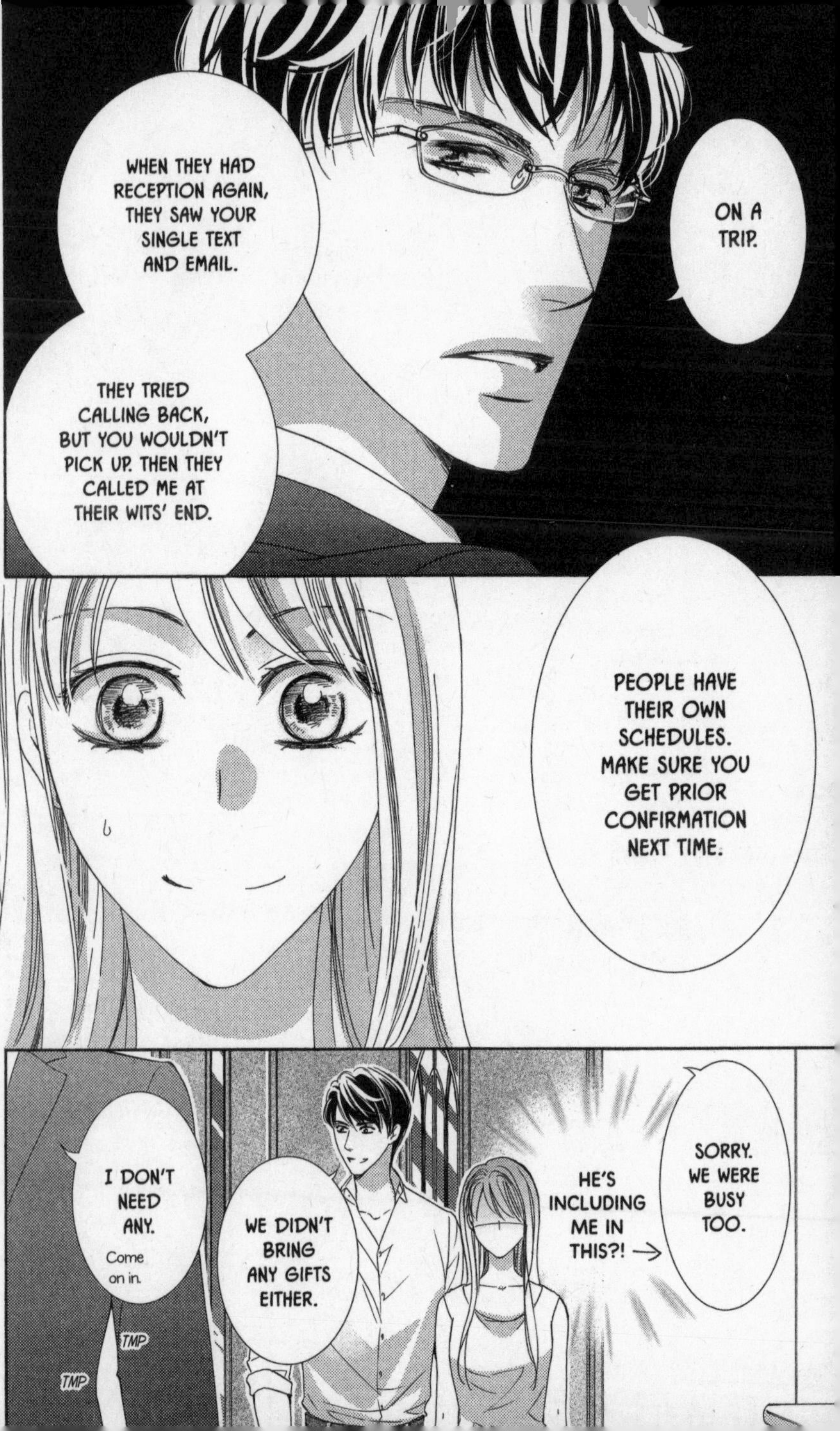
ON A TRIP.
WHEN THEY HAD RECEPTION AGAIN, THEY SAW YOUR SINGLE TEXT AND EMAIL.
THEY TRIED CALLING BACK, BUT YOU WOULDN'T PICK UP. THEN THEY CALLED ME AT THEIR WITS' END.
PEOPLE HAVE THEIR OWN SCHEDULES. MAKE SURE YOU GET PRIOR CONFIRMATION NEXT TIME.
SORRY. WE WERE BUSY TOO.
HE'S INCLUDING ME IN THIS?!
WE DIDN'T BRING ANY GIFTS EITHER.
I DON'T NEED ANY.
Come on in.
TMP
TMP

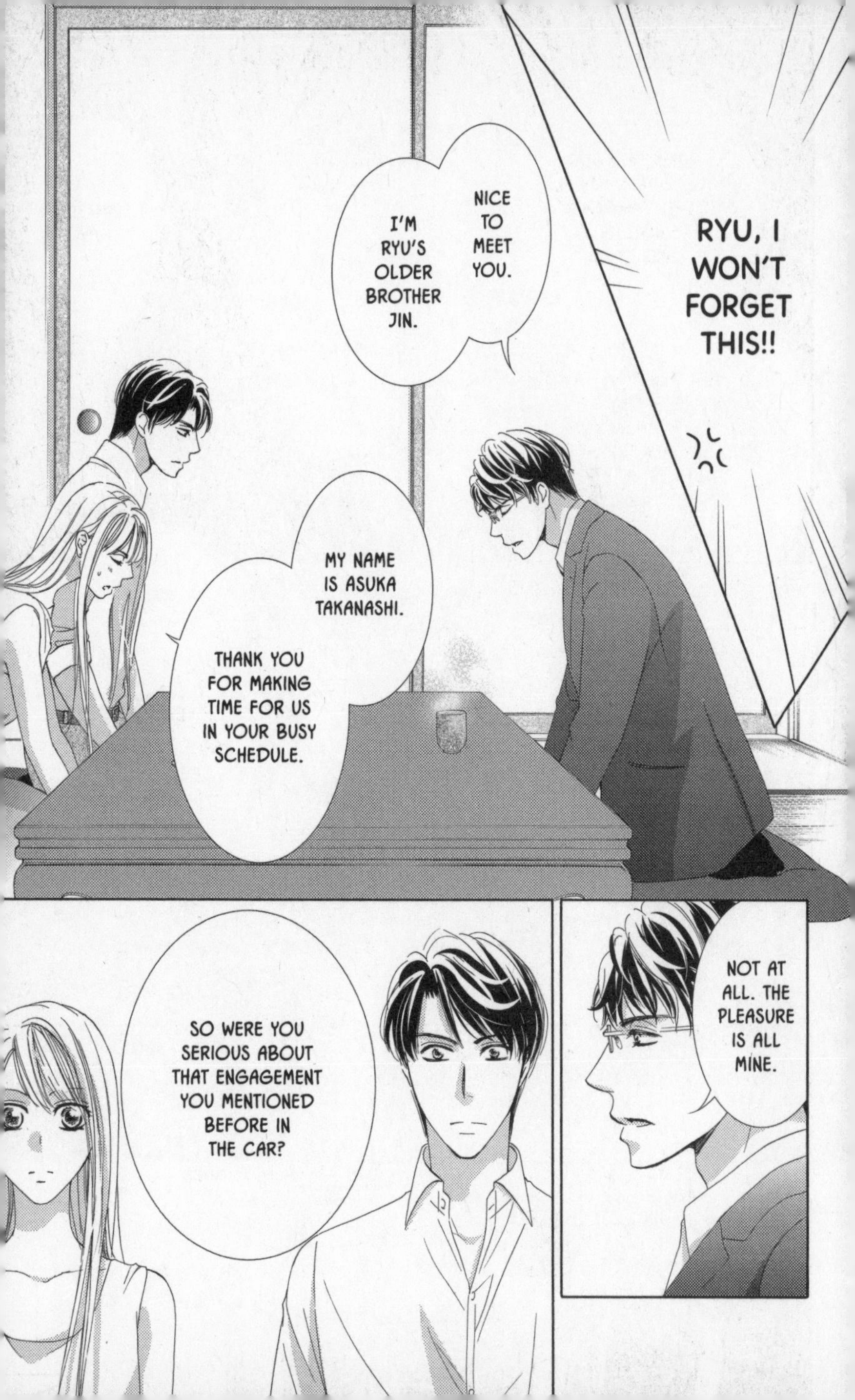
RYU, I WON'T FORGET THIS!!
NICE TO MEET YOU.
I'M RYU'S OLDER BROTHER JIN.
MY NAME IS ASUKA TAKANASHI.
THANK YOU FOR MAKING TIME FOR US IN YOUR BUSY SCHEDULE.
NOT AT ALL. THE PLEASURE IS ALL MINE.
SO WERE YOU SERIOUS ABOUT THAT ENGAGEMENT YOU MENTIONED BEFORE IN THE CAR?

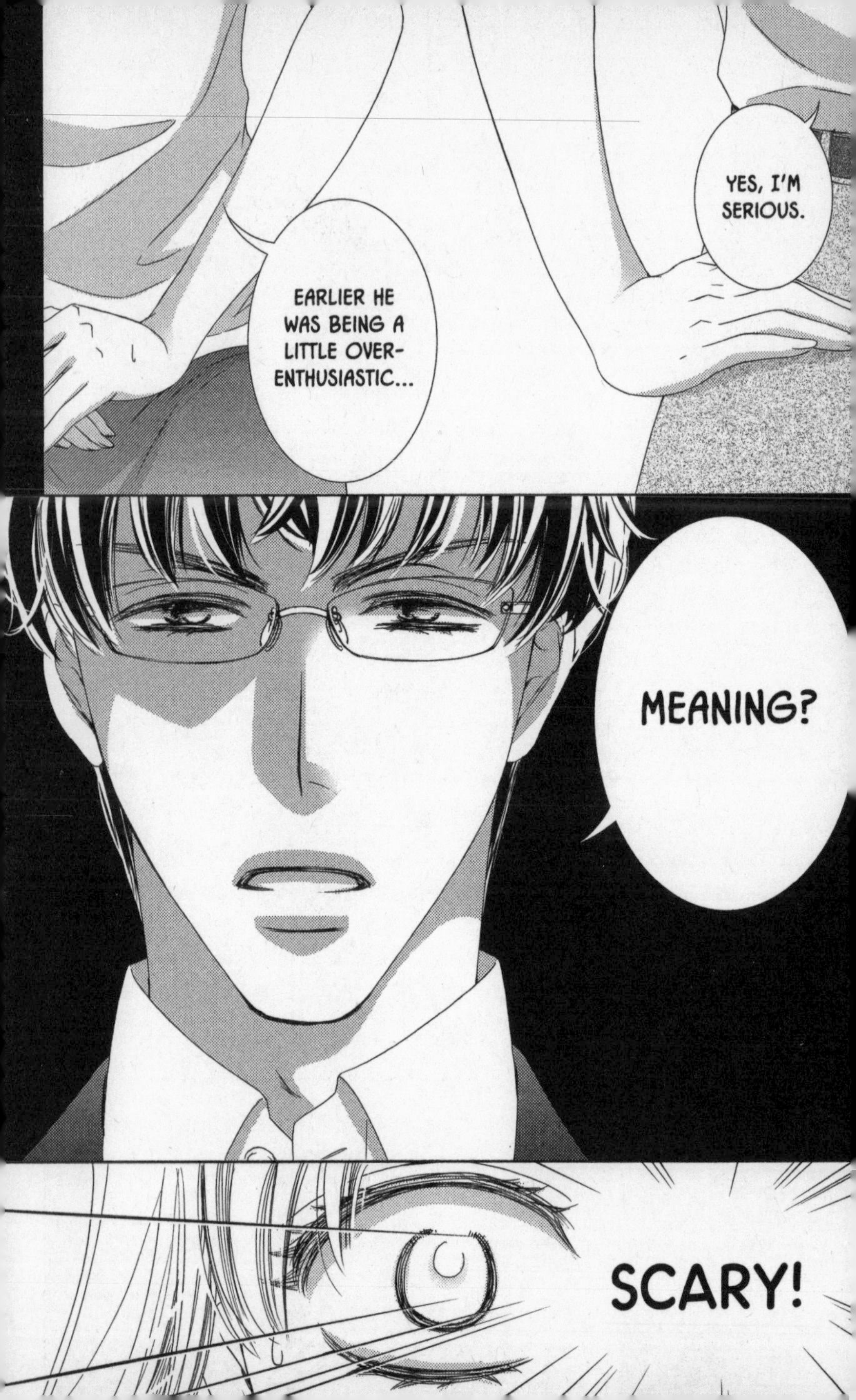
YES, I'M SERIOUS.
EARLIER HE WAS BEING A LITTLE OVER-ENTHUSIASTIC...
MEANING?
SCARY!

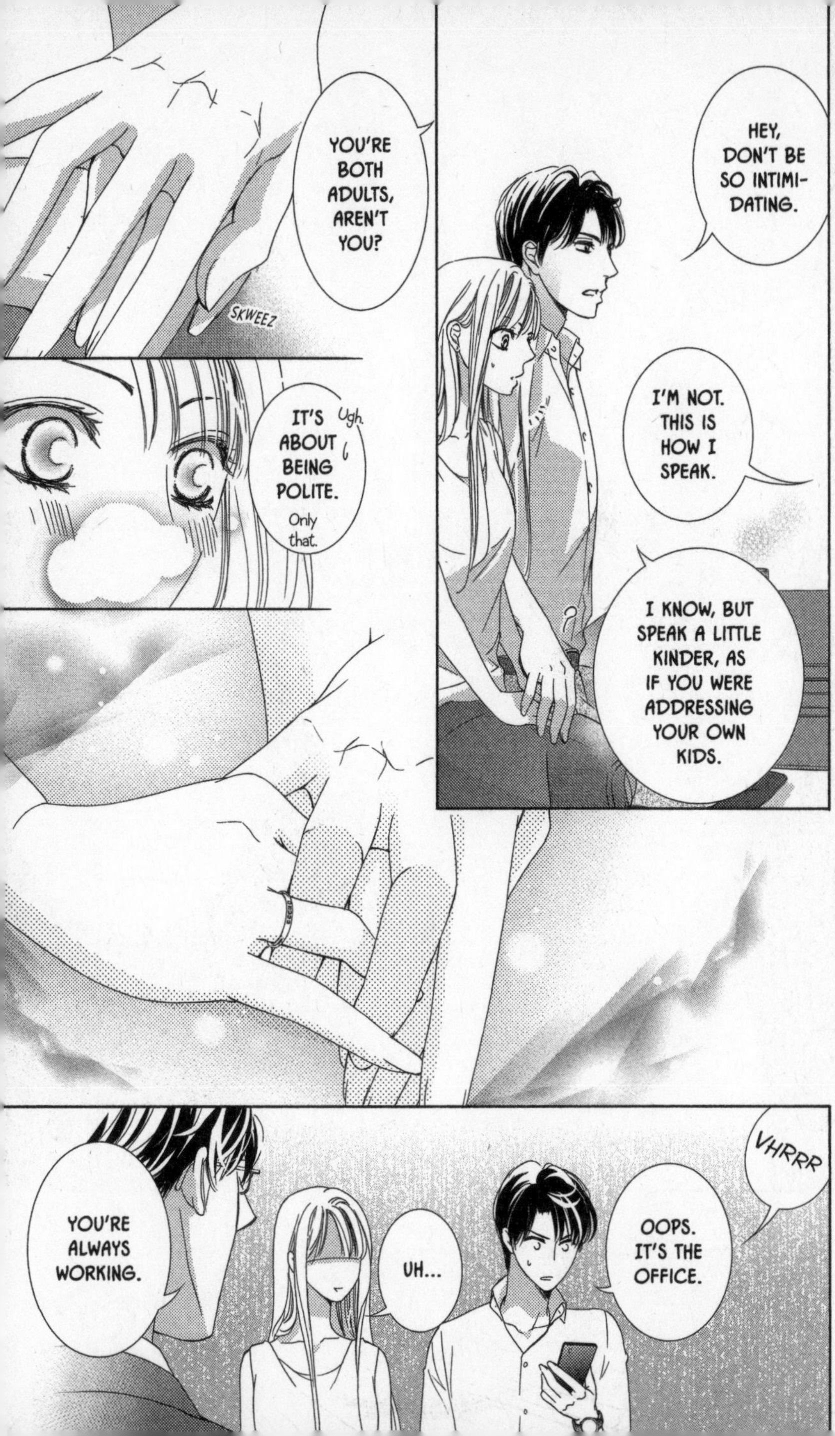
HEY, DON'T BE SO INTIMI-DATING.
I'M NOT. THIS IS HOW I SPEAK.
I KNOW, BUT SPEAK A LITTLE KINDER, AS IF YOU WERE ADDRESSING YOUR OWN KIDS.
YOU'RE BOTH ADULTS, AREN'T YOU?
SKWEEZ
Ugh.
IT'S ABOUT BEING POLITE.
Only that.
VHRRR
OOPS. IT'S THE OFFICE.
UH...
YOU'RE ALWAYS WORKING.

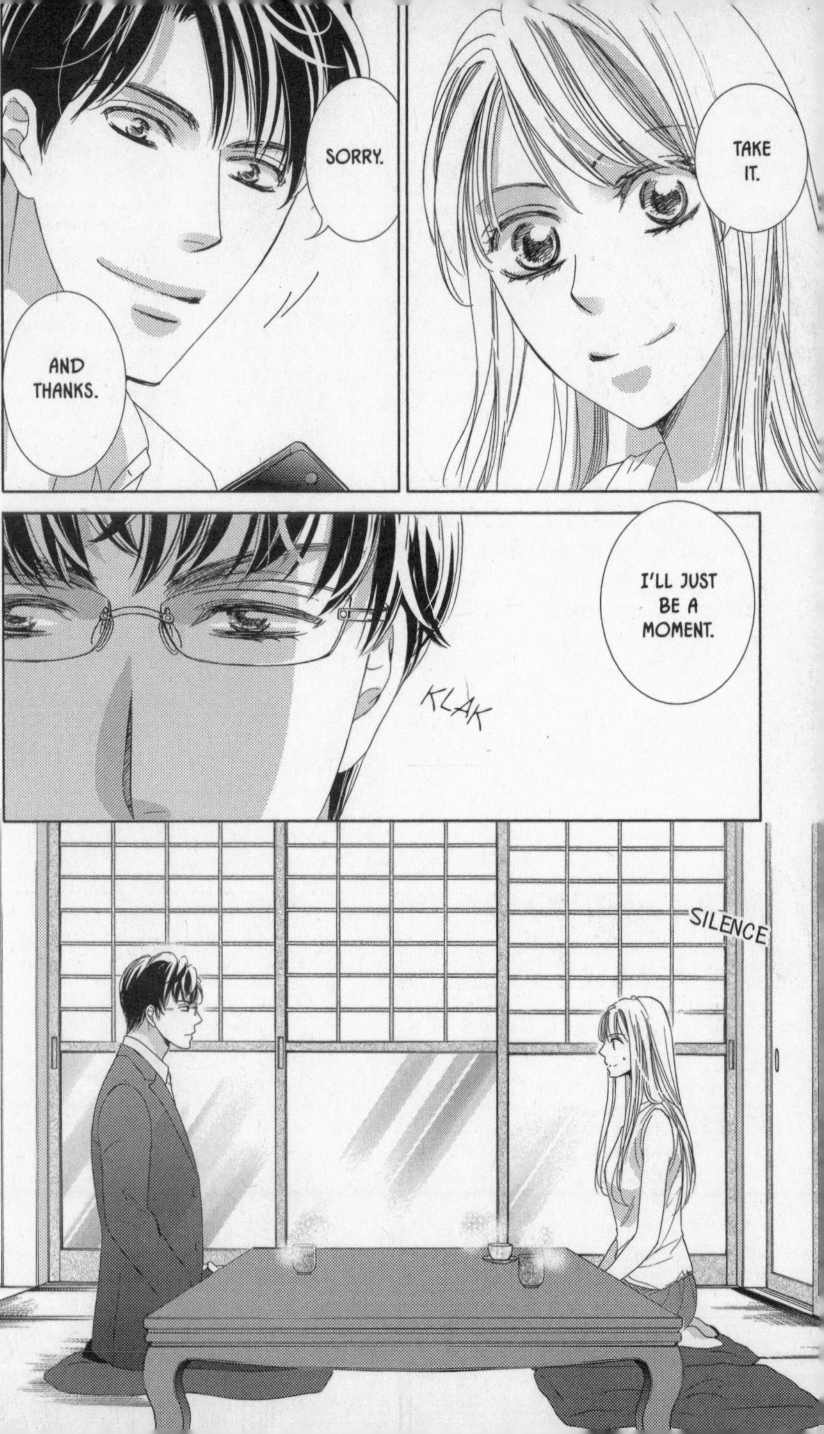
TAKE IT.
SORRY.
AND THANKS.
I'LL JUST BE A MOMENT.
KLAK
SILENCE

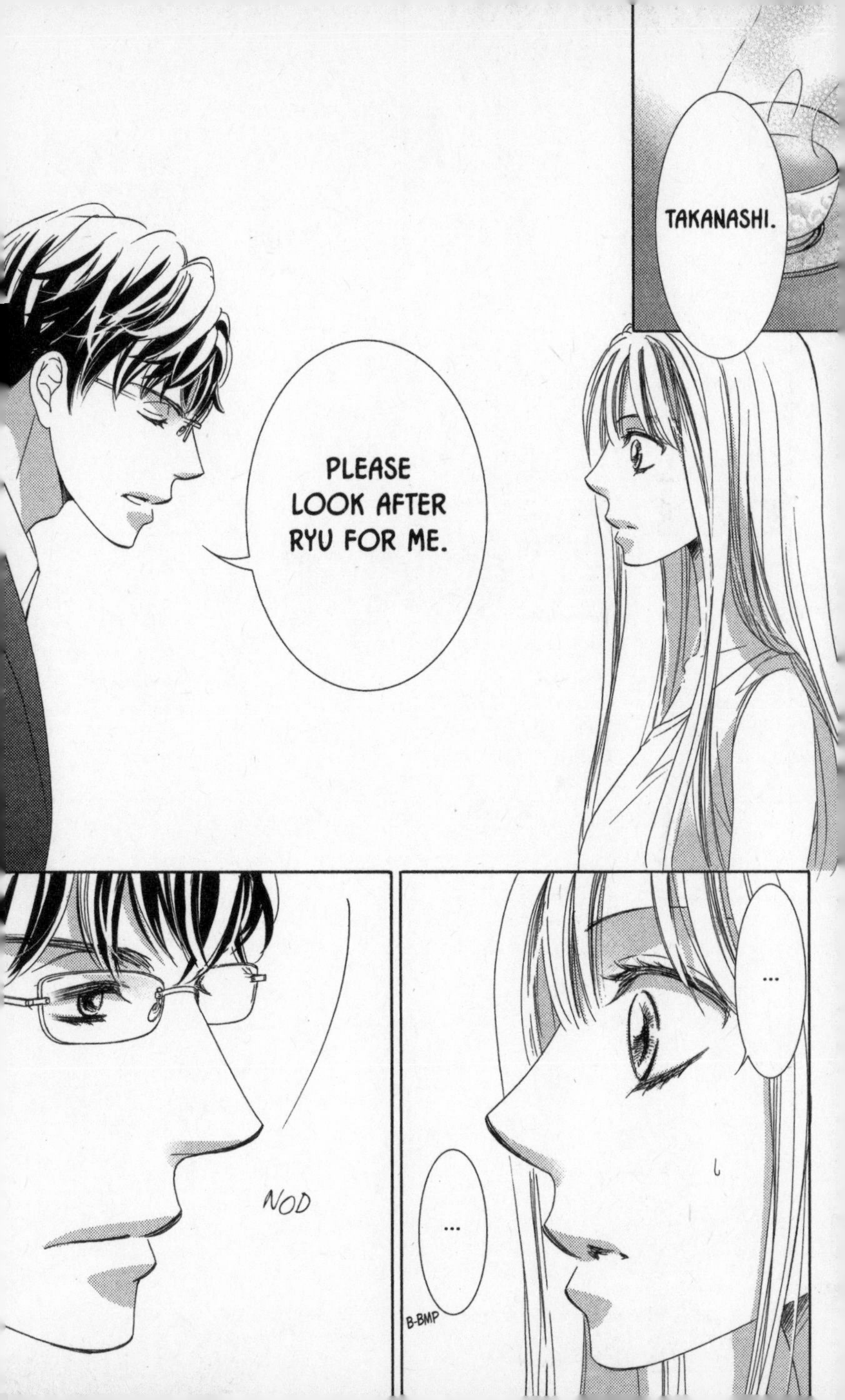
TAKANASHI.
PLEASE LOOK AFTER RYU FOR ME.
...
...
B-BMP
NOD

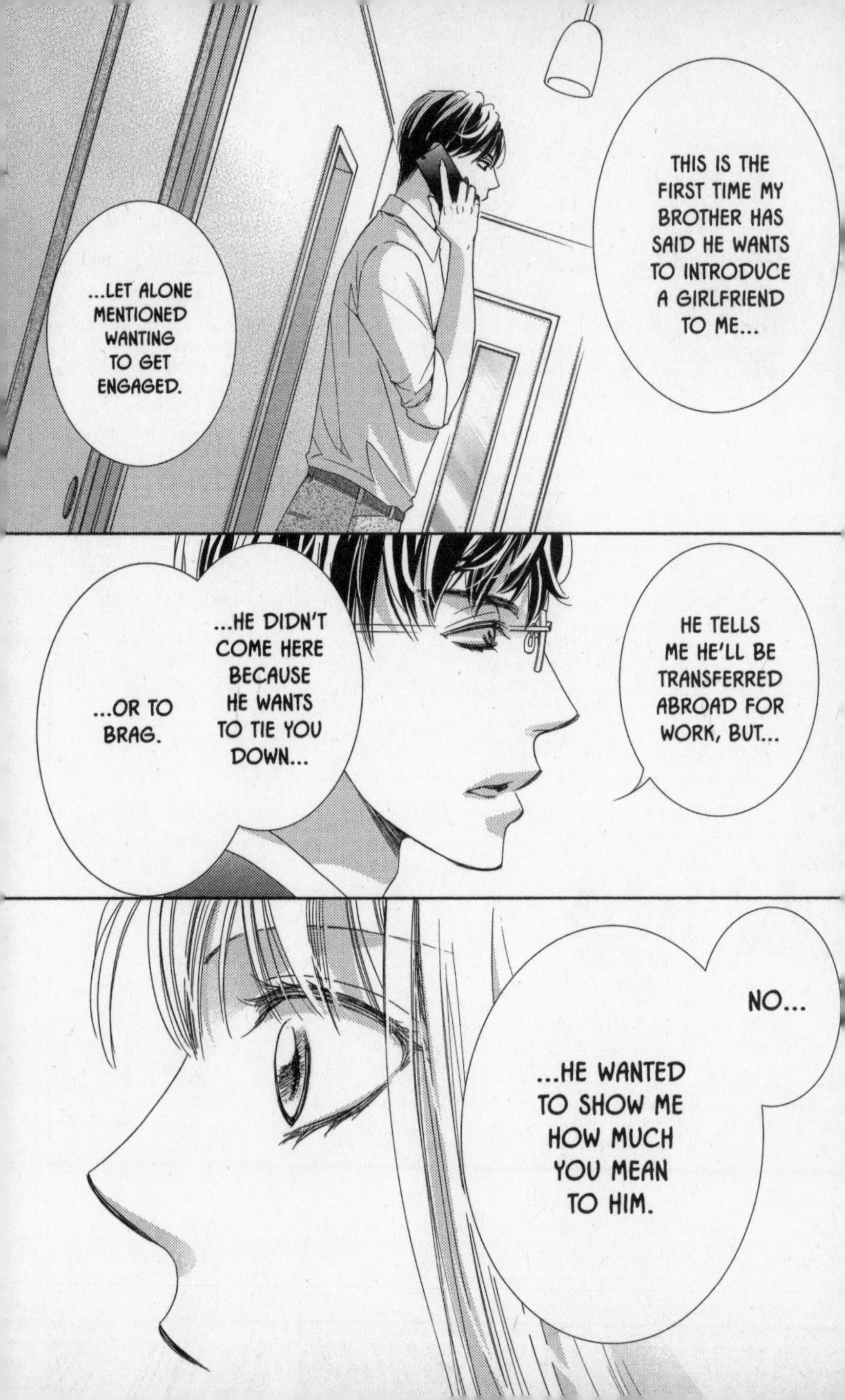
THIS IS THE FIRST TIME MY BROTHER HAS SAID HE WANTS TO INTRODUCE A GIRLFRIEND TO ME...
...LET ALONE MENTIONED WANTING TO GET ENGAGED.
HE TELLS ME HE'LL BE TRANSFERRED ABROAD FOR WORK, BUT...
...HE DIDN'T COME HERE BECAUSE HE WANTS TO TIE YOU DOWN...
...OR TO BRAG.
NO...
...HE WANTED TO SHOW ME HOW MUCH YOU MEAN TO HIM.

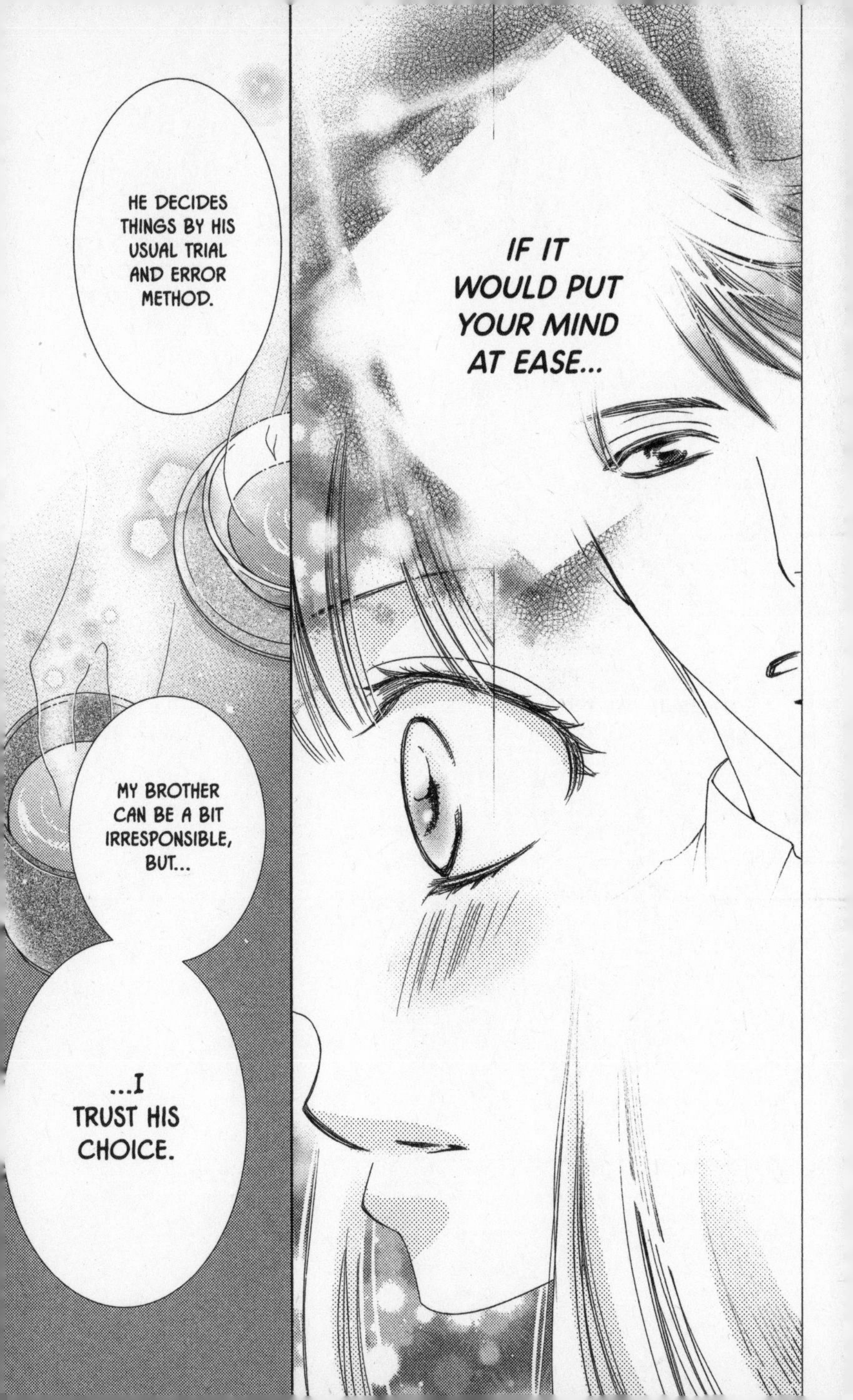
IF IT WOULD PUT YOUR MIND AT EASE...
HE DECIDES THINGS BY HIS USUAL TRIAL AND ERROR METHOD.
MY BROTHER CAN BE A BIT IRRESPONSIBLE, BUT...
...I TRUST HIS CHOICE.

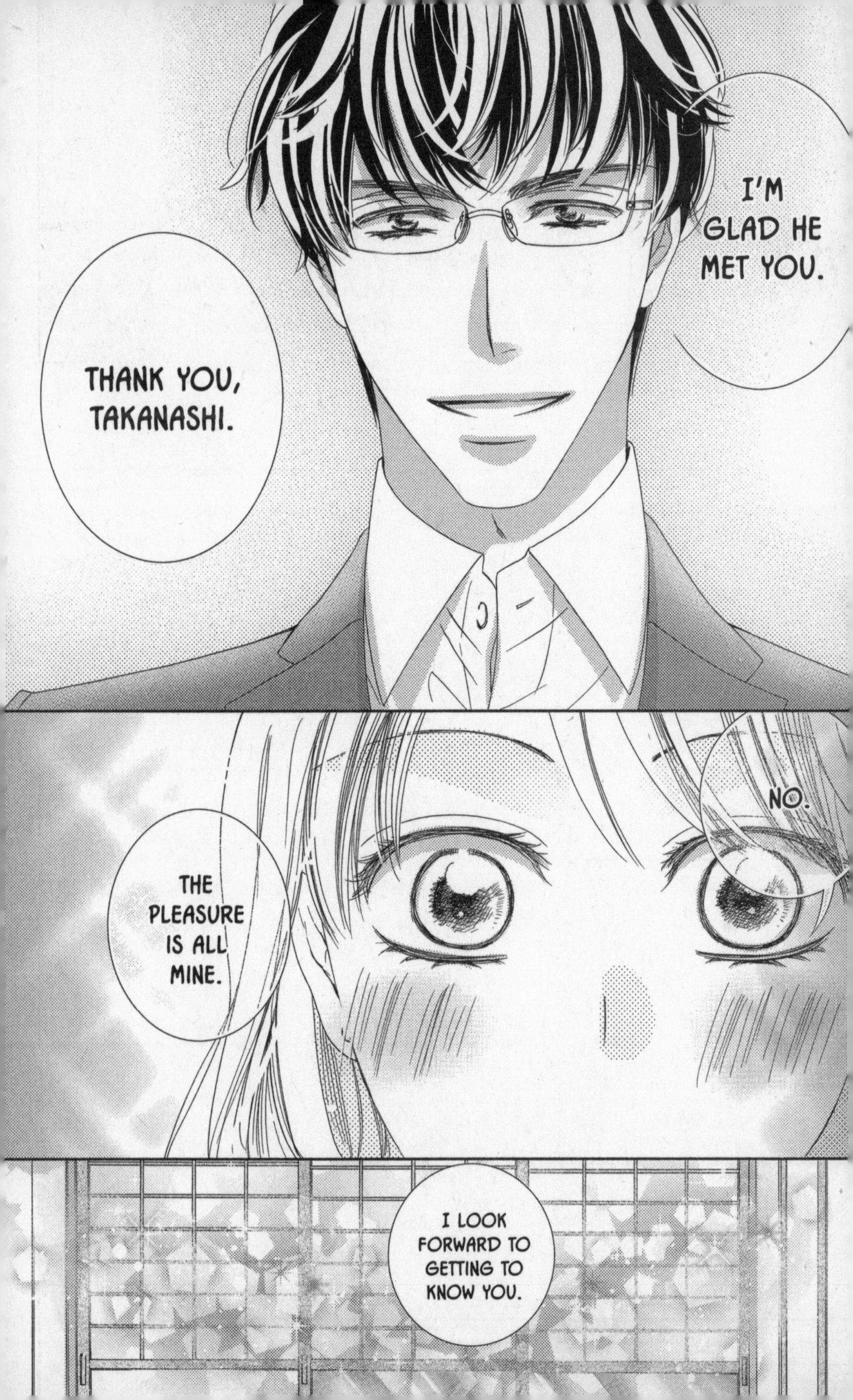
I'M GLAD HE MET YOU.
THANK YOU, TAKANASHI.
NO.
THE PLEASURE IS ALL MINE.
I LOOK FORWARD TO GETTING TO KNOW YOU.

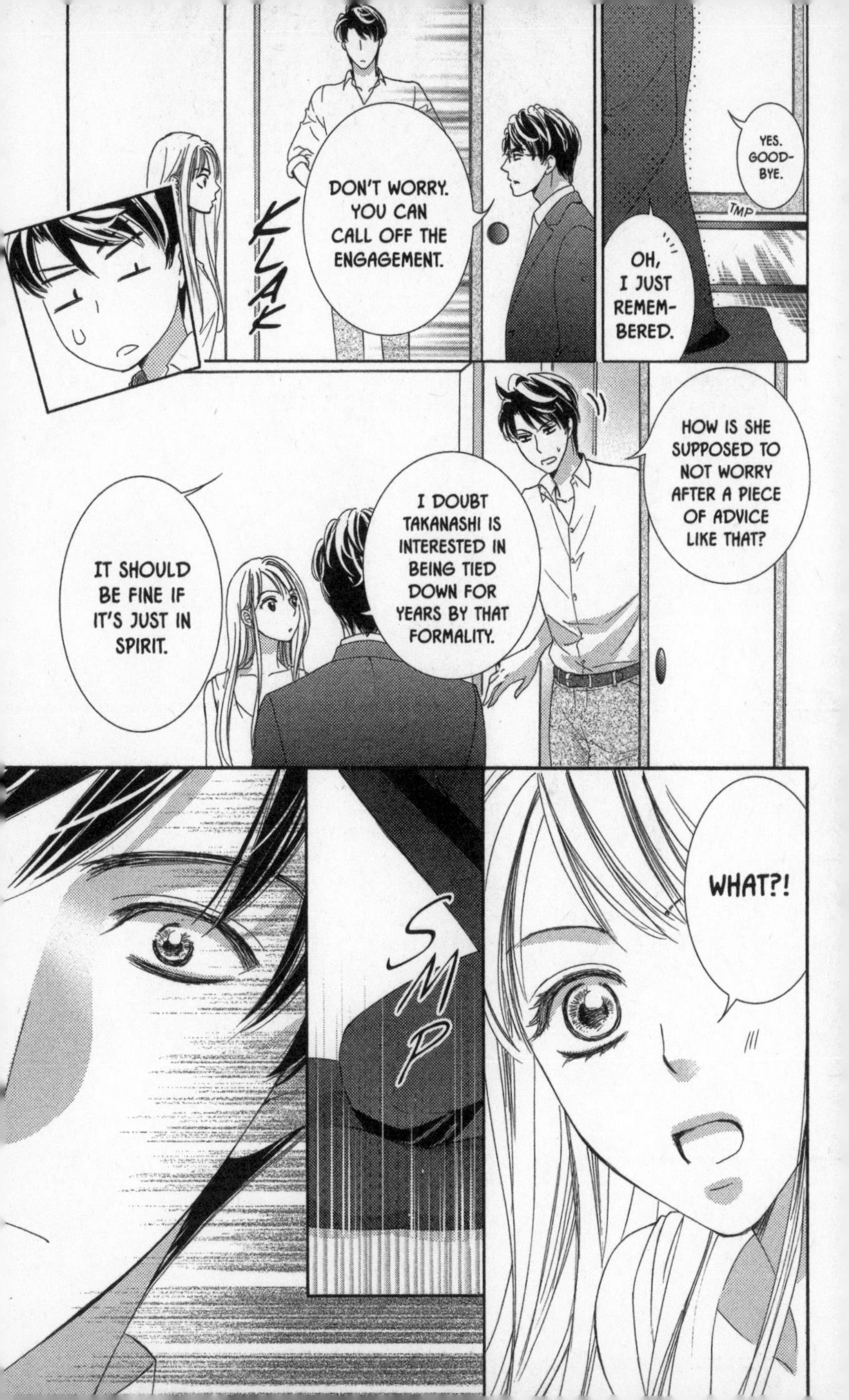
YES. GOOD-BYE.
TMP
OH, I JUST REMEMBERED.
DON'T WORRY. YOU CAN CALL OFF THE ENGAGEMENT.
KLAK
HOW IS SHE SUPPOSED TO NOT WORRY AFTER A PIECE OF ADVICE LIKE THAT?
I DOUBT TAKANASHI IS INTERESTED IN BEING TIED DOWN FOR YEARS BY THAT FORMALITY.
IT SHOULD BE FINE IF IT'S JUST IN SPIRIT.
WHAT?!
SMP

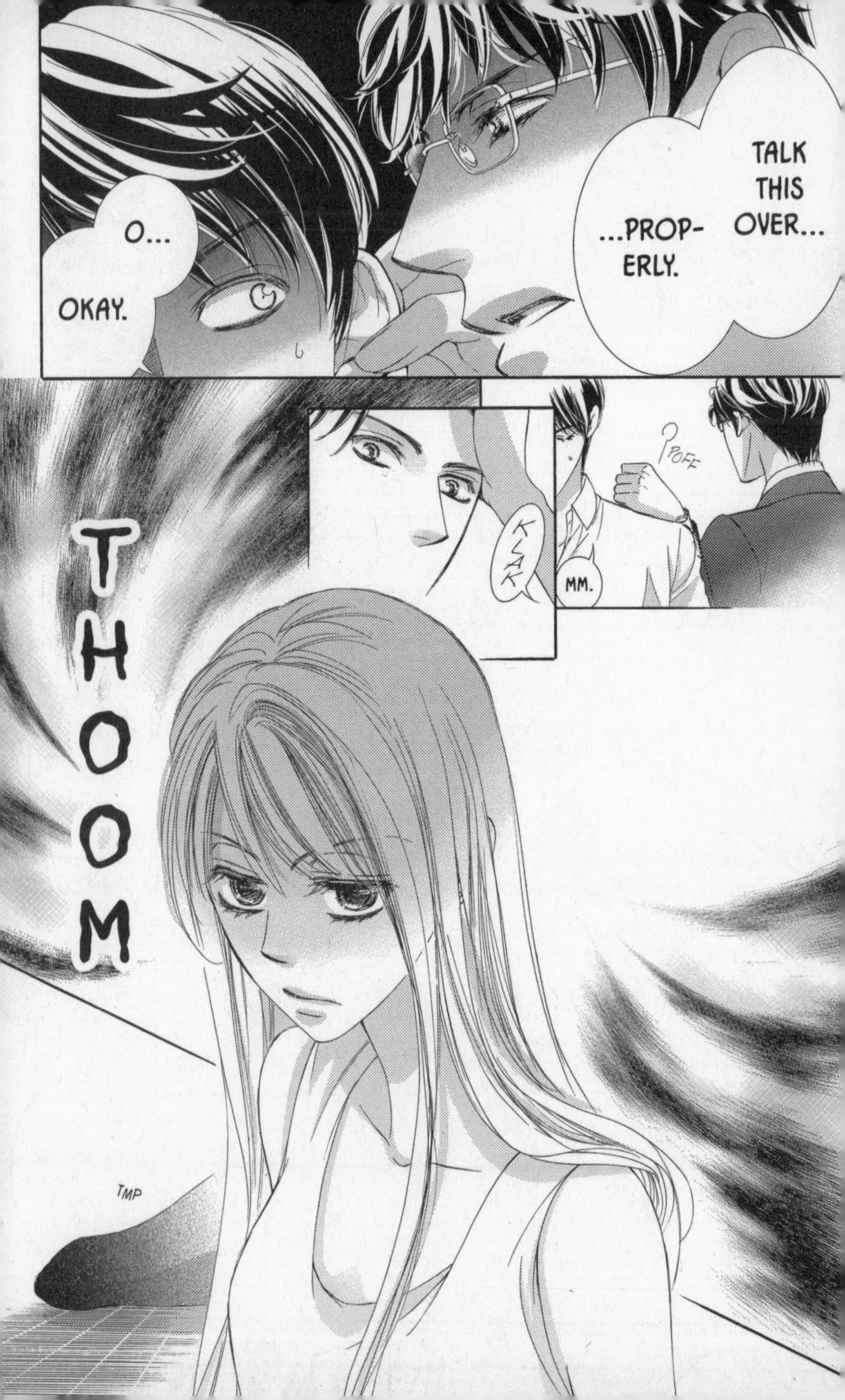
TALK THIS OVER... ...PROPERLY.
O... OKAY.
POFF
MM.
KLAK
THOOM
TMP

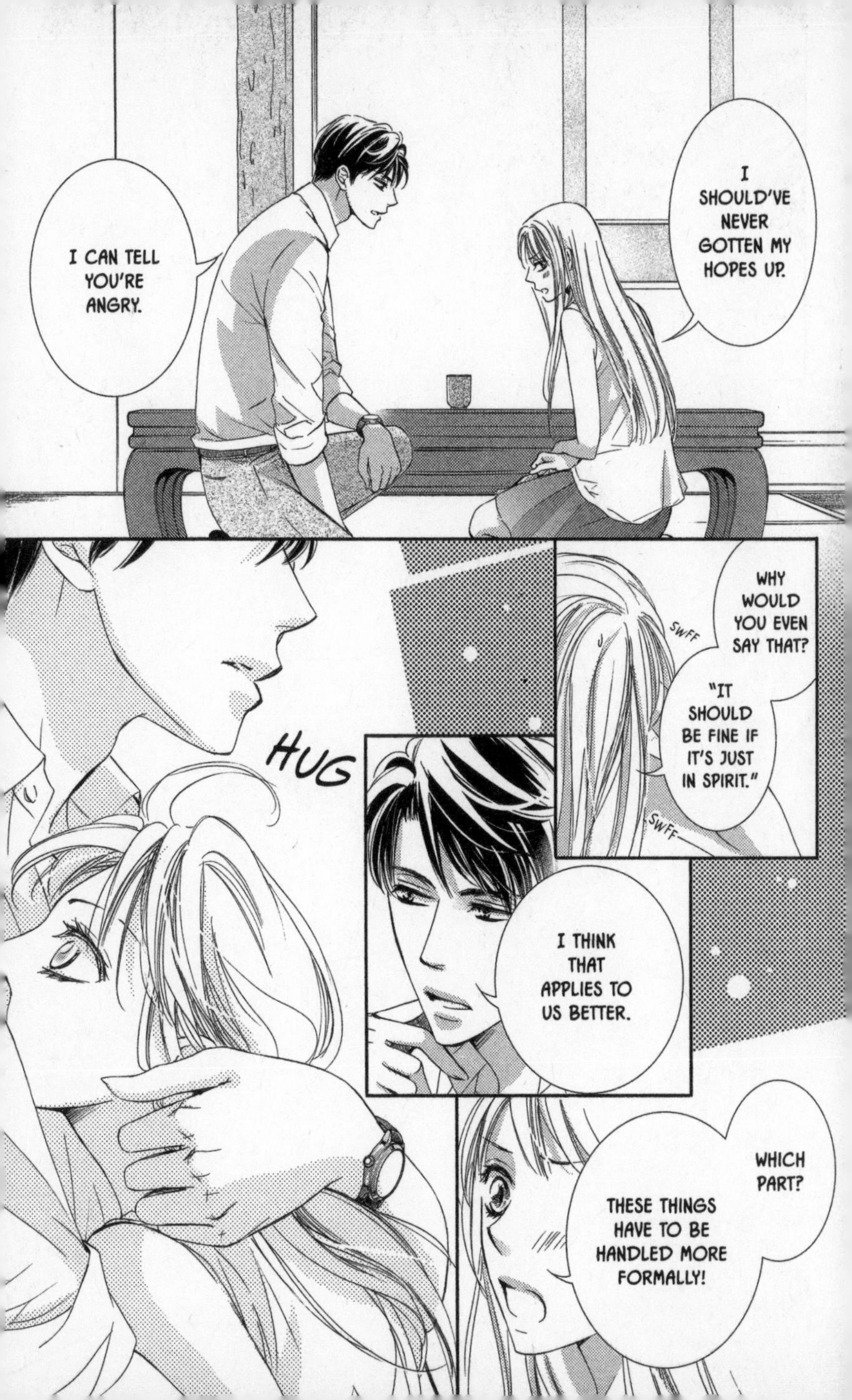
I SHOULD'VE NEVER GOTTEN MY HOPES UP.
I CAN TELL YOU'RE ANGRY.
SWFF
WHY WOULD YOU EVEN SAY THAT?
"IT SHOULD BE FINE IF IT'S JUST IN SPIRIT."
SWFF
I THINK THAT APPLIES TO US BETTER.
WHICH PART?
THESE THINGS HAVE TO BE HANDLED MORE FORMALLY!
HUG

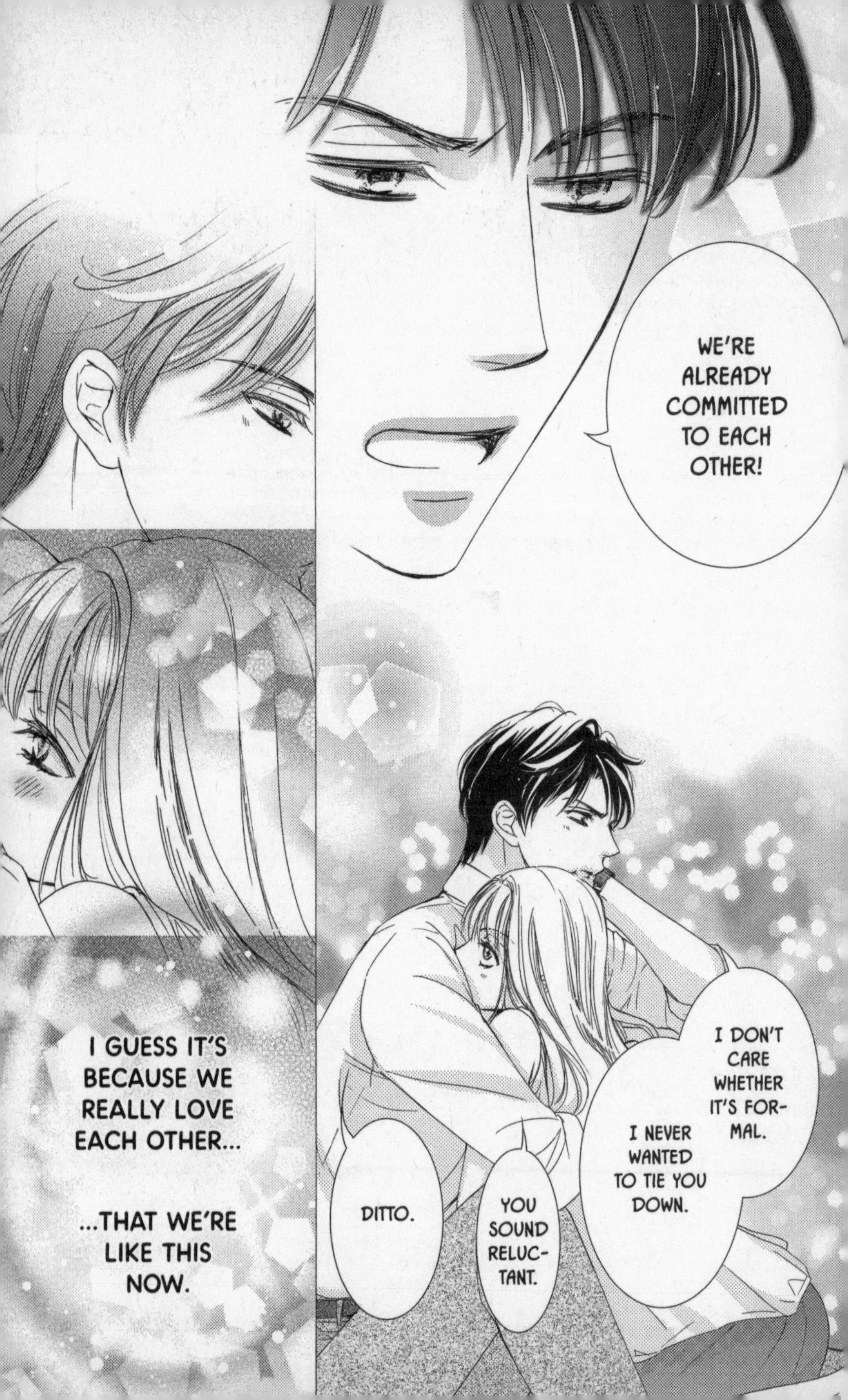
WE'RE ALREADY COMMITTED TO EACH OTHER!
I DON'T CARE WHETHER IT'S FOR-MAL.
I NEVER WANTED TO TIE YOU DOWN.
YOU SOUND RELUC-TANT.
DITTO.
I GUESS IT'S BECAUSE WE REALLY LOVE EACH OTHER...
...THAT WE'RE LIKE THIS NOW.

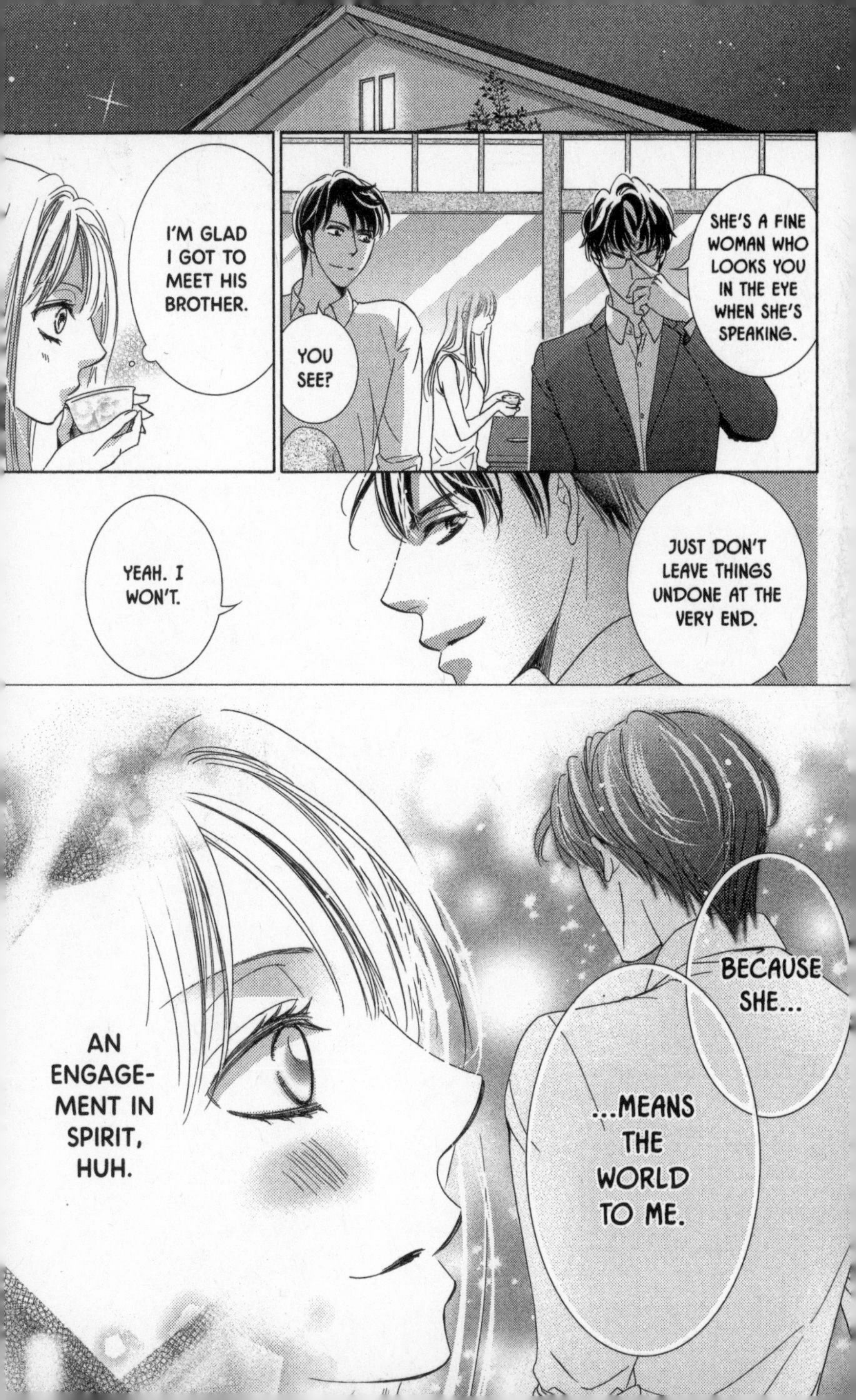

SHE'S A FINE WOMAN WHO LOOKS YOU IN THE EYE WHEN SHE'S SPEAKING.
YOU SEE?
I'M GLAD I GOT TO MEET HIS BROTHER.
JUST DON'T LEAVE THINGS UNDONE AT THE VERY END.
YEAH. I WON'T.
BECAUSE SHE...
...MEANS THE WORLD TO ME.
AN ENGAGE-MENT IN SPIRIT, HUH.

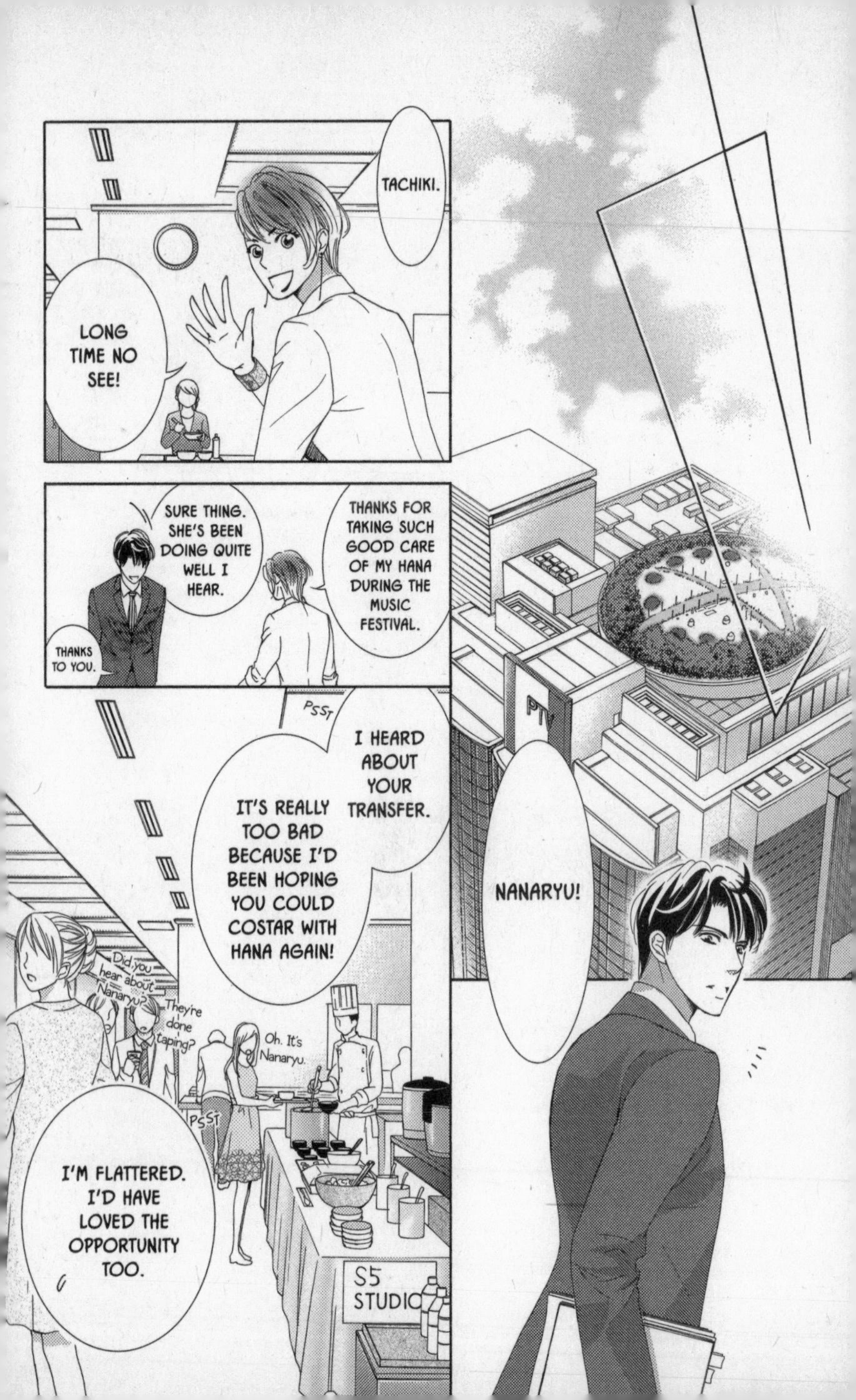
PTV
NANARYU!
TACHIKI.
LONG TIME NO SEE!
THANKS FOR TAKING SUCH GOOD CARE OF MY HANA DURING THE MUSIC FESTIVAL.
SURE THING. SHE'S BEEN DOING QUITE WELL I HEAR.
THANKS TO YOU.
PSST
I HEARD ABOUT YOUR TRANSFER.
IT'S REALLY TOO BAD BECAUSE I'D BEEN HOPING YOU COULD COSTAR WITH HANA AGAIN!
Oh. It's Nanaryu.
They're done taping?
Did you hear about Nanaryu?
PSST
S5 STUDIO
I'M FLATTERED. I'D HAVE LOVED THE OPPORTUNITY TOO.

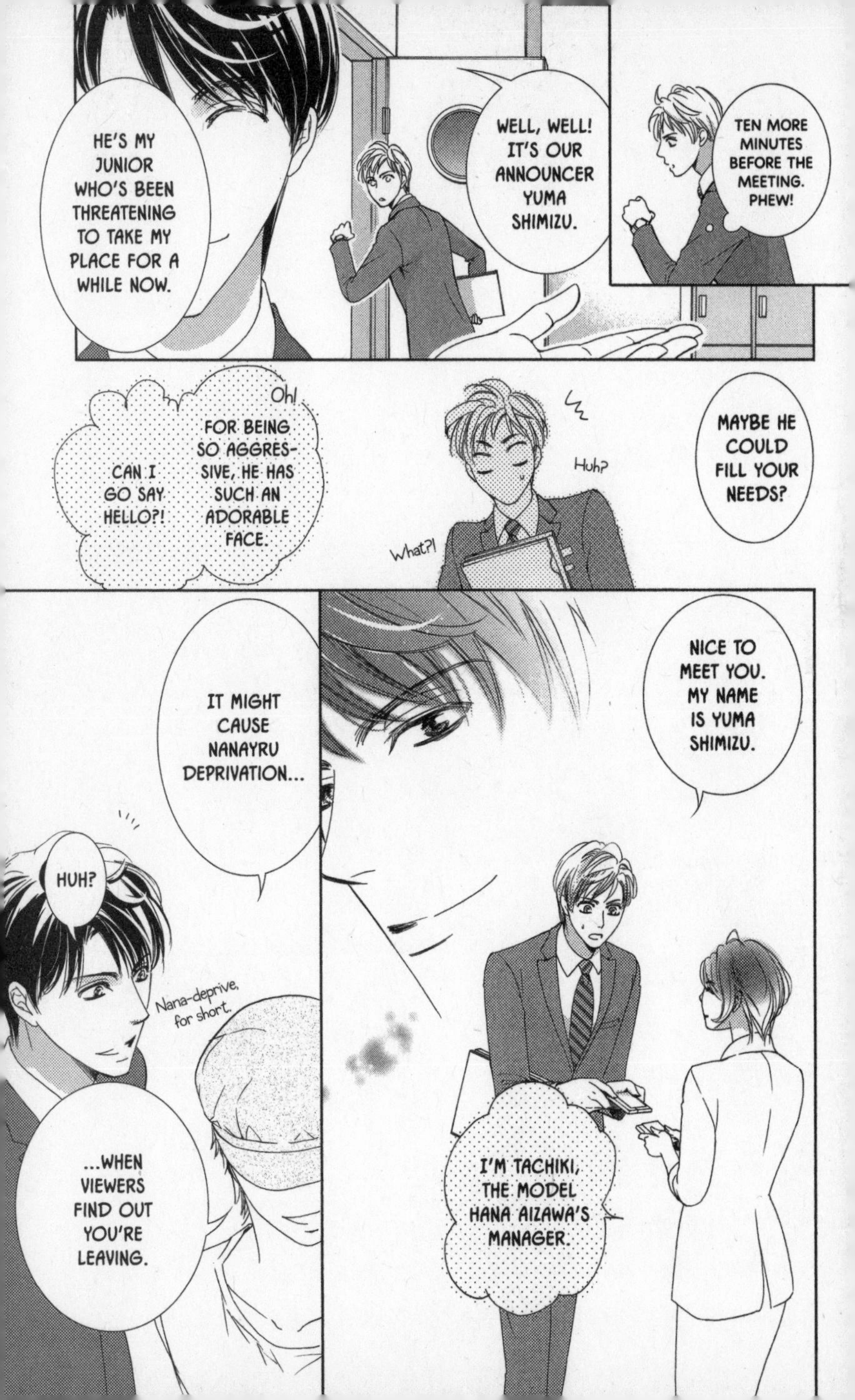
TEN MORE MINUTES BEFORE THE MEETING. PHEW!
WELL, WELL! IT'S OUR ANNOUNCER YUMA SHIMIZU.
HE'S MY JUNIOR WHO'S BEEN THREATENING TO TAKE MY PLACE FOR A WHILE NOW.
MAYBE HE COULD FILL YOUR NEEDS?
Huh?
What?!
Oh!
FOR BEING SO AGGRES-SIVE, HE HAS SUCH AN ADORABLE FACE.
CAN I GO SAY HELLO?!
NICE TO MEET YOU. MY NAME IS YUMA SHIMIZU.
I'M TACHIKI, THE MODEL HANA AIZAWA'S MANAGER.
IT MIGHT CAUSE NANAYRU DEPRIVATION...
HUH?
Nana-deprive, for short.
...WHEN VIEWERS FIND OUT YOU'RE LEAVING.

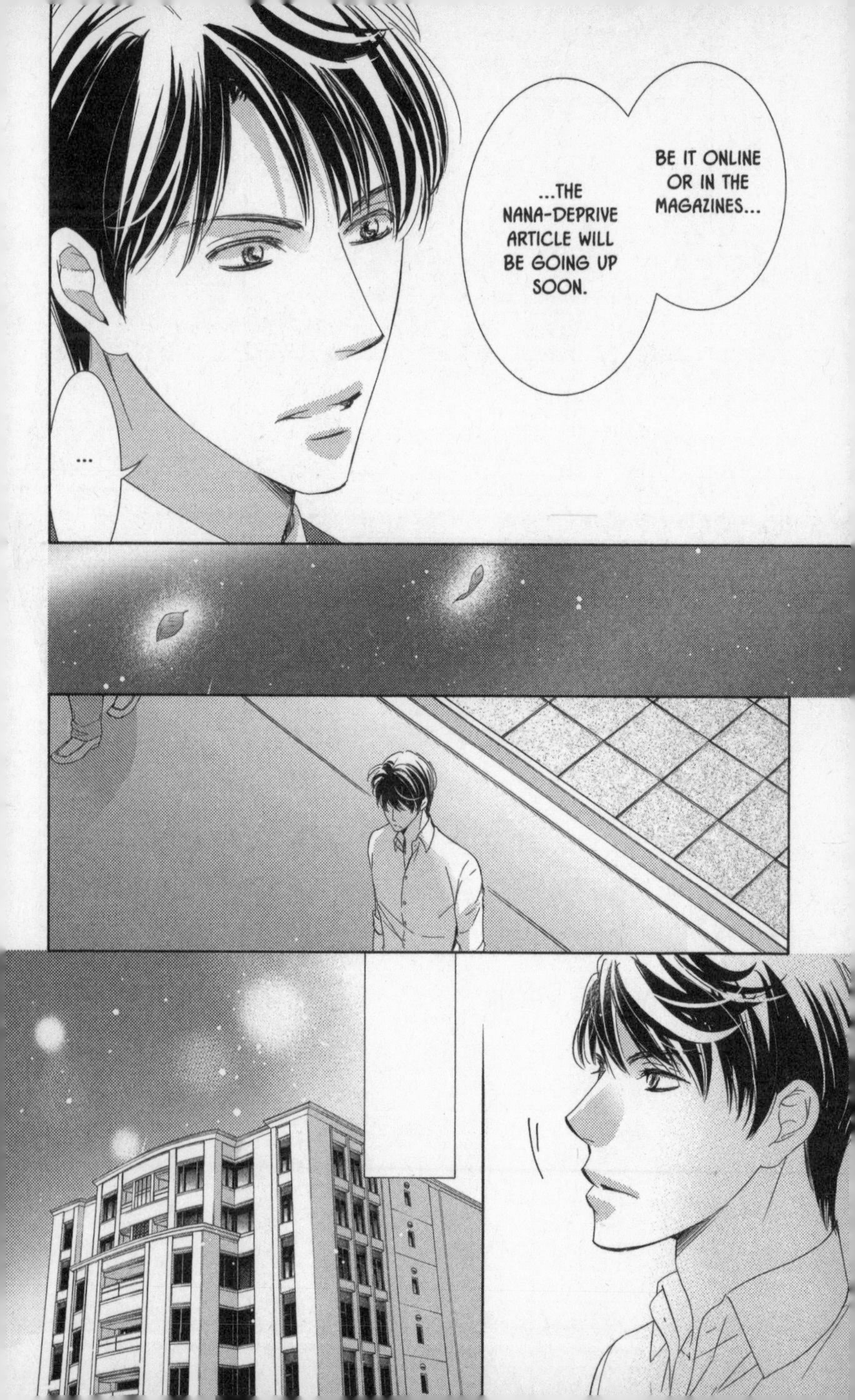
BE IT ONLINE OR IN THE MAGAZINES...
...THE NANA-DEPRIVE ARTICLE WILL BE GOING UP SOON.
...

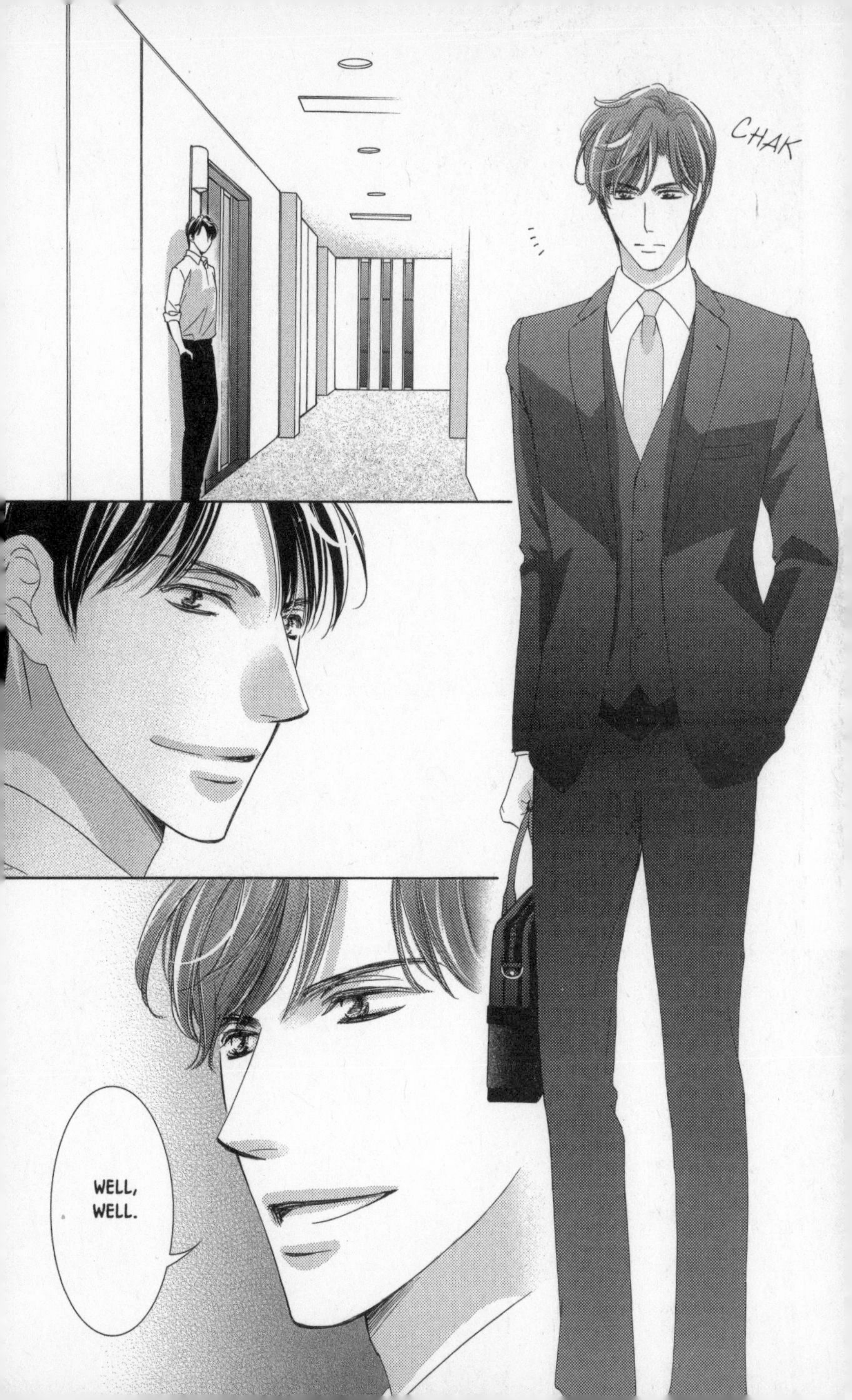
CHAK
WELL, WELL.

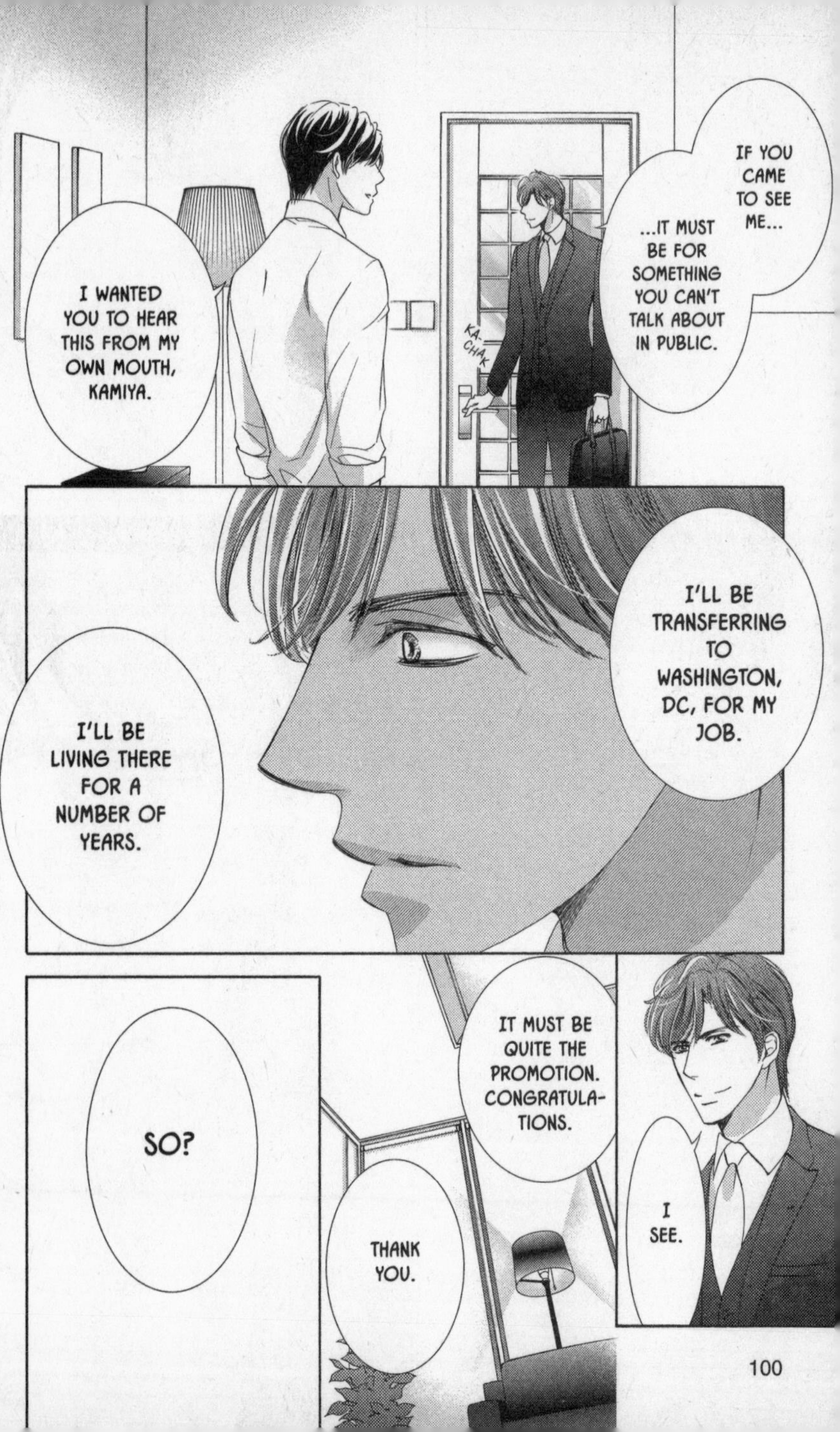
IF YOU CAME TO SEE ME...
...IT MUST BE FOR SOMETHING YOU CAN'T TALK ABOUT IN PUBLIC.
KA-CHAK
I WANTED YOU TO HEAR THIS FROM MY OWN MOUTH, KAMIYA.
I'LL BE TRANSFERRING TO WASHINGTON, DC, FOR MY JOB.
I'LL BE LIVING THERE FOR A NUMBER OF YEARS.
I SEE.
IT MUST BE QUITE THE PROMOTION. CONGRATULA-TIONS.
THANK YOU.
SO?

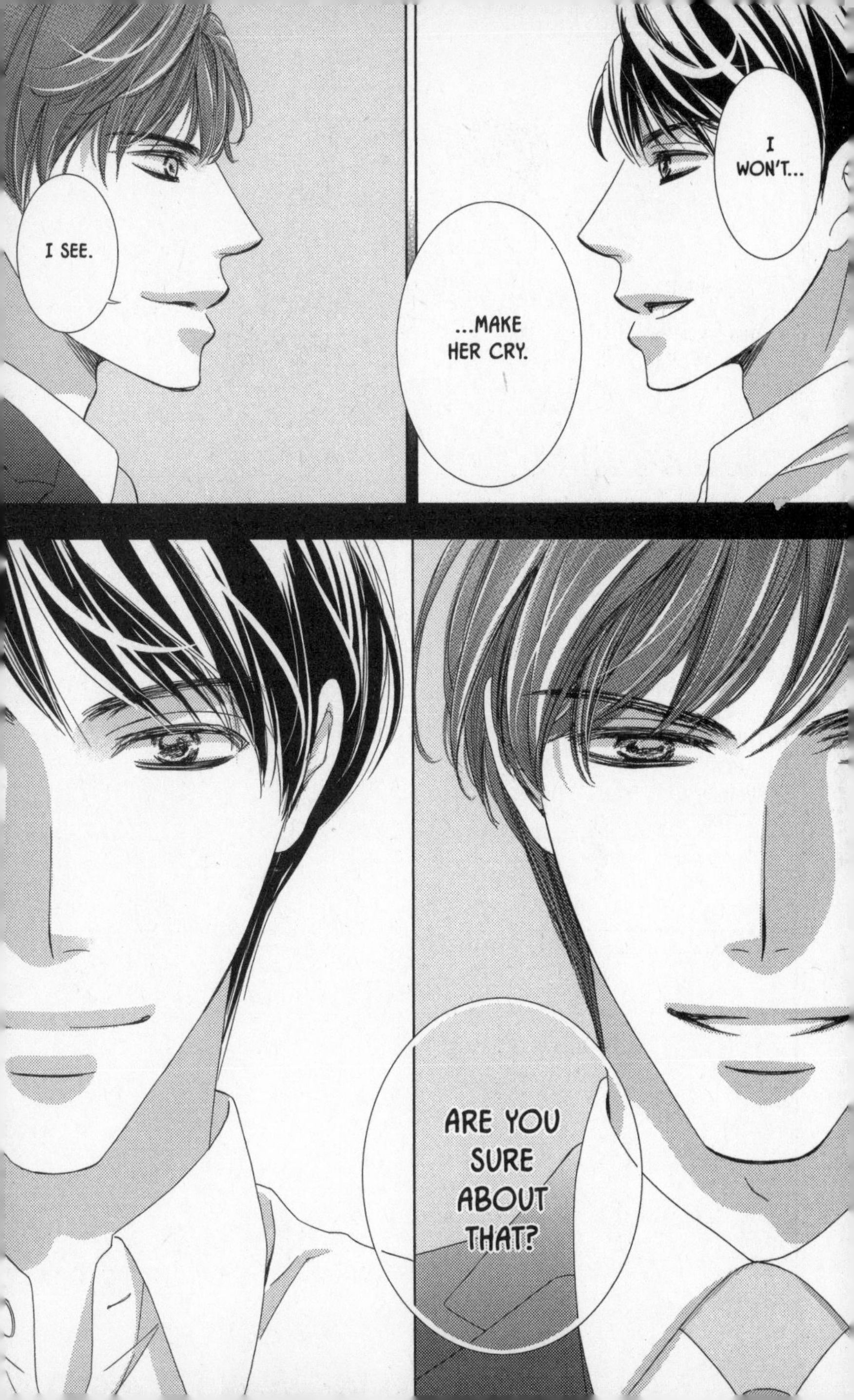
I WON'T...
...MAKE HER CRY.
I SEE.
ARE YOU SURE ABOUT THAT?

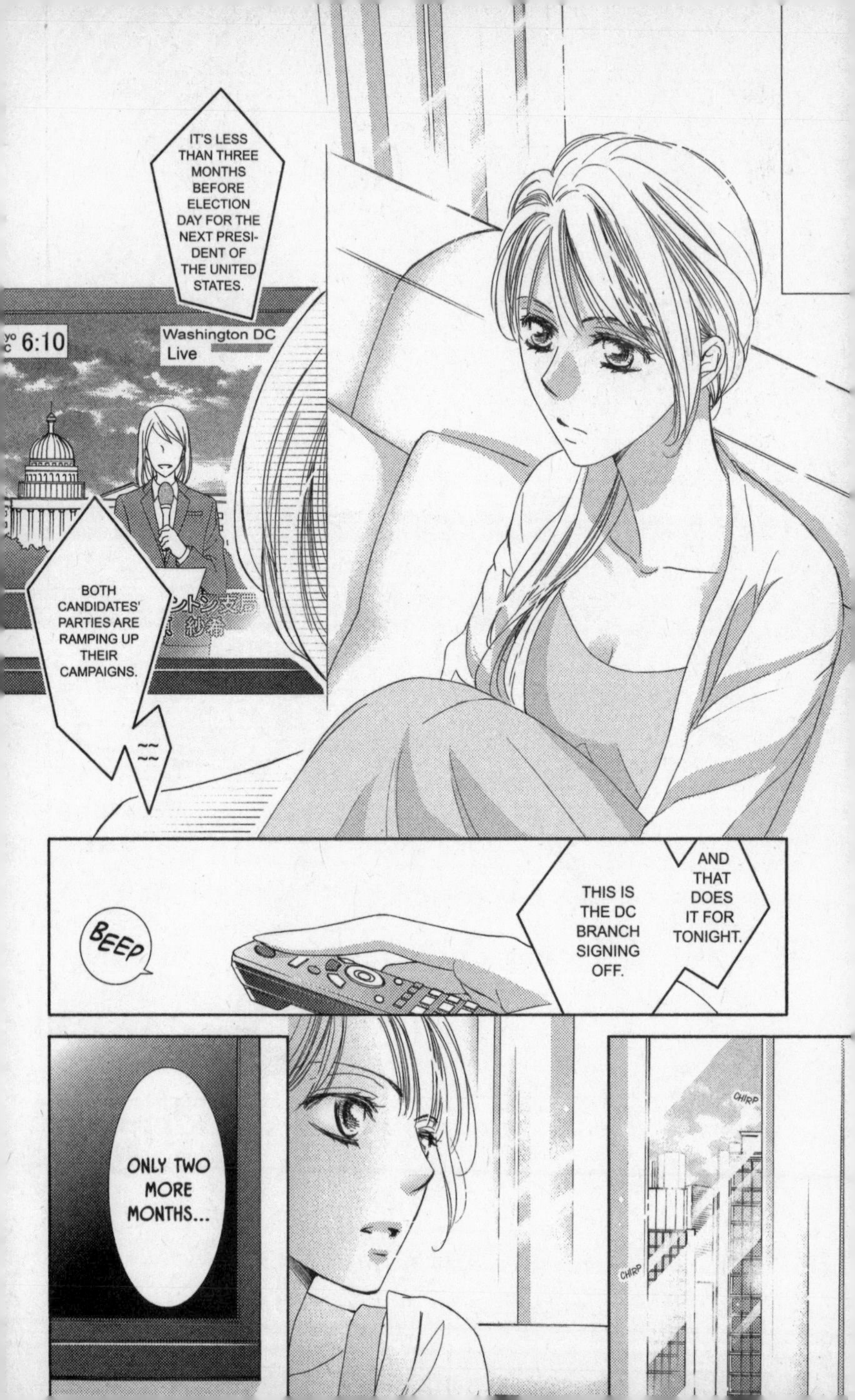

IT'S LESS THAN THREE MONTHS BEFORE ELECTION DAY FOR THE NEXT PRESI-DENT OF THE UNITED STATES.
Washington DC Live
6:10
BOTH CANDIDATES' PARTIES ARE RAMPING UP THEIR CAMPAIGNS.
AND THAT DOES IT FOR TONIGHT.
THIS IS THE DC BRANCH SIGNING OFF.
BEEP
CHIRP
CHIRP
ONLY TWO MORE MONTHS...

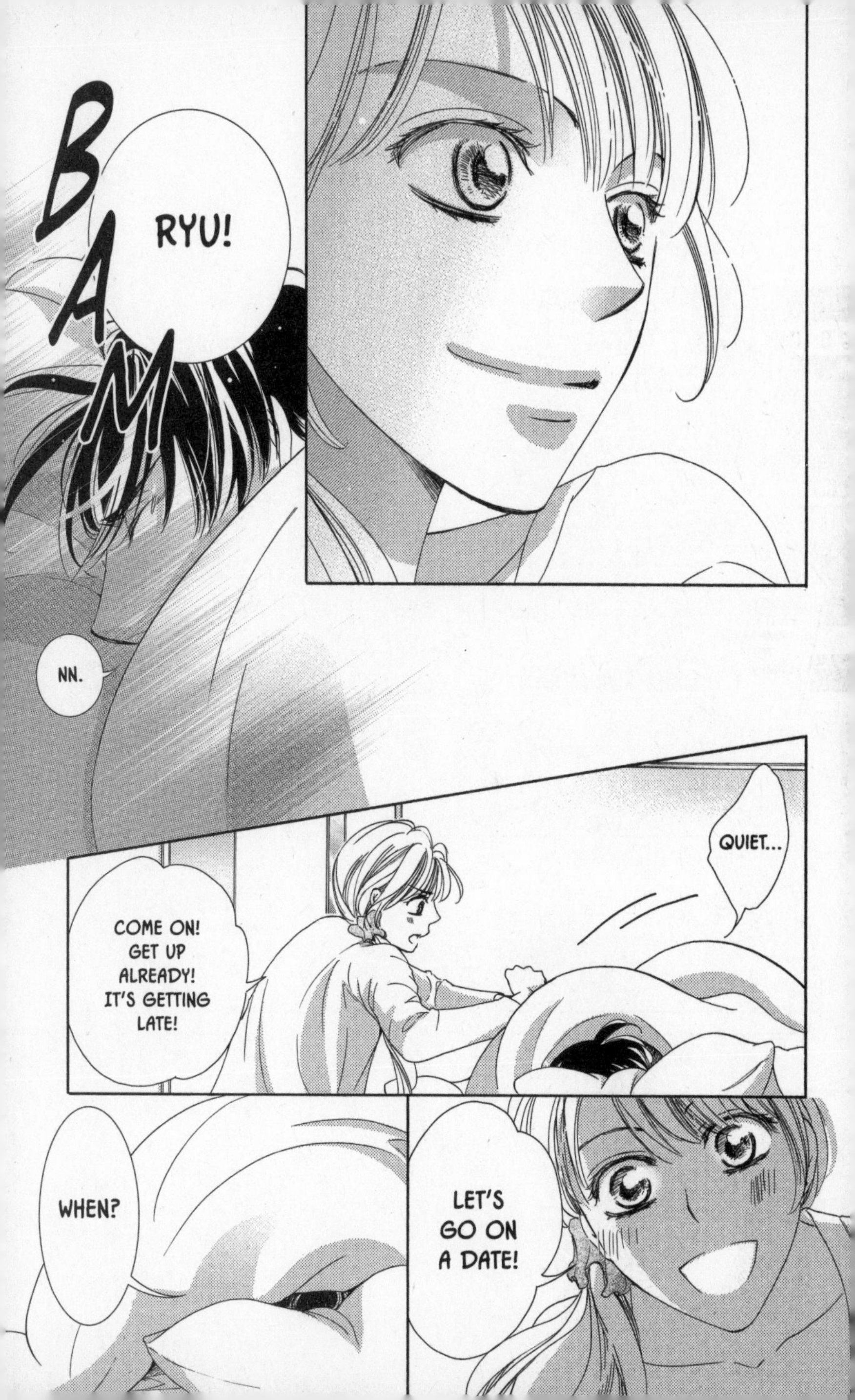
BAM
RYU!
NN.
QUIET...
COME ON! GET UP ALREADY! IT'S GETTING LATE!
LET'S GO ON A DATE!
WHEN?

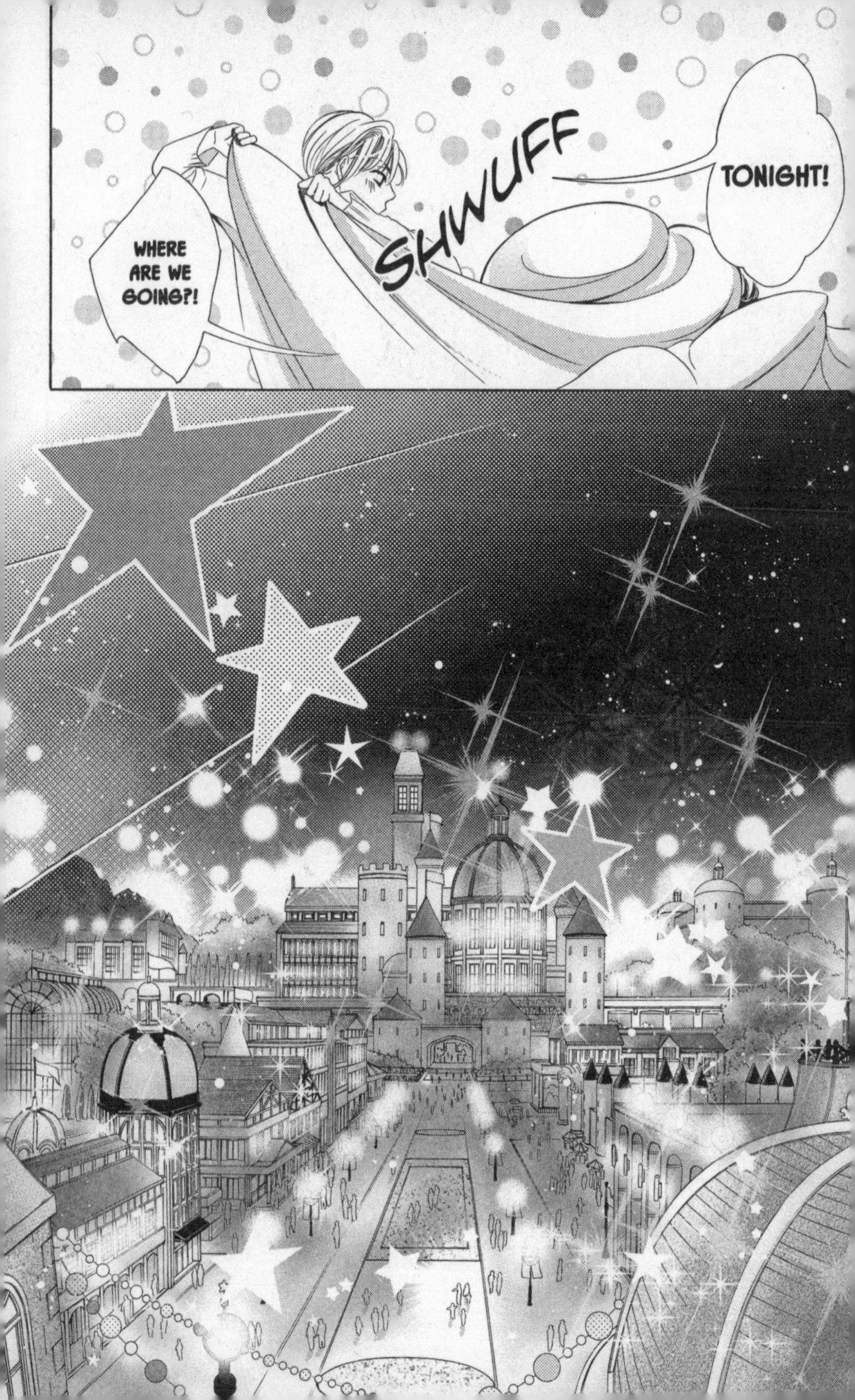
TONIGHT!
SHWUFF
WHERE ARE WE GOING?!

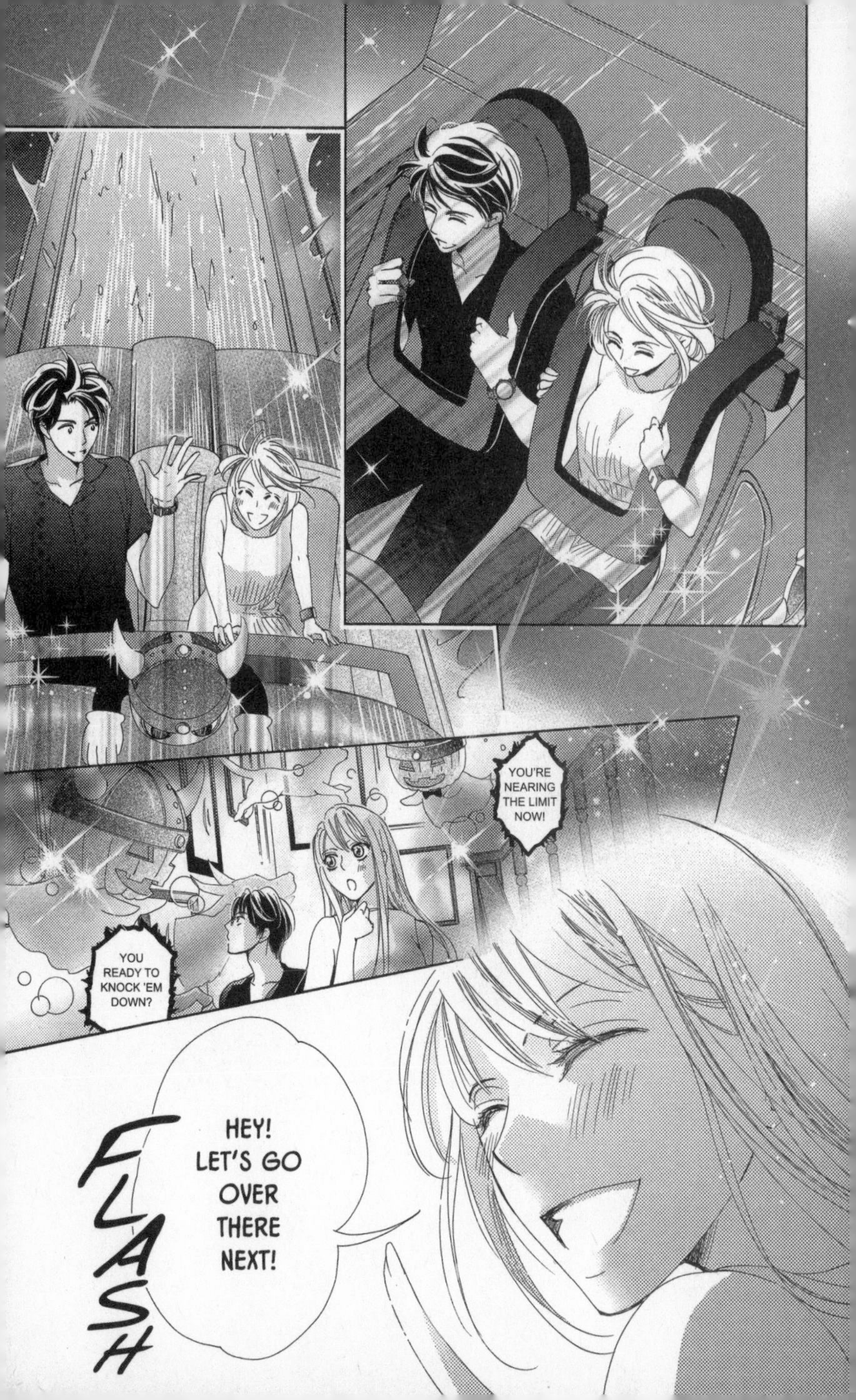
YOU'RE NEARING THE LIMIT NOW!
YOU READY TO KNOCK 'EM DOWN?
HEY! LET'S GO OVER THERE NEXT!
FLASH

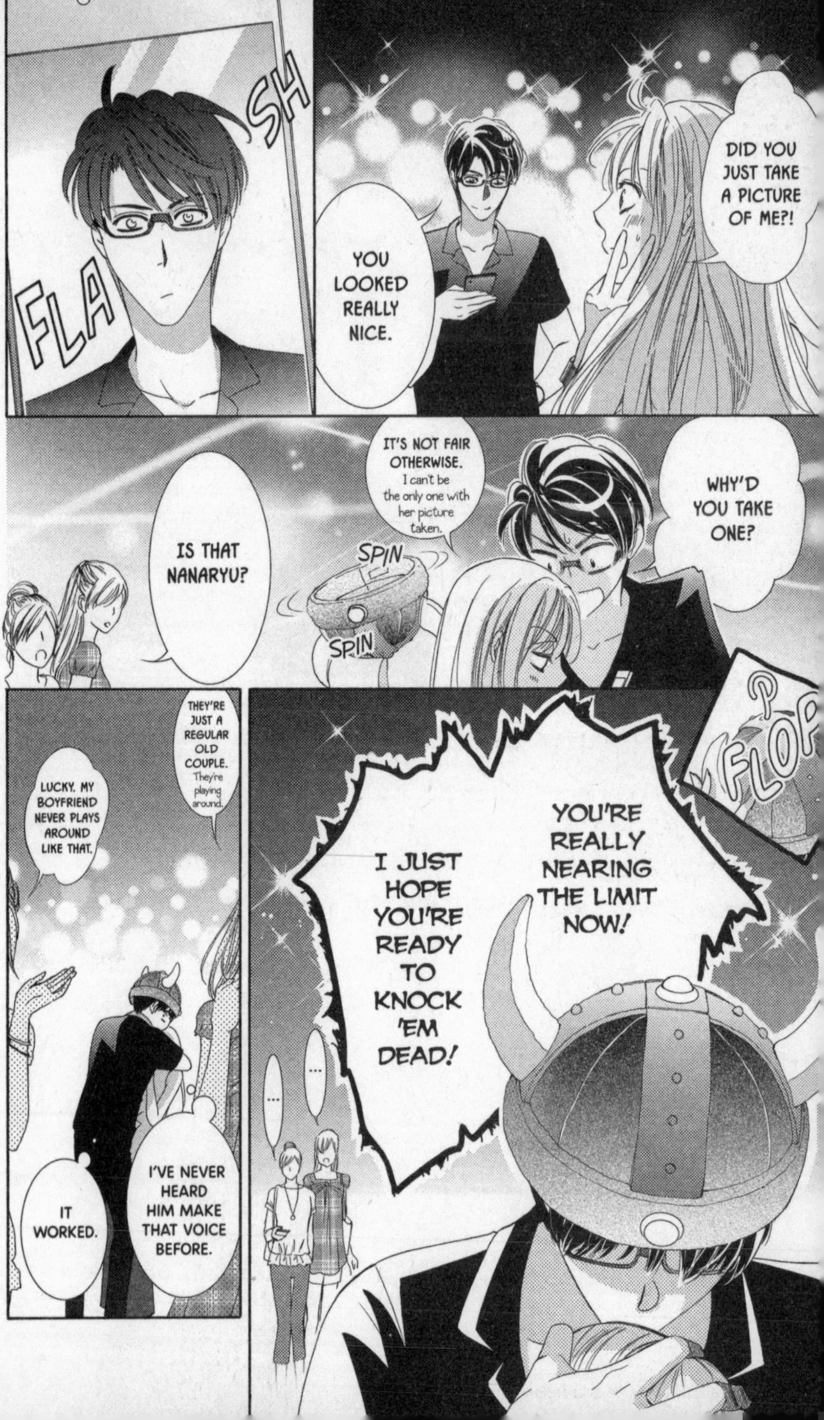
DID YOU JUST TAKE A PICTURE OF ME?!
YOU LOOKED REALLY NICE.
FLA
SH
WHY'D YOU TAKE ONE?
IT'S NOT FAIR OTHERWISE. I can't be the only one with her picture taken.
SPIN
SPIN
IS THAT NANARYU?
P
FLOP
YOU'RE REALLY NEARING THE LIMIT NOW!
I JUST HOPE YOU'RE READY TO KNOCK 'EM DEAD!
...
...
THEY'RE JUST A REGULAR OLD COUPLE. They're playing around.
LUCKY. MY BOYFRIEND NEVER PLAYS AROUND LIKE THAT.
I'VE NEVER HEARD HIM MAKE THAT VOICE BEFORE.
IT WORKED.

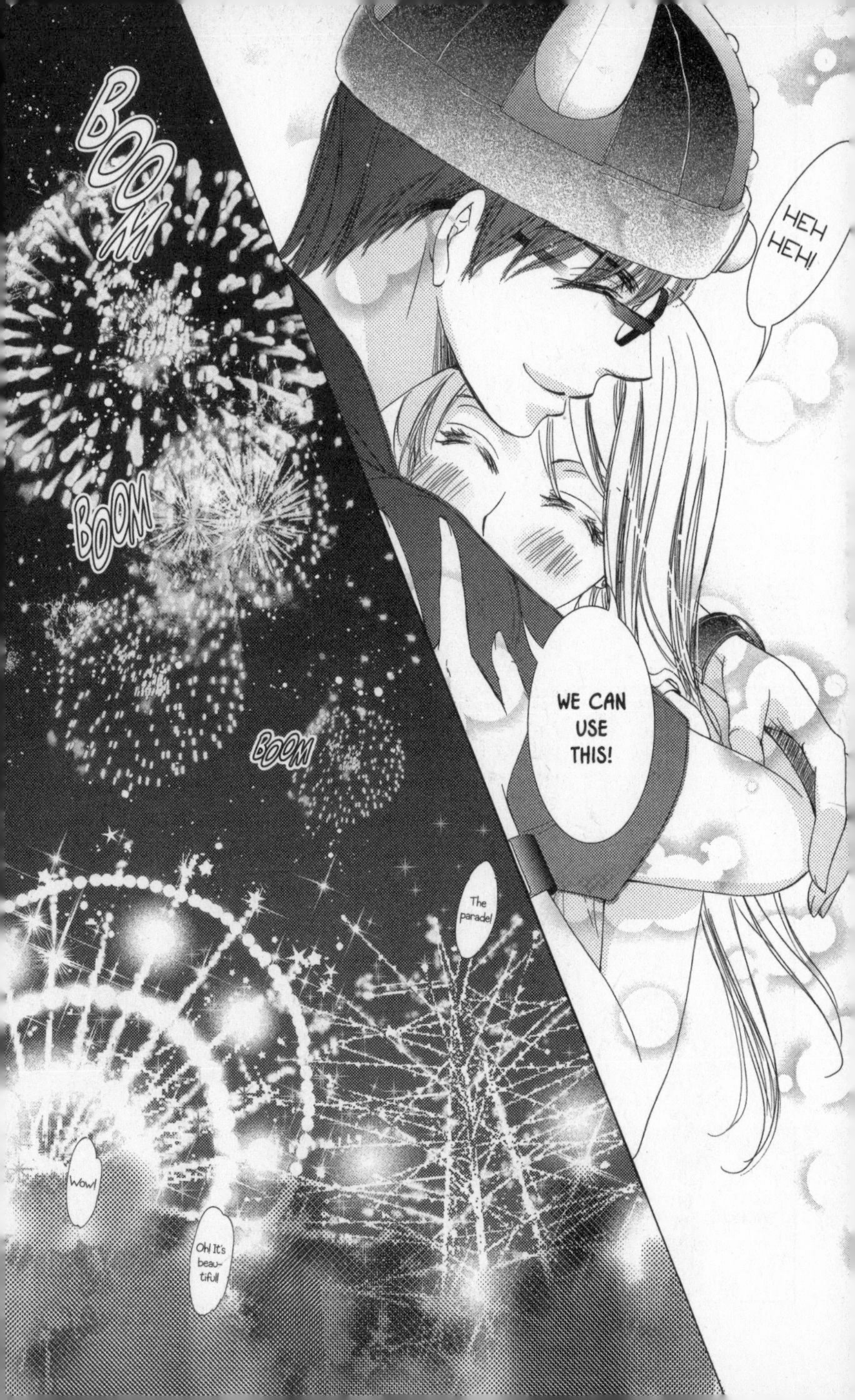
HEH HEH!
WE CAN USE THIS!
BOOM
BOOM
BOOM
The parade!
Wow!
Oh! It's beau-tiful!

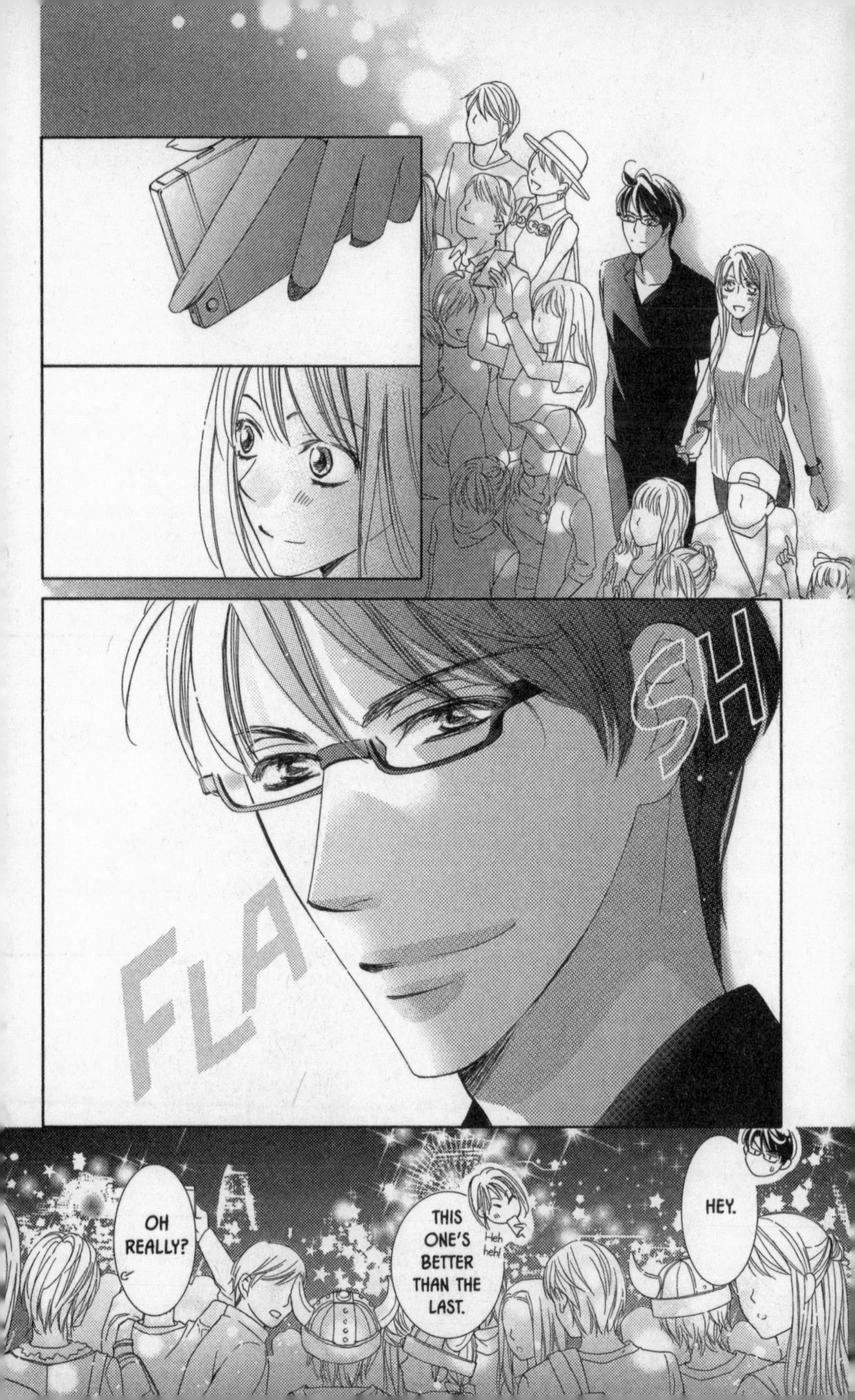
FLA
SH
HEY.
THIS ONE'S BETTER THAN THE LAST.
Heh heh!
OH REALLY?

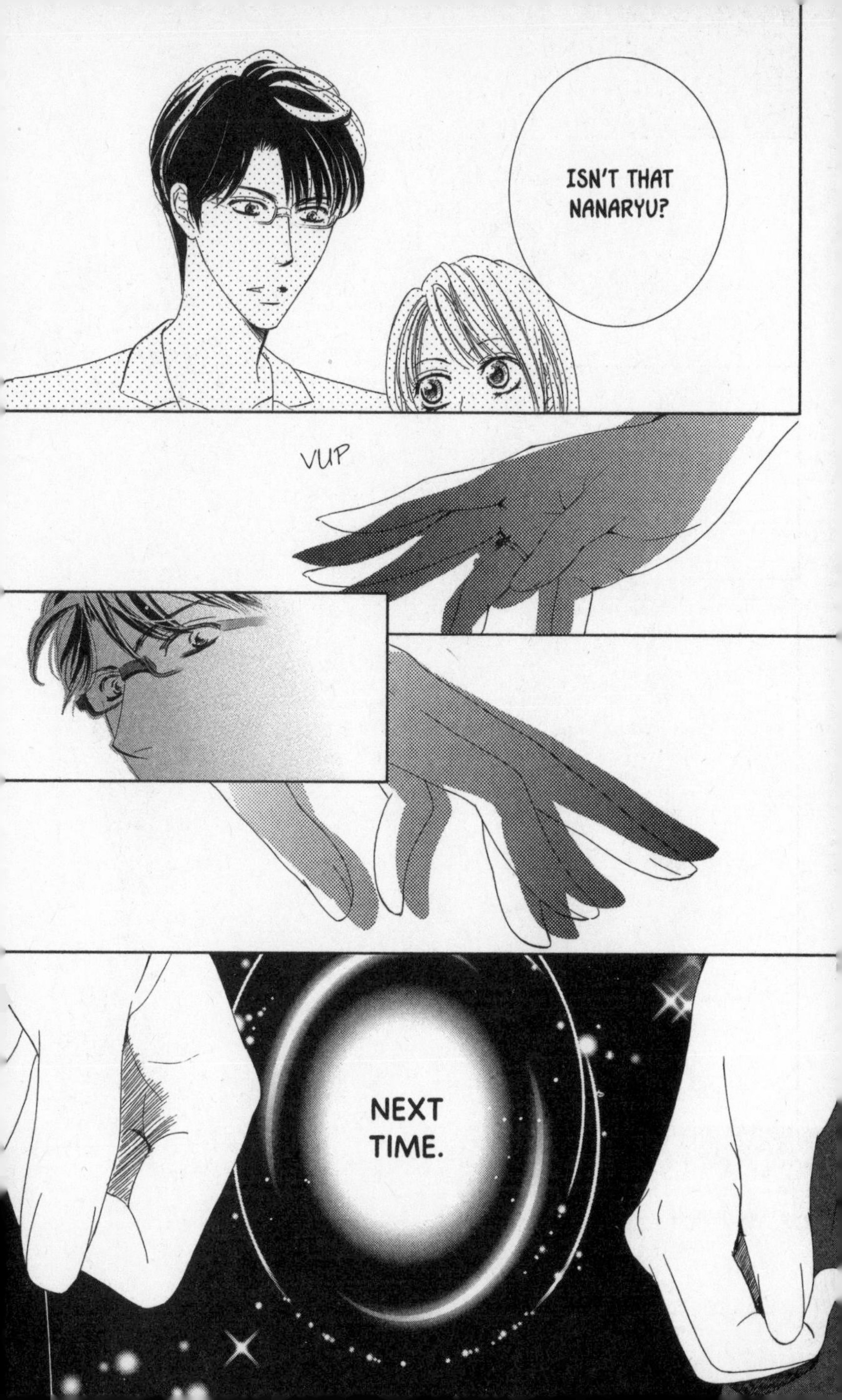
ISN'T THAT NANARYU?
VUP
NEXT TIME.

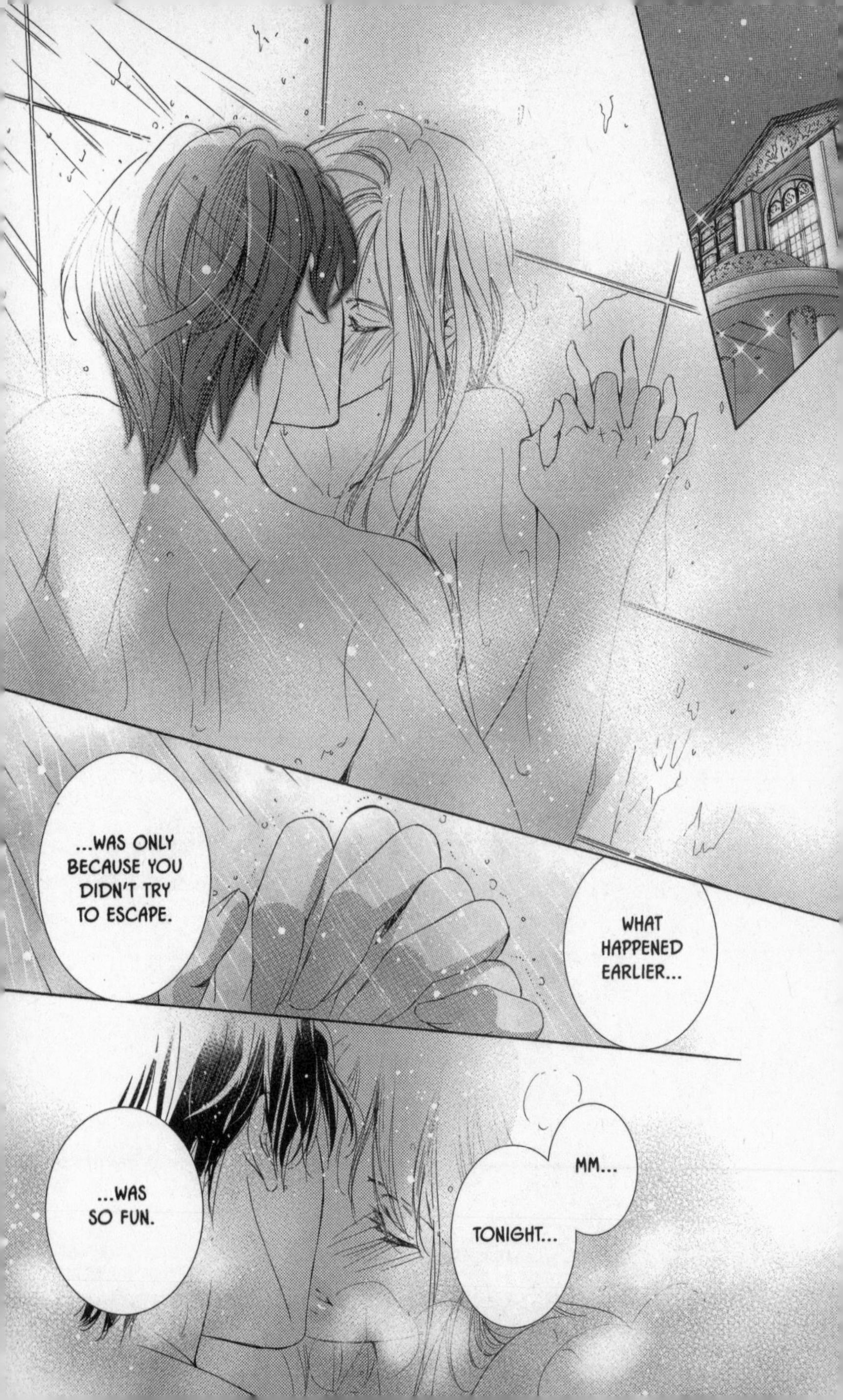
WHAT HAPPENED EARLIER...
...WAS ONLY BECAUSE YOU DIDN'T TRY TO ESCAPE.
MM...
TONIGHT...
...WAS SO FUN.

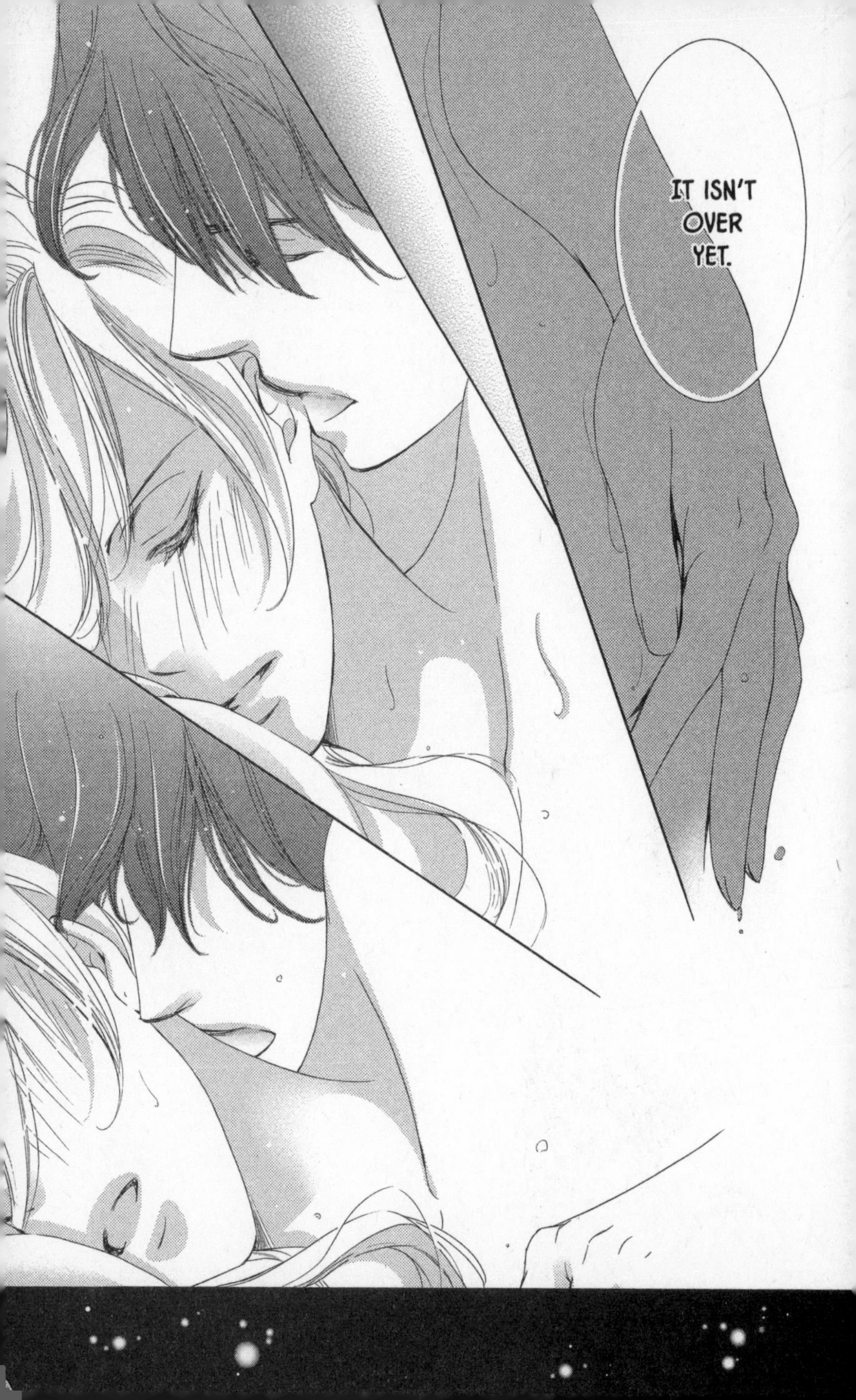
IT ISN'T OVER YET.

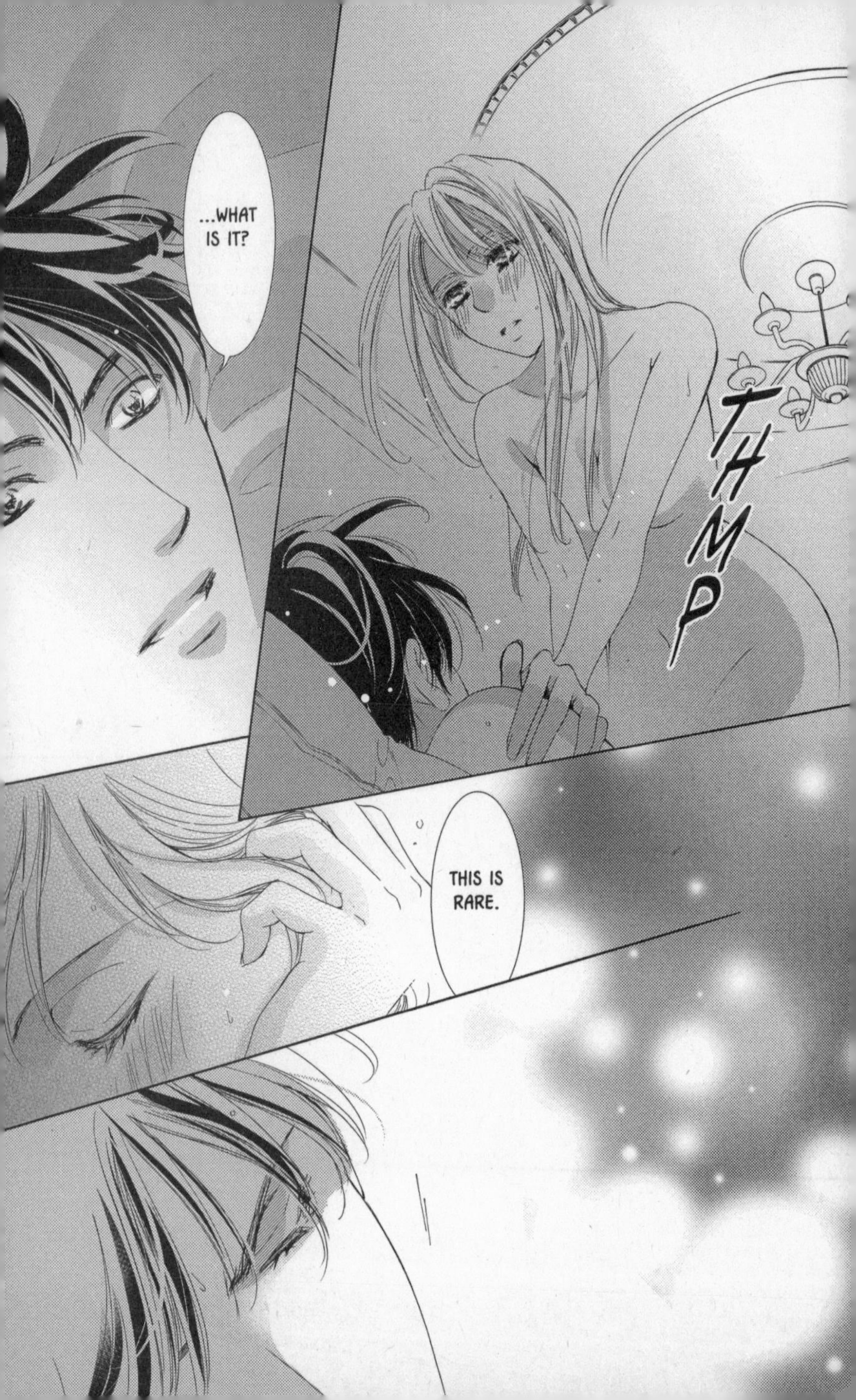
THMP
...WHAT IS IT?
THIS IS RARE.

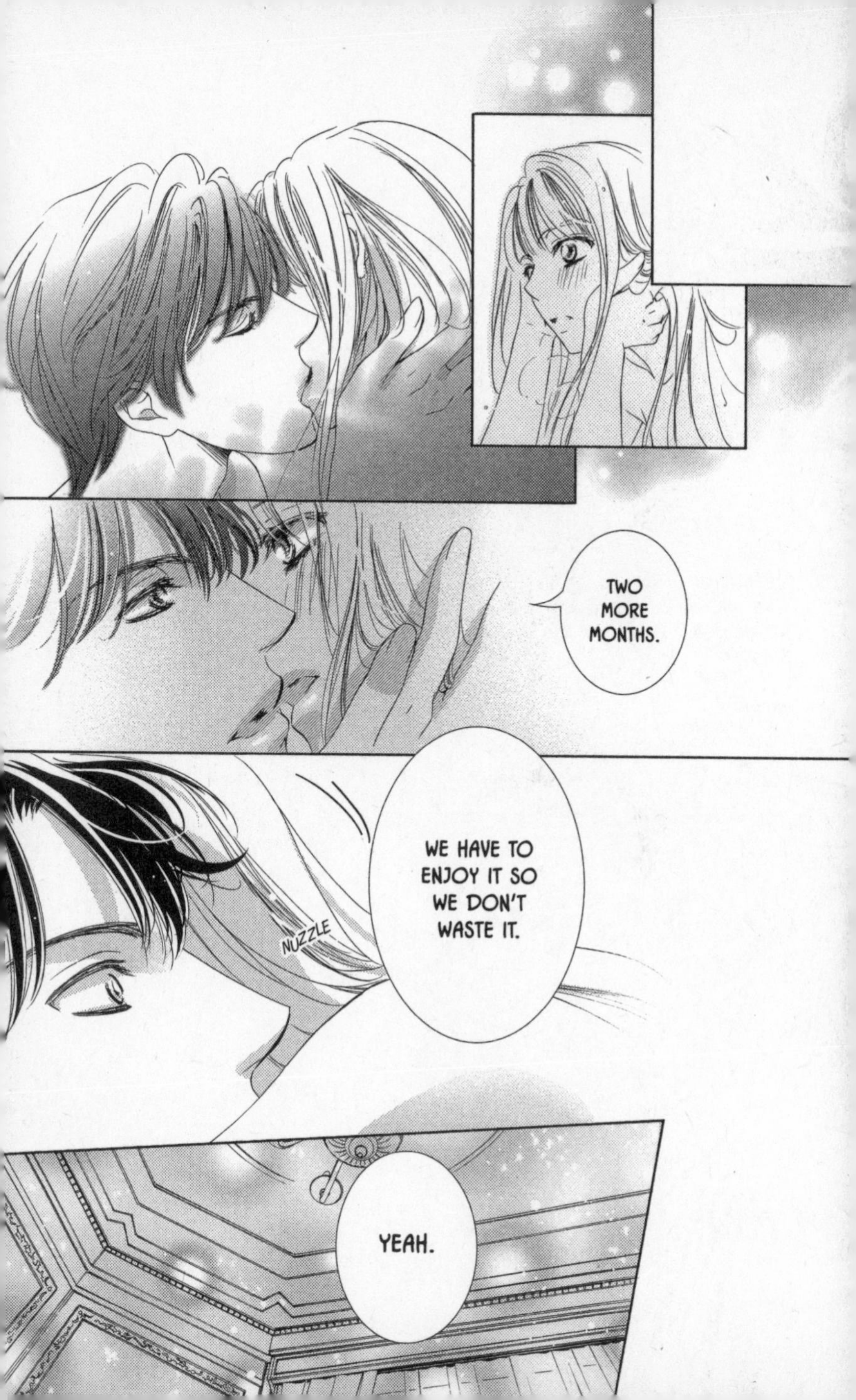
TWO MORE MONTHS.
WE HAVE TO ENJOY IT SO WE DON'T WASTE IT.
NUZZLE
YEAH.

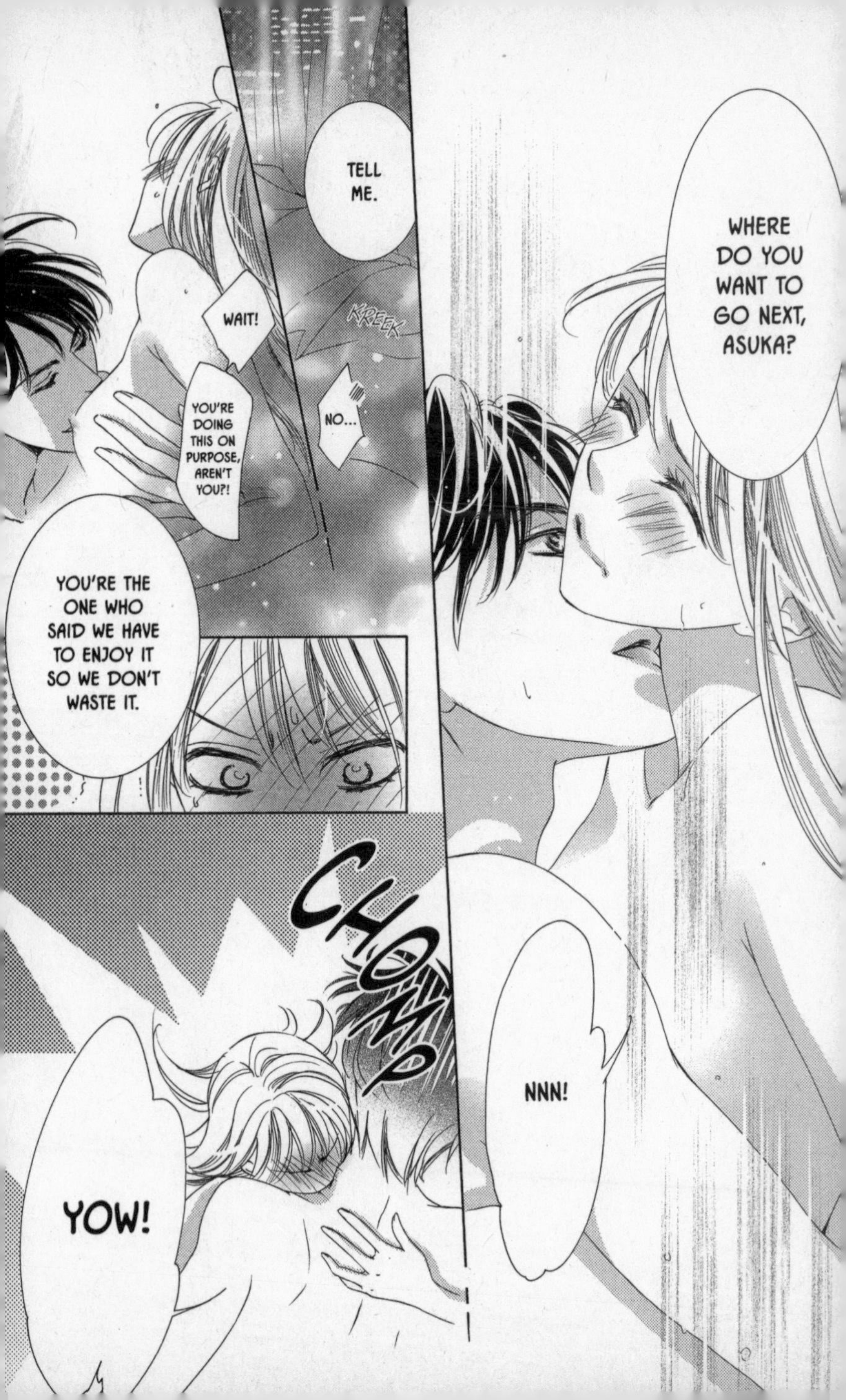
WHERE DO YOU WANT TO GO NEXT, ASUKA?
NNN!
TELL ME.
KREEK
NO...
WAIT!
YOU'RE DOING THIS ON PURPOSE, AREN'T YOU?!
YOU'RE THE ONE WHO SAID WE HAVE TO ENJOY IT SO WE DON'T WASTE IT.
CHOMP
YOW!

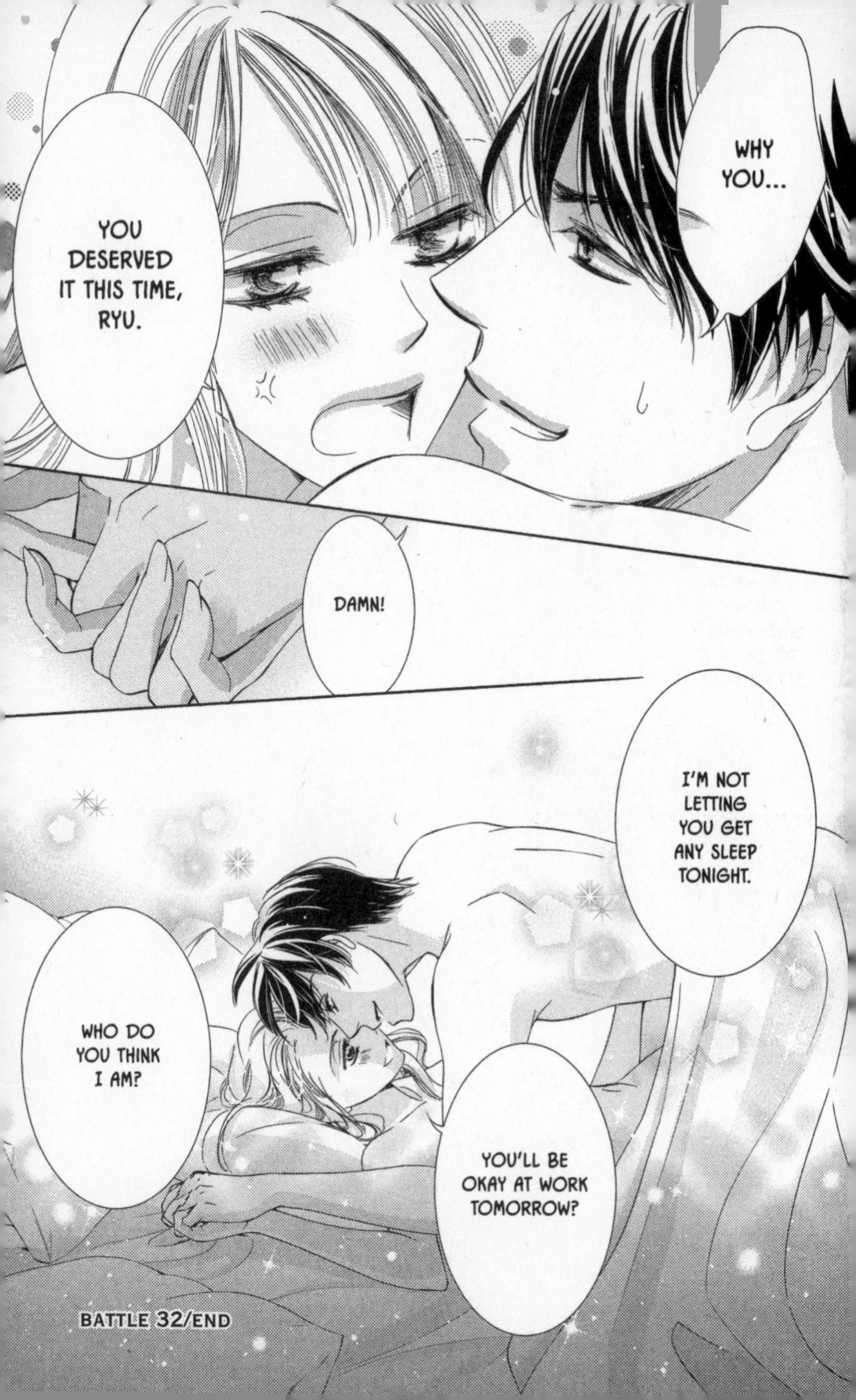
WHY YOU...
YOU DESERVED IT THIS TIME, RYU.
DAMN!
I'M NOT LETTING YOU GET ANY SLEEP TONIGHT.
YOU'LL BE OKAY AT WORK TOMORROW?
WHO DO YOU THINK I AM?
BATTLE 32/END

This is

our precious time.

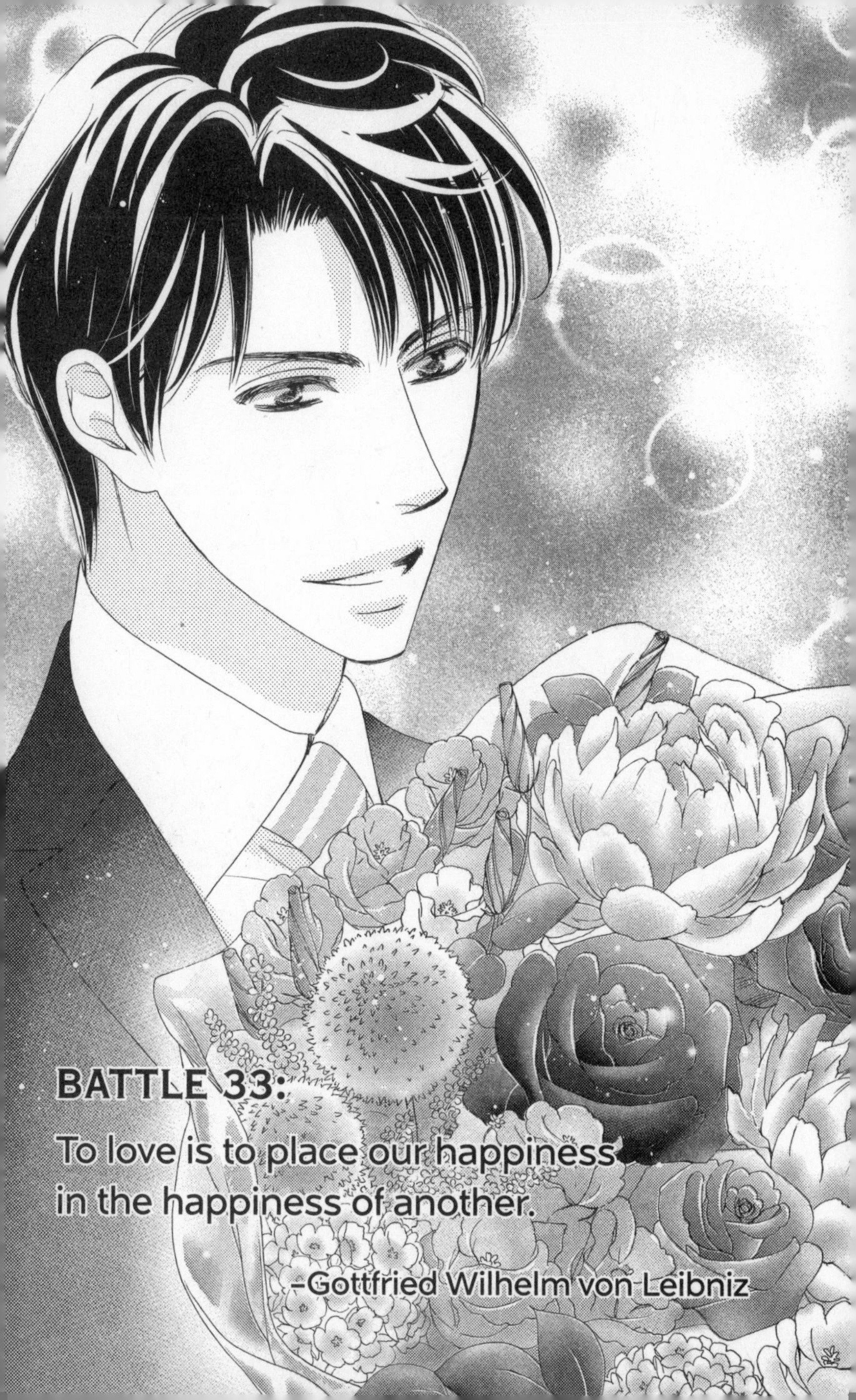
BATTLE 33:
To love is to place our happiness in the happiness of another.
–Gottfried Wilhelm von Leibniz

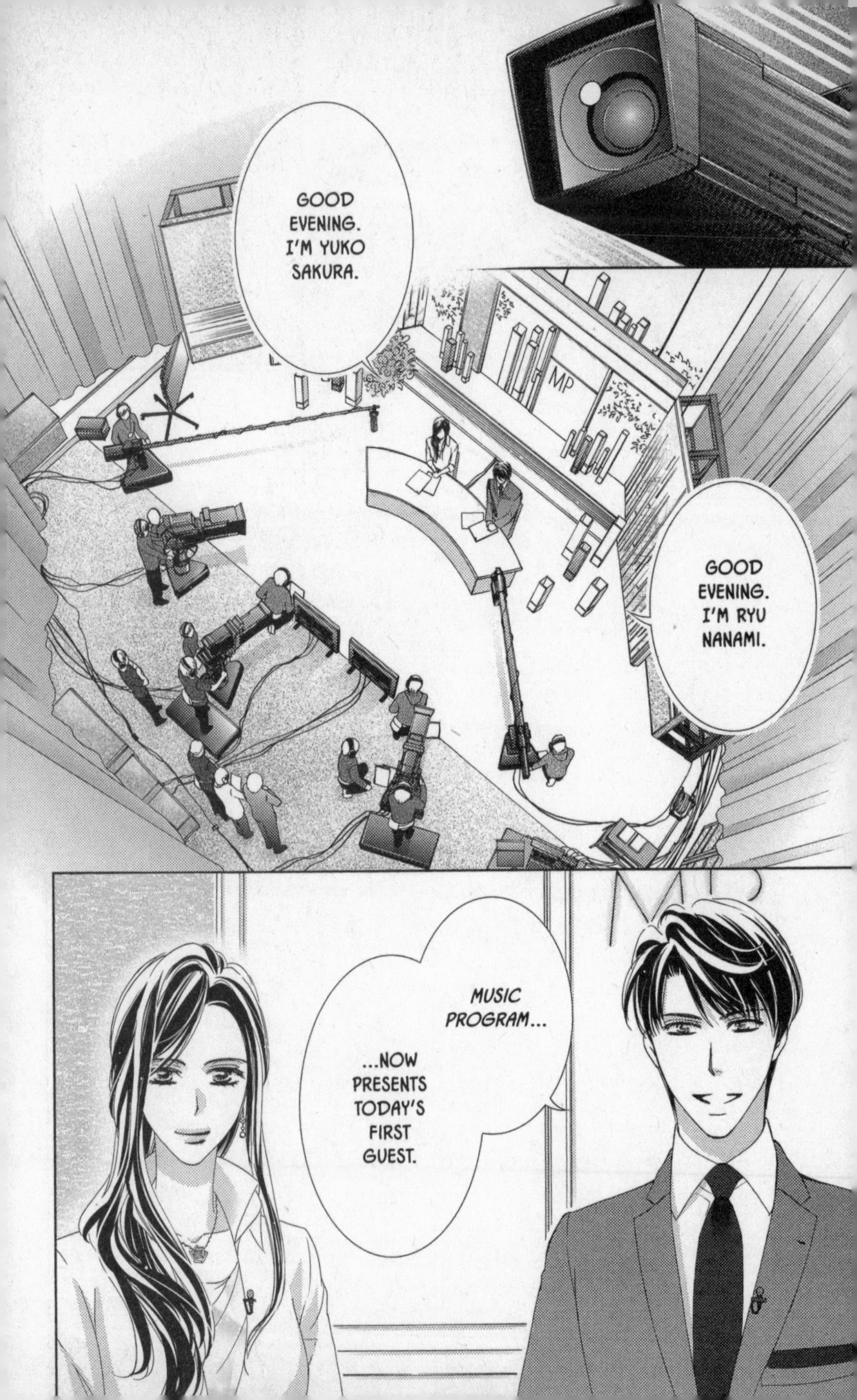
GOOD EVENING. I'M YUKO SAKURA.
GOOD EVENING. I'M RYU NANAMI.
MUSIC PROGRAM...
...NOW PRESENTS TODAY'S FIRST GUEST.

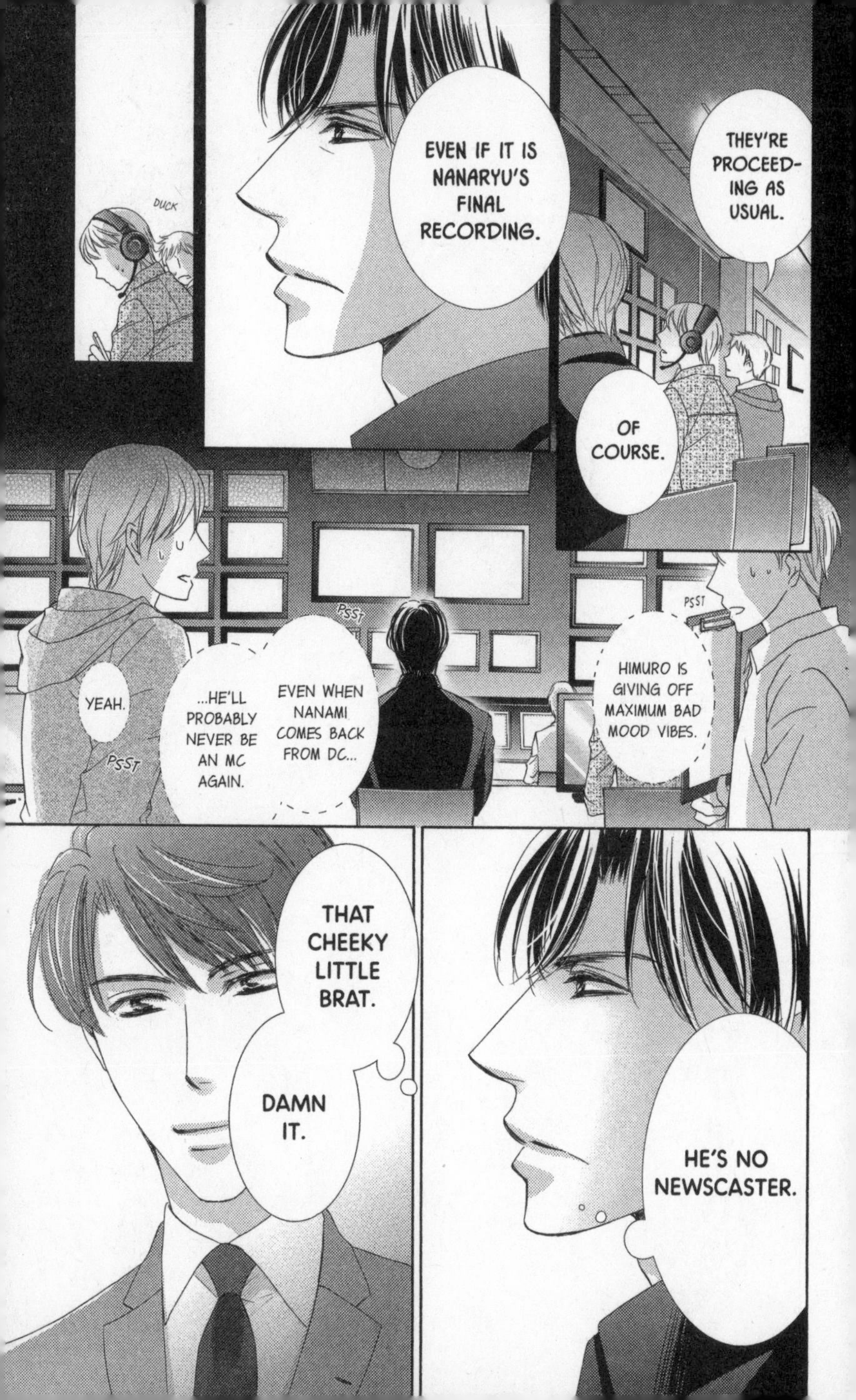
THEY'RE PROCEED-ING AS USUAL.
OF COURSE.
EVEN IF IT IS NANARYU'S FINAL RECORDING.
DUCK
PSST
HIMURO IS GIVING OFF MAXIMUM BAD MOOD VIBES.
PSST
EVEN WHEN NANAMI COMES BACK FROM DC...
...HE'LL PROBABLY NEVER BE AN MC AGAIN.
YEAH.
PSST
HE'S NO NEWSCASTER.
THAT CHEEKY LITTLE BRAT.
DAMN IT.

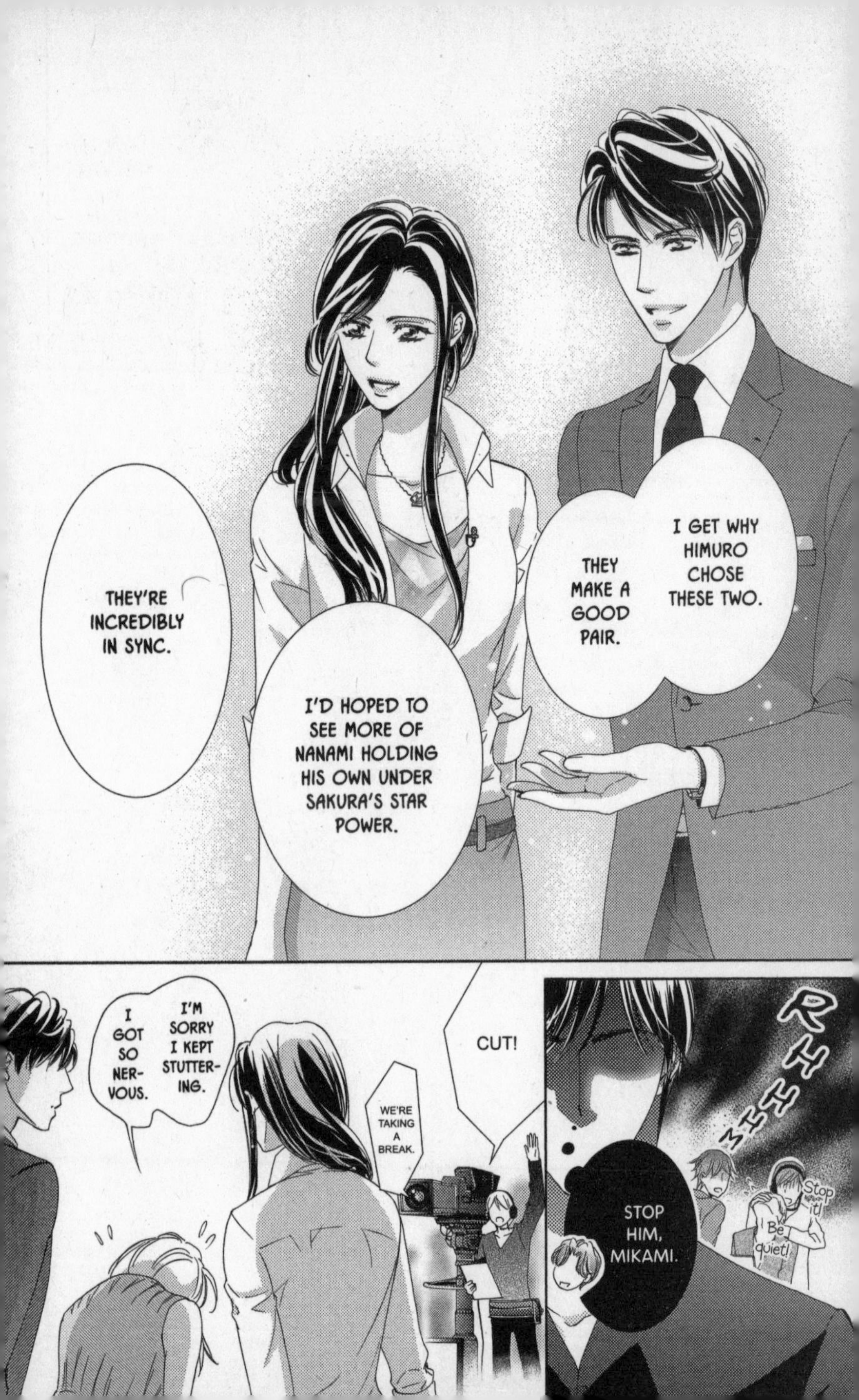
I GET WHY HIMURO CHOSE THESE TWO.
THEY MAKE A GOOD PAIR.
I'D HOPED TO SEE MORE OF NANAMI HOLDING HIS OWN UNDER SAKURA'S STAR POWER.
THEY'RE INCREDIBLY IN SYNC.
RHHHM
STOP HIM, MIKAMI.
Stop it!
Be quiet!
CUT!
WE'RE TAKING A BREAK.
I'M SORRY I KEPT STUTTER-ING.
I GOT SO NER-VOUS.

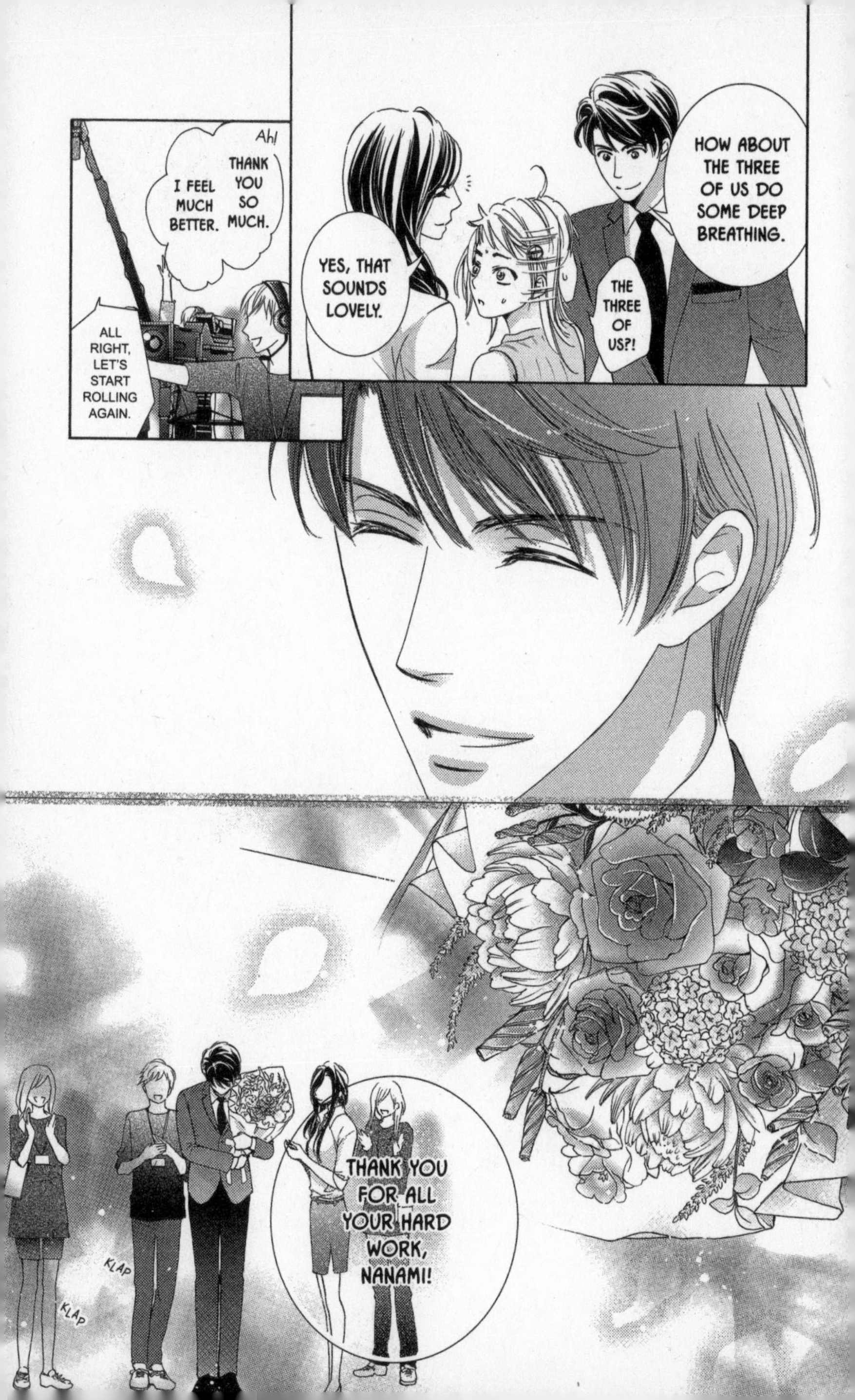
HOW ABOUT THE THREE OF US DO SOME DEEP BREATHING.
THE THREE OF US?!
YES, THAT SOUNDS LOVELY.
Ah!
THANK YOU SO MUCH.
I FEEL MUCH BETTER.
ALL RIGHT, LET'S START ROLLING AGAIN.
THANK YOU FOR ALL YOUR HARD WORK, NANAMI!
KLAP
KLAP

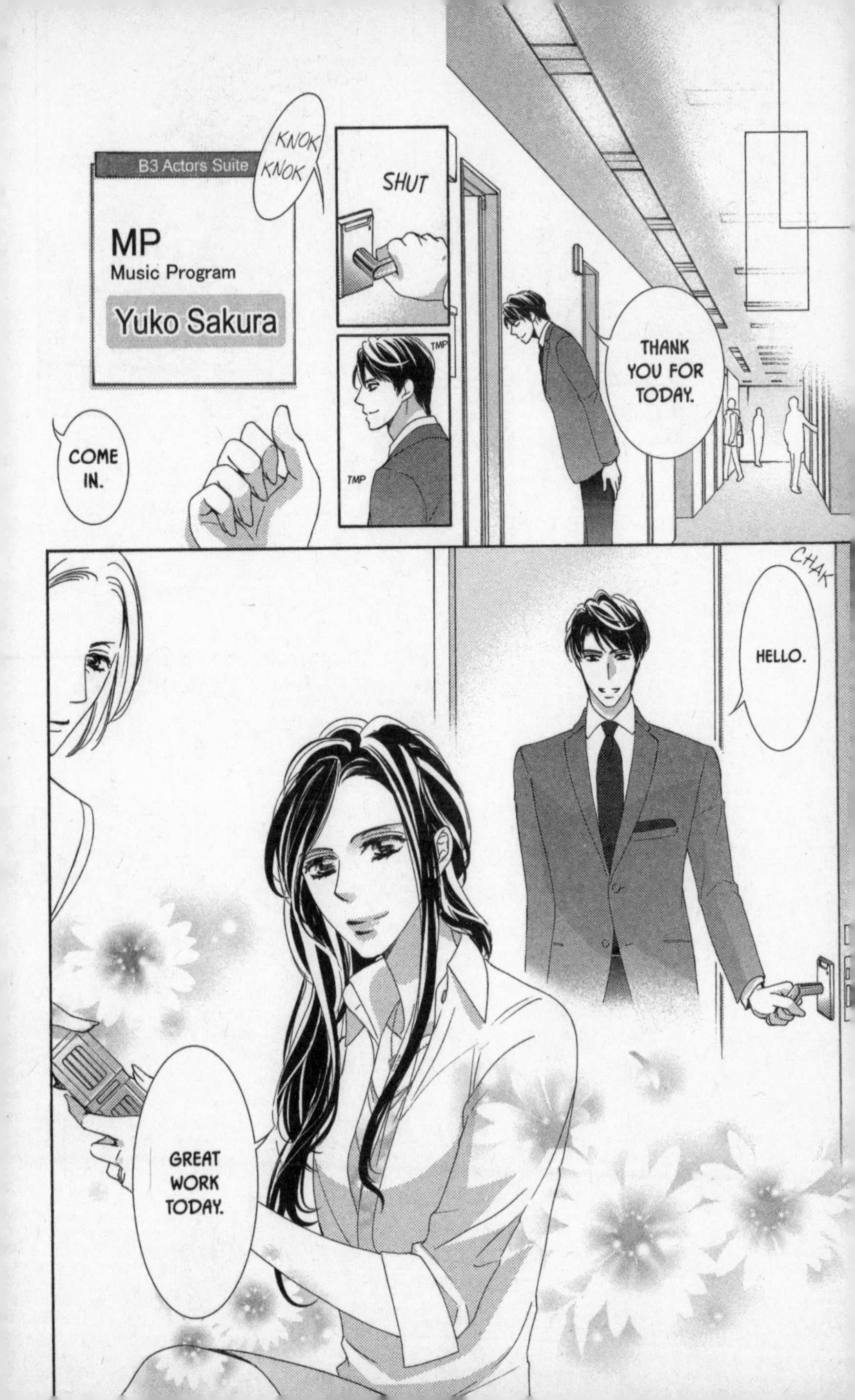
THANK YOU FOR TODAY.
SHUT
TMP
TMP
KNOK KNOK
B3 Actors Suite
MP
Music Program
Yuko Sakura
COME IN.
CHAK
HELLO.
GREAT WORK TODAY.

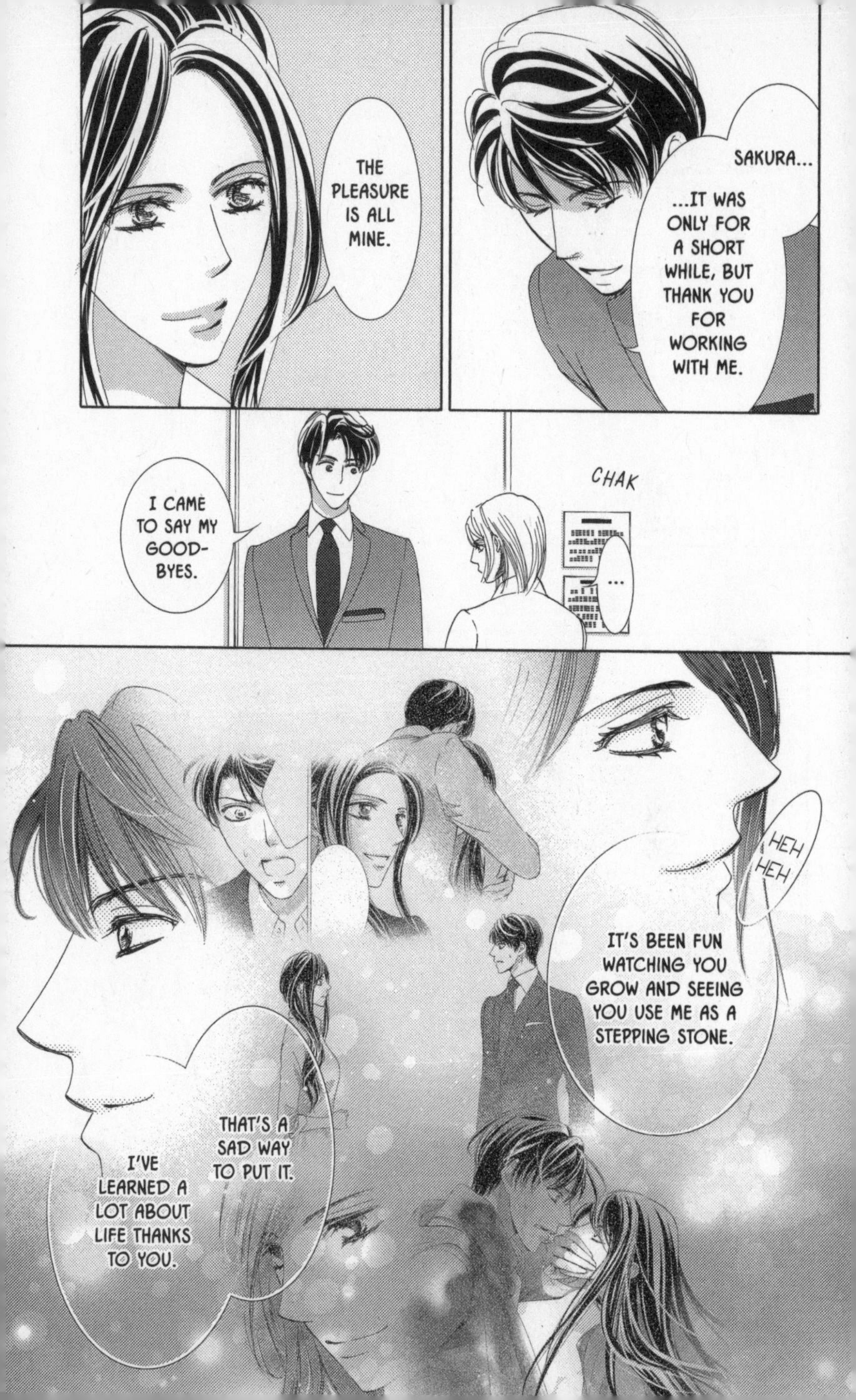
SAKURA...
...IT WAS ONLY FOR A SHORT WHILE, BUT THANK YOU FOR WORKING WITH ME.
THE PLEASURE IS ALL MINE.
CHAK
...
I CAME TO SAY MY GOOD-BYES.
HEH HEH
IT'S BEEN FUN WATCHING YOU GROW AND SEEING YOU USE ME AS A STEPPING STONE.
THAT'S A SAD WAY TO PUT IT.
I'VE LEARNED A LOT ABOUT LIFE THANKS TO YOU.

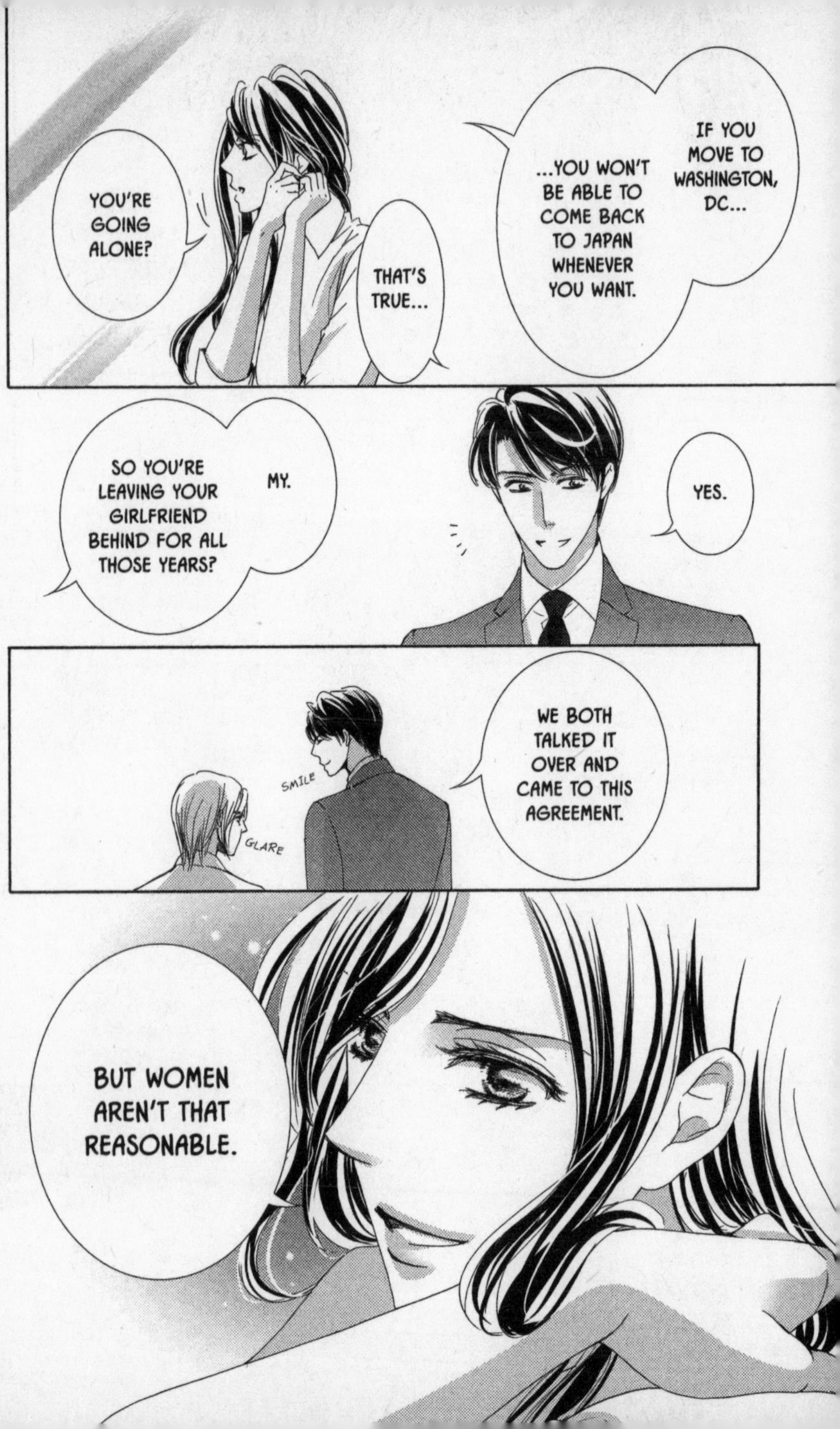
IF YOU MOVE TO WASHINGTON, DC...
...YOU WON'T BE ABLE TO COME BACK TO JAPAN WHENEVER YOU WANT.
THAT'S TRUE...
YOU'RE GOING ALONE?
YES.
MY.
SO YOU'RE LEAVING YOUR GIRLFRIEND BEHIND FOR ALL THOSE YEARS?
WE BOTH TALKED IT OVER AND CAME TO THIS AGREEMENT.
SMILE
GLARE
BUT WOMEN AREN'T THAT REASONABLE.

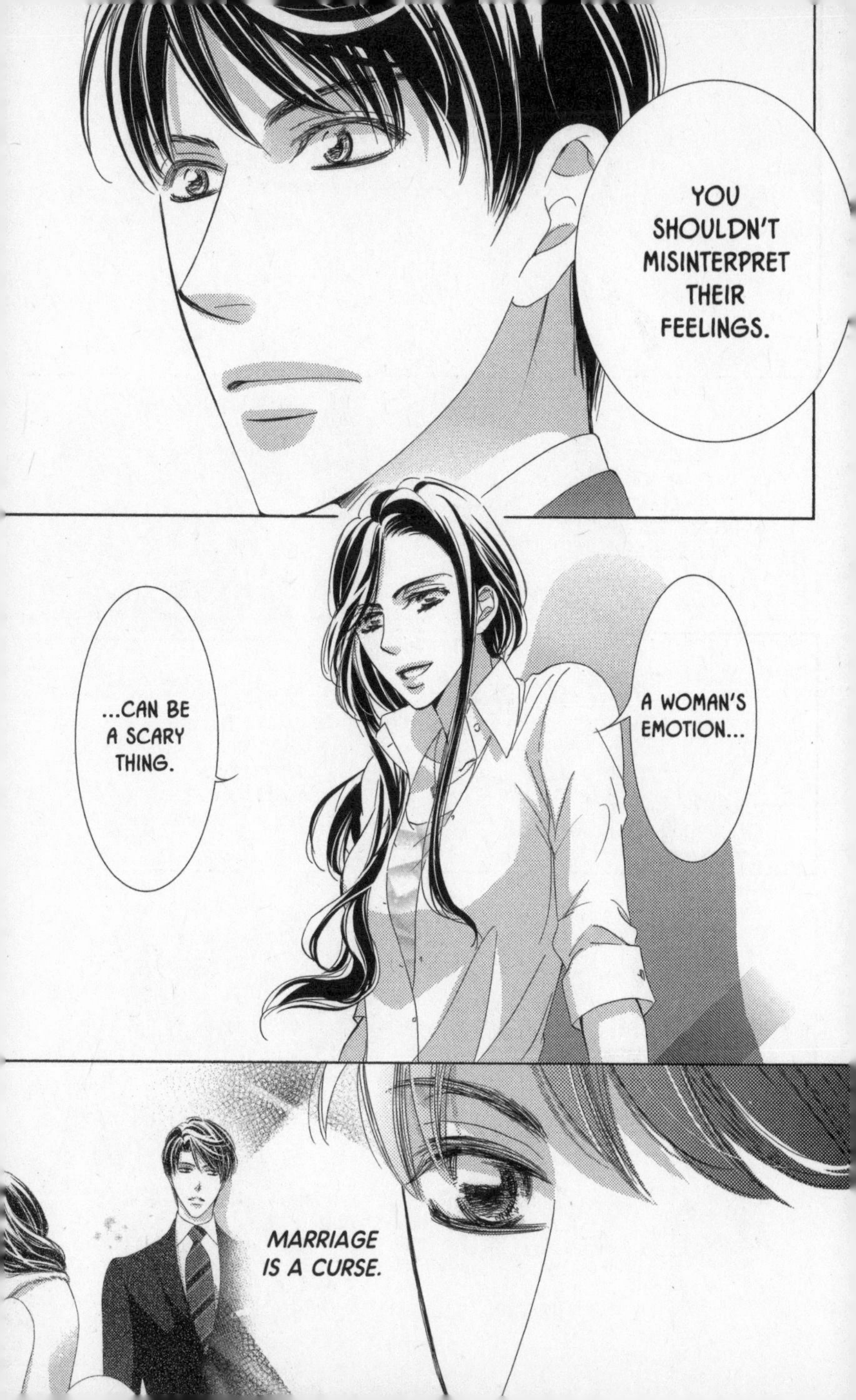
YOU SHOULDN'T MISINTERPRET THEIR FEELINGS.
A WOMAN'S EMOTION...
...CAN BE A SCARY THING.
MARRIAGE IS A CURSE.

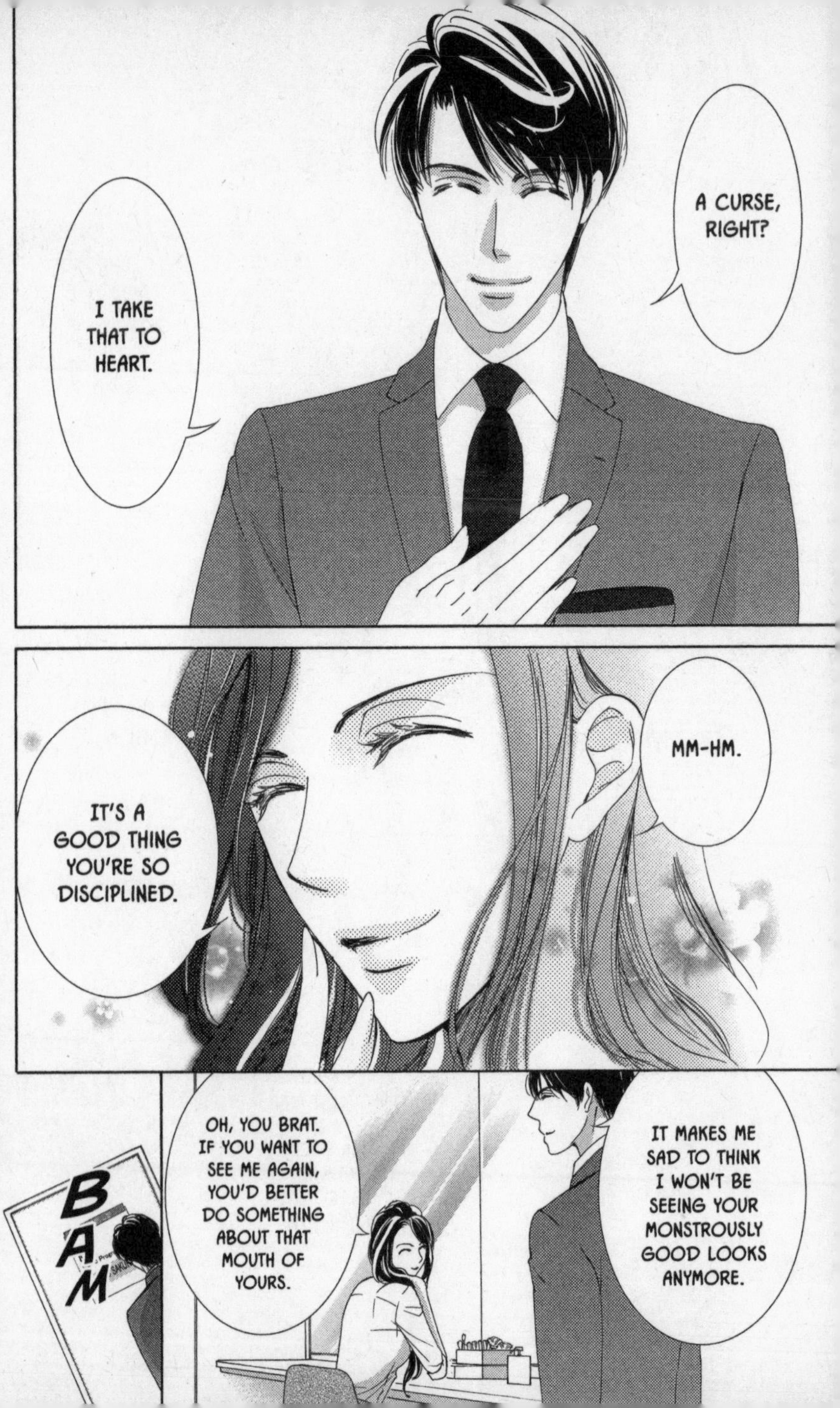
A CURSE, RIGHT?
I TAKE THAT TO HEART.
MM-HM.
IT'S A GOOD THING YOU'RE SO DISCIPLINED.
IT MAKES ME SAD TO THINK I WON'T BE SEEING YOUR MONSTROUSLY GOOD LOOKS ANYMORE.
OH, YOU BRAT. IF YOU WANT TO SEE ME AGAIN, YOU'D BETTER DO SOMETHING ABOUT THAT MOUTH OF YOURS.
BAM

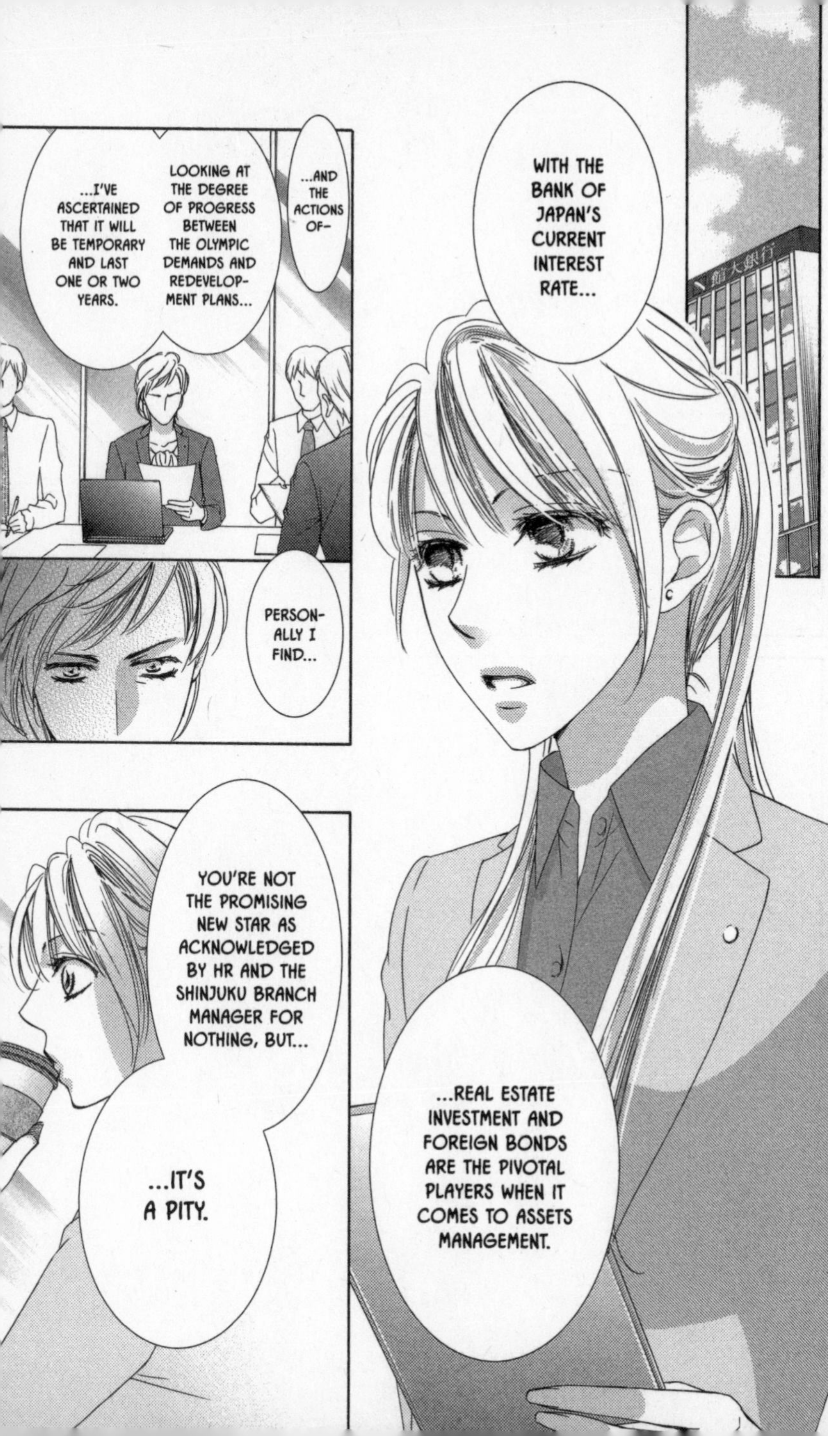
WITH THE BANK OF JAPAN'S CURRENT INTEREST RATE...
...REAL ESTATE INVESTMENT AND FOREIGN BONDS ARE THE PIVOTAL PLAYERS WHEN IT COMES TO ASSETS MANAGEMENT.
...AND THE ACTIONS OF-
LOOKING AT THE DEGREE OF PROGRESS BETWEEN THE OLYMPIC DEMANDS AND REDEVELOPMENT PLANS...
...I'VE ASCERTAINED THAT IT WILL BE TEMPORARY AND LAST ONE OR TWO YEARS.
PERSONALLY I FIND...
YOU'RE NOT THE PROMISING NEW STAR AS ACKNOWLEDGED BY HR AND THE SHINJUKU BRANCH MANAGER FOR NOTHING, BUT...
...IT'S A PITY.

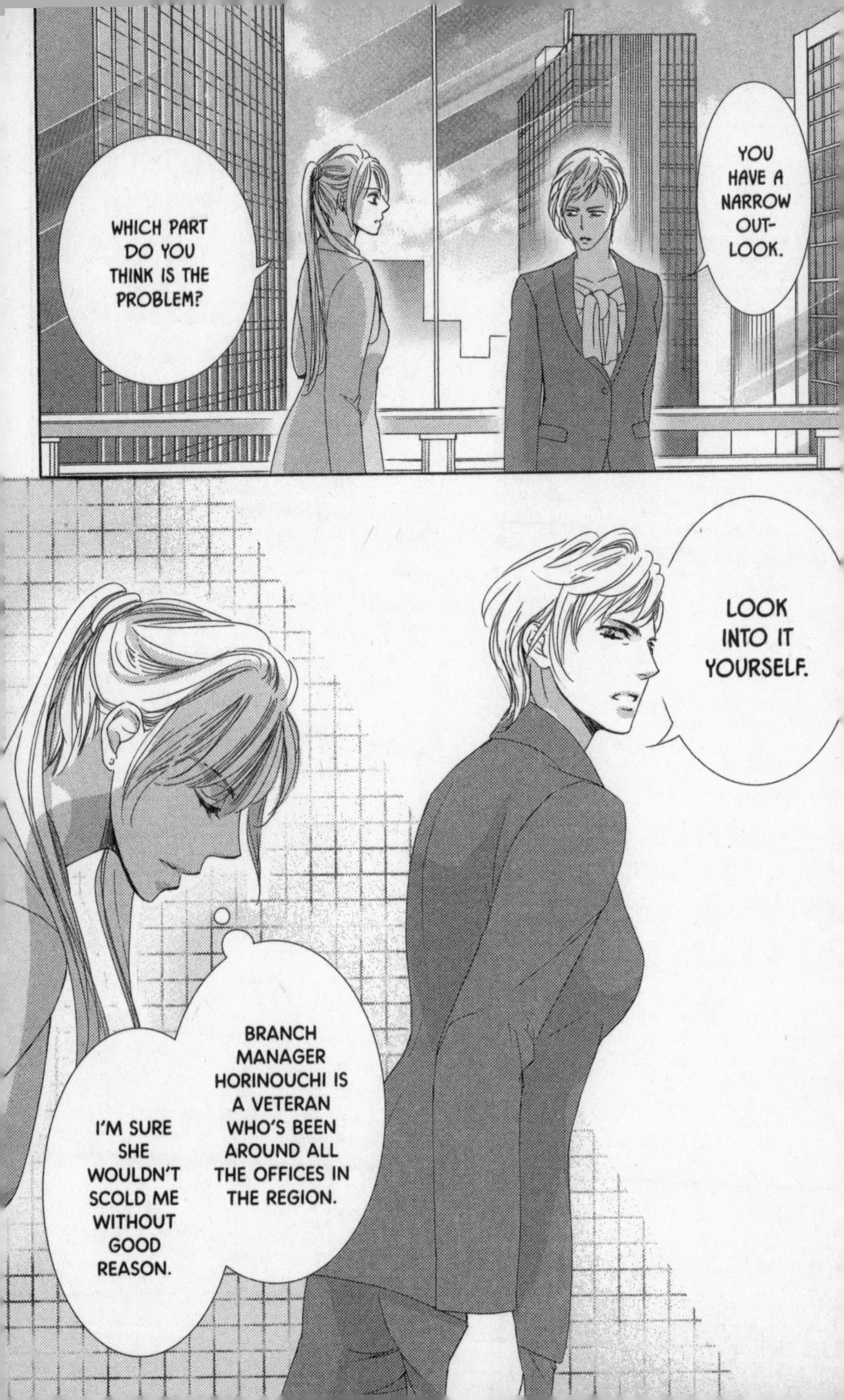
YOU HAVE A NARROW OUT-LOOK.
WHICH PART DO YOU THINK IS THE PROBLEM?
LOOK INTO IT YOURSELF.
BRANCH MANAGER HORINOUCHI IS A VETERAN WHO'S BEEN AROUND ALL THE OFFICES IN THE REGION.
I'M SURE SHE WOULDN'T SCOLD ME WITHOUT GOOD REASON.

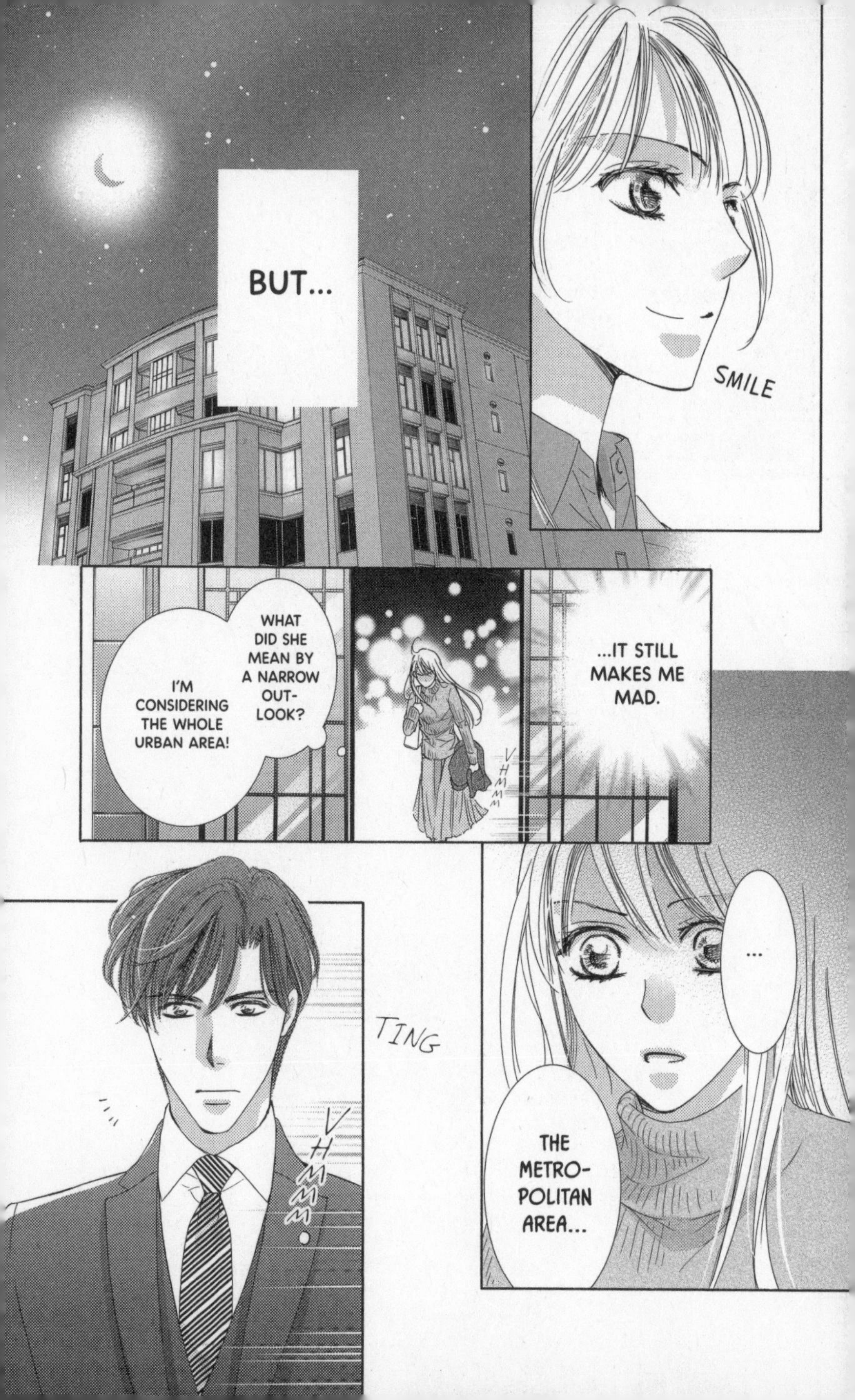
SMILE
BUT...
...IT STILL MAKES ME MAD.
VHMMMM
WHAT DID SHE MEAN BY A NARROW OUT-LOOK?
I'M CONSIDERING THE WHOLE URBAN AREA!
...
THE METRO-POLITAN AREA...
TING
VHMMMM

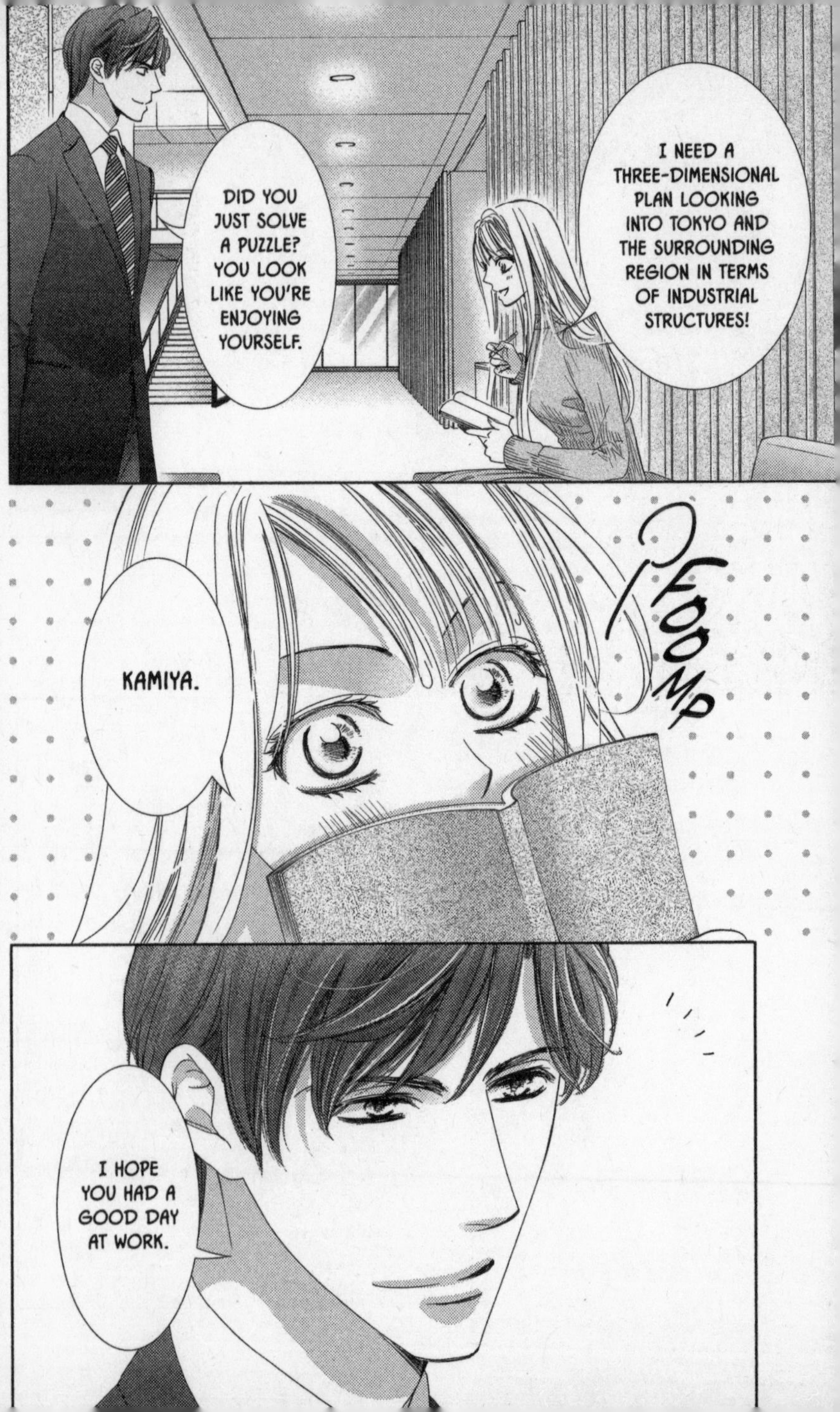
I NEED A THREE-DIMENSIONAL PLAN LOOKING INTO TOKYO AND THE SURROUNDING REGION IN TERMS OF INDUSTRIAL STRUCTURES!
DID YOU JUST SOLVE A PUZZLE? YOU LOOK LIKE YOU'RE ENJOYING YOURSELF.
PFOOMP
KAMIYA.
I HOPE YOU HAD A GOOD DAY AT WORK.

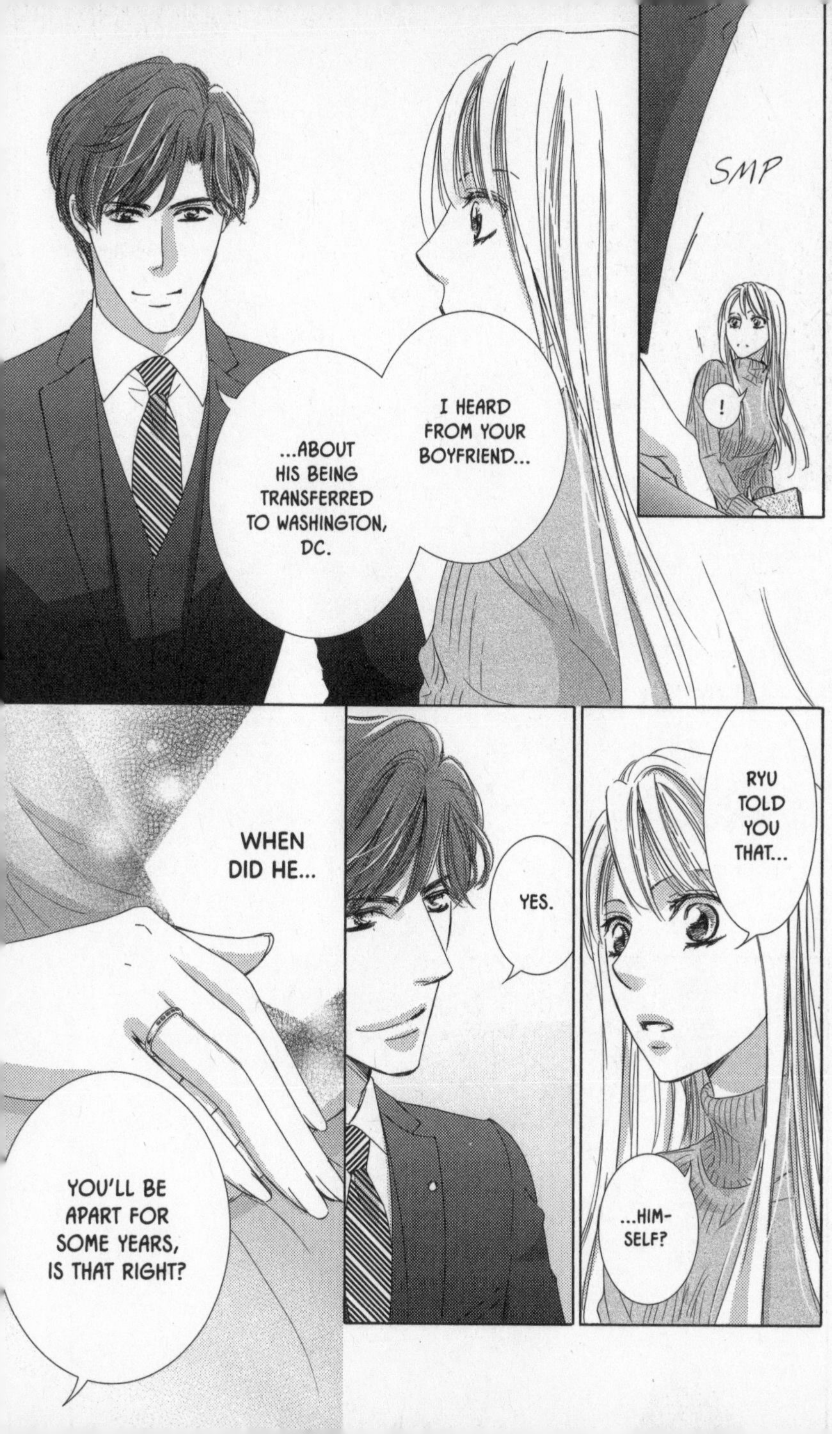
SMP
!
I HEARD FROM YOUR BOYFRIEND...
...ABOUT HIS BEING TRANSFERRED TO WASHINGTON, DC.
RYU TOLD YOU THAT...
...HIM-SELF?
YES.
WHEN DID HE...
YOU'LL BE APART FOR SOME YEARS, IS THAT RIGHT?

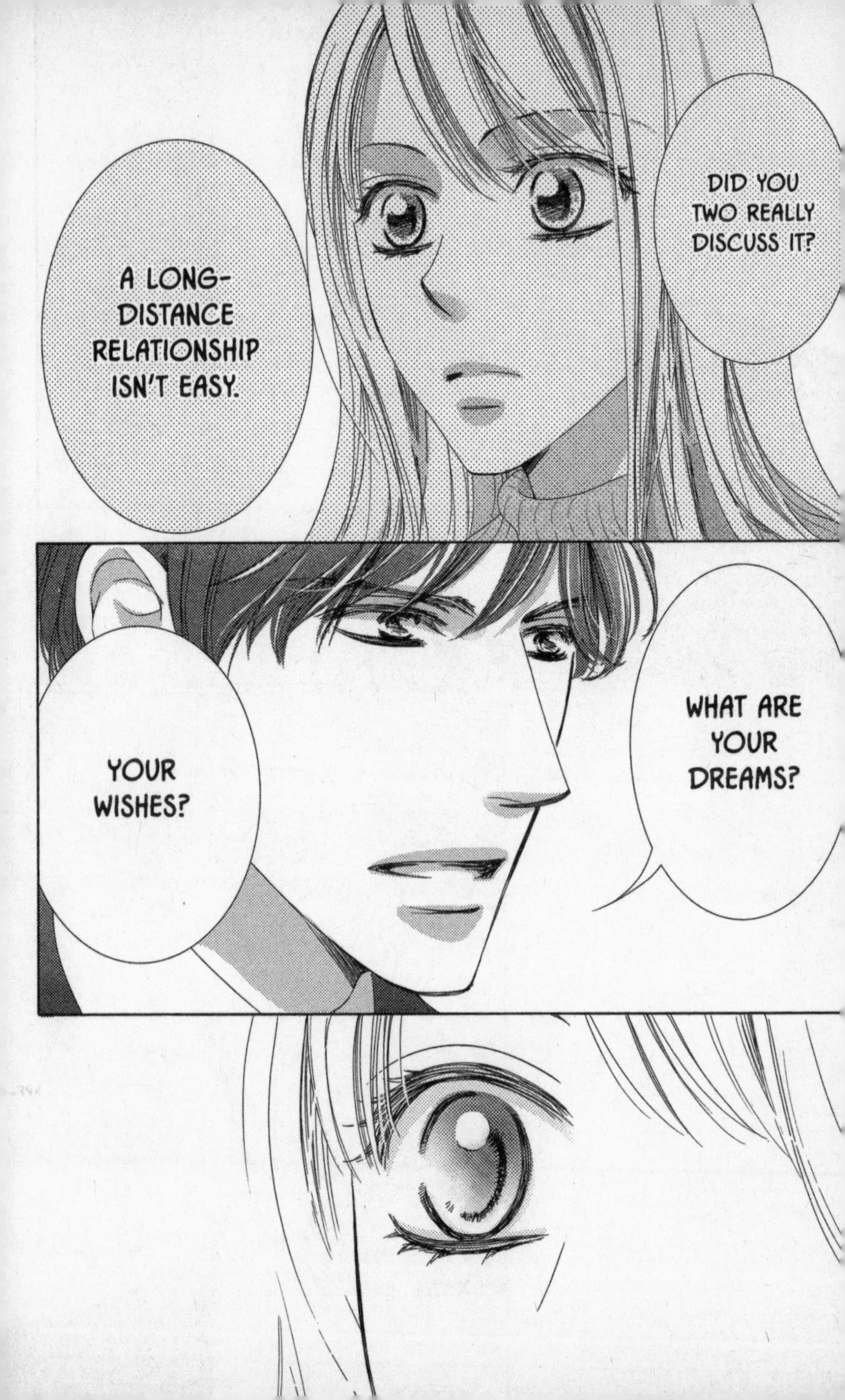
DID YOU TWO REALLY DISCUSS IT?
A LONG-DISTANCE RELATIONSHIP ISN'T EASY.
WHAT ARE YOUR DREAMS?
YOUR WISHES?

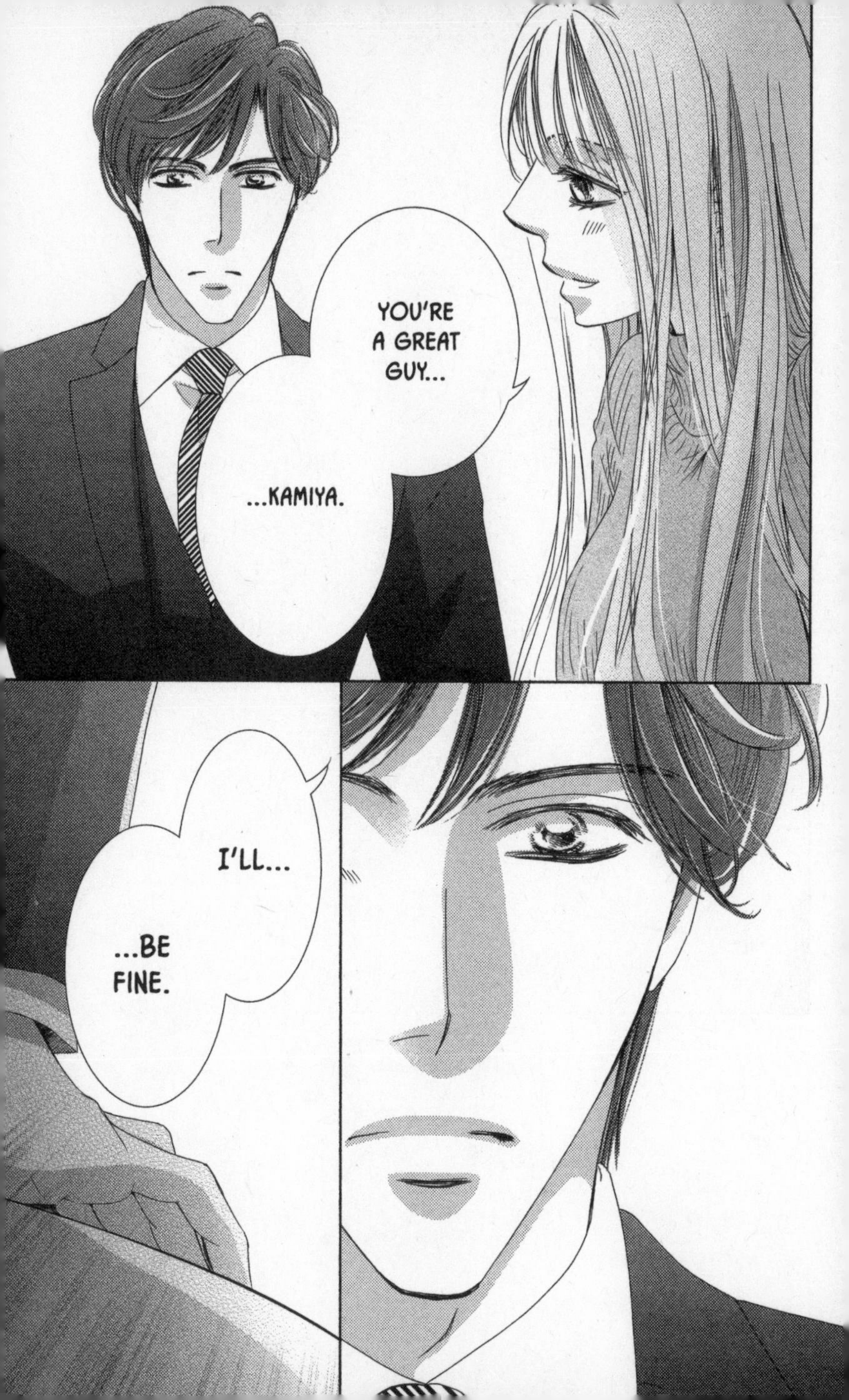
YOU'RE A GREAT GUY...
...KAMIYA.
I'LL...
...BE FINE.

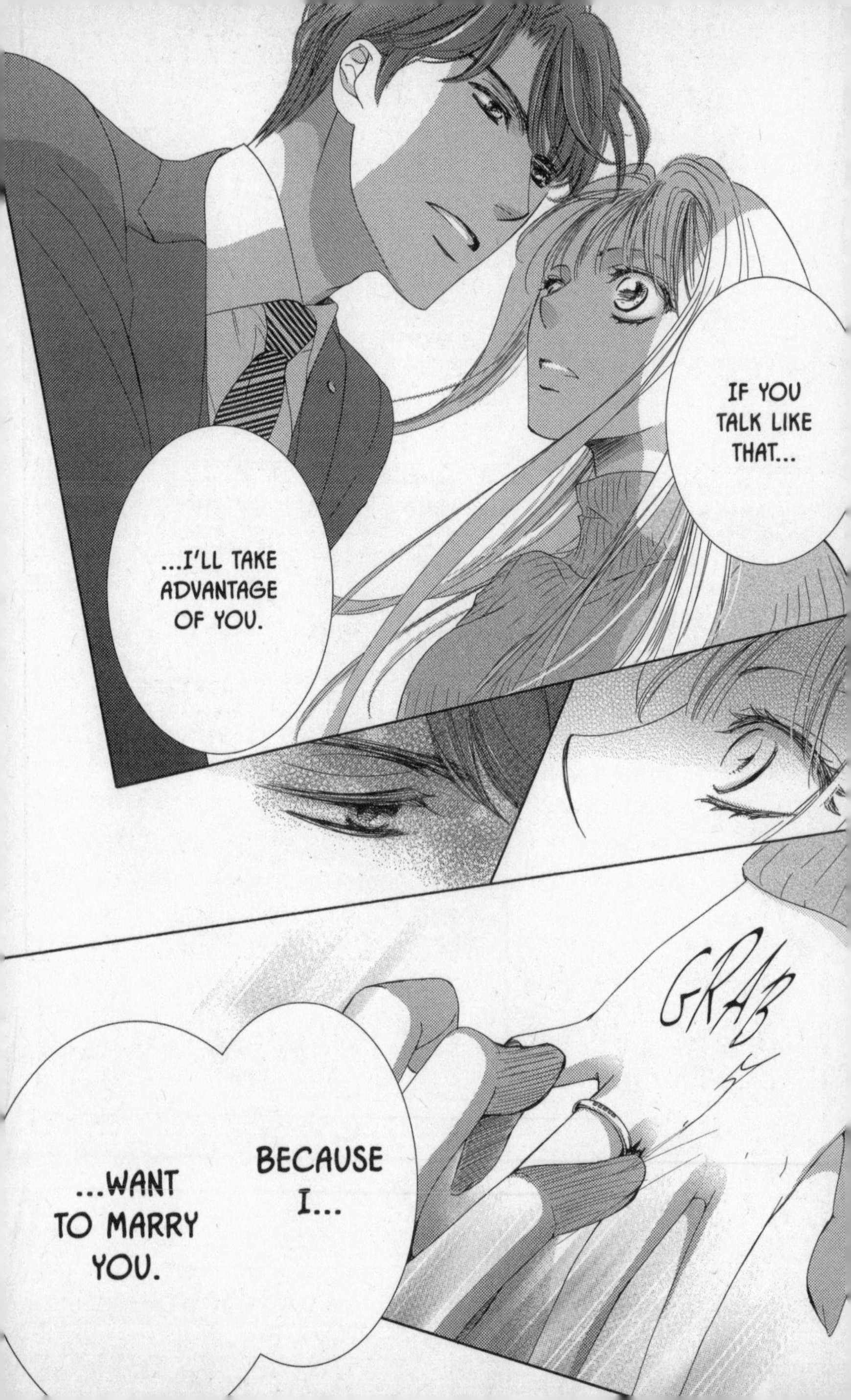
IF YOU TALK LIKE THAT...
...I'LL TAKE ADVANTAGE OF YOU.
GRAB
BECAUSE I...
...WANT TO MARRY YOU.

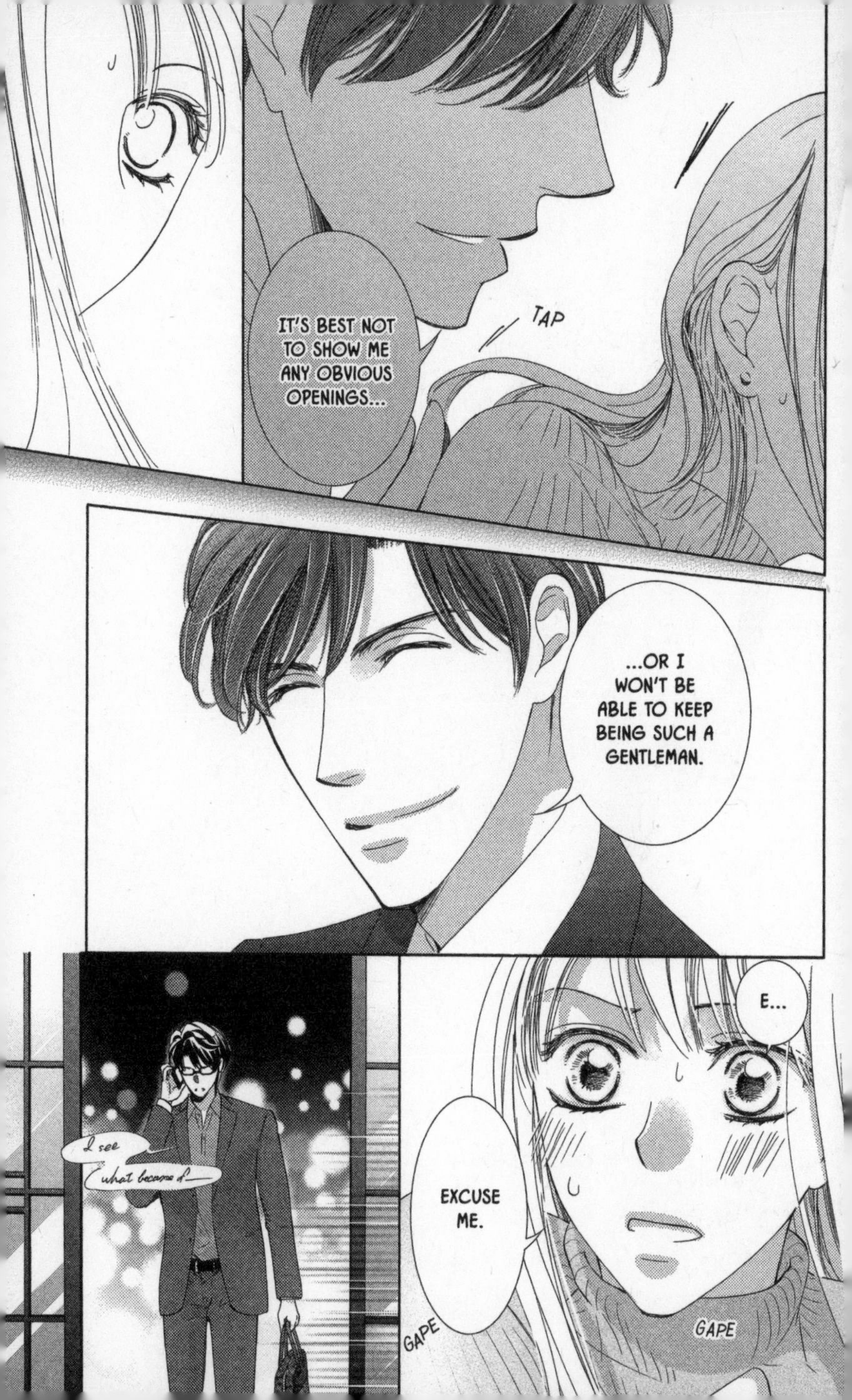
TAP
IT'S BEST NOT TO SHOW ME ANY OBVIOUS OPENINGS...
...OR I WON'T BE ABLE TO KEEP BEING SUCH A GENTLEMAN.
E...
EXCUSE ME.
GAPE
GAPE
I see
what became of—

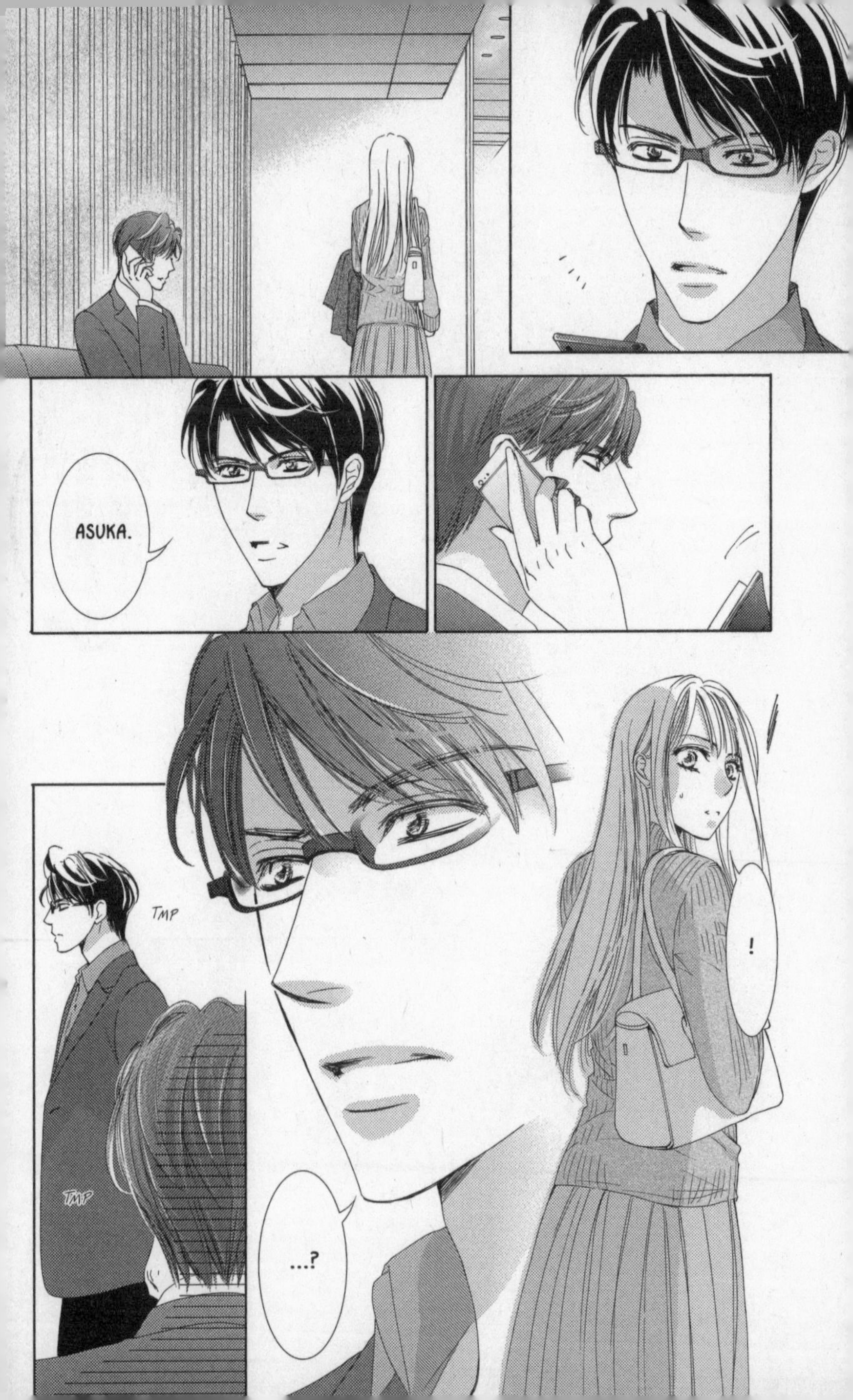
ASUKA.
!
TMP
TMP
...?

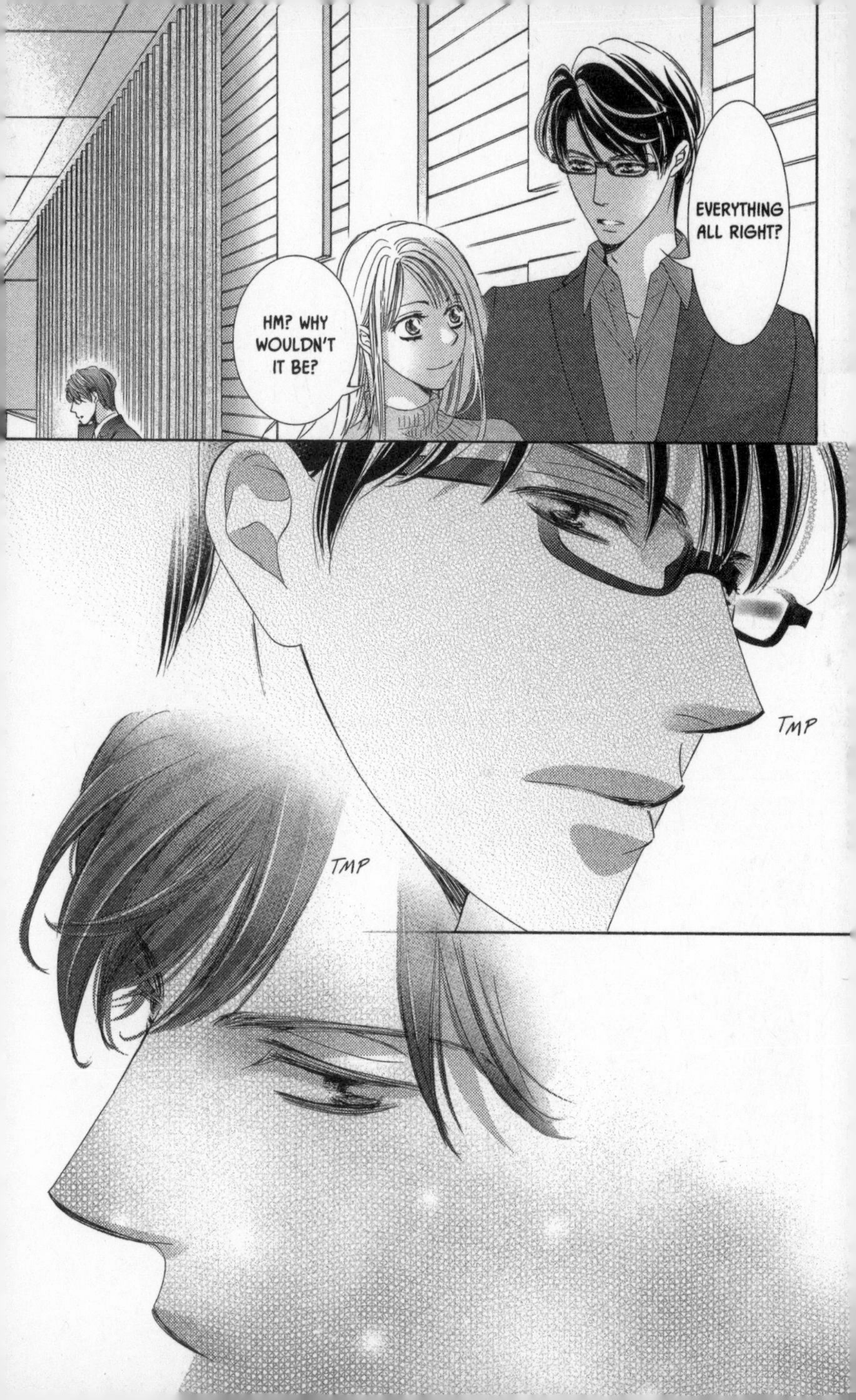
EVERYTHING ALL RIGHT?
HM? WHY WOULDN'T IT BE?
TMP
TMP

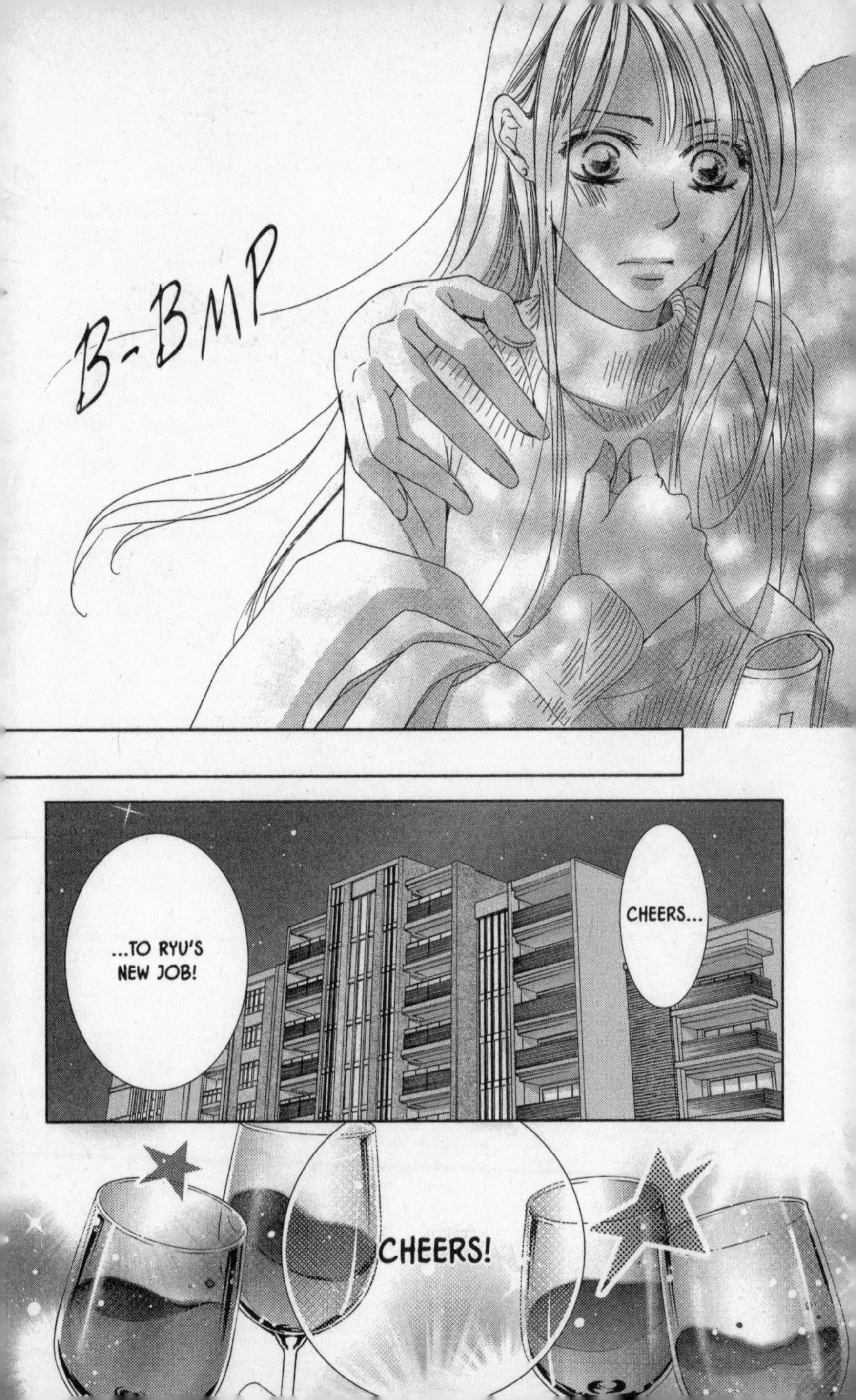
B-BMP
CHEERS...
...TO RYU'S NEW JOB!
CHEERS!

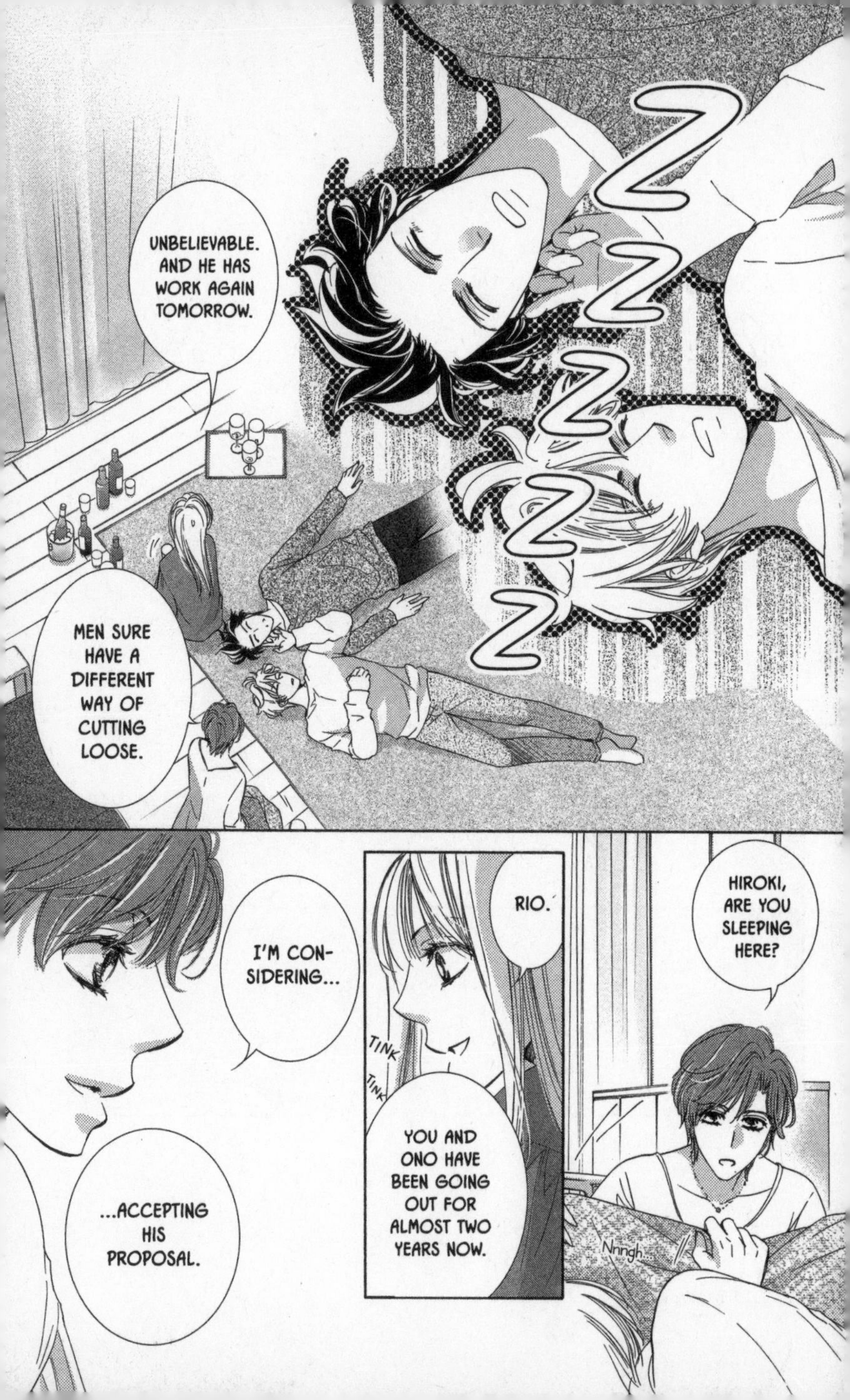
ZZZZZ
UNBELIEVABLE. AND HE HAS WORK AGAIN TOMORROW.
MEN SURE HAVE A DIFFERENT WAY OF CUTTING LOOSE.
HIROKI, ARE YOU SLEEPING HERE?
Nnngh...
RIO.
TINK TINK
YOU AND ONO HAVE BEEN GOING OUT FOR ALMOST TWO YEARS NOW.
I'M CONSIDERING...
...ACCEPTING HIS PROPOSAL.

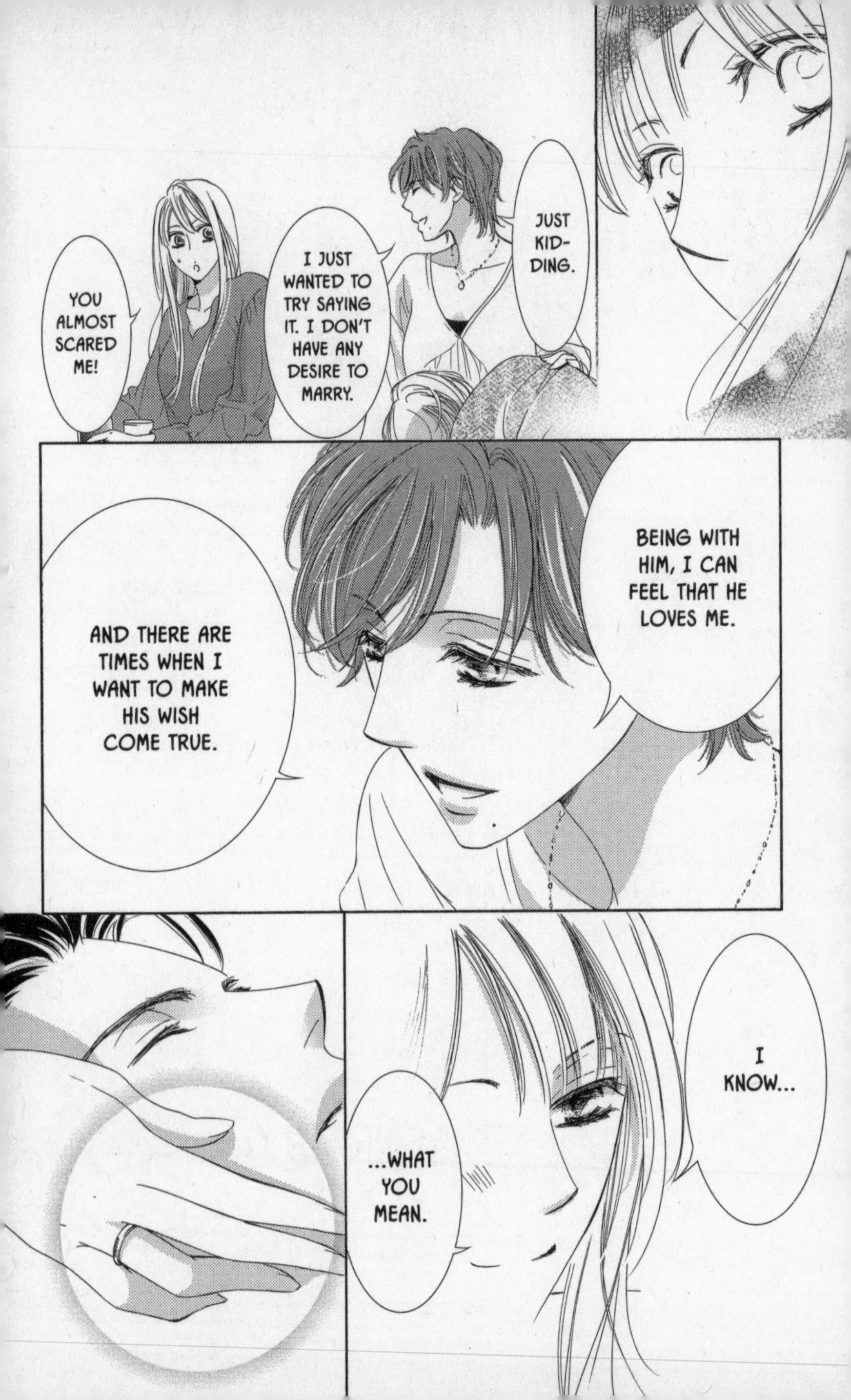
JUST KID-DING.
I JUST WANTED TO TRY SAYING IT. I DON'T HAVE ANY DESIRE TO MARRY.
YOU ALMOST SCARED ME!
BEING WITH HIM, I CAN FEEL THAT HE LOVES ME.
AND THERE ARE TIMES WHEN I WANT TO MAKE HIS WISH COME TRUE.
I KNOW...
...WHAT YOU MEAN.

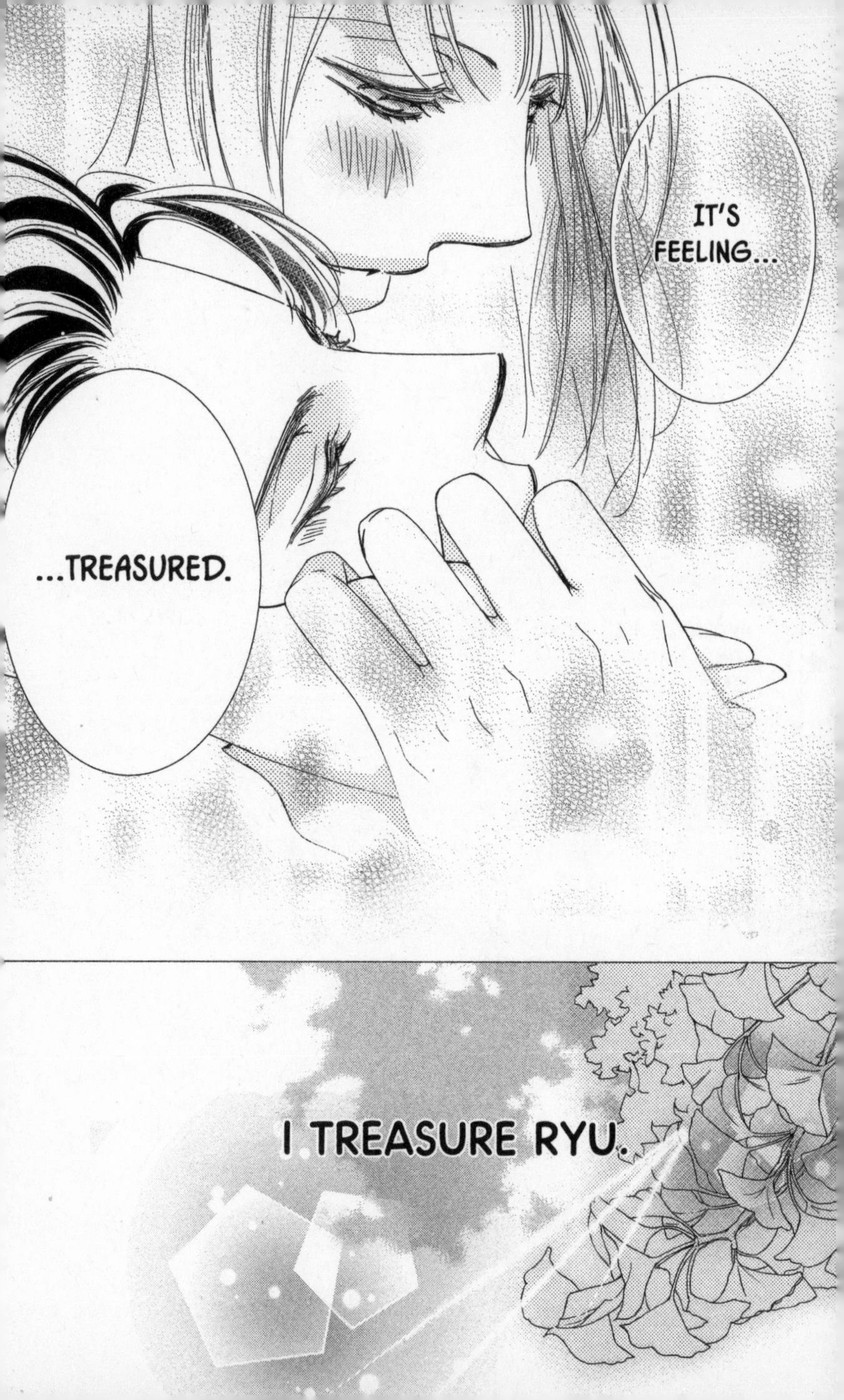
IT'S FEELING...
...TREASURED.
I TREASURE RYU.

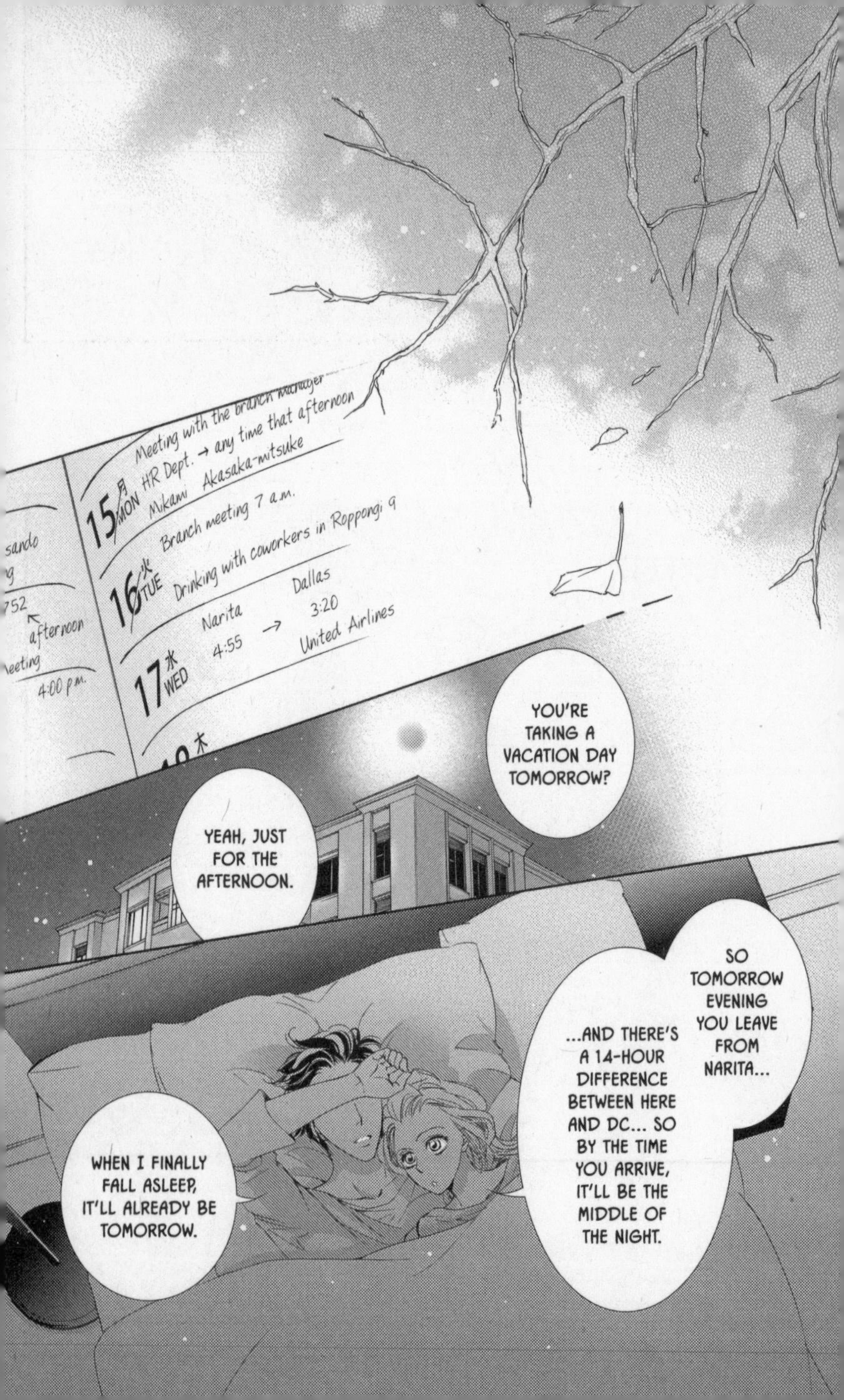

15 月 MON Meeting with the branch manager
HR Dept. → any time that afternoon
Mikami Akasaka-mitsuke
16 火 TUE Branch meeting 7 a.m.
Drinking with coworkers in Roppongi 9
17 水 WED Narita 4:55 → Dallas 3:20
United Airlines
afternoon
4:00 p.m.
YOU'RE TAKING A VACATION DAY TOMORROW?
YEAH, JUST FOR THE AFTERNOON.
SO TOMORROW EVENING YOU LEAVE FROM NARITA...
...AND THERE'S A 14-HOUR DIFFERENCE BETWEEN HERE AND DC... SO BY THE TIME YOU ARRIVE, IT'LL BE THE MIDDLE OF THE NIGHT.
WHEN I FINALLY FALL ASLEEP, IT'LL ALREADY BE TOMORROW.

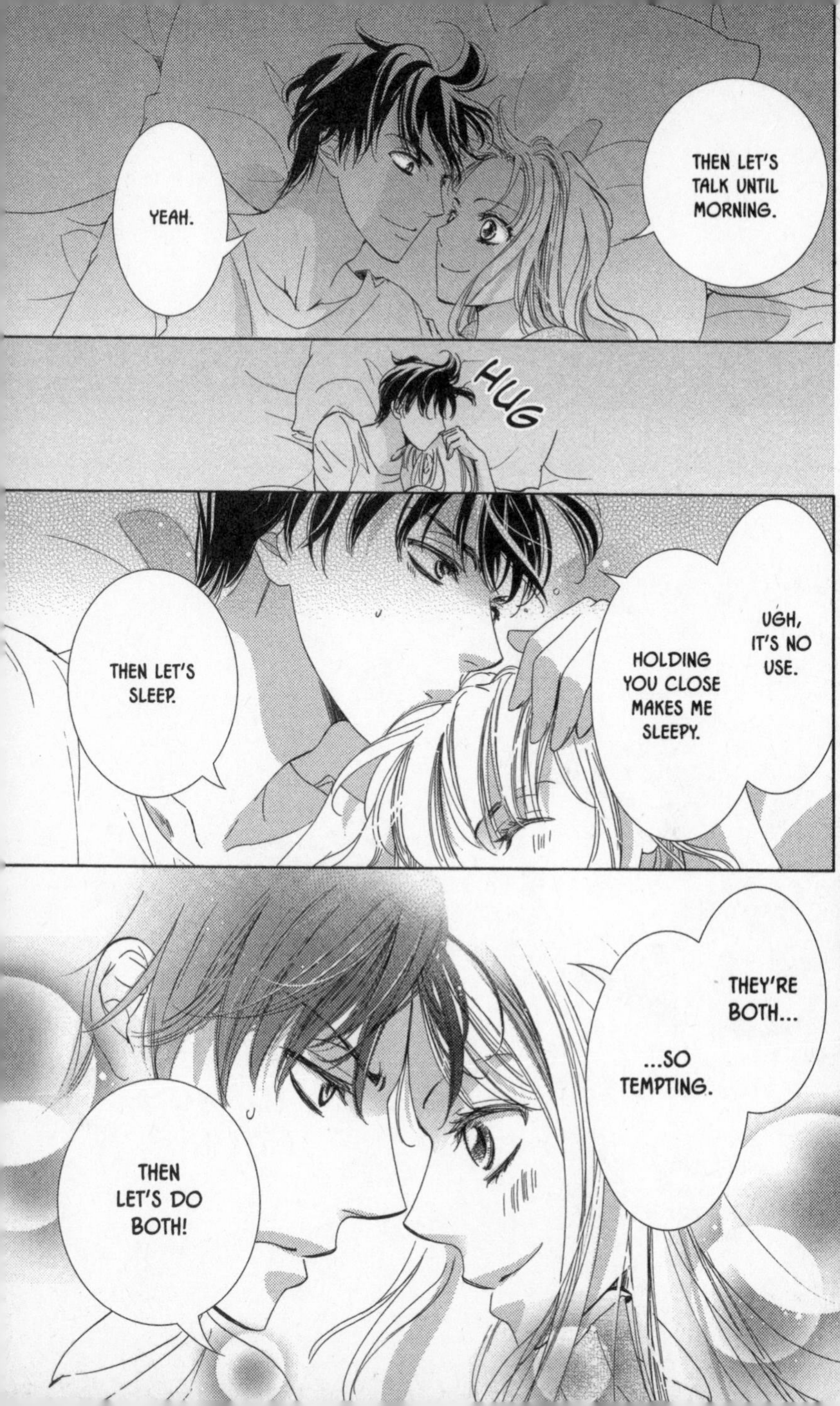
THEN LET'S TALK UNTIL MORNING.
YEAH.
HUG
UGH, IT'S NO USE.
HOLDING YOU CLOSE MAKES ME SLEEPY.
THEN LET'S SLEEP.
THEY'RE BOTH...
...SO TEMPTING.
THEN LET'S DO BOTH!

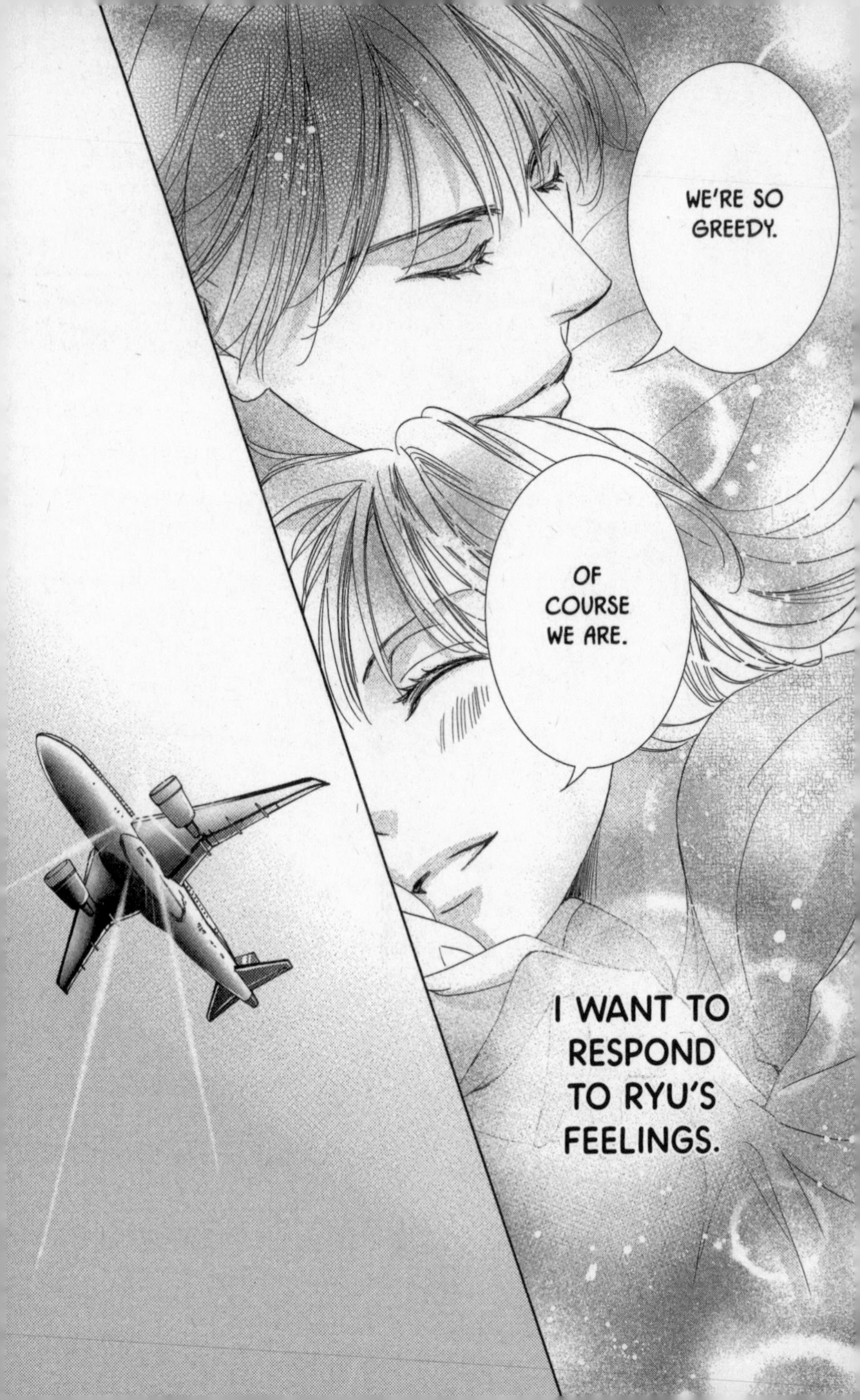
WE'RE SO GREEDY.
OF COURSE WE ARE.
I WANT TO RESPOND TO RYU'S FEELINGS.

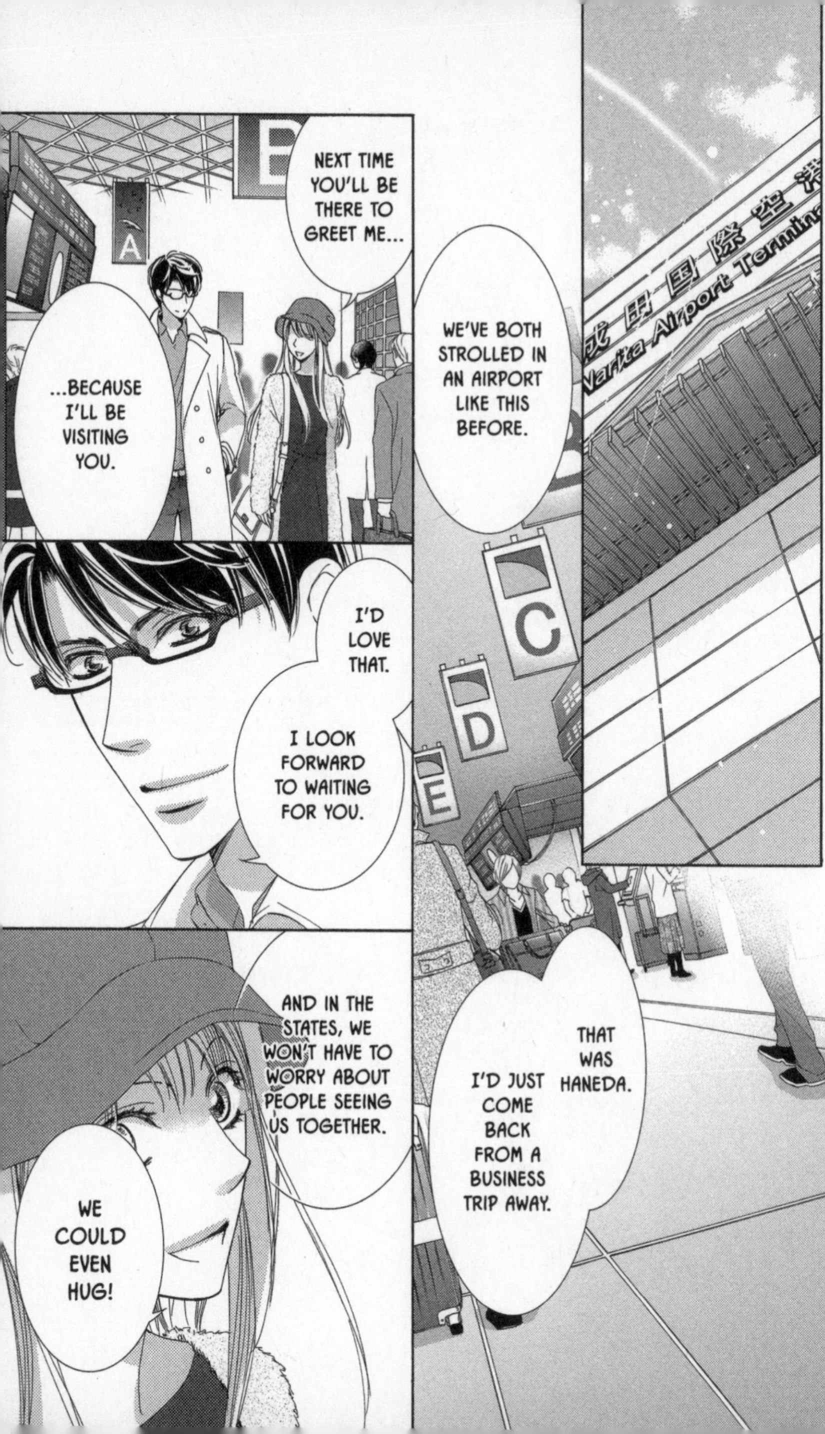
WE'VE BOTH STROLLED IN AN AIRPORT LIKE THIS BEFORE.
THAT WAS HANEDA. I'D JUST COME BACK FROM A BUSINESS TRIP AWAY.
NEXT TIME YOU'LL BE THERE TO GREET ME...
...BECAUSE I'LL BE VISITING YOU.
I'D LOVE THAT.
I LOOK FORWARD TO WAITING FOR YOU.
AND IN THE STATES, WE WON'T HAVE TO WORRY ABOUT PEOPLE SEEING US TOGETHER.
WE COULD EVEN HUG!

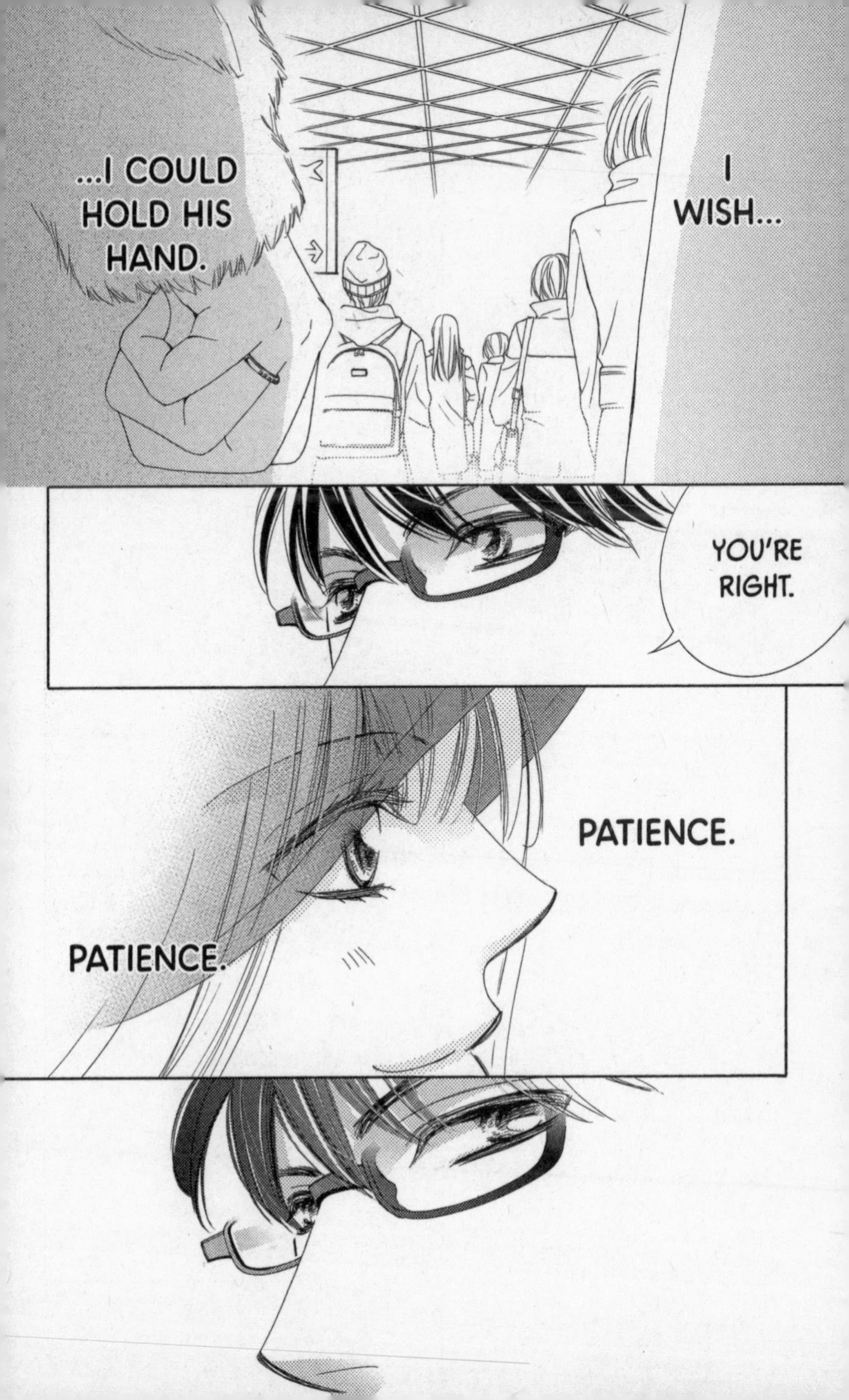
I WISH...
...I COULD HOLD HIS HAND.
YOU'RE RIGHT.
PATIENCE.
PATIENCE.

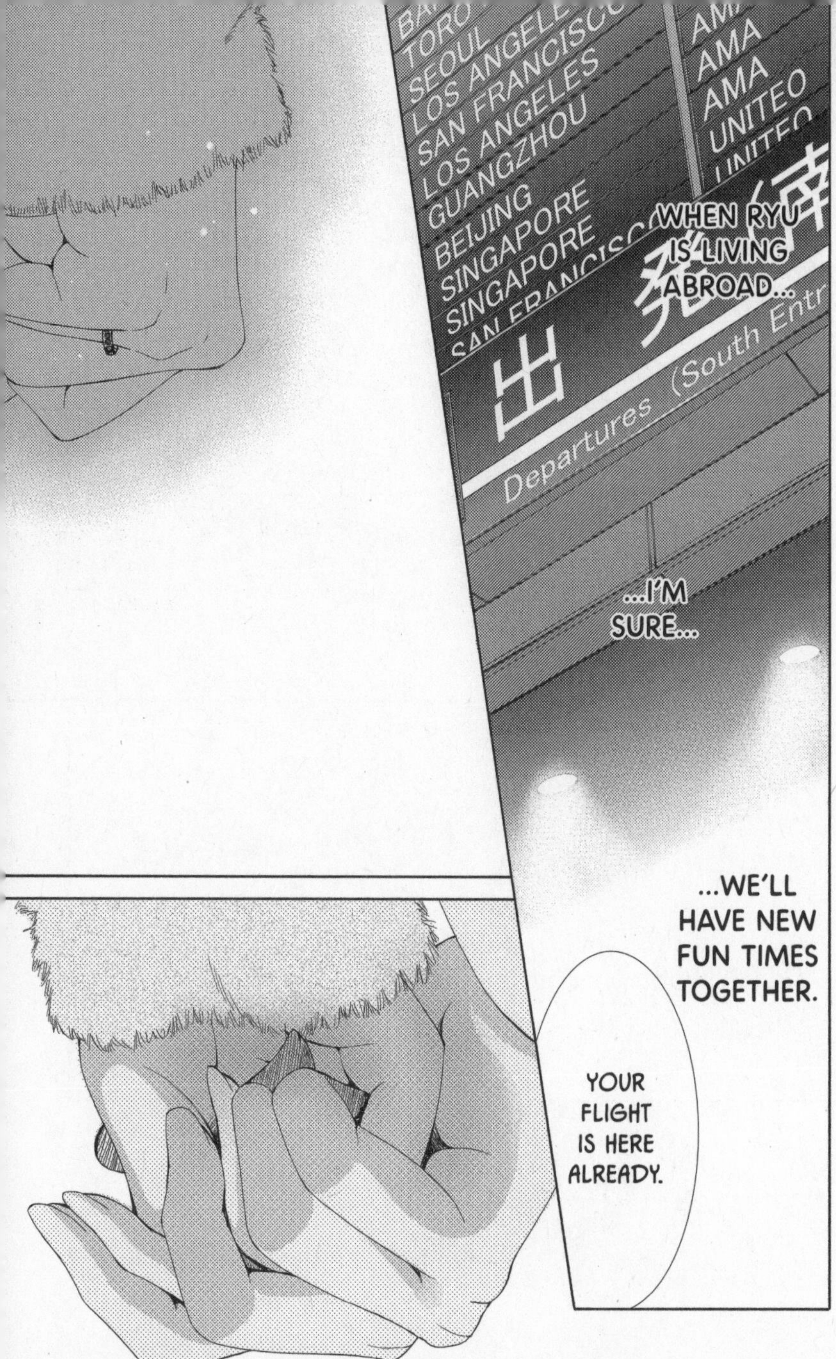
SEOUL
SAN FRANCISCO
LOS ANGELES
GUANGZHOU
BEIJING
SINGAPORE
SINGAPORE
AMA
AMA
UNITED
Departures
WHEN RYU IS LIVING ABROAD...
...I'M SURE...
...WE'LL HAVE NEW FUN TIMES TOGETHER.
YOUR FLIGHT IS HERE ALREADY.

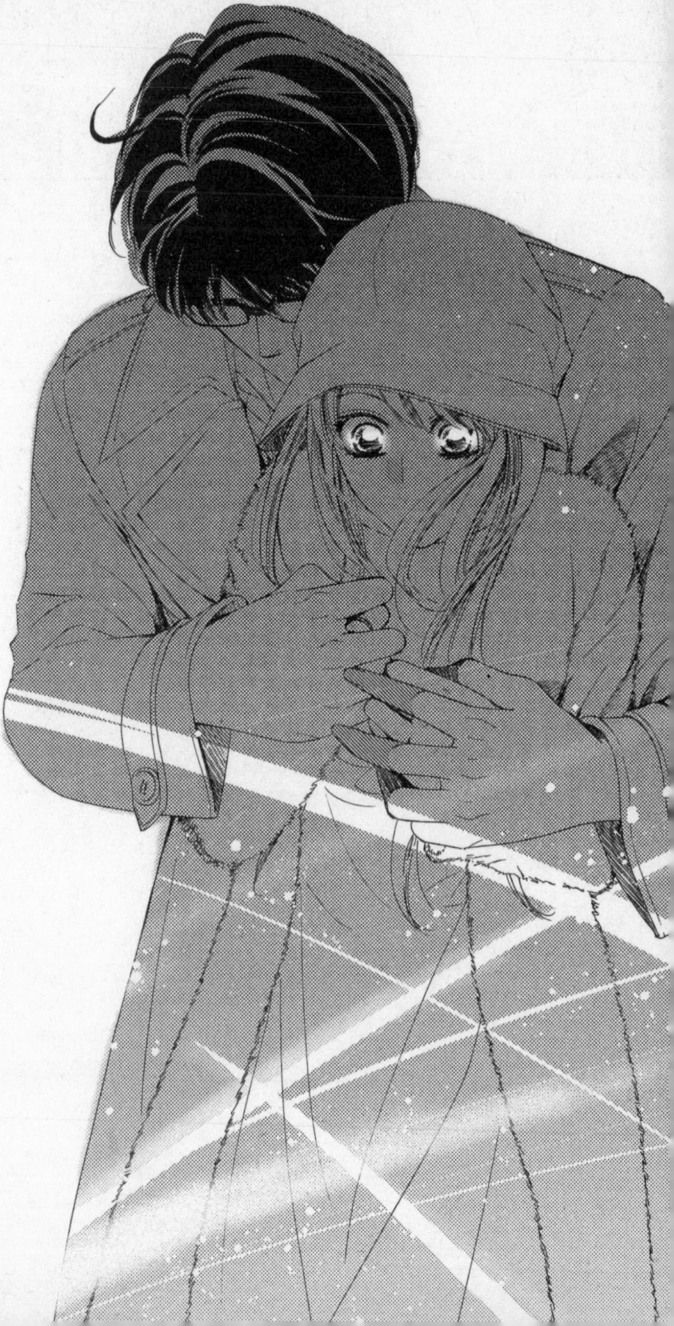

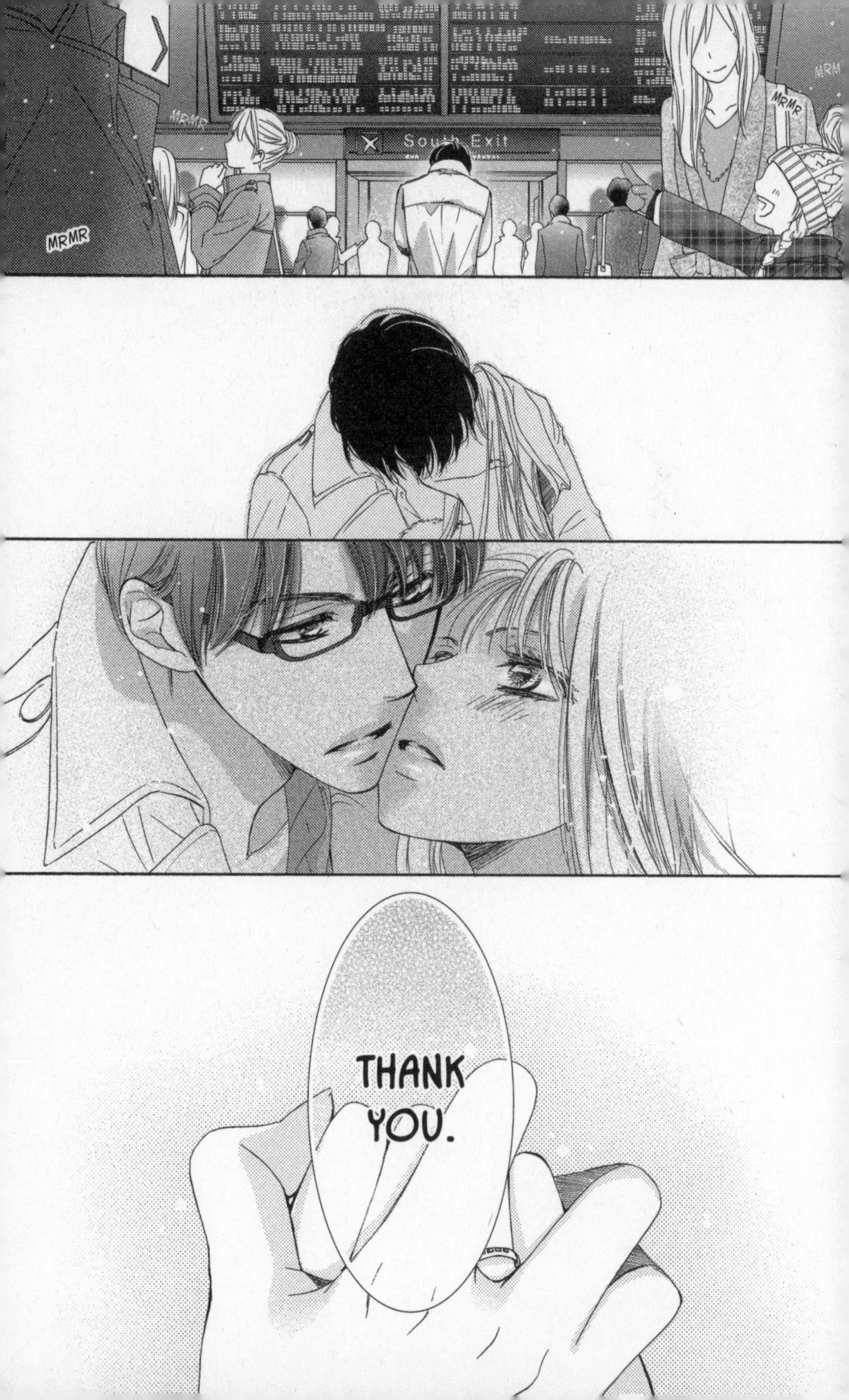
MRMR
MRMR
South Exit
MRMR
MRMR
THANK YOU.

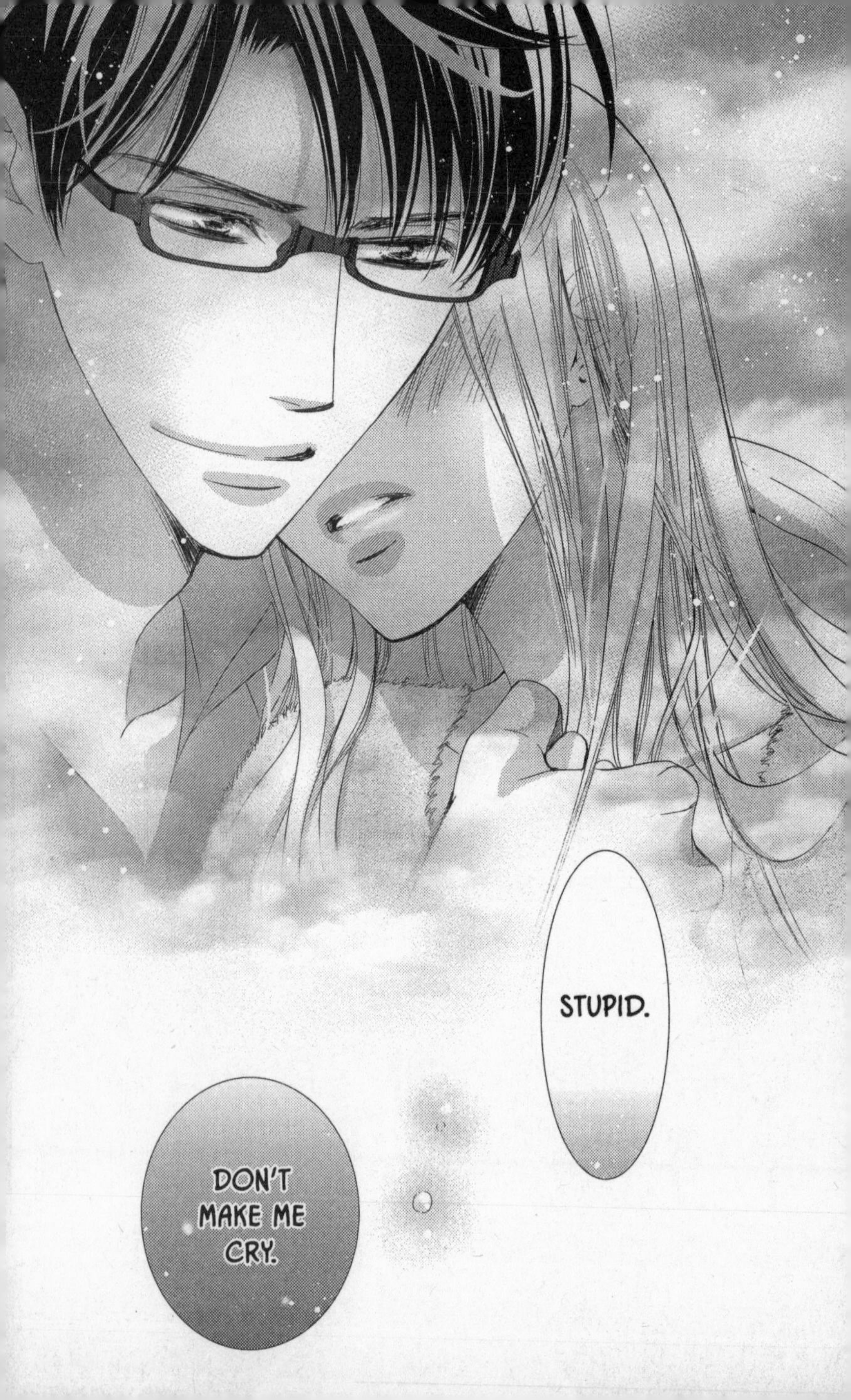
STUPID.
DON'T MAKE ME CRY.

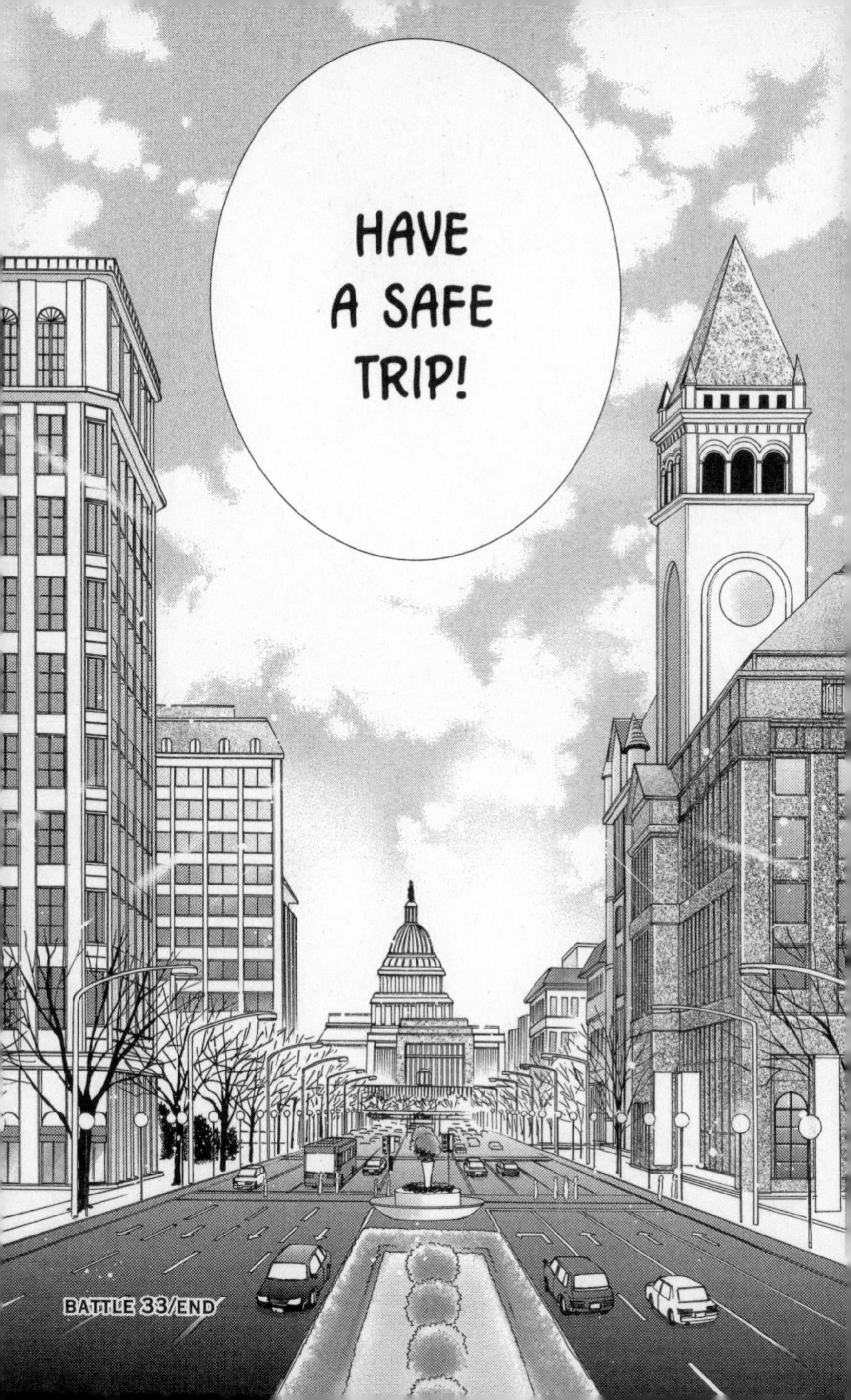
HAVE A SAFE TRIP!
BATTLE 33/END

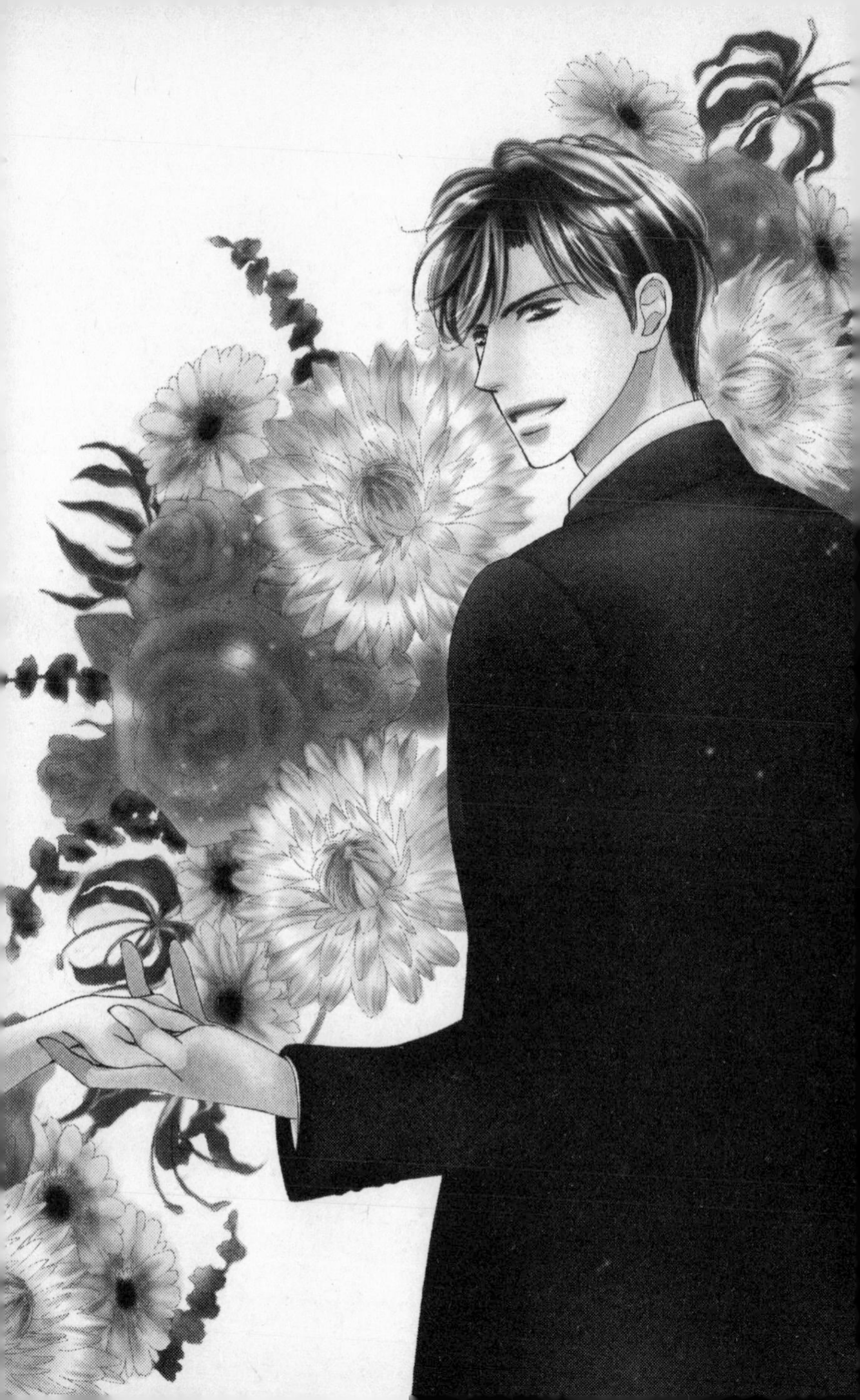

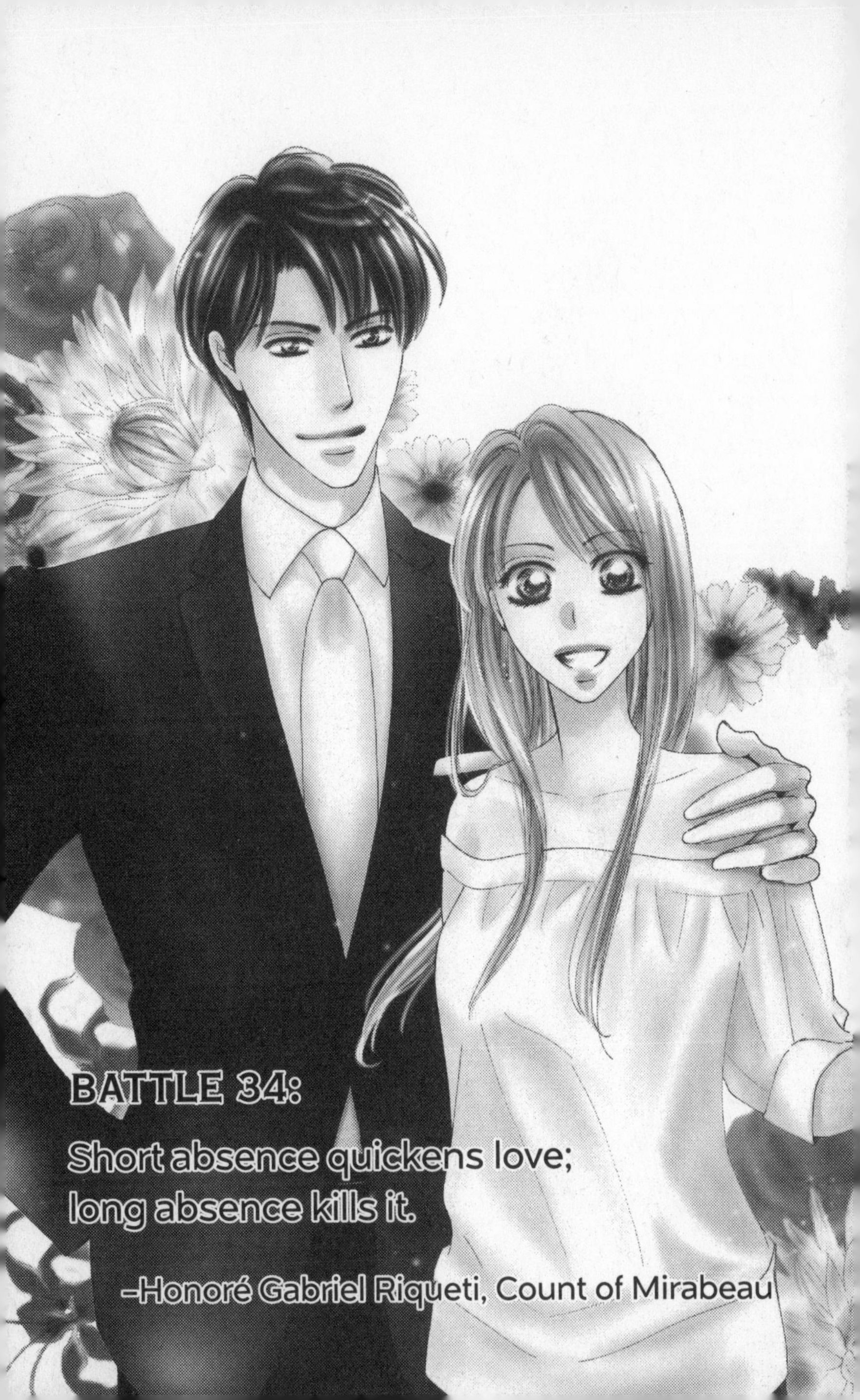
BATTLE 34:
Short absence quickens love;
long absence kills it.
–Honoré Gabriel Riqueti, Count of Mirabeau

Everyone's
Getting
Married

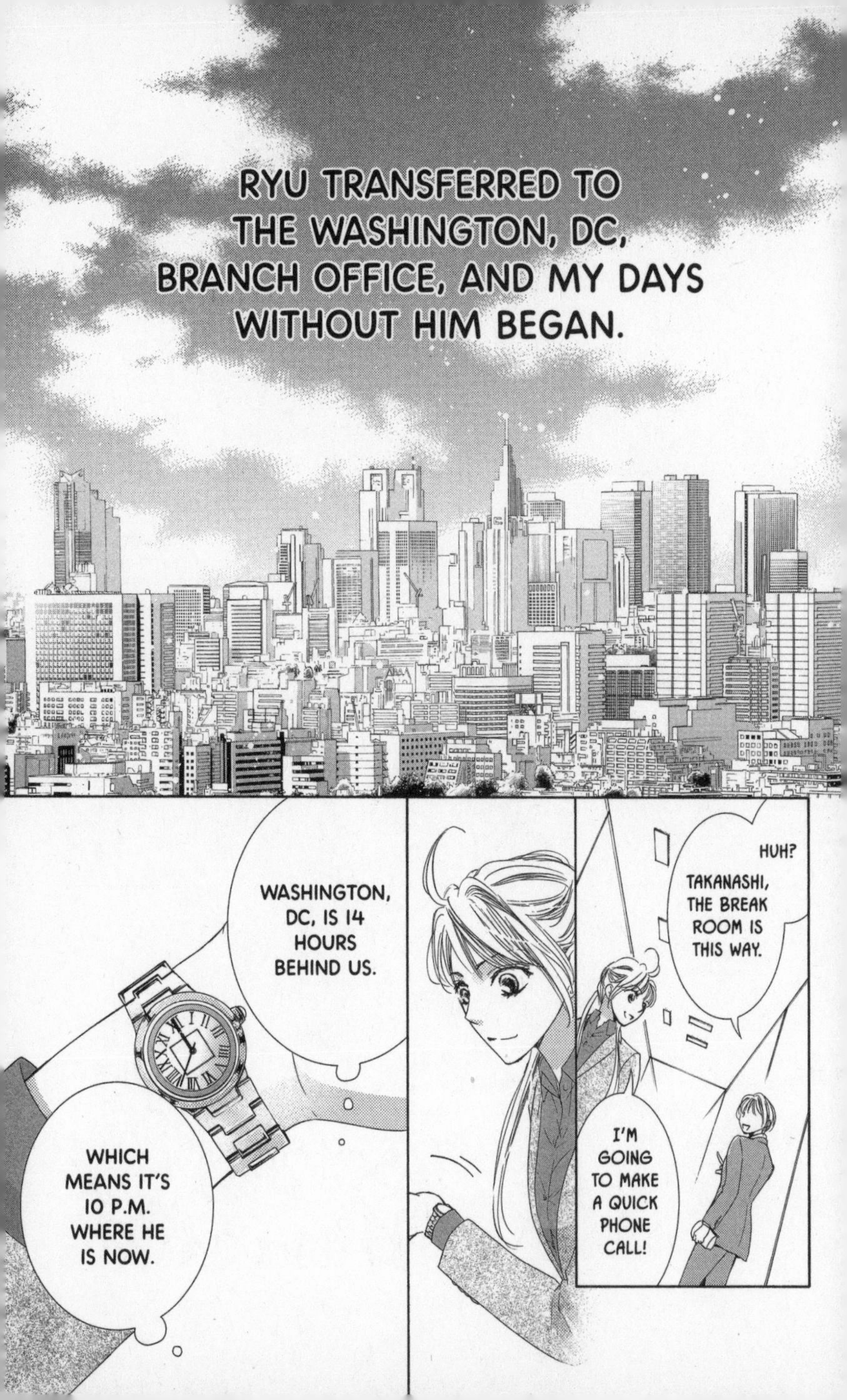
RYU TRANSFERRED TO THE WASHINGTON, DC, BRANCH OFFICE, AND MY DAYS WITHOUT HIM BEGAN.
HUH?
TAKANASHI, THE BREAK ROOM IS THIS WAY.
I'M GOING TO MAKE A QUICK PHONE CALL!
WASHINGTON, DC, IS 14 HOURS BEHIND US.
WHICH MEANS IT'S 10 P.M. WHERE HE IS NOW.

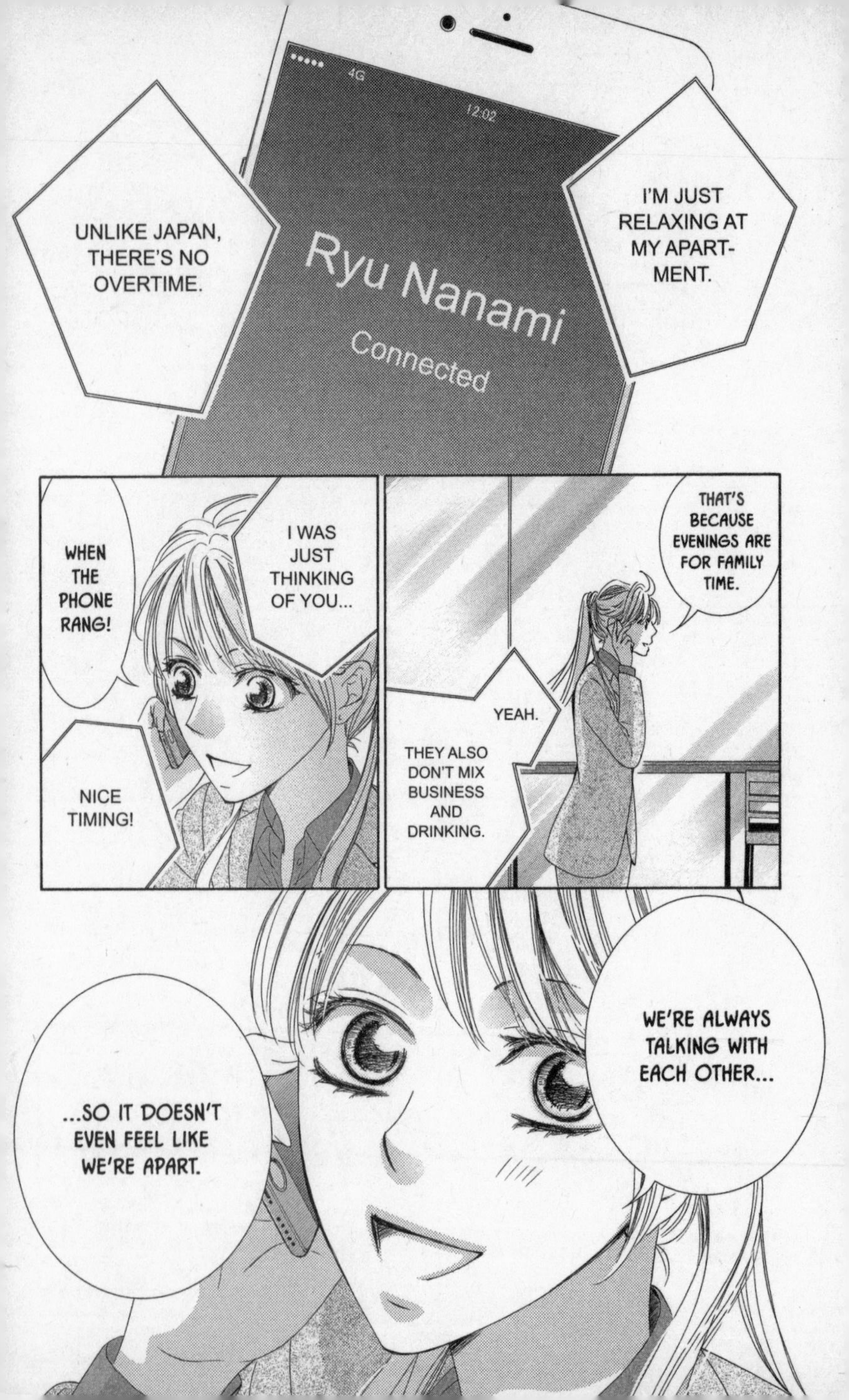
4G
12:02
Ryu Nanami
Connected
I'M JUST RELAXING AT MY APART-MENT.
UNLIKE JAPAN, THERE'S NO OVERTIME.
THAT'S BECAUSE EVENINGS ARE FOR FAMILY TIME.
YEAH.
THEY ALSO DON'T MIX BUSINESS AND DRINKING.
I WAS JUST THINKING OF YOU...
WHEN THE PHONE RANG!
NICE TIMING!
WE'RE ALWAYS TALKING WITH EACH OTHER...
...SO IT DOESN'T EVEN FEEL LIKE WE'RE APART.

FOR THE FIRST WEEK THAT RYU WAS ABROAD...

...MY EVERYDAY LIFE DIDN'T CHANGE.

...

EVEN IF YOUR WEEKDAY NIGHTS ARE FREE...

...YOU STILL DO WORK ON YOUR DAYS OFF, RIGHT?

YEAH. THIS WEEK I'M GOING GOLFING WITH THE EMBASSY CORRESPONDENTS.

AND NEXT WEEK THERE'S A SYMPOSIUM.

GOOD LUCK WITH ALL THAT WORK!

I HAD TO DO STUFF LIKE THIS BACK AT THE NEW YORK OFFICE TOO, SO...

...IT FEELS A LITTLE FAMILIAR.

EVEN THOUGH OUR DAY-TO-DAY LIFE HASN'T CHANGED...

...NOT GETTING TO SEE HIM IN PERSON IS HARD.

IT'S KILLING ME THAT I CAN'T HOLD YOU.

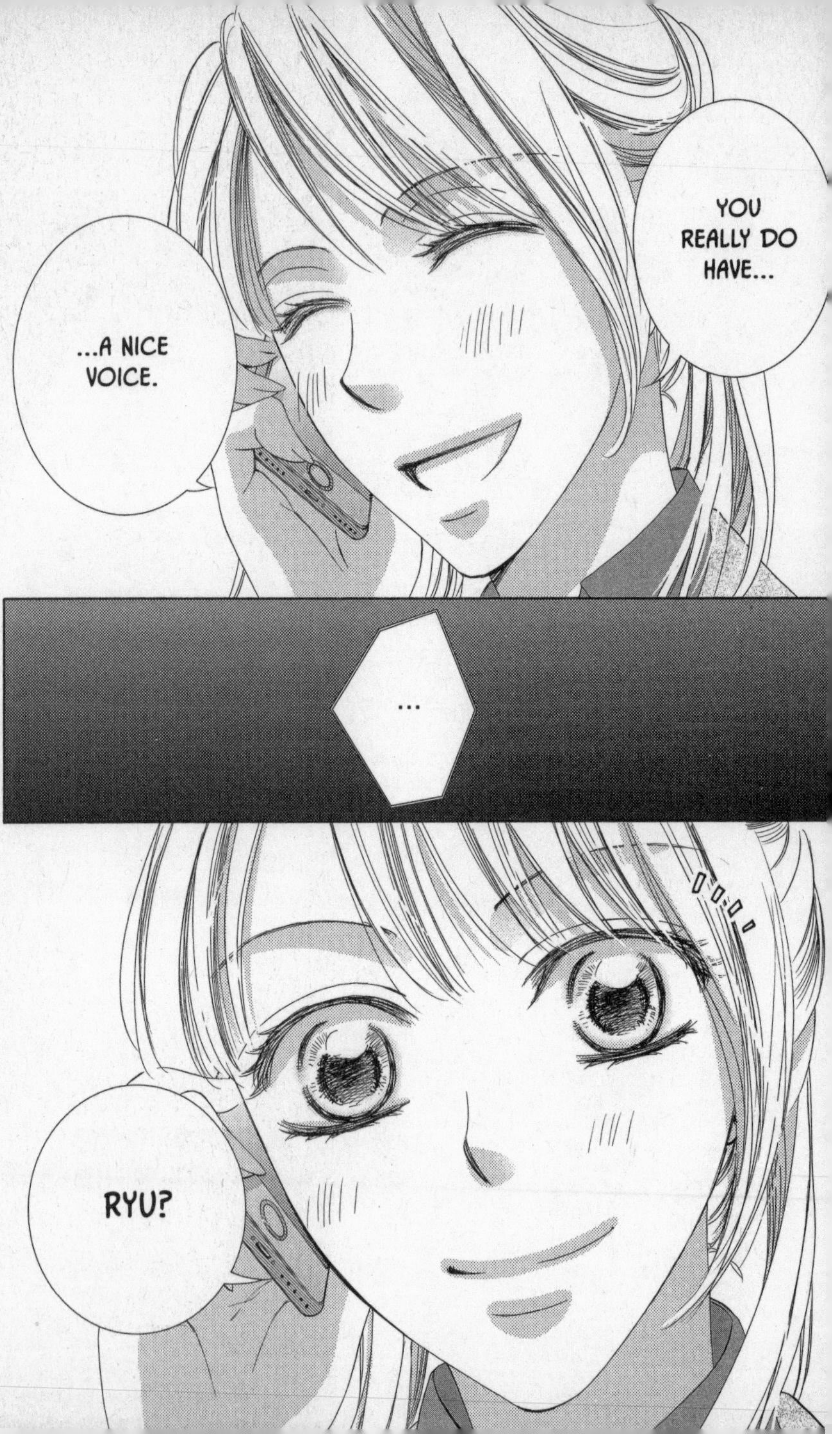
YOU REALLY DO HAVE...
...A NICE VOICE.
...
RYU?

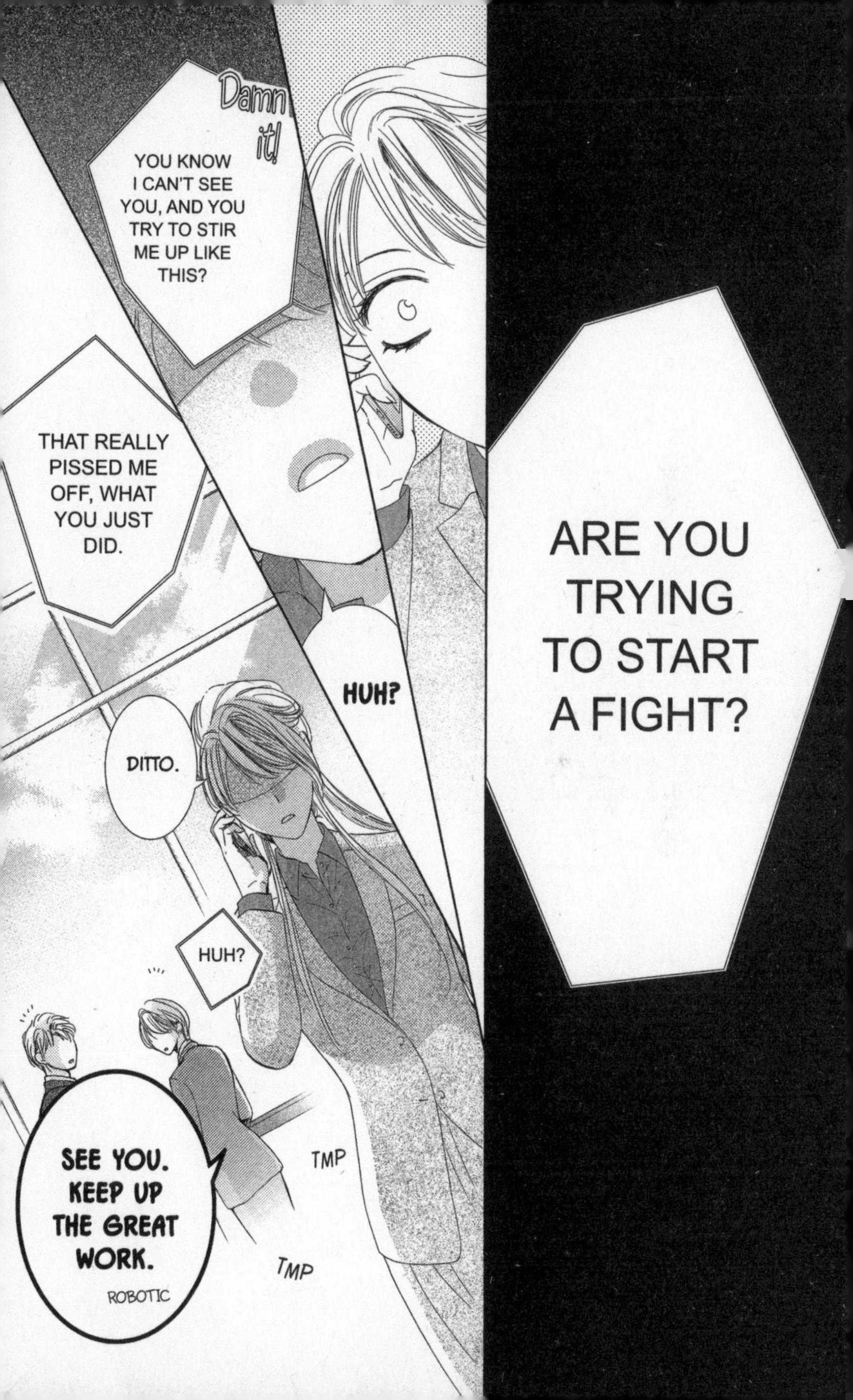
ARE YOU TRYING TO START A FIGHT?
Damn it!
YOU KNOW I CAN'T SEE YOU, AND YOU TRY TO STIR ME UP LIKE THIS?
THAT REALLY PISSED ME OFF, WHAT YOU JUST DID.
HUH?
DITTO.
HUH?
TMP
SEE YOU. KEEP UP THE GREAT WORK.
ROBOTIC
TMP

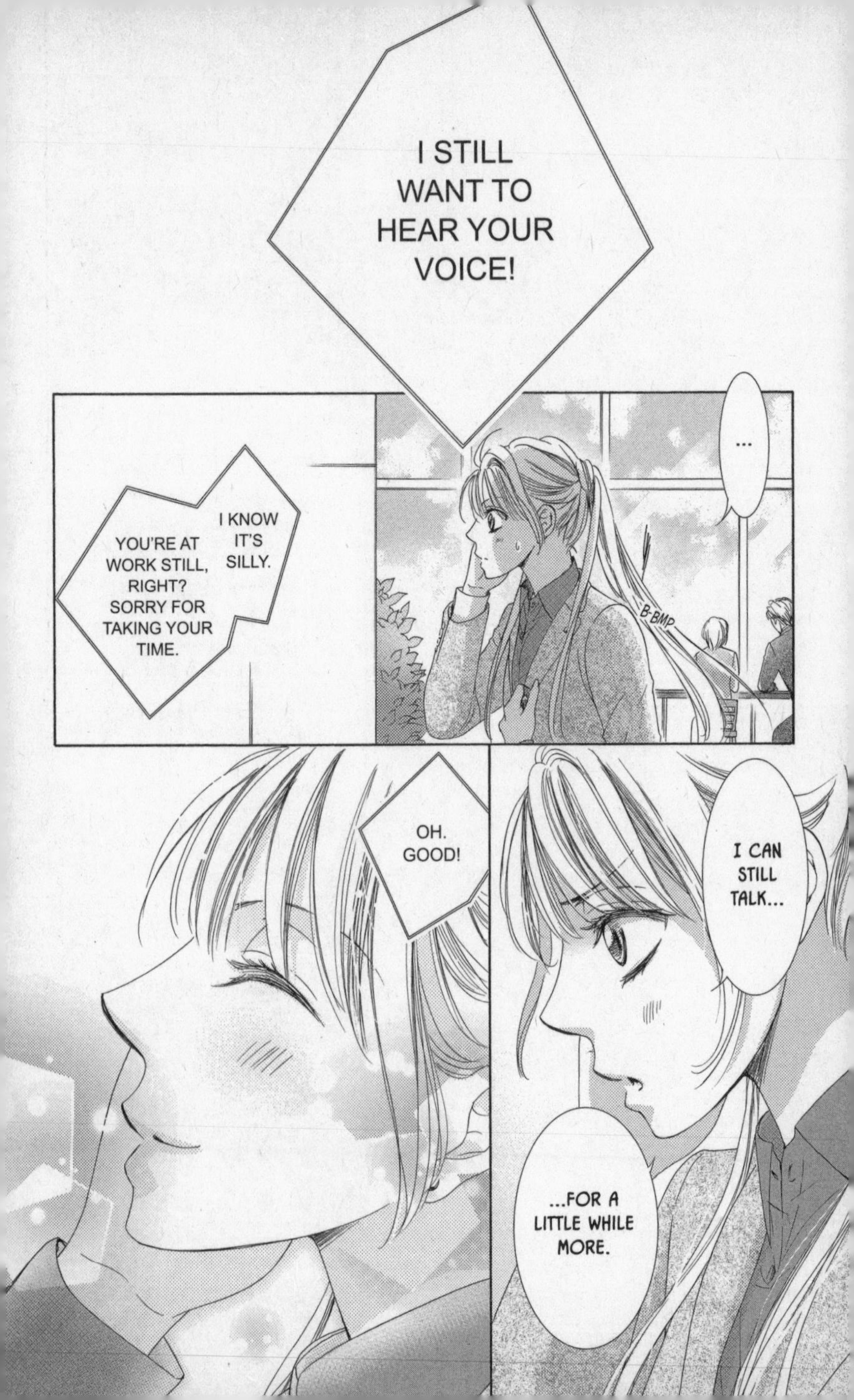
I STILL WANT TO HEAR YOUR VOICE!
...
B-BMP
I KNOW IT'S SILLY.
YOU'RE AT WORK STILL, RIGHT? SORRY FOR TAKING YOUR TIME.
I CAN STILL TALK...
...FOR A LITTLE WHILE MORE.
OH. GOOD!

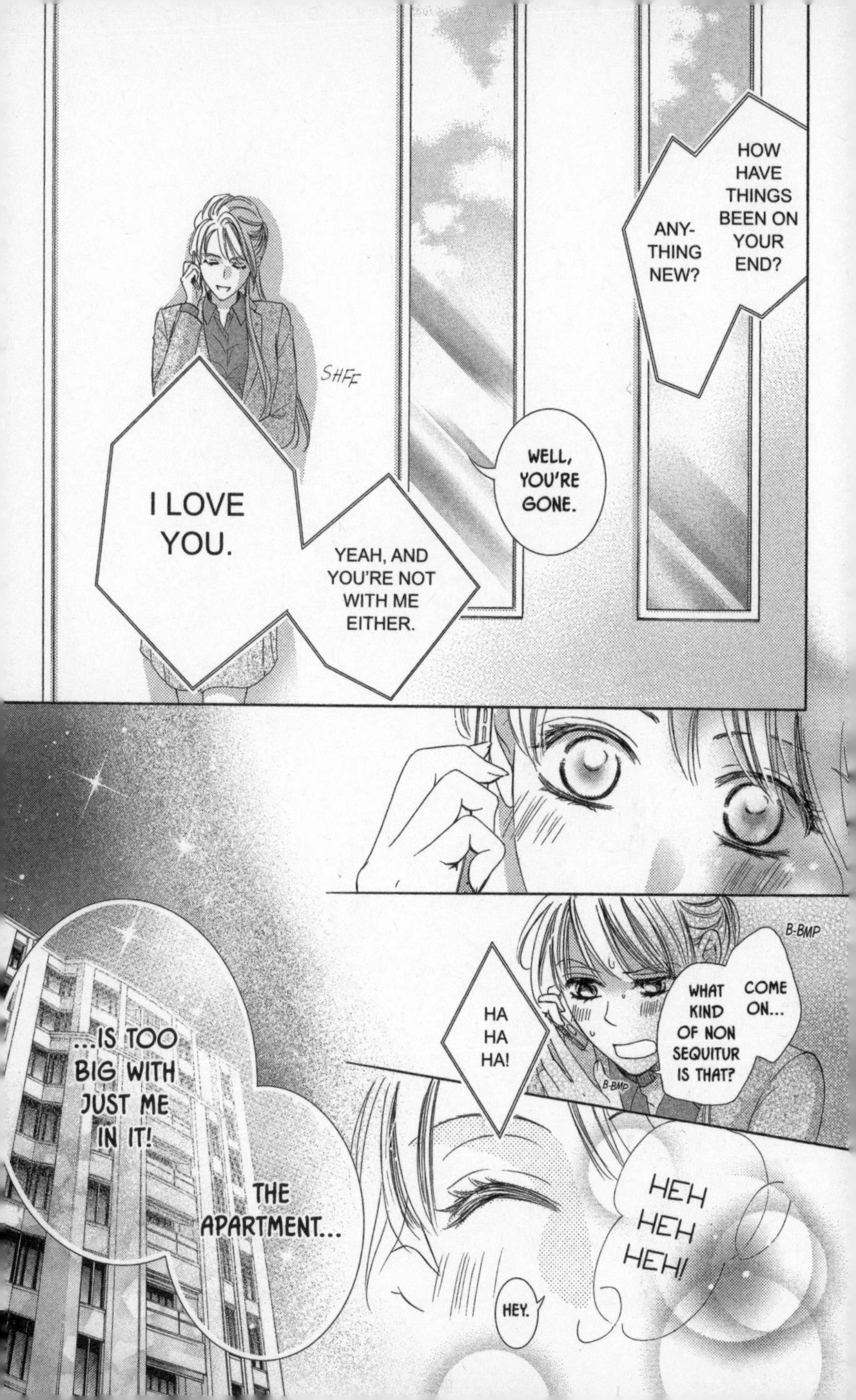
HOW HAVE THINGS BEEN ON YOUR END?
ANY-THING NEW?
SHFF
WELL, YOU'RE GONE.
YEAH, AND YOU'RE NOT WITH ME EITHER.
I LOVE YOU.
B-BMP
COME ON...
WHAT KIND OF NON SEQUITUR IS THAT?
B-BMP
HA HA HA!
HEH HEH HEH!
HEY.
THE APARTMENT...
...IS TOO BIG WITH JUST ME IN IT!

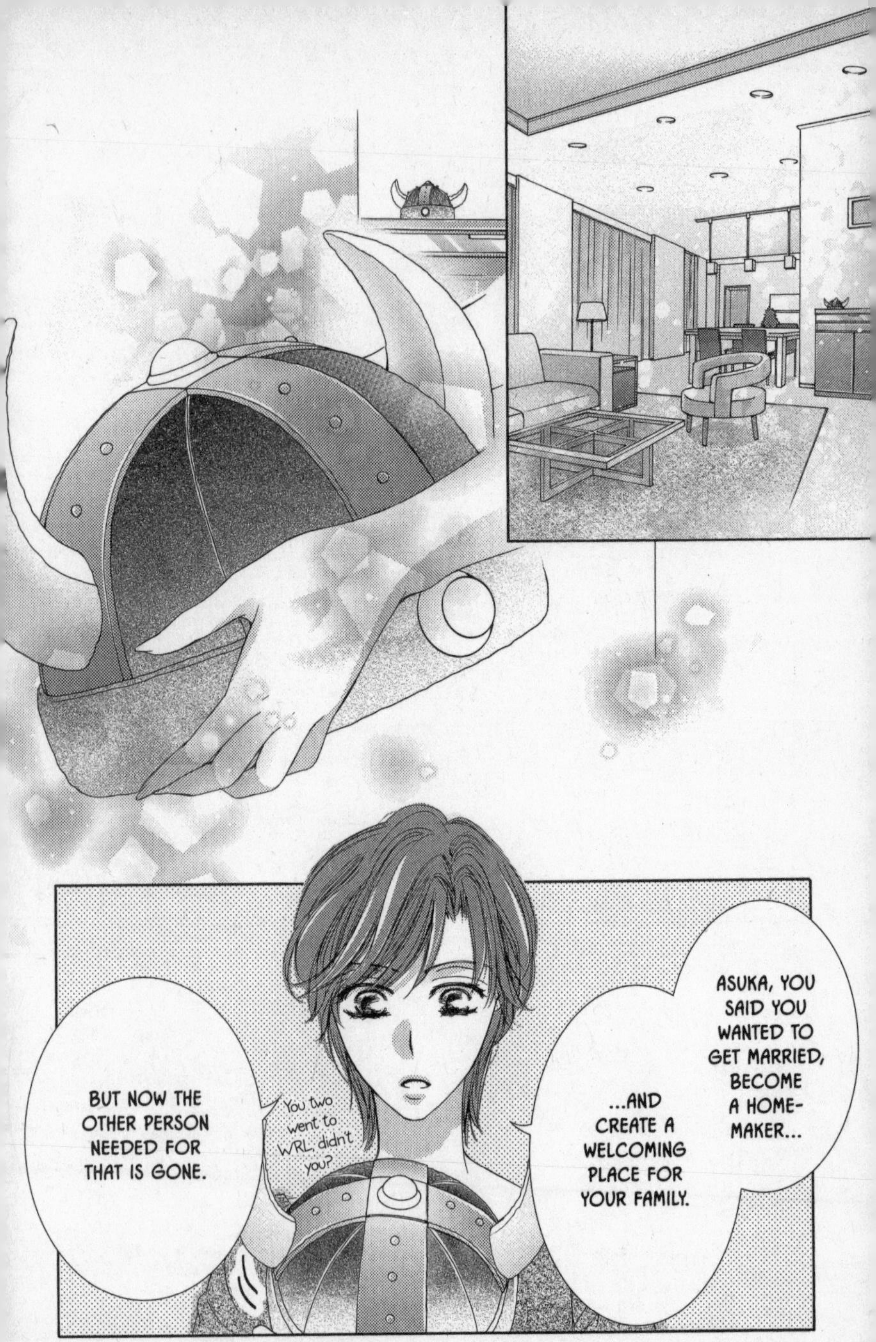
ASUKA, YOU SAID YOU WANTED TO GET MARRIED, BECOME A HOME-MAKER...
...AND CREATE A WELCOMING PLACE FOR YOUR FAMILY.
You two went to WRL, didn't you?
BUT NOW THE OTHER PERSON NEEDED FOR THAT IS GONE.

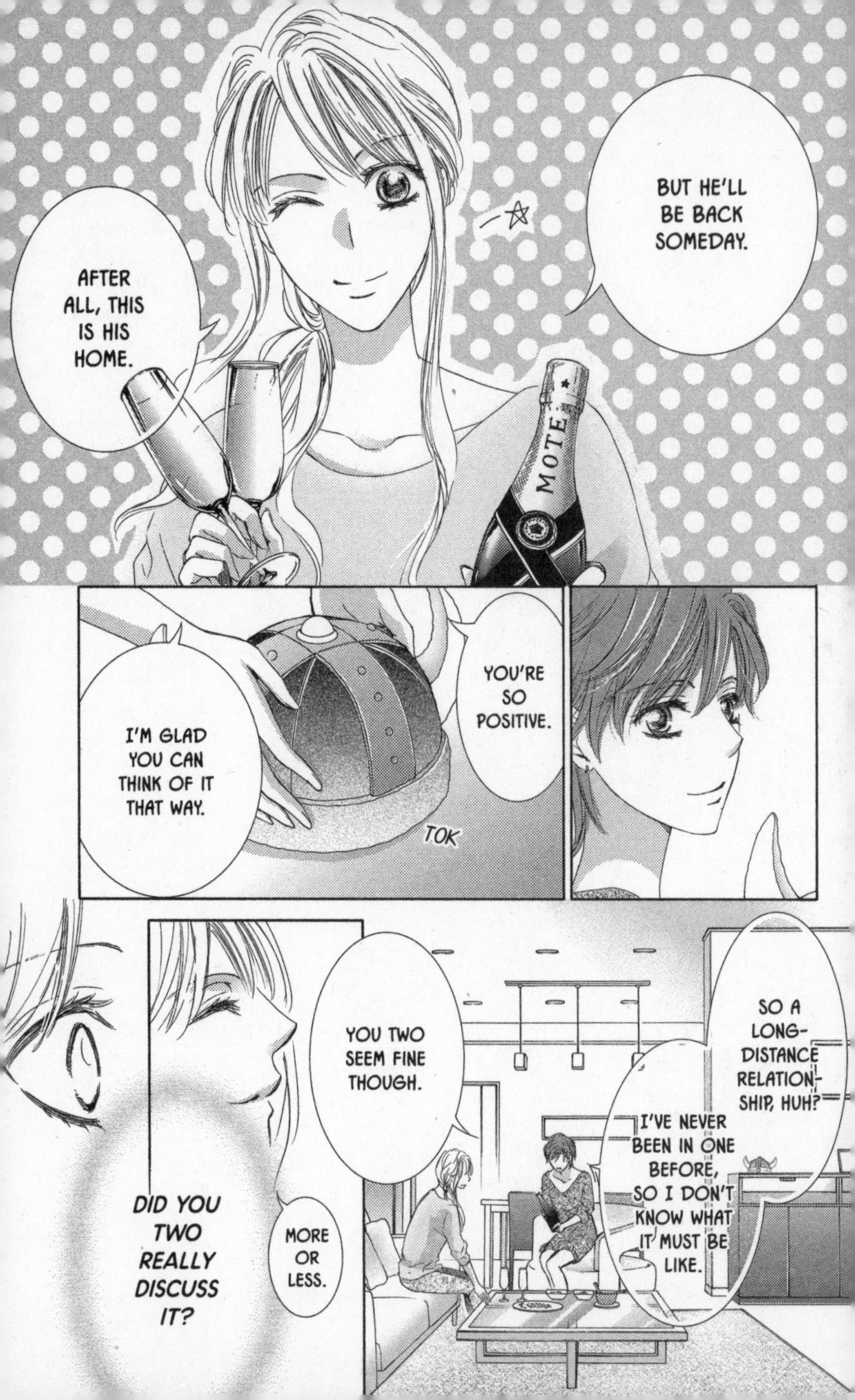
BUT HE'LL BE BACK SOMEDAY.
AFTER ALL, THIS IS HIS HOME.
YOU'RE SO POSITIVE.
I'M GLAD YOU CAN THINK OF IT THAT WAY.
TOK
SO A LONG-DISTANCE RELATIONSHIP, HUH?
I'VE NEVER BEEN IN ONE BEFORE, SO I DON'T KNOW WHAT IT MUST BE LIKE.
YOU TWO SEEM FINE THOUGH.
MORE OR LESS.
DID YOU TWO REALLY DISCUSS IT?

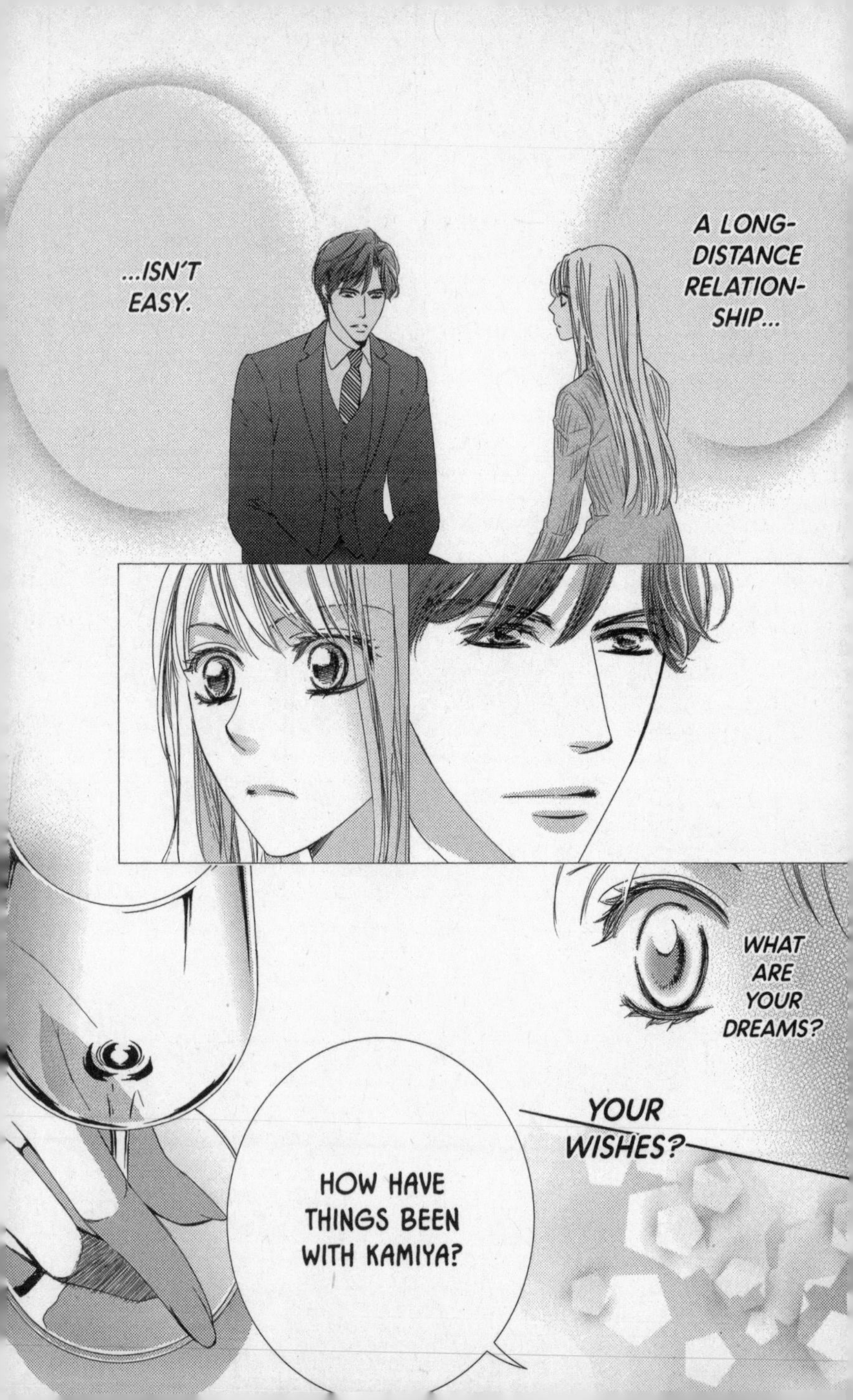
A LONG-DISTANCE RELATIONSHIP...
...ISN'T EASY.
WHAT ARE YOUR DREAMS?
YOUR WISHES?
HOW HAVE THINGS BEEN WITH KAMIYA?

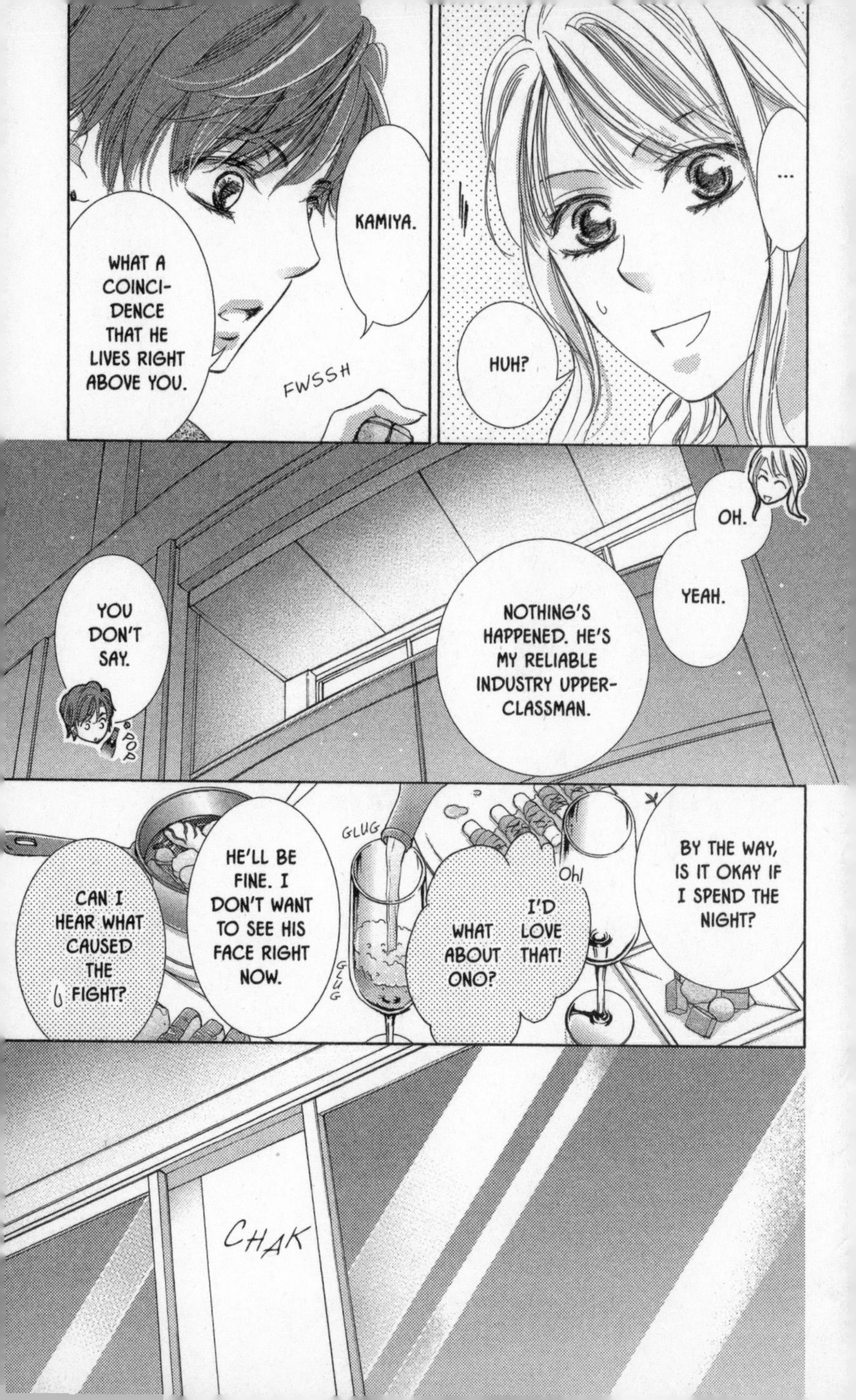
...
HUH?
KAMIYA.
WHAT A COINCIDENCE THAT HE LIVES RIGHT ABOVE YOU.
FWSSH
OH.
YEAH.
NOTHING'S HAPPENED. HE'S MY RELIABLE INDUSTRY UPPERCLASSMAN.
YOU DON'T SAY.
POP
BY THE WAY, IS IT OKAY IF I SPEND THE NIGHT?
Oh!
I'D LOVE THAT!
WHAT ABOUT ONO?
GLUG
HE'LL BE FINE. I DON'T WANT TO SEE HIS FACE RIGHT NOW.
GLUG
CAN I HEAR WHAT CAUSED THE FIGHT?
CHAK

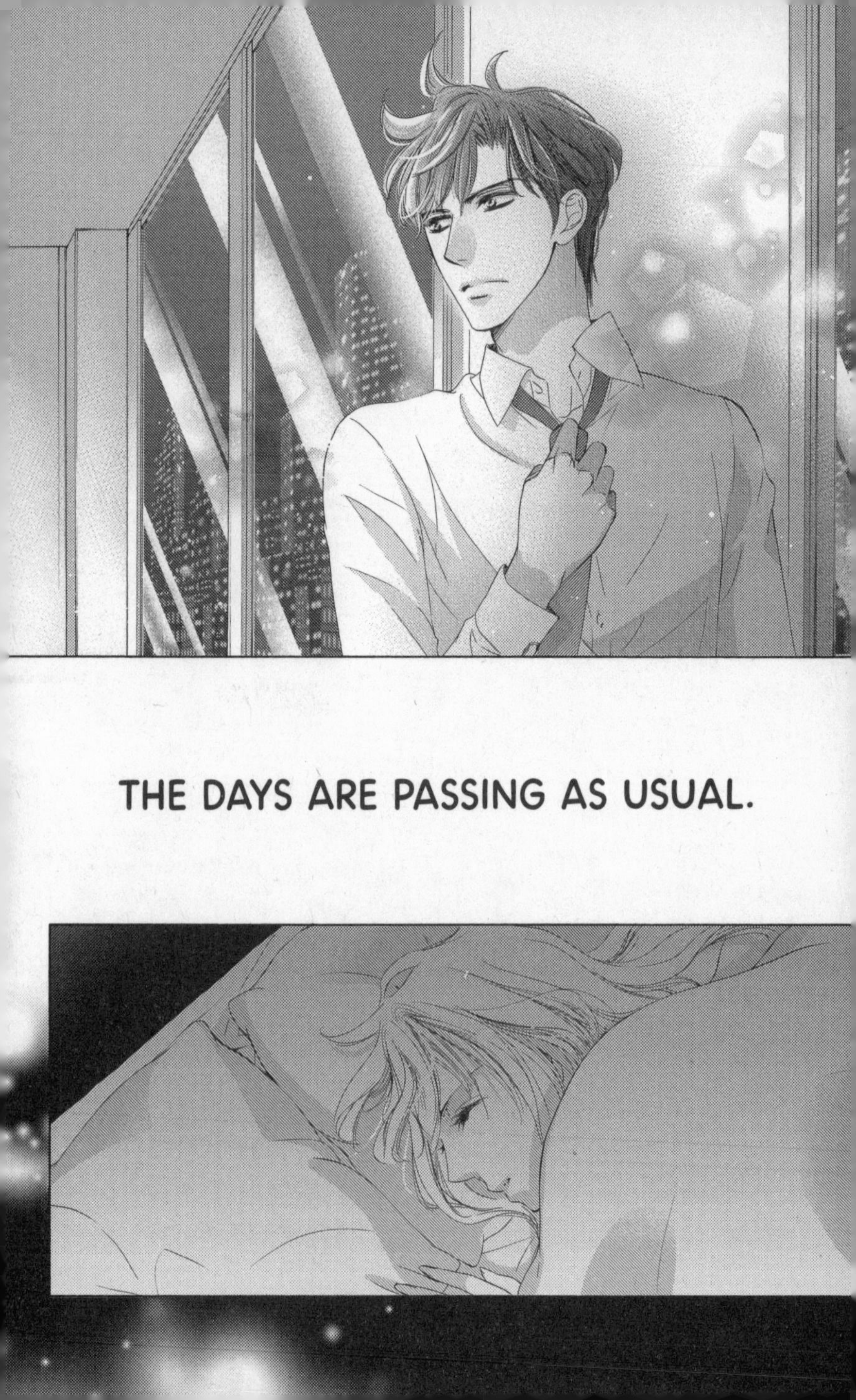
THE DAYS ARE PASSING AS USUAL.

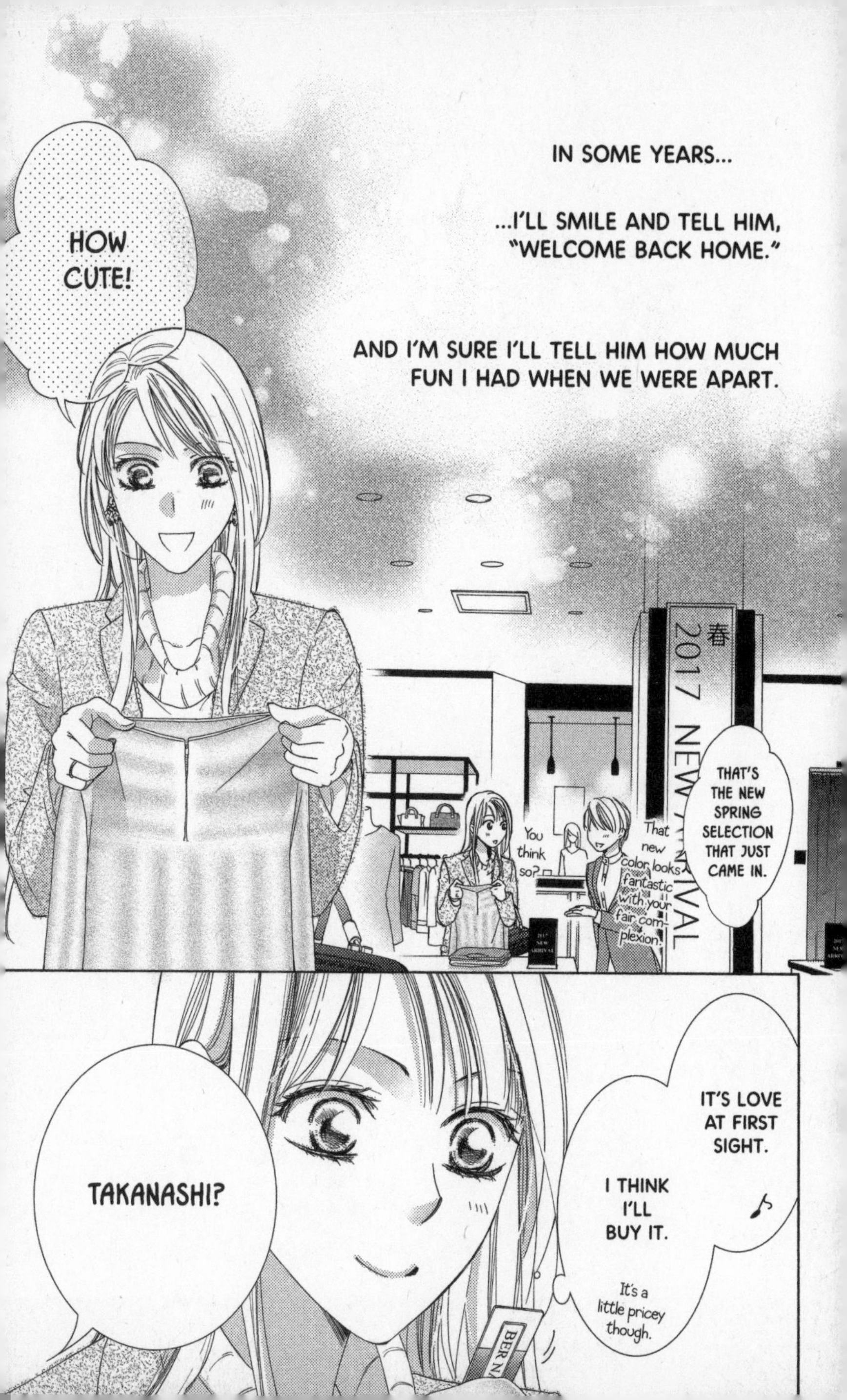
IN SOME YEARS...
...I'LL SMILE AND TELL HIM, "WELCOME BACK HOME."
AND I'M SURE I'LL TELL HIM HOW MUCH FUN I HAD WHEN WE WERE APART.
HOW CUTE!
THAT'S THE NEW SPRING SELECTION THAT JUST CAME IN.
That new color looks fantastic with your fair complexion!
You think so?
IT'S LOVE AT FIRST SIGHT.
I THINK I'LL BUY IT.
It's a little pricey though.
TAKANASHI?

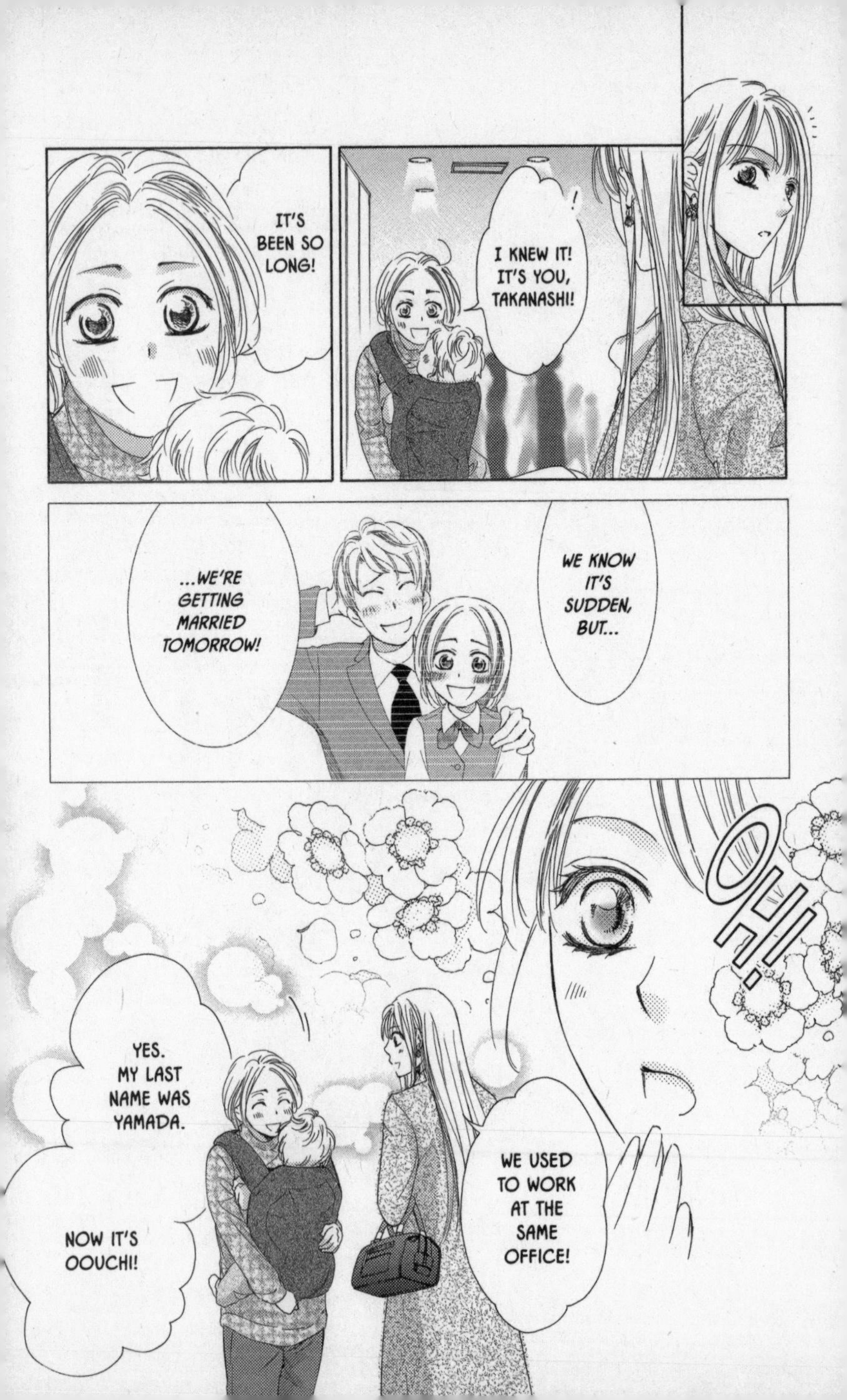
!
I KNEW IT! IT'S YOU, TAKANASHI!
IT'S BEEN SO LONG!
WE KNOW IT'S SUDDEN, BUT...
...WE'RE GETTING MARRIED TOMORROW!
OH!!
WE USED TO WORK AT THE SAME OFFICE!
YES. MY LAST NAME WAS YAMADA.
NOW IT'S OOUCHI!

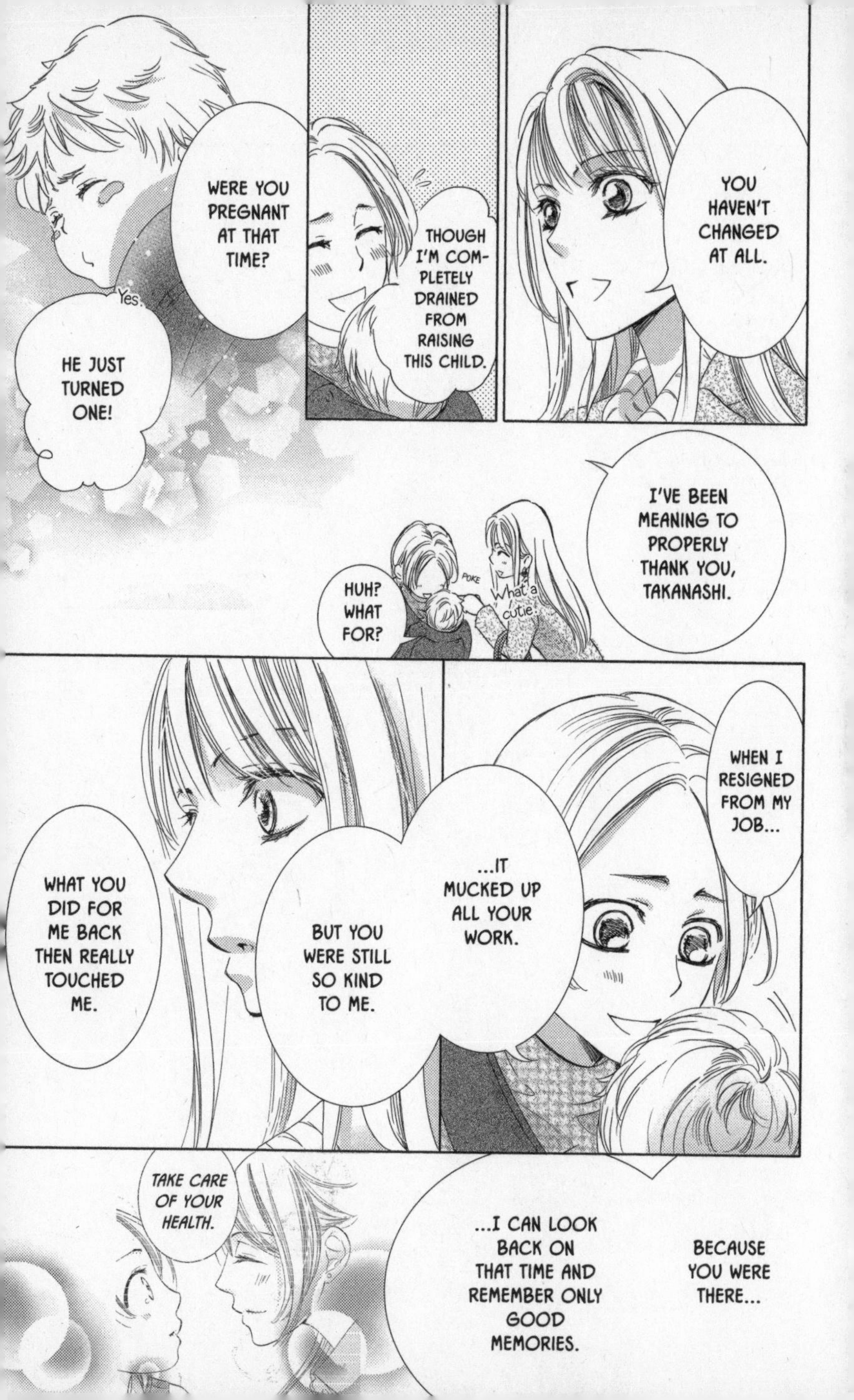
YOU HAVEN'T CHANGED AT ALL.
THOUGH I'M COM-PLETELY DRAINED FROM RAISING THIS CHILD.
WERE YOU PREGNANT AT THAT TIME?
Yes.
HE JUST TURNED ONE!
I'VE BEEN MEANING TO PROPERLY THANK YOU, TAKANASHI.
What a cutie
POKE
HUH? WHAT FOR?
WHEN I RESIGNED FROM MY JOB...
...IT MUCKED UP ALL YOUR WORK.
BUT YOU WERE STILL SO KIND TO ME.
WHAT YOU DID FOR ME BACK THEN REALLY TOUCHED ME.
BECAUSE YOU WERE THERE...
...I CAN LOOK BACK ON THAT TIME AND REMEMBER ONLY GOOD MEMORIES.
TAKE CARE OF YOUR HEALTH.

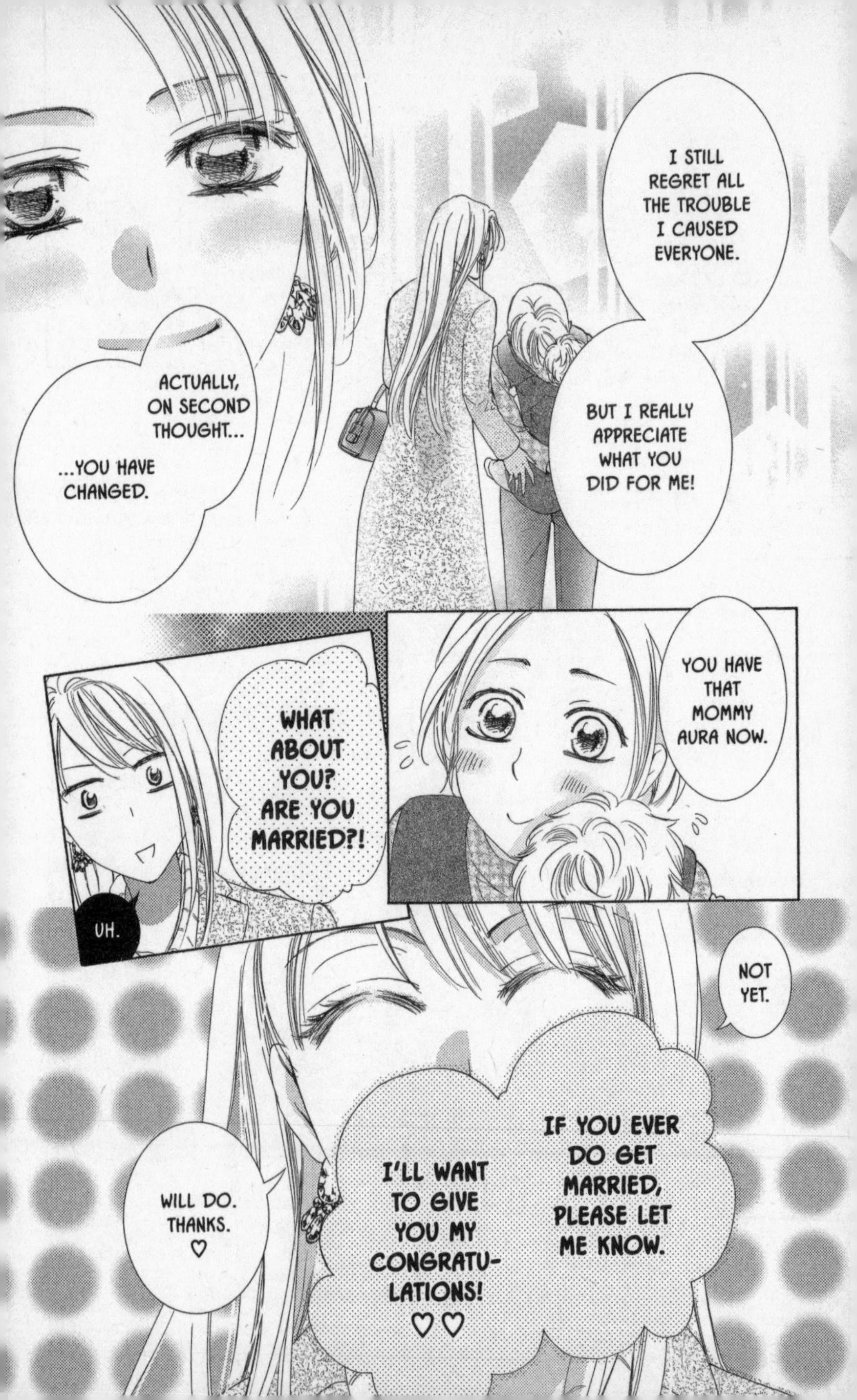
I STILL REGRET ALL THE TROUBLE I CAUSED EVERYONE.
BUT I REALLY APPRECIATE WHAT YOU DID FOR ME!
ACTUALLY, ON SECOND THOUGHT...
...YOU HAVE CHANGED.
YOU HAVE THAT MOMMY AURA NOW.
WHAT ABOUT YOU? ARE YOU MARRIED?!
UH.
NOT YET.
IF YOU EVER DO GET MARRIED, PLEASE LET ME KNOW.
I'LL WANT TO GIVE YOU MY CONGRATU-LATIONS! ♡♡
WILL DO. THANKS. ♡

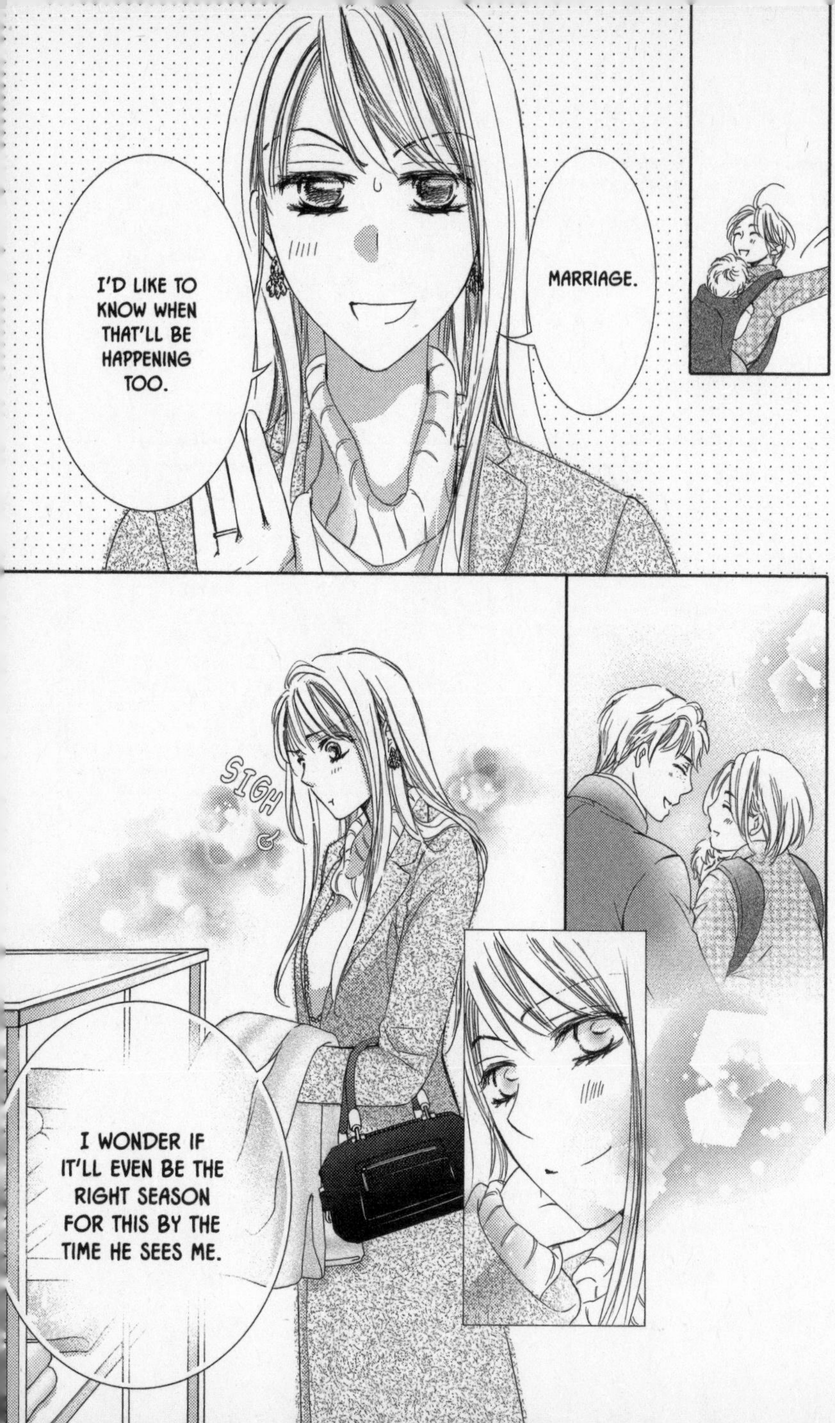
MARRIAGE.
I'D LIKE TO KNOW WHEN THAT'LL BE HAPPENING TOO.
SIGH
I WONDER IF IT'LL EVEN BE THE RIGHT SEASON FOR THIS BY THE TIME HE SEES ME.

I WONDER WHEN I'LL GET TO SEE HIM AGAIN.

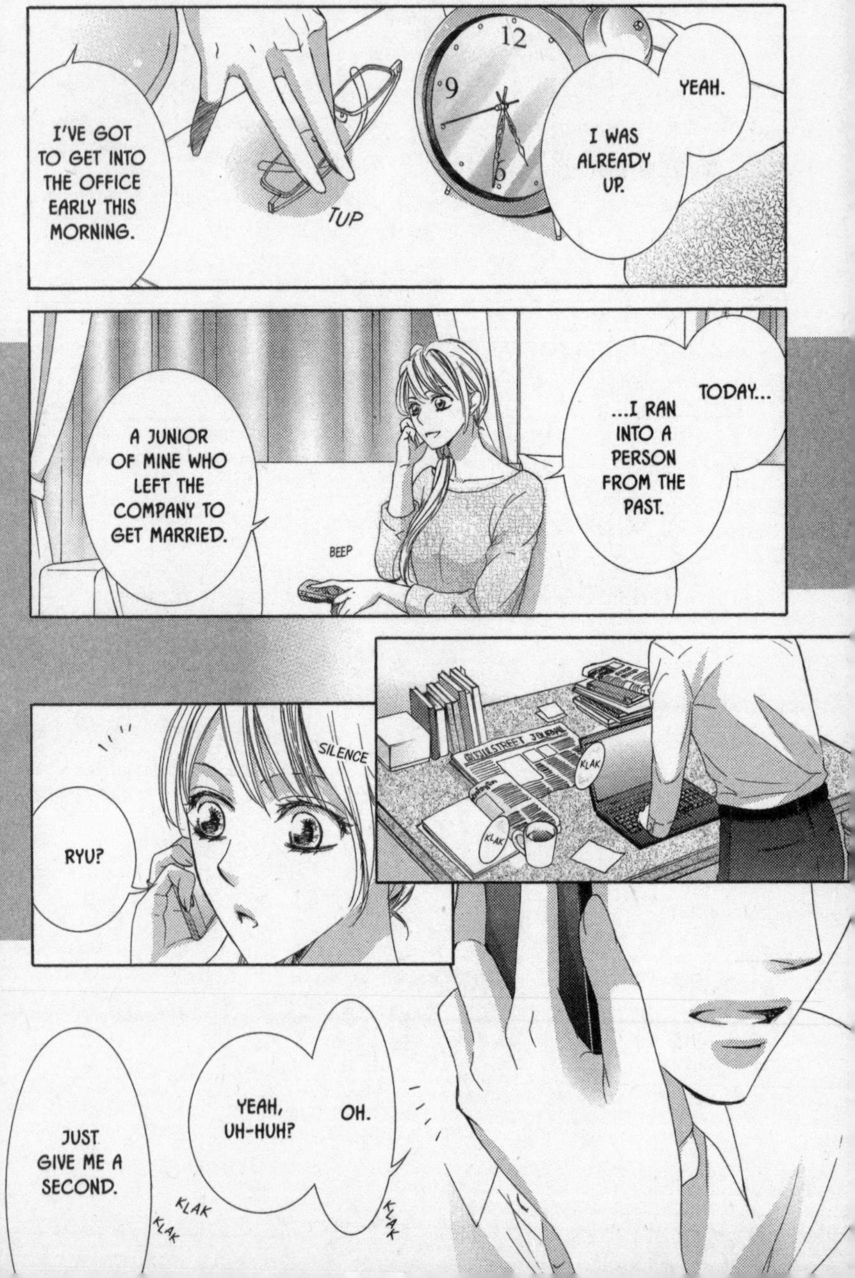
YEAH.
I WAS ALREADY UP.
I'VE GOT TO GET INTO THE OFFICE EARLY THIS MORNING.
TUP
TODAY...
...I RAN INTO A PERSON FROM THE PAST.
BEEP
A JUNIOR OF MINE WHO LEFT THE COMPANY TO GET MARRIED.
KLAK
KLAK
SILENCE
RYU?
OH.
YEAH, UH-HUH?
KLAK
JUST GIVE ME A SECOND.
KLAK
KLAK

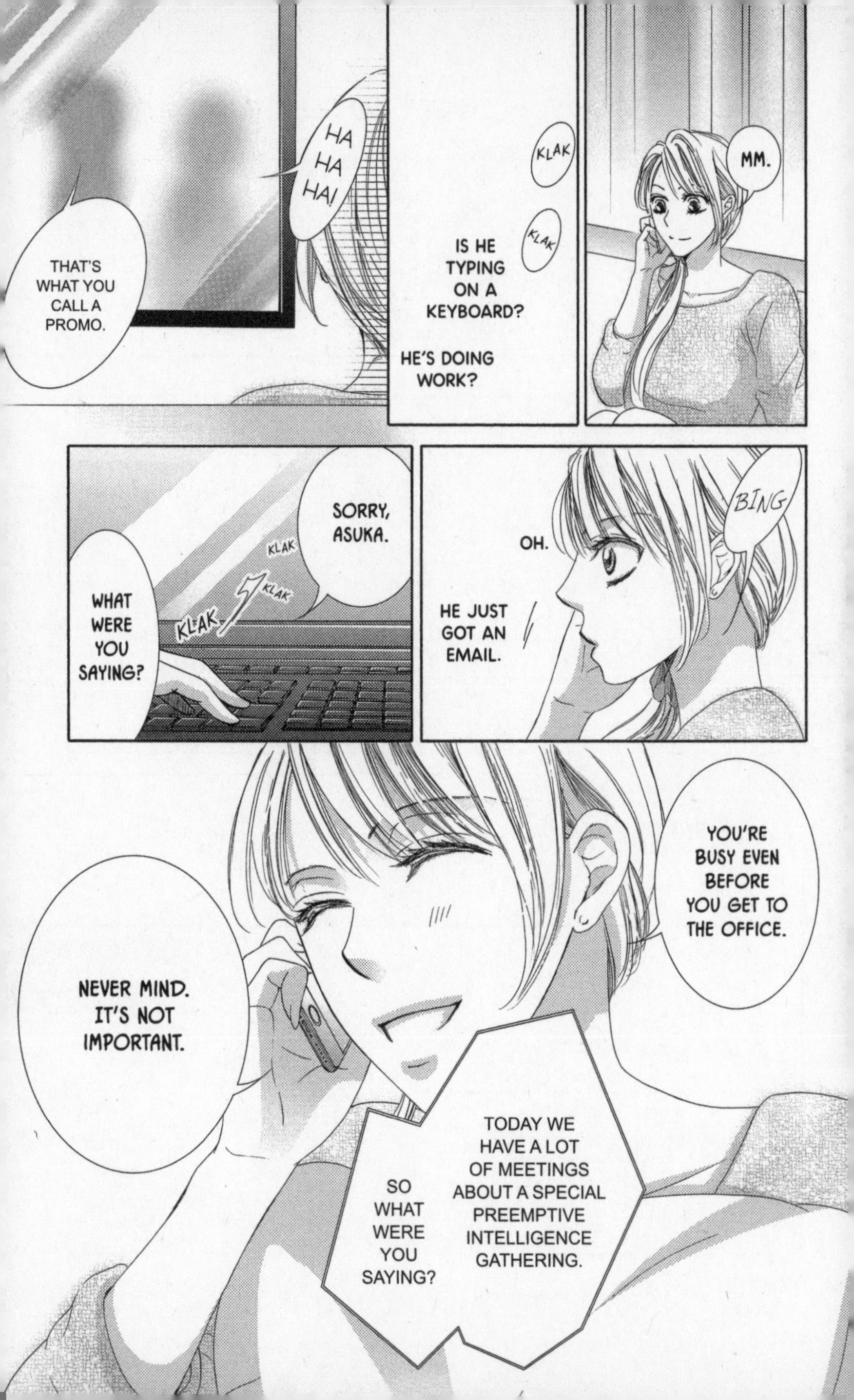
MM.
KLAK
KLAK
IS HE TYPING ON A KEYBOARD?
HE'S DOING WORK?
HA HA HA!
THAT'S WHAT YOU CALL A PROMO.
BING
OH.
HE JUST GOT AN EMAIL.
SORRY, ASUKA.
KLAK
KLAK
KLAK
WHAT WERE YOU SAYING?
YOU'RE BUSY EVEN BEFORE YOU GET TO THE OFFICE.
NEVER MIND. IT'S NOT IMPORTANT.
TODAY WE HAVE A LOT OF MEETINGS ABOUT A SPECIAL PREEMPTIVE INTELLIGENCE GATHERING.
SO WHAT WERE YOU SAYING?

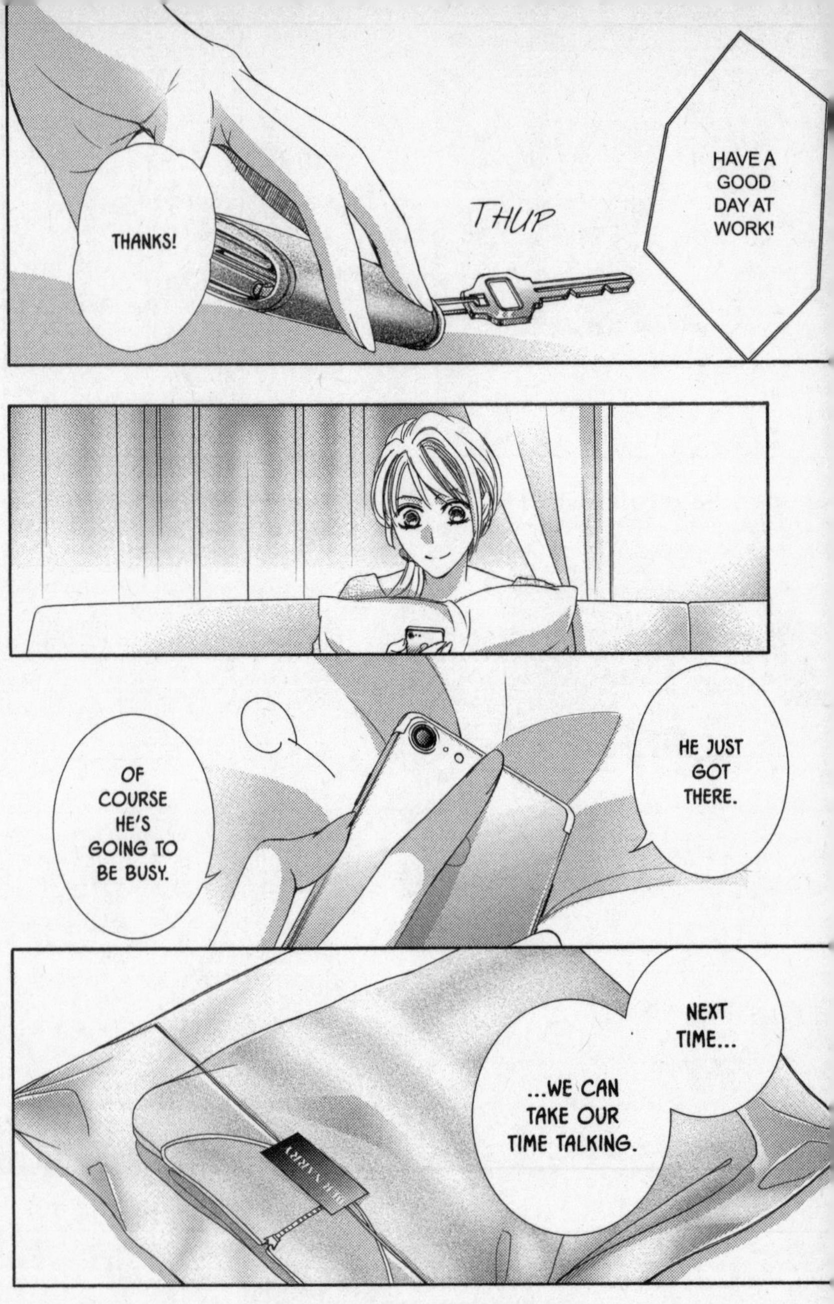
HAVE A GOOD DAY AT WORK!
THUP
THANKS!
HE JUST GOT THERE.
OF COURSE HE'S GOING TO BE BUSY.
NEXT TIME...
...WE CAN TAKE OUR TIME TALKING.

IT'S JUST HOW IT IS.

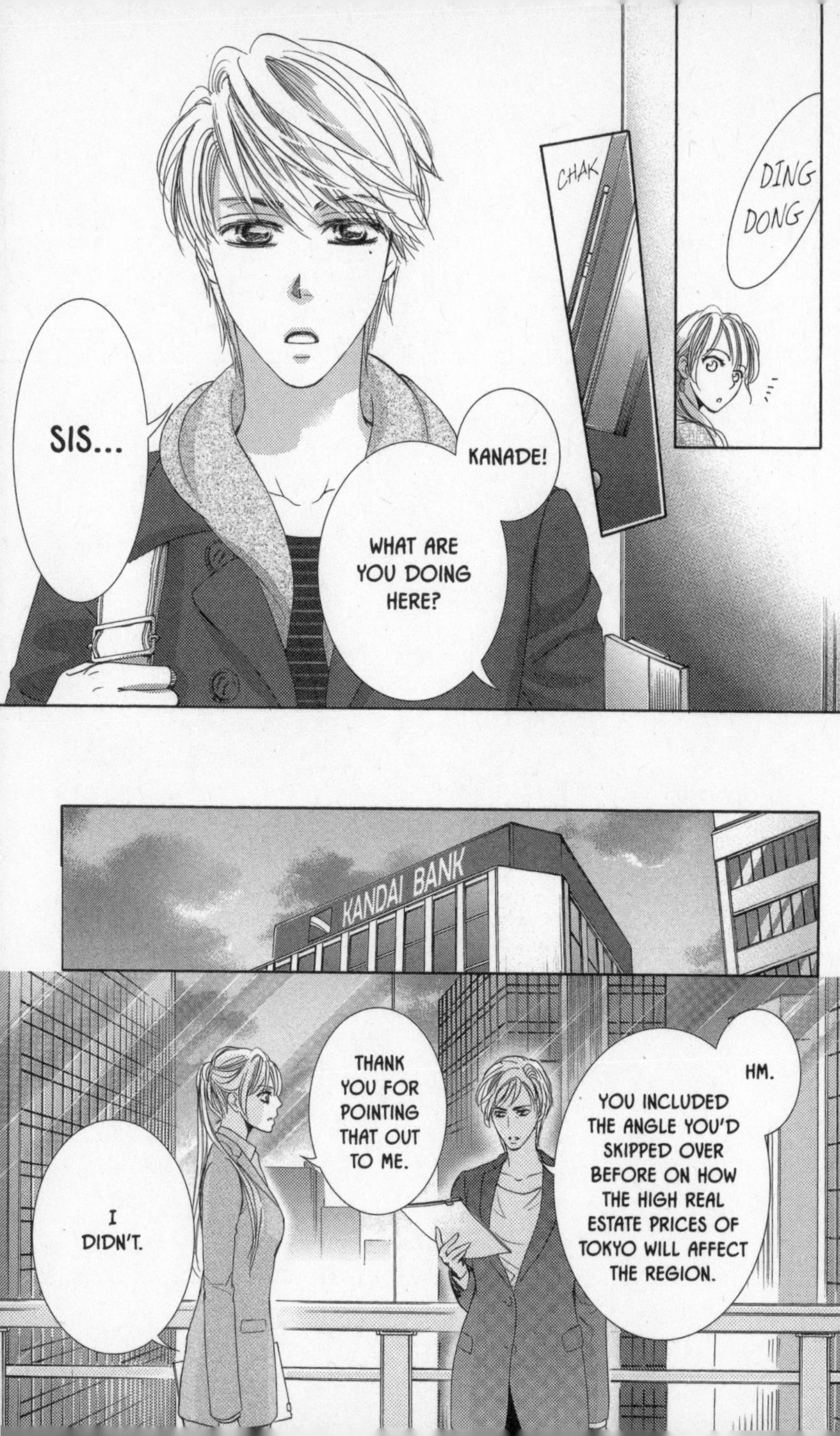
DING DONG
CHAK
KANADE!
WHAT ARE YOU DOING HERE?
SIS...
KANDAI BANK
HM.
YOU INCLUDED THE ANGLE YOU'D SKIPPED OVER BEFORE ON HOW THE HIGH REAL ESTATE PRICES OF TOKYO WILL AFFECT THE REGION.
THANK YOU FOR POINTING THAT OUT TO ME.
I DIDN'T.

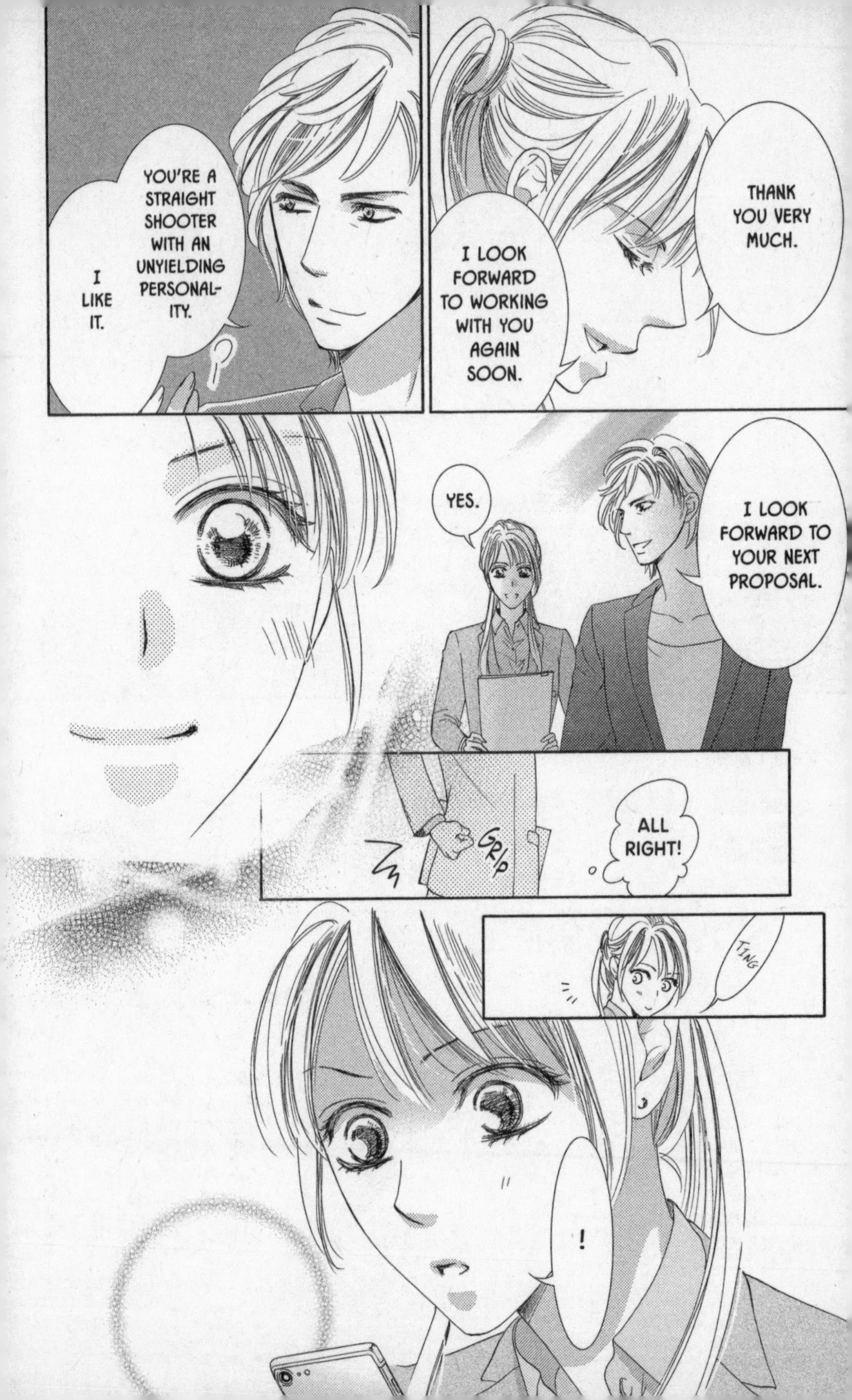
THANK YOU VERY MUCH.
I LOOK FORWARD TO WORKING WITH YOU AGAIN SOON.
YOU'RE A STRAIGHT SHOOTER WITH AN UNYIELDING PERSONAL-ITY.
I LIKE IT.
I LOOK FORWARD TO YOUR NEXT PROPOSAL.
YES.
ALL RIGHT!
GRIP
TING
!

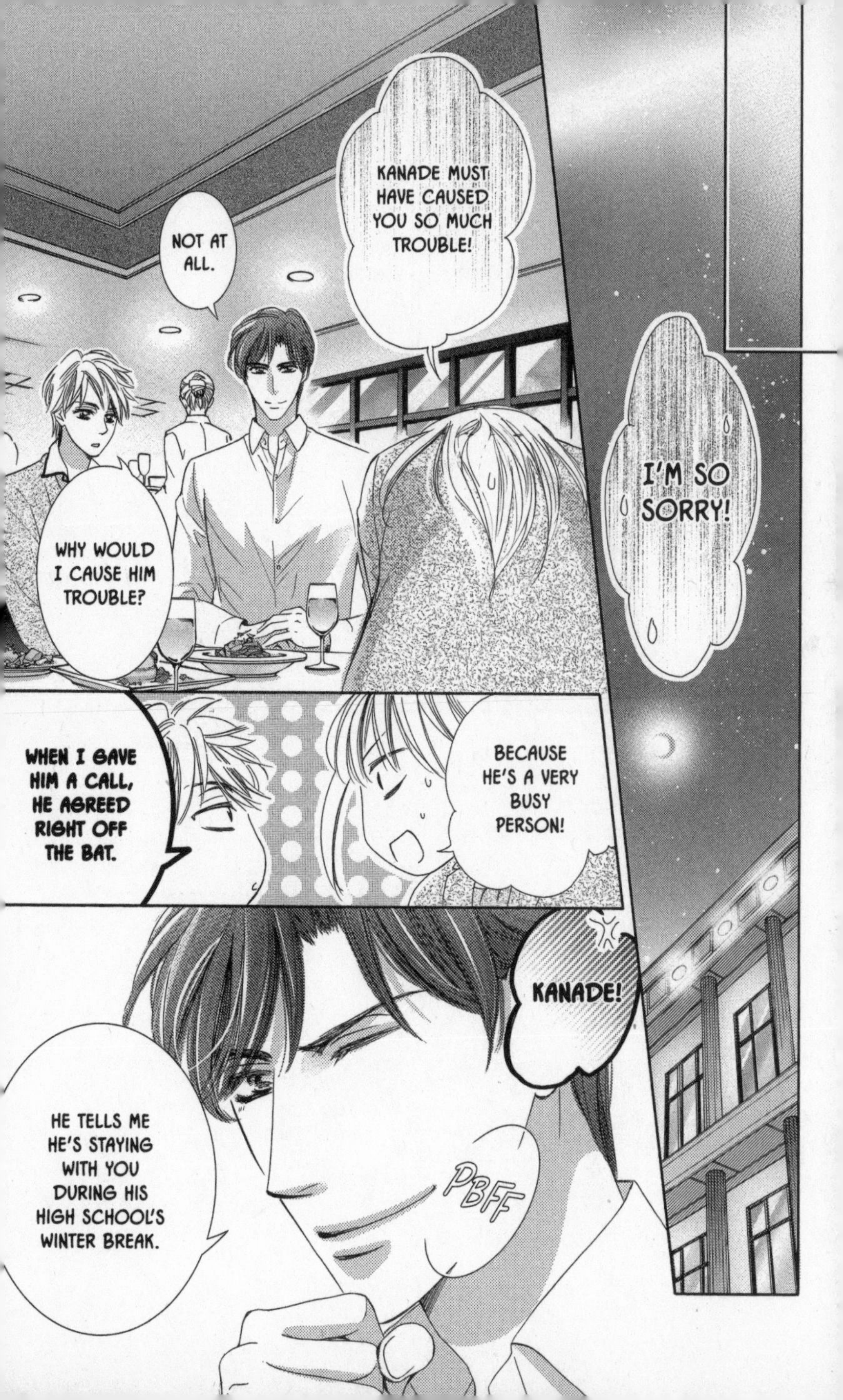
KANADE MUST HAVE CAUSED YOU SO MUCH TROUBLE!
I'M SO SORRY!
NOT AT ALL.
WHY WOULD I CAUSE HIM TROUBLE?
BECAUSE HE'S A VERY BUSY PERSON!
WHEN I GAVE HIM A CALL, HE AGREED RIGHT OFF THE BAT.
KANADE!
HE TELLS ME HE'S STAYING WITH YOU DURING HIS HIGH SCHOOL'S WINTER BREAK.
PBFF

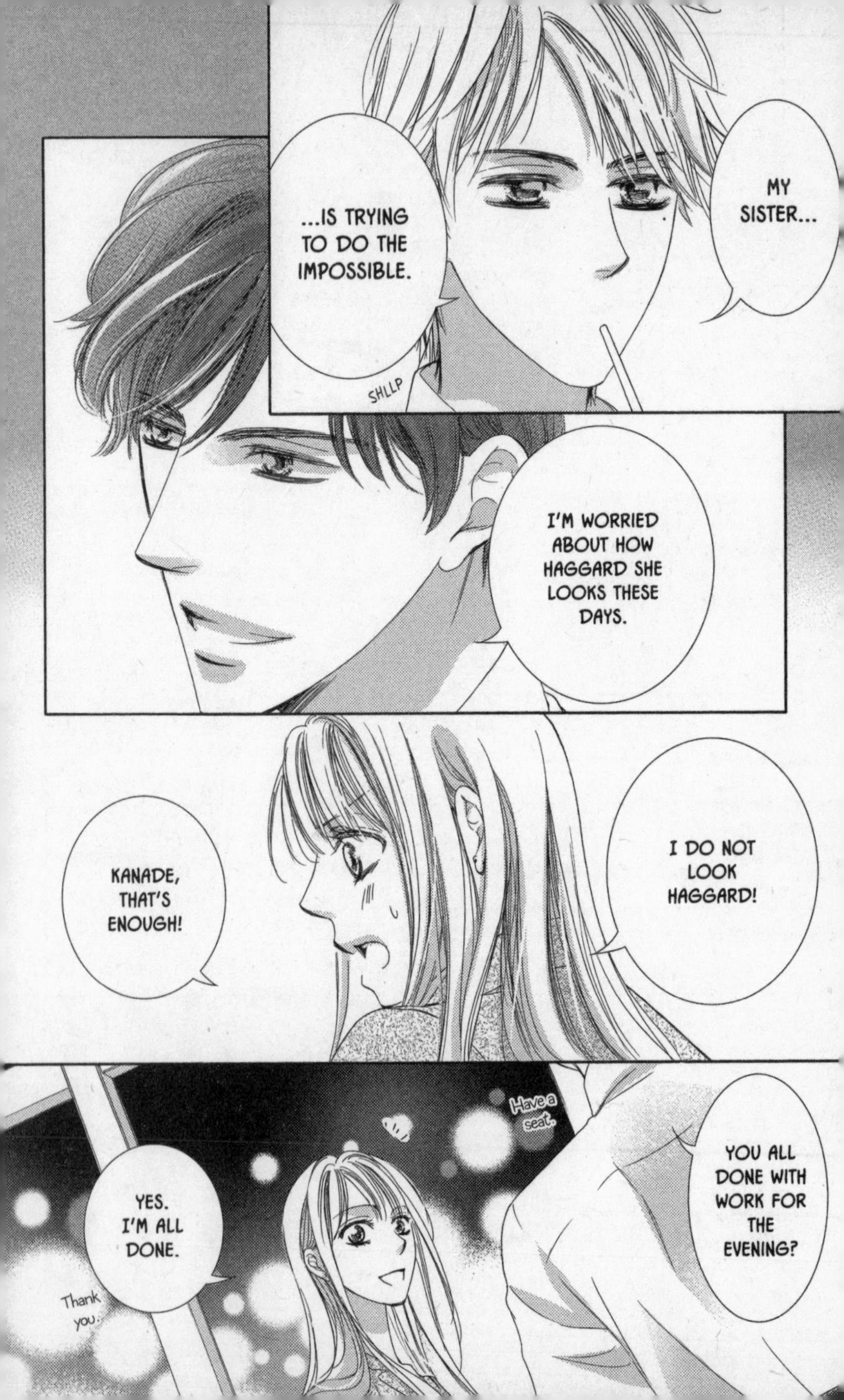
MY SISTER...
...IS TRYING TO DO THE IMPOSSIBLE.
SHLLP
I'M WORRIED ABOUT HOW HAGGARD SHE LOOKS THESE DAYS.
I DO NOT LOOK HAGGARD!
KANADE, THAT'S ENOUGH!
YOU ALL DONE WITH WORK FOR THE EVENING?
Have a seat.
YES. I'M ALL DONE.
Thank you.

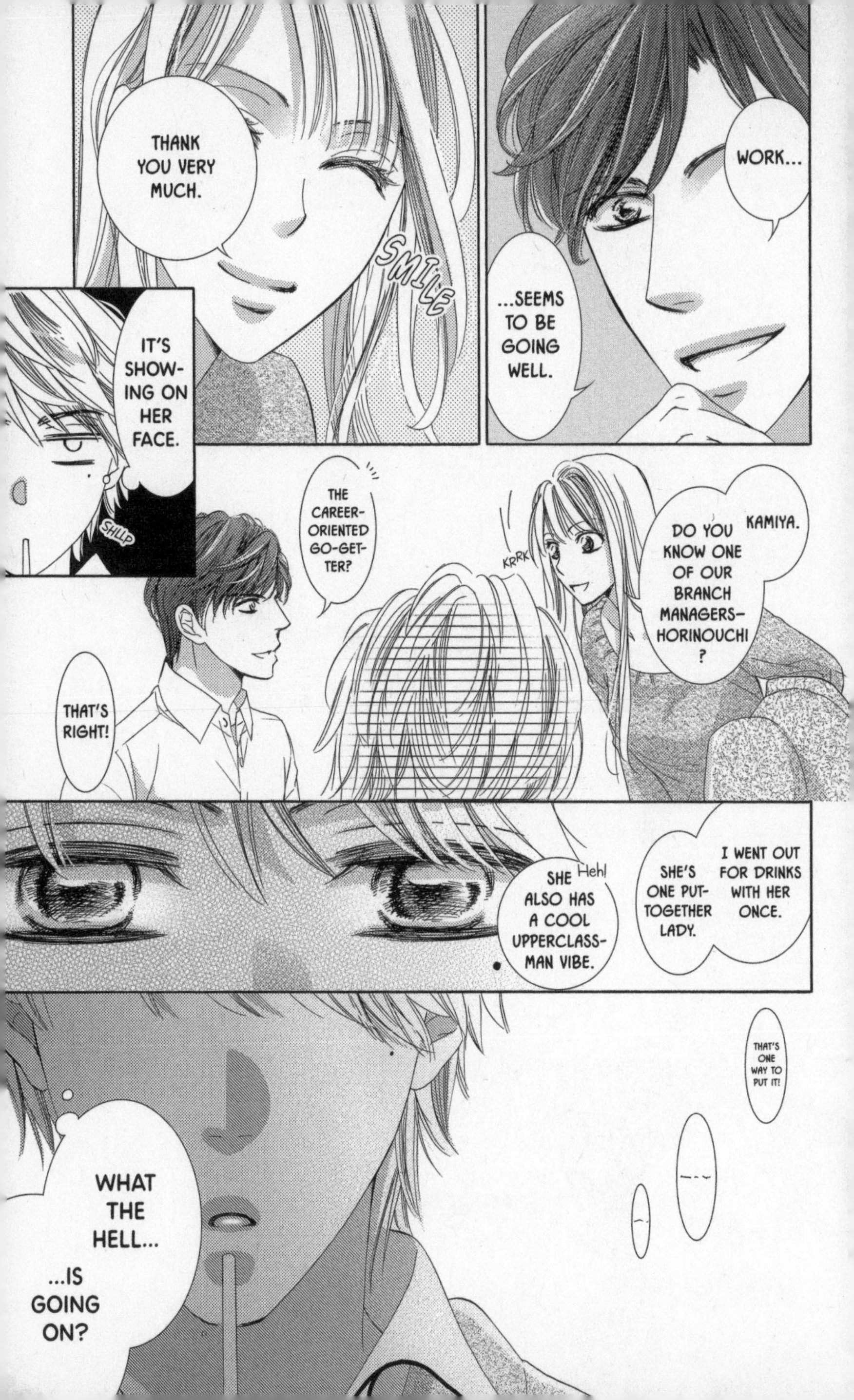
WORK...
...SEEMS TO BE GOING WELL.
THANK YOU VERY MUCH.
SMILE
IT'S SHOWING ON HER FACE.
SHLLP
KAMIYA.
DO YOU KNOW ONE OF OUR BRANCH MANAGERS-HORINOUCHI?
KRRK
THE CAREER-ORIENTED GO-GETTER?
THAT'S RIGHT!
I WENT OUT FOR DRINKS WITH HER ONCE.
SHE'S ONE PUT-TOGETHER LADY.
SHE ALSO HAS A COOL UPPERCLASSMAN VIBE.
Heh!
THAT'S ONE WAY TO PUT IT!
WHAT THE HELL...
...IS GOING ON?

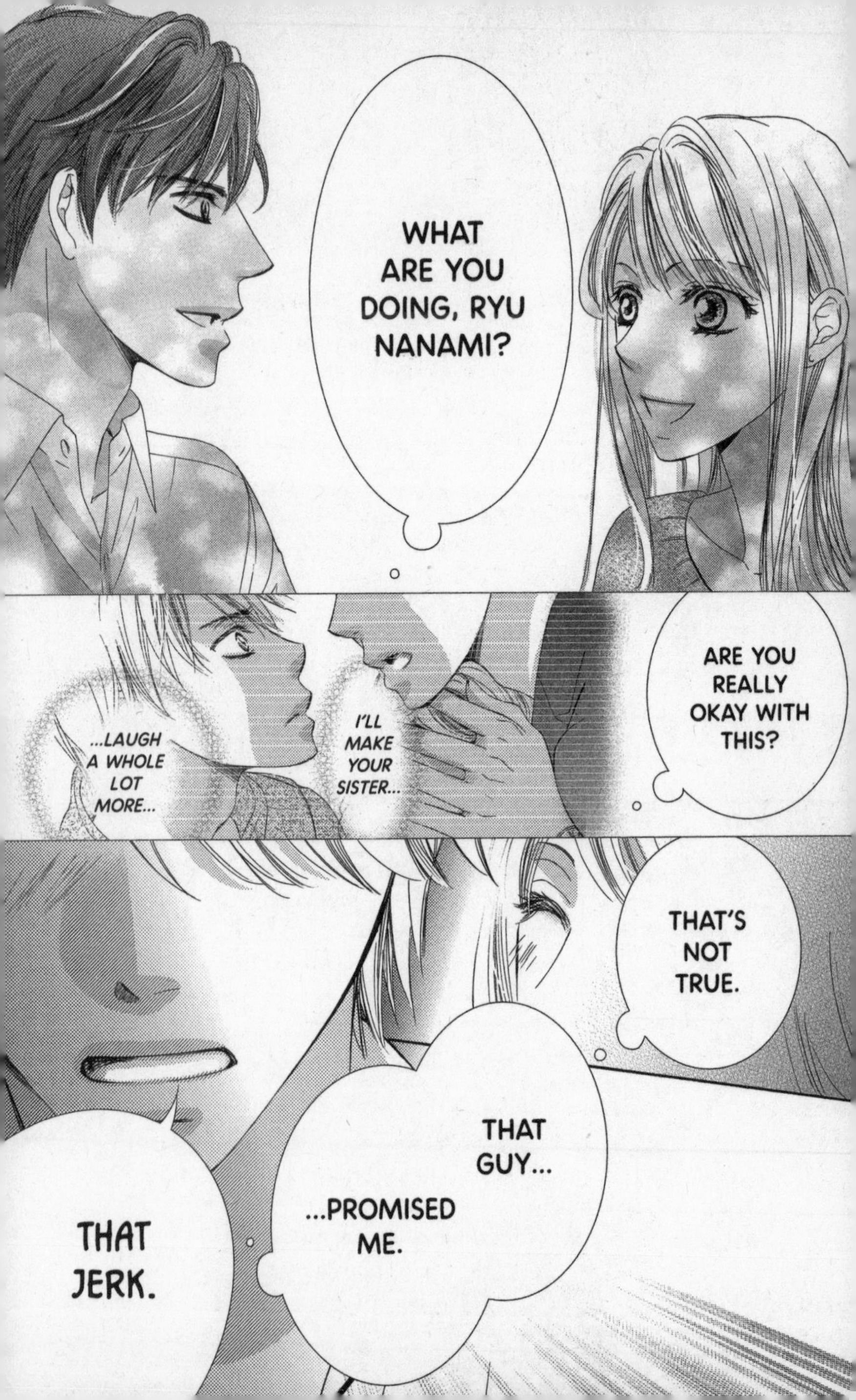
WHAT ARE YOU DOING, RYU NANAMI?
ARE YOU REALLY OKAY WITH THIS?
I'LL MAKE YOUR SISTER...
...LAUGH A WHOLE LOT MORE...
THAT'S NOT TRUE.
THAT GUY...
...PROMISED ME.
THAT JERK.

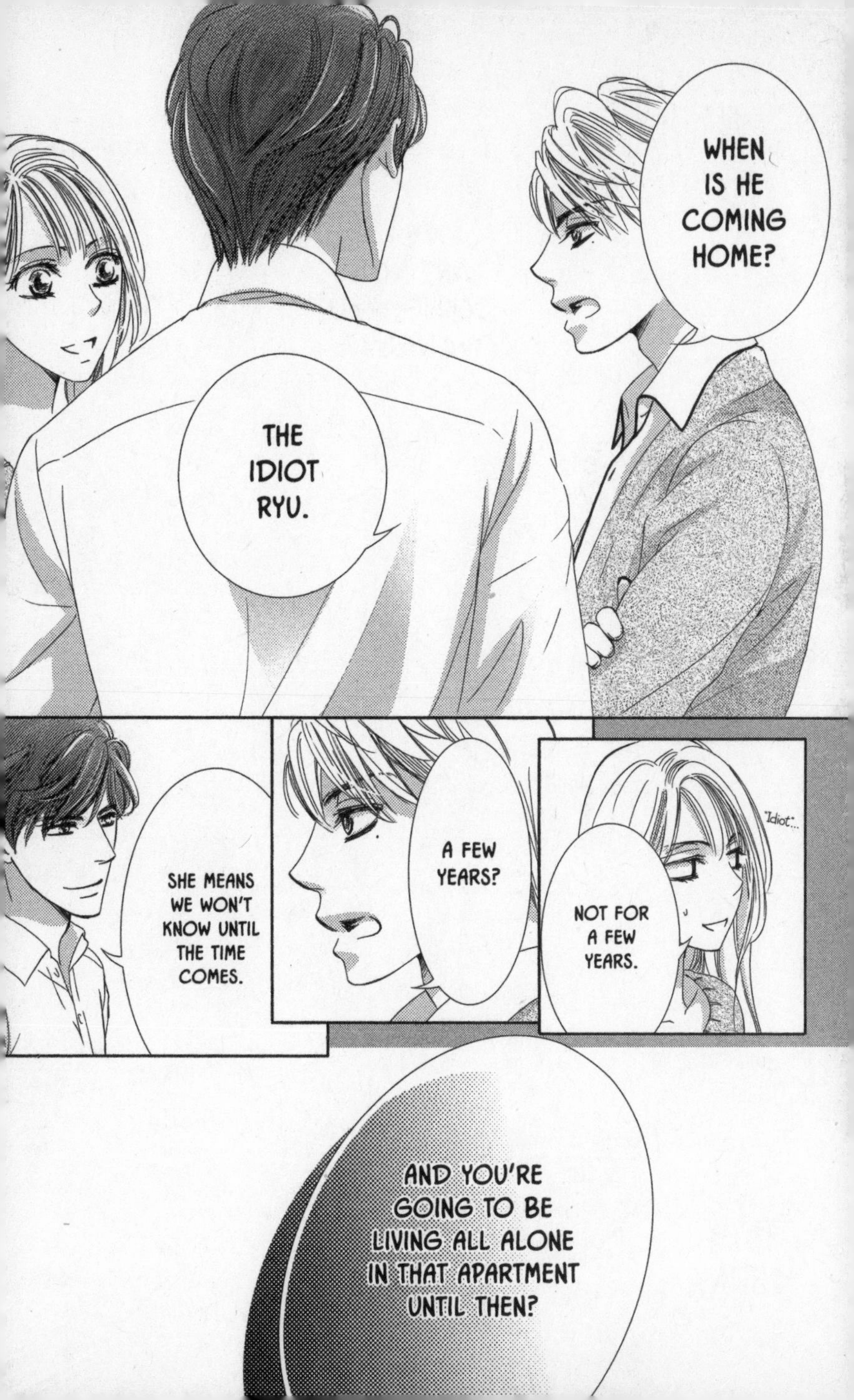
WHEN IS HE COMING HOME?
THE IDIOT RYU.
"Idiot"...
NOT FOR A FEW YEARS.
A FEW YEARS?
SHE MEANS WE WON'T KNOW UNTIL THE TIME COMES.
AND YOU'RE GOING TO BE LIVING ALL ALONE IN THAT APARTMENT UNTIL THEN?

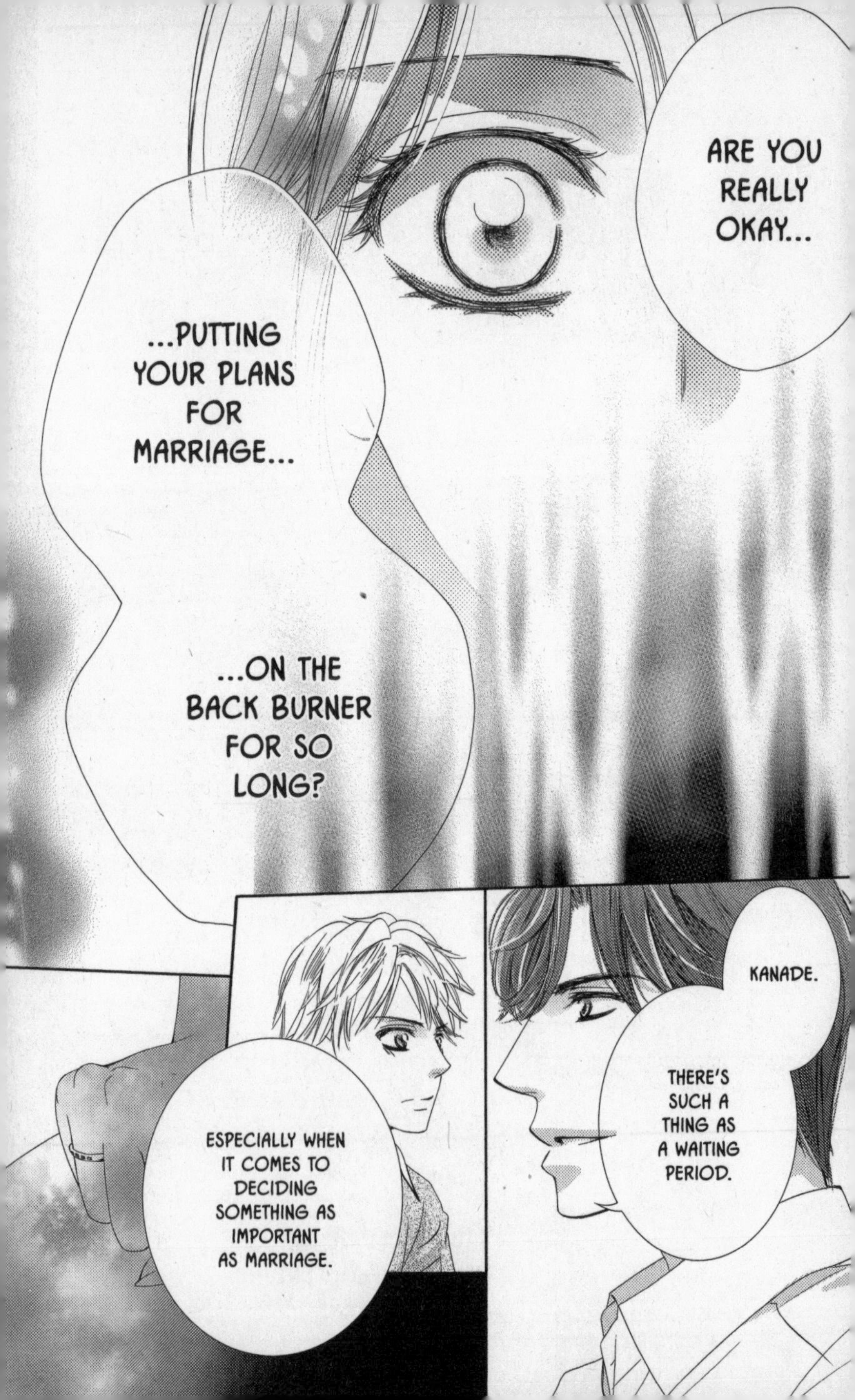
ARE YOU REALLY OKAY...
...PUTTING YOUR PLANS FOR MARRIAGE...
...ON THE BACK BURNER FOR SO LONG?
KANADE.
THERE'S SUCH A THING AS A WAITING PERIOD.
ESPECIALLY WHEN IT COMES TO DECIDING SOMETHING AS IMPORTANT AS MARRIAGE.

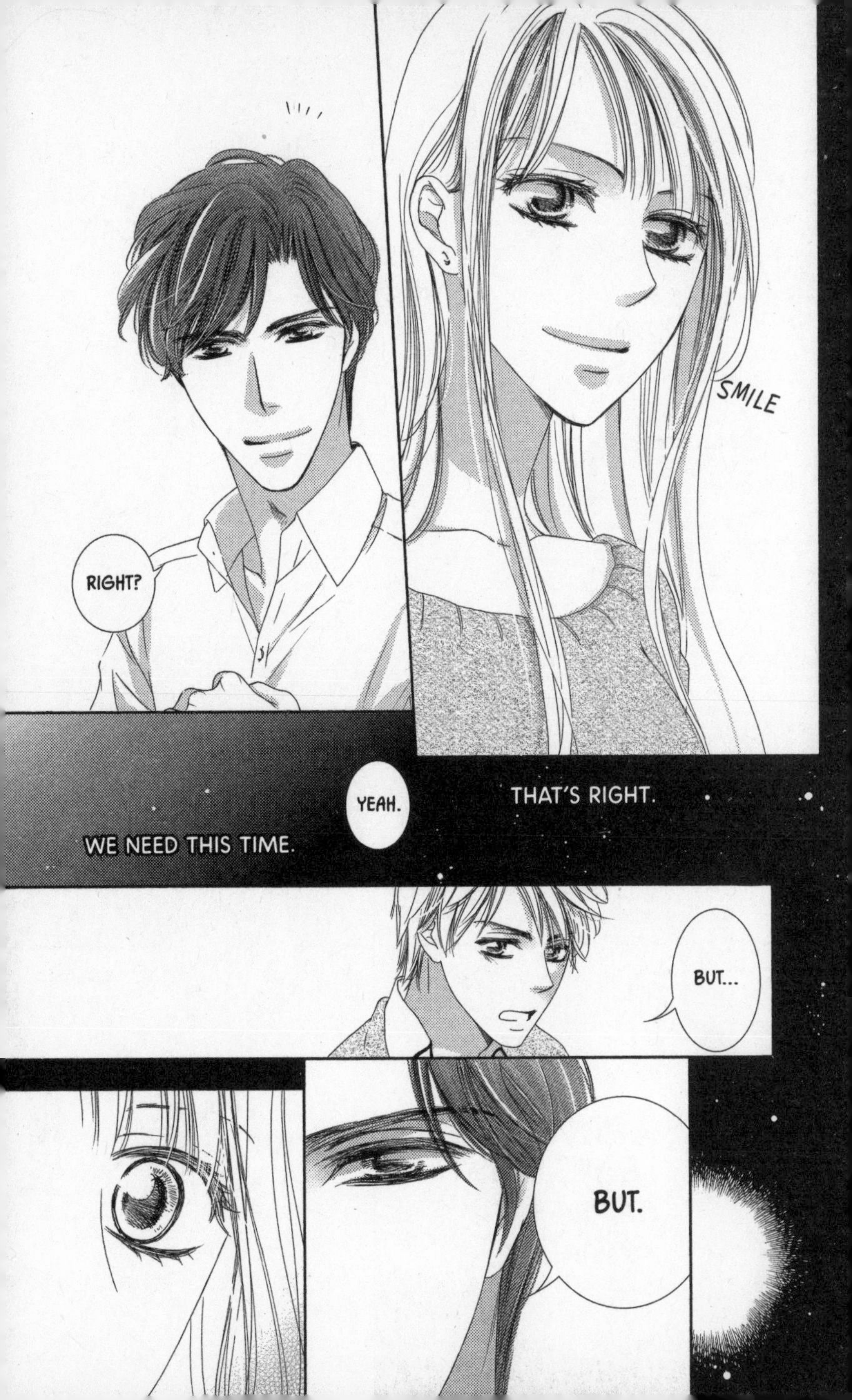
SMILE
RIGHT?
THAT'S RIGHT.
YEAH.
WE NEED THIS TIME.
BUT...
BUT.

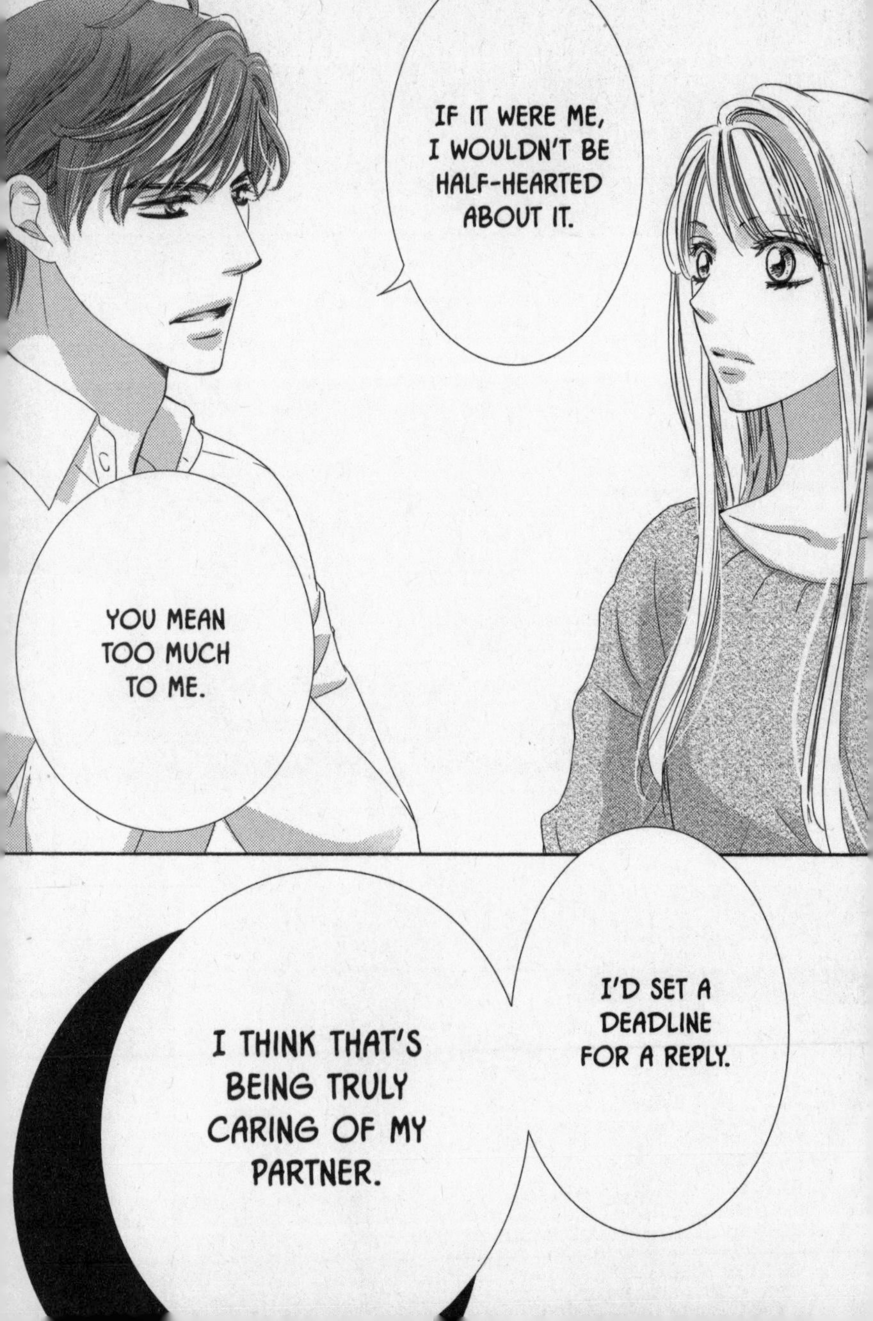
IF IT WERE ME, I WOULDN'T BE HALF-HEARTED ABOUT IT.
YOU MEAN TOO MUCH TO ME.
I'D SET A DEADLINE FOR A REPLY.
I THINK THAT'S BEING TRULY CARING OF MY PARTNER.

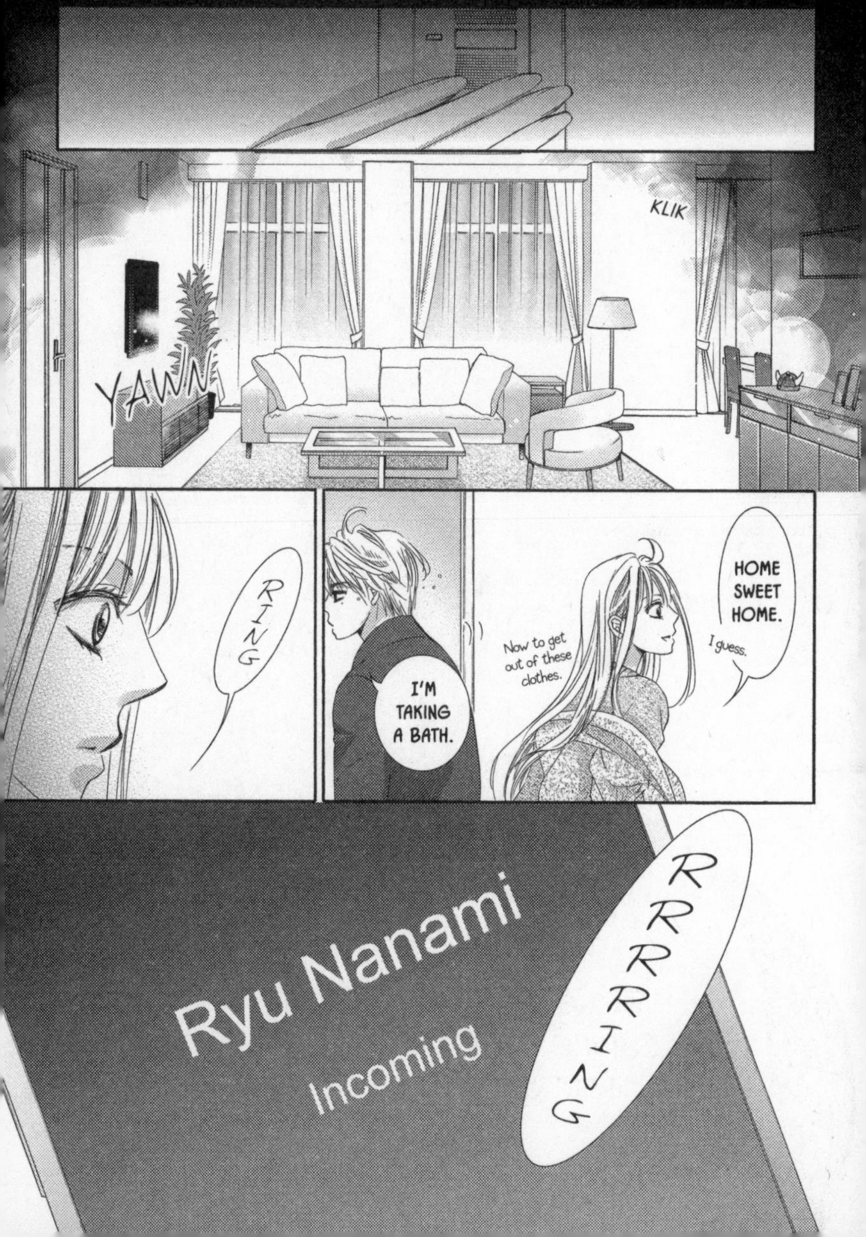
KLIK
YAWN
HOME SWEET HOME.
I guess.
Now to get out of these clothes.
I'M TAKING A BATH.
RING
RRRRING
Ryu Nanami
Incoming

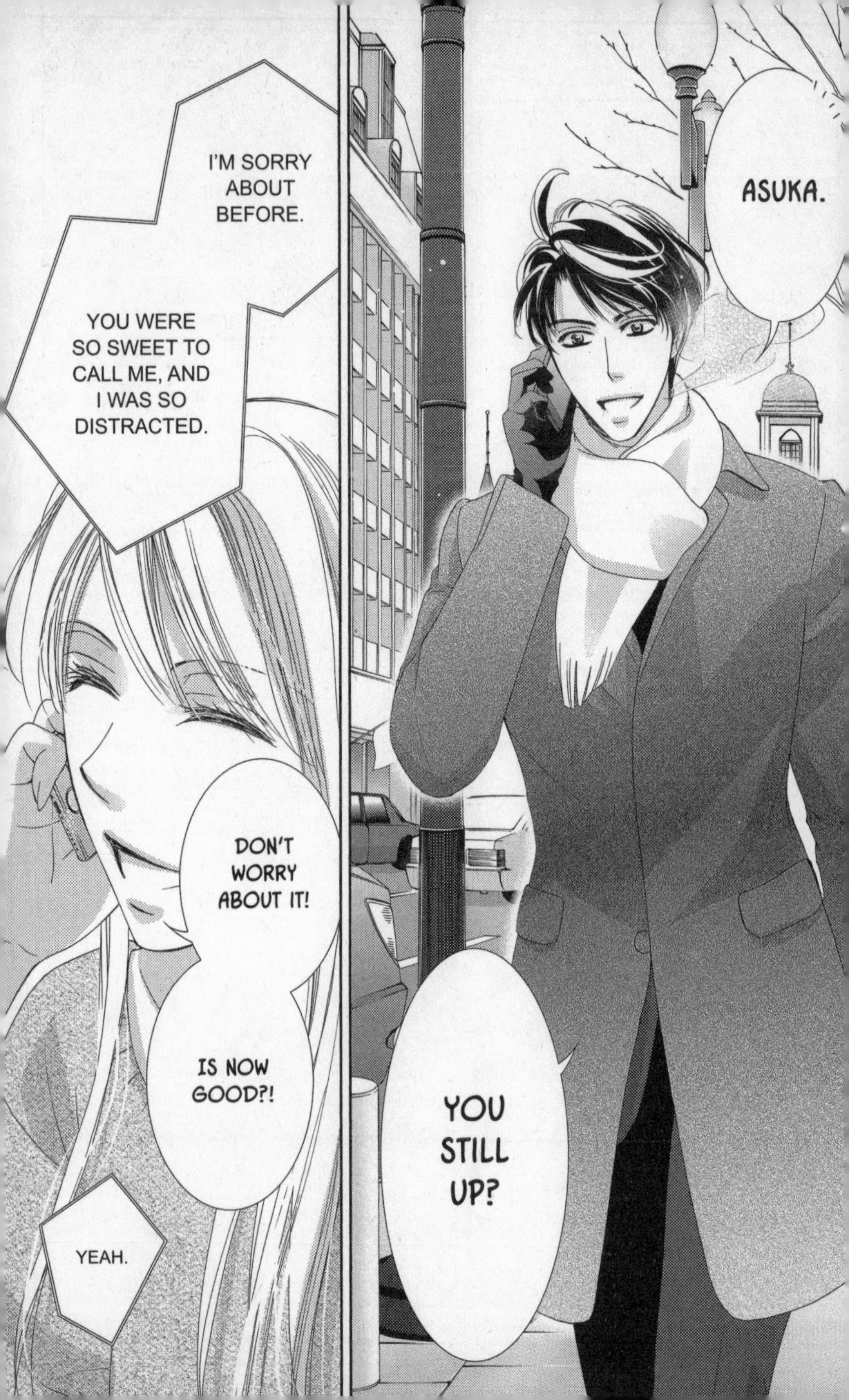
ASUKA.
YOU STILL UP?
I'M SORRY ABOUT BEFORE.
YOU WERE SO SWEET TO CALL ME, AND I WAS SO DISTRACTED.
DON'T WORRY ABOUT IT!
IS NOW GOOD?!
YEAH.

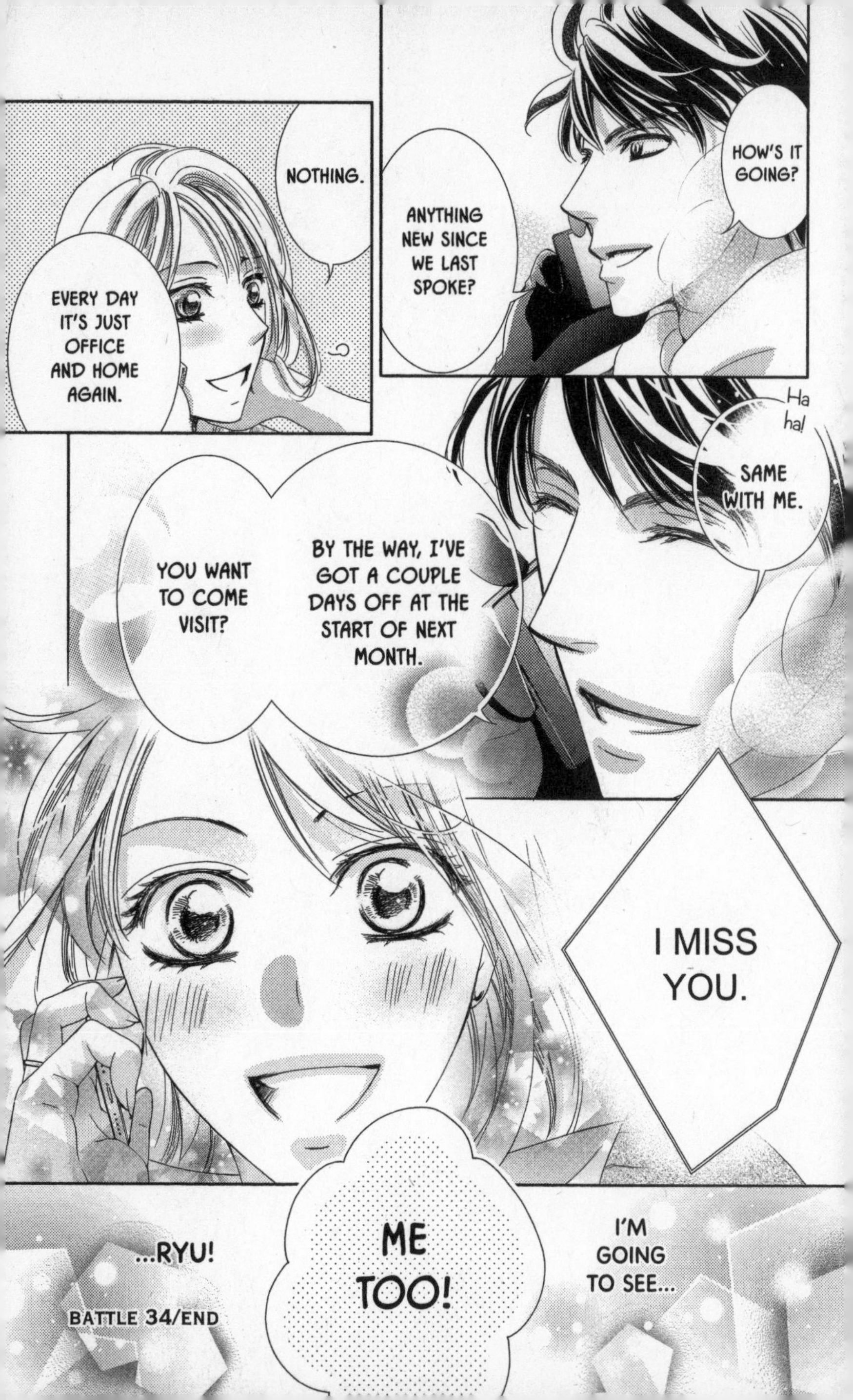
HOW'S IT GOING?
ANYTHING NEW SINCE WE LAST SPOKE?
NOTHING.
EVERY DAY IT'S JUST OFFICE AND HOME AGAIN.
Ha ha!
SAME WITH ME.
BY THE WAY, I'VE GOT A COUPLE DAYS OFF AT THE START OF NEXT MONTH.
YOU WANT TO COME VISIT?
I MISS YOU.
ME TOO!
I'M GOING TO SEE...
...RYU!
BATTLE 34/END

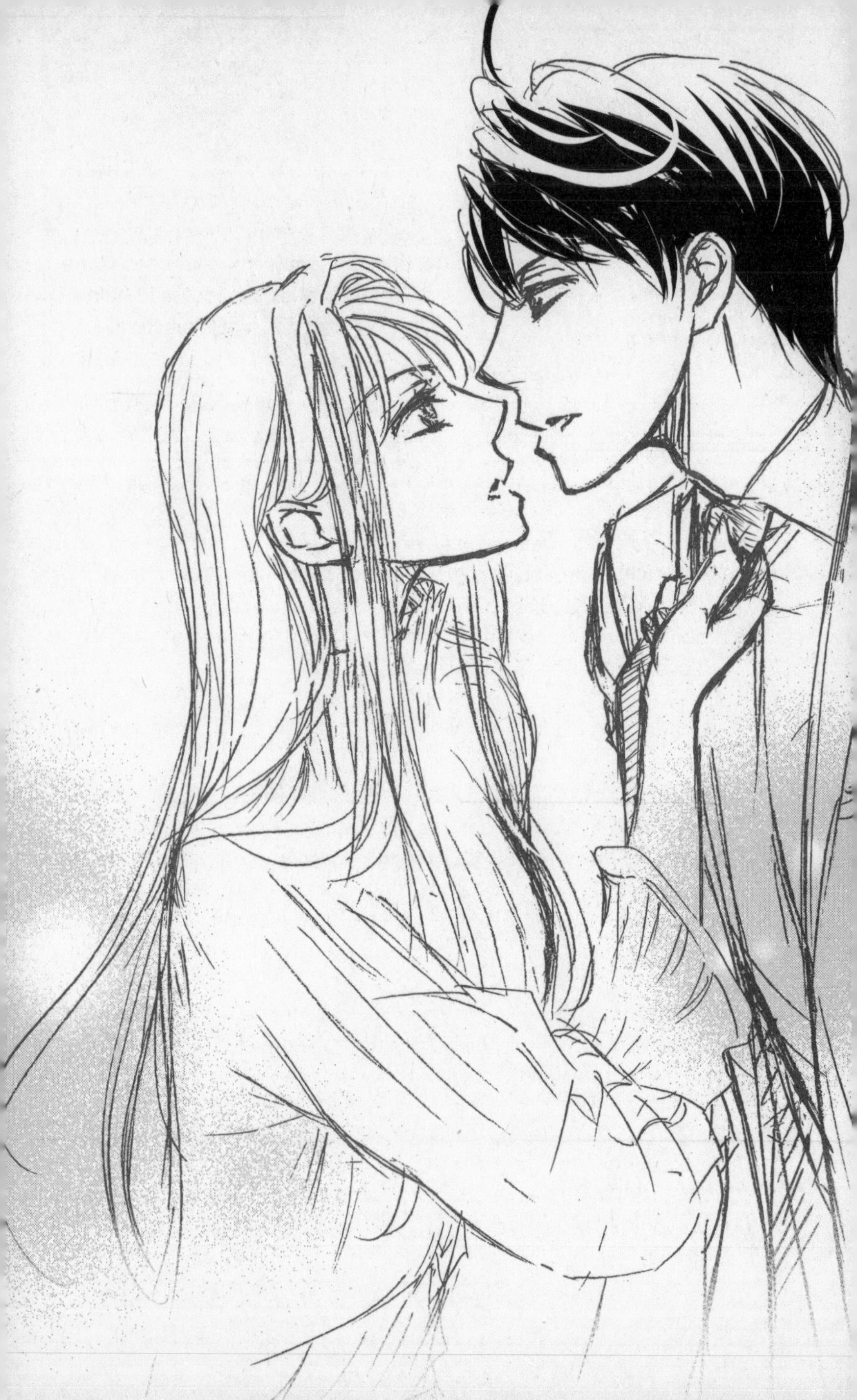

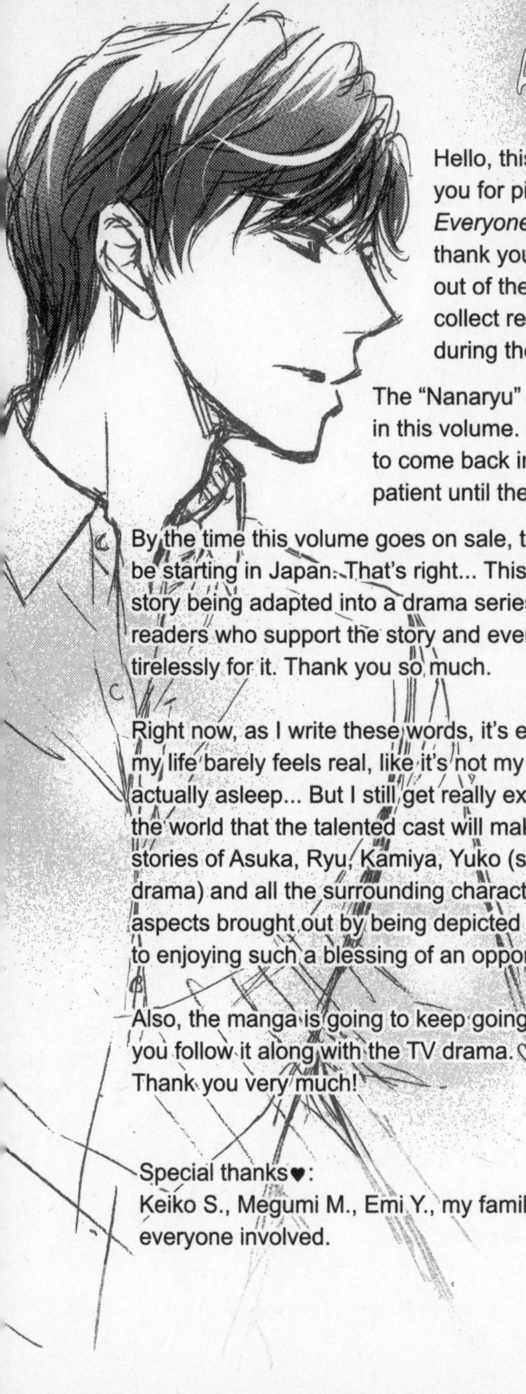

AFTERWORD

Hello, this is Izumi Miyazono. Thank you for picking up volume 7 of *Everyone's Getting Married.* And thank you to everyone who took time out of their busy schedules to help collect reference materials for me during the making of it.

The "Nanaryu" bonus stories took a break in this volume. (But they're scheduled to come back in volume 8, so please be patient until then...!)

By the time this volume goes on sale, the television drama should be starting in Japan. That's right... This time I was able to enjoy this story being adapted into a drama series. This is all thanks to my readers who support the story and everyone involved who works tirelessly for it. Thank you so much.

Right now, as I write these words, it's early January... To be honest, my life barely feels real, like it's not my own... I ask myself if I'm actually asleep... But I still get really excited when I start to envision the world that the talented cast will make for EGM. I'm sure the stories of Asuka, Ryu, Kamiya, Yuko (spelled slightly different in the drama) and all the surrounding characters will have new and unique aspects brought out by being depicted on the screen. I look forward to enjoying such a blessing of an opportunity with you all!

Also, the manga is going to keep going for a little while more. I hope you follow it along with the TV drama.♡ And see you next volume. Thank you very much!

Special thanks♥:
Keiko S., Megumi M., Emi Y., my family, my editor and everyone involved.

This is volume 7 (*nana*) of Nanaryu. I'd always thought how nice it'd be to reach nana volumes, but I never would have imagined that the story would then be adapted into a live-action drama. (Shock...) Thank you for taking it in a new direction!! Starting with the adorable Mariya Nishiuchi-san and the handsome Ryuta Yamamura-san, I am thoroughly pleased with all the cast and crew involved in bringing us this drama. ♡

IZUMI MIYAZONO

IZUMI MIYAZONO is from Niigata Prefecture in Japan. She debuted in 2005 with *Shunmin Shohousen* (A Prescription for Sleep). In 2014 she began serializing *Everyone's Getting Married* in *Petit Comic*. This series was also adapted for a live-action TV drama in Japan.